GORBACHEV

· · · · ·

GORBACHEV

Martin McCauley

LONGMAN
London and New York

Addison Wesley Longman Limited
Edinburgh Gate,
Harlow, Essex CM20 2JE, United Kingdom
and Associated Companies throughout the world

*Published in the United States of America
by Addison Wesley Longman Inc., New York*

© Addison Wesley Longman Limited 1998

First published 1998

ISBN 0 582 21597 8 CSD
ISBN 0 528 21598 6 PPR

British Library Cataloguing in Publication Data

A catalogue record for this book is available from the British Library

Library of Congress Cataloging-in-Publication Data

McCauley, Martin.
   Gorbachev / Martin McCauley.
      p. cm. — (Profiles in power)
   Includes bibliographical references and index.
   ISBN 0–582–21598–6 (ppr). — ISBN 0–582–21597–8 (csd)
   1. Gorbachev, Mikhail Sergeevich, 1931–   . 2. Heads of state—
Soviet Union—Biography.   3. Soviet Union—Politics and
government—1985–1991.   4. Russia (Federation)—Politics and
government—1991– I. Title.   II. Series: Profiles in power
(London, England)
DK290.3.G67M38   1998
947.085′4′092—dc21
[B]   97–38886
                                                                  CIP

Set by 35 in 11/12pt Baskerville
Produced by Addison Wesley Longman Singapore (Pte) Ltd.,
Printed in Singapore

CONTENTS

FOR MARTA

PREFACE

The magnificent seven made and unmade perestroika. They also restructured the Soviet Union out of existence. First there were seven: Mikhail Gorbachev, Eduard Shevardnadze, Aleksandr Yakovlev, Egor Ligachev, Nikolai Ryzhkov, Boris Yeltsin and Georgy Razumovsky. Then there were six when Ligachev left in the summer of 1988. Then there were five when Yeltsin departed. Eventually there was only one, Mikhail Sergeevich Gorbachev. He had fallen out with everyone, or perhaps they had fallen out with him. Then there were the *faux amis*, fair-weather friends. Anatoly Lukyanov, Vladimir Kryuchkov, Sergei Akhromeev, Boris Pugo, Valentin Pavlov, Gennady Yanaev, Dmitry Yazov, Valery Boldin, Oleg Shenin, and many more. They betrayed the leader, or, as they would put it, they tried to save the Soviet Union from the leader. Advisers also came and went, but two influential ones remained: Anatoly Chernyaev and Georgy Shakhnazarov. Gorbachev aroused passions. Ligachev, Shevardnadze, Ryzhkov and Yeltsin are bitter about their treatment. They feel they were dumped like a sack of potatoes. Some had second thoughts. Shevardnadze and Yakovlev repaired their relationship with the leader, when it was too late.

Such a man must have been extraordinary. He headed the Party and resigned voluntarily as general secretary. Yet he emasculated the Party and the state it ran. This testifies to extraordinary gifts of charm, persuasion, prevarication, camouflage, manipulation, cunning and tactical skill. He must have had luck on his side. He achieved the almost impossible feat, for a Soviet Party leader, of becoming more popular abroad than at home. Nowhere was he more of a hit than in America, the land of capitalism, the arch enemy of communism.

He charmed two US Presidents, Reagan and Bush, who were instinctively anti-communist, and reached agreements with them that no one, in 1985, would have believed feasible. His words abroad took on meaning. He declared the Soviet Union wanted to leave Afghanistan. So convinced were CIA officers that he was lying, that they bet money with one another that the Soviet Army would stay. He so charmed Margaret Thatcher, a free marketeer, that she became a passionate advocate of his domestic reforms.

And yet he failed. The prophet ended up unemployed, without a country. He set trends in motion which he dimly understood and lacked the insight to perceive where they were heading. His original reforms were based on false assumptions, as were many more. His blind spots were economics and nationality affairs. He paid dearly for his lack of insight and empathy for non-Russians. Why did he survive as long as he did? Amongst the contributory factors were his undimmed self-confidence, the belief that he could persuade anyone to do anything, and the conviction that what he was doing was right and this would be acknowledged, sooner or later. He was young enough to sense he had to move with the times, that the time and the world wait for no man.

Assessing his career is extraordinarily difficult. There is a wealth of material and testimony about him. Yet his character remains elusive. He is a remarkably difficult man to get close to and to know. He had an authoritarian streak which alienated many. He was brusque with his aides and officials. He trampled on their sensitivities and did not notice it. He omitted to praise his cohorts so as to inspire them to achieve more. He would not have made a successful football manager, capable of perceiving human weaknesses and building up the players so that the team can become more than the sum of its parts. He was willing to listen to foreigners but became very impatient with natives. He can be seen as a great transitional leader, the F. W. de Klerk of the Soviet Union. Both perceived that the value systems they had served were false. They then embraced their opposites without demur.

No attempt is made in this study to cover the history of the period 1985–91. Only those aspects of it which illuminate Gorbachev's journey are selected. Vast areas of intellectual endeavour, literature, religion, science, are hardly mentioned. Gorbachev was a remarkable man who changed the world. No two persons will ever agree on the legacy he bequeathed to the world. All politicians ultimately fail, but some fail more miserably than others. If Gorbachev failed, he failed gloriously.

The main sources of this book are Gorbachev's writings, especially his memoirs, and the books by Archie Brown and Jack F. Matlock, Jr.

NOTE ON THE PARTY AND THE GOVERNMENT

The USSR was sometimes described as a Party–government state. The main features of the relationship between the Party and the government are shown below. The approximate equivalence of Party and governmental bodies is given at each territorial level.

PARTY	GOVERNMENT
Politburo (Presidium 1952–66), Communist Party of the Soviet Union (CPSU)	Presidium of the USSR Council of Ministers
Central Committee (CC)	USSR Council of Ministers
CPSU Congress	Presidium of the USSR Supreme Soviet
Republican (e.g. Ukrainian) Party Secretariat	Republican Council of Ministers
Republican CC	Presidium of Republican Supreme Soviet
Republican Party Congress	Republican Supreme Soviet
Regional (krai, oblast) Party Committee	City, krai or oblast soviet
Regional Party Conference	No equivalent
District (raion, etc.) Party bodies	Raion-village soviet

District Party Conference	No equivalent
Primary Party Organisations (enterprises, collective farm, etc.)	No equivalent
Rank and file Party members	Voters

NOTE ON RUSSIAN NAMES

Russian names consist of a first name, patronymic (father's name) and a surname. Hence Mikhail Sergeevich Gorbachev, or Mikhail, the son of Sergei Gorbachev. A sister would have been called Anna Sergeevna (the daughter of Sergei) Gorbacheva. Gorbachev's wife was Raisa Maksimovna, or Raisa, the daughter of Maksim, née Titorenko. (Titorenko is a Ukrainian name, hence does not end in the feminine a.) Another Russian name is Rimashevsky (masculine) and Rimashevskaya (feminine). The latter denotes both the daughter and the wife.

Many Russian names end in ov and ev. This is the genitive plural. Gorbachev (pronounced Gorba-choff) has an ev ending because it follows ch. The stress is at the end, on the ev. He would have been addressed formally as Mikhail Sergeevich, as the title gospodin (mister or lord) had been dropped in 1917. It is now again in use in Russia. He could also be addressed as Tovarishch (Comrade) Gorbachev.

Most Russian names have a diminutive: Sasha for Aleksandr, Volodya for Vladimir, Kolya for Nikolai, Seryozha for Sergei, Misha for Mikhail, Nadya for Nadezhda, Tanya for Tatyana, Raya for Raisa, and so on. Children, animals and close friends are addressed with the diminutive. There is also Ivan Ivanovich Ivanov: Ivan (John), the son of Ivan Johnson. Donald MacDonald, or Donald, the son of Donald, would be Donald Donaldovich Donaldov in Russian.

Ukrainian names sometimes end in a: e.g. Kuchma, but this is both masculine and feminine. As above Titorenko is masculine and feminine. Some names end in o: e.g. Chernenko. This would be Chernenkov in Russian. There are also

names ending in enko, chenko, lenko, denoting the diminutive: e.g. Kirilenko, little Kiril or Cyril; Mikhailichenko, little
Mikhail or Michael. A common Armenian surname ending
is yan: e.g. Mikoyan (the stress is always at the end). Common
Georgian surname endings are vili, adze, elli: e.g. Dzhugashvili
(or Djugashvili), Shevardnadze, Tseretelli, Chekhidze. Muslim surnames adopt the Russian ending ov or ev: e.g. Aliev,
Kunaev, Rakhmonov, Nazarbaev.

In this book the Russian endings -ii, yi have been rendered
y: e.g. Malinovsky, Podgorny. The phonetic y has been omitted:
e.g. Efimov, not Yefimov. The exception is Yeltsin as this is
now the accepted English spelling. The soft sign in Russian
has been omitted throughout.

The present day names of the republics are given in the
text. Hence Moldova, not Moldavia; Kyrgyzstan, not Kirgiziya.

LIST OF MAPS

Chapter 1

BACKGROUND: THE KINGDOM
OF CERTAINTY

The career of Mikhail Gorbachev is incomprehensible without an appreciation of the political development of the Soviet
Union. This chapter therefore provides a brief survey of the
Soviet system since its inception in 1917. Lenin changed his
mind about how the country could develop several times
but the framework of the Soviet system was in place when
he died in 1924. His successors competed for primacy during the 1920s and the victory of Stalin signalled the end of
the market economy and the onset of central planning. This
centralised political and economic power in Moscow around
Stalin and his cohorts. It became less efficient over time but
it was only after Stalin's death, in 1953, that attempts were
made to reform it. Khrushchev attempted many radical reforms but never overcame the tension of a decentralised
economy and centralised political power. Kosygin made a
valiant effort to transfer more decision-making to the enterprise, but the Czechoslovak events of 1968 fatally weakened
his concepts.

The Soviet Union was sometimes referred to as a party-
state. Local government was exercised through the soviets.
These complex relationships are looked at as they hold the
key to Gorbachev's advance.

.   .   .

THE LEGACY OF LENINISM

Karl Marx, in his dynamic version of classical economics,[1]
never refers to forecasting. He belonged to the pre-1914 era
when human beings dreamed that one day they would know
everything they needed to know and that certainty would

1

replace uncertainty. The belief that he had discovered the laws of human existence led Marx to perceive the conflict between capital and labour, between management and workers, as a drama in which the actors play pre-ordained roles which they are powerless to change. The denouement – revolution – is inevitable and therefore certain. This *Weltanschauung*, or world view, was seized upon by Lenin and the Bolsheviks with religious zeal. They were convinced the future was knowable and that it would be an extension of the past and the present, only better. Even more important, they thought they could shape the future according to their own preferences. A striking factor about Lenin was his will-power, the belief that he and the Bolshevik Party could transform Russian society in their own image. How did his views about the future of Russia evolve over time?[2] It should be pointed out that Nikolai Bukharin and Lev Trotsky influenced his perceptions, so that what follows can be described as a product of the combined labour of the triumvirate.

Lenin was much taken by the German war economy and came to see advanced capitalism as a stepping stone to socialism.

> Capitalism has created an accounting *apparatus* in the shape of the banks, syndicates, postal service ... *Without big banks socialism would be impossible* ... The big banks are the 'state apparatus' which we *need* to bring about socialism, and which we *take ready-made* from capitalism ... A single State Bank, the biggest of the big, with branches in every rural district, in every factory, will constitute as much as nine tenths of the *socialist* apparatus.[3]

This vision of a state of clerks then fades and Lenin advocates the destruction of the state. To him, it cannot be reformed so has to be smashed. A commune state would replace it, one which soviets, cooperatives, trade unions, factory committees and other representative institutions would run. The affairs of state would be carried out by elected officials, accountable to their constituents, subject to recall at any time and paid an average workman's wages. This vision of socialism dissolves society into the state. The name of the Bolshevik Party was changed in 1918 to Russian Communist Party to underline the commitment to commune socialism.[4] Little concern was paid to the conduct of elections, access to the media, the immunity of elected representatives and civil rights. This was because Lenin did not regard the state or politics (understood by Lenin as the relations between capitalists and workers) as having any permanence since both would melt away as the exploitation of man by man disappeared. The primary objective for Lenin was to eliminate exploitation and thereby eliminate classes. When this was achieved there would be no need for the state or politics. Society would become autonomous and self-governing.

In 1920–1 Lenin, Bukharin and Trotsky reformulated their view of the state.[5] They concluded that socialism could no longer be identified with mass popular participation in the management of political, economic and social affairs. Workers' control, factory committees, trade unions, soviets, people's militias and cooperatives were now viewed as the first, destructive phase of the revolution. They had produced nothing positive, in fact they had almost brought ruin to Soviet Russia. Lenin now concluded that socialism should no longer be linked to altering the power relations among men but rather to transforming their productive potential so that economic growth would eventually lead to abundance. For the first time Bolshevik leaders made a distinction between socialism and communism – hitherto these terms had been used almost interchangeably. Now communism was a long, long way off. The dictatorship of the proletariat was redefined and could no longer be exercised by the working class as a whole. Only the avant-garde of the working class was capable of leading the proletariat and administering the state. That avant-garde was to be found in the Party.

> The proletariat is still so divided, so degraded, so corrupted in parts ... that an organisation taking in the whole proletariat cannot directly exercise proletarian dictatorship. It can be exercised only by a vanguard that has absorbed the revolutionary energy of the class.[6]

Communists were a small minority and this sharpened Lenin's definition of dictatorship: 'nothing more or less than authority untrammelled by any laws, absolutely unrestricted by any rules whatsoever, and based directly on force'.[7]

Given limited public support, this vision led to state terror and coercion. Lenin, in a flash of candour, acknowledged that he and the Bolsheviks were imitating the imperialist states they wanted destroyed. As long as the conflict between capitalism and socialism lasted, the Bolsheviks did not promise 'any freedom or any democracy'.[8] Workers had to be consolidated into a class and to achieve this they had to be concentrated into a single political party. Lenin put it succinctly: 'Henceforth less politics will be the best politics'.[9]

At the 2nd Congress of the Communist International (Comintern), Lenin, for the first time, defined the organisational structure of a Communist Party. The core of it was democratic centralism, which meant that no member or organisation could oppose instructions from a superior body. Offenders could be expelled. At the 10th Party Congress, in 1921, Lenin, exasperated by criticism, fumed: 'We are not a debating society'.[10] A resolution was passed banning factionalism (opposition).

Hence Leninism means the gradual elimination of politics from public life. The chief task of the Party and government was to draft a national plan which made optimal use of the capital and labour available. Under war communism (1918–20) an attempt was made to create a national agency which would run the economy, the Supreme Council of the National Economy (VSNKh), but it never functioned smoothly due to the civil war. The New Economic Policy (NEP), introduced in March 1921, was a retreat from socialism and the rational state.

The ban on factionalism permitted the Party Central Committee (CC) to expel CC members who challenged Party decisions. This Leninist innovation was skilfully used later by Stalin to remove his opponents from the leadership. With the wisdom of hindsight this was one of the most fateful decisions taken by Lenin as it stifled discussion at the top and at all levels in the Party. To be fair to Lenin, he envisaged the ban as a temporary measure, until the Party came to terms with NEP, which in turn was a temporary stop on the road to socialism. Unfortunately for the Soviet Union, Lenin died in 1924 and left the resolution in place.

Lenin was convinced he knew the future and this is the major factor in his political thinking. He was a child of the pre-1914 era of certainty. In the rest of Europe, the First World War shattered this dream that man could know everything and ushered in the modern era of uncertainty. The profound malaise of the post-1918 era in Europe prompted radical, new thinking and new solutions. It has emerged that the explosion of knowledge over time makes life more uncertain and, consequently, the world more difficult to comprehend. In 1917 the Bolsheviks deliberately cut Russia off from the rest of Europe and hence continued along the road of certainty. This fateful decision led to totalitarian politics as the beleaguered Bolshevik Party, with minimal support, forced its vision of the future on the working class and the rest of the population.

Lenin and the Bolsheviks, certain of their views, became embroiled in a struggle which in essence consisted of forcing Russians to be free. This was not an original Marxist concept as Engels had already intimated that man might have to be forced to be free.[11] This boosted the self-confidence of the Bolsheviks, and Stalin, revealing his grasp of what the public would respond to, adopted the slogan of 'socialism in one country'. Russia was a special country and, as such, the world leader. He also underlined that Party members were the elect during a speech on the eve of Lenin's funeral. 'We communists are people of a special mould. We are made of special stuff.'

Soviet Russia had become a federal state and Lenin made much of the right of self-determination of nations. They could even secede if they so desired. However, this was a remnant of the commune democracy stage of Russia's development. In his Testament, Lenin was blunt and to the point:

> There are instances when the right to self-determination conflicts with another, higher right – the right of the working class to consolidate its power. In such cases – and one must be blunt – the right of self-determination cannot and must not be an obstacle to the working class in exercising its dictatorship.[12]

Given that the leadership of the Communist Party decided what was in the best interests of the working class, the above made abundantly clear that Russian communists would decide what was best for non-Russians. This was imperialism in a new guise. The Communist Party, on paper, was a federal party, but in reality Moscow decided. At the 8th Party Congress, in March 1918, this was spelled out:

All decisions of the Russian Communist Party and its leading organs are unconditionally binding on all elements of the Party, irrespective of their national composition. The Central Committees of the Lithuanian, Latvian, and Ukrainian communists have the right of regional committees of the Party and are completely subordinate to the Central Committee of the Russian Communist Party.[13]

Hence the organisation of the Party did not go through the two phases experienced by the state: commune democracy and rigid centralism. The Party was always subject to democratic centralism, the expression used to underline the centre's right to rule.

. . .

THE PARTY AND THE ECONOMY

The mixed economy flourished during the 1920s and this put socialism back on the agenda. Russia was a developing state with almost 80 per cent of its population on the land. To protect themselves from alternative political pressures, the Communists banned all other political parties. The fierce struggle to succeed Lenin ended in 1929 with Stalin the victor. He astutely formed coalitions against his main rivals, first and foremost Trotsky, and concealed his real ambition, to become a strong leader, from everyone. Lenin, enamoured by the minutiae of government, concentrated his energies on government, as chair of the Council of People's Commissars (Sovnarkom). Stalin, made general secretary of the Party in 1922, used the potential of the Party apparatus to construct his political base. By 1921 the Party Politburo was the key decision-making body and the battles of the 1920s took place there. One may speak of Stalin being absolute ruler from 1934. He acted like a Russian Tsar and autocrat (in fact he was an assimilated Great Russian, having being born a Georgian) and concentrated all decision-making in Moscow. Stalinism is a mélange of Imperial Russian and Soviet political and economic cultures.

The planned economy (also called the command economy) emerged after 1928 and was rationality personified. It was based on the logical assumption that if all the resources of the state were brought together and deployed optimally, the result would be superior to anything achieved in a market economy. Marx wrote of the anarchy of the market; surely central planning had to be superior? Implicit in Stalin's economic model was the belief that no economic actor (managers, workers) harboured interests which were different to those of the state. Hence self-interest and the general interest coincided. This proved to be a fundamental misconception, one which prevailed right up to Gorbachev.

Marxism legitimised Stalin's concentration of power at the centre. Only the leadership of the Communist Party had the knowledge to implement the laws of human development and only it was in possession of the necessary information to effect this. Other institutions and groups only had access to partial information; it was all brought together at the centre. The Five Year Plans were a natural extension of the attempts by the Supreme Council of the National Economy (VSNKh) to administer Russia as a single economic space. The most radical Bolsheviks even thought that they were no longer bound by the laws of mathematics. They certainly did not accept the innovations of Francis Galton, for instance the concept of regression to the mean. He demonstrated that change and motion from the outer limits towards the centre are constant, inevitable, foreseeable. The driving force is always towards the average, towards the restoration of normality.[14] Of course, the mean changes location. It is not surprising that Bolsheviks rejected Galton's conclusions. During the 1930s they downgraded statistics, psychology, sociology and all other disciplines concerned with the measurement of society. Stalin and his team were not primarily concerned with the measurement of existing society, they concentrated on building a new world.

The Five Year Plans were attempts to manage uncertainty out of existence by making the plans law. The government then issued detailed decrees to implement the conclusions of the planners. Hence they were deliberately attempting to eliminate risk. By doing this enterprises did not need to concern themselves with the laws of probability and to attempt to calculate the optimal mix of output. The plan told them what to produce and provided the inputs. The state also disposed of their output. Since the Bolshevik planners did not accept (after 1936 when socialism had been built) that there could be antagonistic contradictions (conflicts of interests between management and labour which could undermine the plan), they did not need information about managers' and workers' motives and how these could affect labour productivity. A major problem for Stalin's planners was how to increase labour productivity, how to get more work out of the workers. Stakhanovism, socialist competition and other campaigns were launched in an effort to achieve more output from available resources. Workers were treated as a cheap resource, just as they had been viewed before 1917. Stalin spoke of trade unions being transmission belts for higher output. The race for greater and greater output led to quantity taking precedence over quality.

Decline in quality led to less interest in innovation. The risk was that if an innovation did not achieve its potential, the enterprise could be penalised. Hence the tendency was to become risk-averse and, in consequence, innovation-shy. By the late 1930s severe economic problems were looming and there were calls to afford enterprises greater autonomy. This implied that the planner did not know best. However, the onset of war ended these debates and the wartime economy allowed the enterprises greater decision-making powers as they attempted to maximise output from the resources they had.

The passivity of management and labour was a constant concern of Khrushchev (1953–64). He intuitively grasped what was lacking in Soviet society and initiated reform after reform to promote greater efficiency. He removed coercion and fear from everyday life for most people, believing that fear was a poor motivator. Almost all his reforms were concerned with raising labour productivity. However, since the Soviet establishment had decided that psychology could teach them little, he was denied access to studies on motivation. This would have saved him from some of his more egregious errors. He did not permit himself to be restricted by probability and forecasting. He decided what was needed and expected it to be achieved. So convinced was he that communism (to each according to need, from each according to ability) was attainable in his generation that he predicted in 1961 that it would begin in 1980. Here was a man who was certain about the future! Had he heard of Francis Galton he would have been aware that rising growth rates, essential for the construction of communism, could only continue for a time and then decline to the mean or average. In

8

reality, it was impossible to predict when communism would arrive. Khrushchev undermined the concepts of reform and communism. Afterwards they were sparingly used until under Gorbachev communism slipped out of the leader's vocabulary.

The most radical attempt at economic reform in the post-Stalin period was undertaken in 1965 by Aleksei Kosygin, the Soviet Prime Minister. This allowed greater decision-making autonomy to enterprises, which were permitted to link up with end users and could also shed surplus labour. The invasion of Czechoslovakia in August 1968 crippled these initiatives as the centre reasserted itself. There was an ongoing debate during the 1970s about improving the economic mechanism. This term involved increasing output within the existing economic system. A key question, that of ownership, was not addressed. Proposals that cooperatives could be more efficient than state-owned enterprises and that private farms were more productive than collective or state farms were ruled out of court by the Party. There could not be private ownership of the means of production under socialism.

The Brezhnev era was one of stability. In the early 1970s the United States acknowledged nuclear parity with the Soviet Union and the latter was accepted as a superpower. This was wonderful for the Russian ego, but pride comes before a fall. The rapid growth of oil revenues in the 1970s obscured the fact that the Soviet economy was slowing down. Self-satisfaction bred corruption, and leadership at the centre became weak after 1976. As Brezhnev became addicted to drugs, so the establishment became addicted to the easy life. The Soviet body politic needed a stimulant and risk would have provided it. Russia in the 1970s is an example of a society which became passive *vis-à-vis* the future due to the elimination of risk. The physical decline of Soviet leaders from 1979 reflected the physical decline of the country. To return to Francis Galton, the succession of old, infirm leaders was bound to end and a healthy one was due to make his appearance.

· · ·

THE PARTY, THE GOVERNMENT AND THE SOVIETS

In order to grasp the world in which Gorbachev was to operate, it is opportune to consider three institutions: the Party, the government and the soviets. According to the statutes of the Party, the supreme policy-making body was the Congress, which convened every four or five years, but annually in the early post-revolutionary period. Congresses were normally meticulously planned and every speech was checked and rechecked. It was like a play which unfolds, but the audience was also expected to participate yet not contradict the actors. Between Congresses, the Central Committee (CC) was the highest policy-making body and it was an assembly which Party leaders after Stalin took seriously. However, whereas under Khrushchev it met quite often, under Brezhnev it convened twice or three times annually, and the same under Gorbachev, revealing that it was not the institution which ran the country on a day-to-day basis. That role was performed by the CC Secretariat. Its apparatus consisted of departments, most of which paralleled, by design, government ministries. Each department had a head and secretaries of the CC supervised groups of departments. Some CC secretaries were also members of the Politburo and this marked them out as powerful men (rarely women) and potential future Party leaders. The relationship between a CC secretary and a minister changed over time. After 1957, the CC secretary was normally superior to the minister. The top secretary was called the general secretary, responsible for all other secretaries, and indeed the Party.

When Stalin died in 1953 there was uncertainty which institution, the Party or government, took precedence. When obliged to choose, Malenkov decided to be Prime Minister and the way was then clear for Khrushchev to promote the Party as his political base. After Khrushchev's defeat, in 1957, of the Anti-Party Group, so called because of their opposition to a greater role for the Party in the economy, the primary position in the state became the head of the Communist Party. This remained the case until Gorbachev was elected President in 1990. There were 20 departments of the CC Secretariat in 1988 before Gorbachev began pruning them back in line with his decision to exclude the Secretariat from the management of the economy. The general department worked most closely with the general secretary, drafting the agenda for Politburo meetings and preparing background papers. The organisational department was responsible for cadres or personnel. The administrative organs department supervised the Ministry of Civil Aviation, the Ministry of Defence, the KGB, the Ministry of Internal Affairs, the Ministry of Justice, the Procuracy, the Supreme Court and the civil defence apparatus.

Each republic had its own Communist Party, except the Russian Federation until 1990. They were headed by a bureau (except in Ukraine where it was called a Politburo) which was elected by a Central Committee at a Congress. There was also a CC Secretariat and secretaries. The top Party boss was the first secretary. Meetings of the CC between Congresses were called plenums, as at the all-Union level. Republics were divided administratively into oblasts and krais, with the latter containing within its territory a non-Slav autonomous oblast. Hence Stavropol krai contained a non-Slav ethnic territory. Oblasts, krais and cities were divided into raions. The Party leader was the first secretary. In this book the first secretary of a krai, oblast, city and raion is referred to as first secretary of the kraikom, obkom, gorkom and raikom. The backbone of the Party were the kraikom and obkom first secretaries. The Komsomol (Communist Party for youth) mirrored the Communist Party organisation and it was normal for officials to begin their careers in the Komsomol, prove themselves and then be promoted to Party work. Patronage was very important in the Komsomol and Communist Party. Rising officials gathered around themselves reliable and effective men (and a few women) so that when they rose, their faithful retinue rose as well. Gorbachev's patrons were Kulakov and Andropov. When Gorbachev became general secretary he brought a large number of officials from Stavropol krai to Moscow to work with him there.

State institutions consisted of the government (the executive) and the soviets (the elected agencies). The Constitution stated that supreme power in the state rested with the USSR Supreme Soviet, which elected the government and passed all the main legislation. In reality, the Politburo was the supreme policy-making body, with the general secretary taking precedence over the Prime Minister. Until the reforms of 1989, there was almost always only one candidate in elections to the soviets at all levels. The USSR Supreme Soviet (bicameral, consisting of the Soviet of the Union and the Soviet of Nationalities, of equal status) only met twice a year, a week in all, and rubber-stamped decisions taken elsewhere.

Local soviets (all soviets below the level of republic) were responsible for local government, were financed from Moscow and subordinate to the local Party boss. If the Party secretary thought the soviets were not performing their duties he could take decisions for them and order their implementation.

The USSR Council of Ministers was the Soviet government and each republic and autonomous republic had its own Council of Ministers. Some ministries were all-Union, in other words responsible for the whole of the Soviet Union. All the key ministries were all-Union: the Ministry of Defence, the Ministry for Light Machine Building Industry (which produced nuclear weapons for the military), etc. Other ministries were Union-republican, that is individual ministries operated in each republic but were subordinate to an all-Union ministry. The Ministry of Agriculture was a case in point. Economic ministries and the enterprises subordinate to them were powerful as they sought to become monopolies. It was very difficult to reform them as there was no market and all high technology ministries were connected with the military-industrial complex. They defeated Khrushchev's attempts to make them more accountable to the Party leadership, and under Kosygin (1964–80) there were no reforms which threatened their interests.

The ruling class, the nomenklatura, jealously guarded its privileges. In the early 1970s academician Andrei Sakharov gloomily reflected on the nature of Soviet society:

> Our society is infested with apathy, hypocrisy, petty egoism, open cruelty. Most representatives of its upper layer – the Party and the state managers, the highest circles of the prosperous intelligentsia – firmly hold on to their secret and open privileges. They are deeply indifferent to human rights' violations, the interests of progress, the problems of security and the future of the world.[15]

. . .

NOTES

1. Classical economists believed in the power of market forces and the self-correcting nature of the economy. When growth declined, wages and interest rates would eventually fall to levels low enough to encourage new investment. Investment, in turn, would increase employment and incomes and the

economy would expand again until rising prices brought the next decline.

2. A penetrating and lucid analysis of Lenin and Leninism is to be found in N. Harding, *Leninism* (London, Macmillan, 1996).
3. V. I. Lenin, *Collected Works* (Moscow, Progress, 1963–70); here vol. 26, p. 106.
4. Harding, *Leninism*, p. 151.
5. Ibid., chapter 6, passim.
6. Lenin, *Collected Works*, vol. 32, p. 21.
7. Ibid., vol. 31, p. 353.
8. Ibid., vol. 32, p. 495.
9. Ibid., vol. 31, p. 525.
10. Ibid., vol. 32, p. 252.
11. The concept of forcing man to be free has a long history. A lucid expositor was Jean Michelet, the eminent French historian of the French Revolution. Another exponent was Thomas Jefferson, a supporter of the French Revolution, and consequently an enemy of monarchy. To him, it was legitimate to force republicanism on the British. This would occur after French armies occupied Britain, something he would have welcomed.
12. J. V. Stalin, *Works* (Moscow, Foreign Language Publishing House, 1953), vol. 5, pp. 269–70.
13. *KPSS v rezolyutsiyakh i resheniyakh sezdov, konferentsii i plenumov*, 7th edn, part 1 (1898–1925), (Moscow, Gospolizdat, 1953), p. 443.
14. P. L. Bernstein, *Against the Gods: The Remarkable Story of Risk* (New York, Wiley, 1996), p. 170. This is a brilliant study of the mathematics of risk taking.
15. Quoted in Alexander A. Danilov et al., *The History of Russia: The Twentieth Century* (New York, The Heron Press, 1996), p. 324.

Chapter 2

THE RISING STAR

The probability of a radical reformer rising to the top of the Communist Party of the Soviet Union (CPSU) was slight during a period when the leadership was complacent about its achievements. It would increase if those choosing the new leader perceived that there was a systemic crisis, a crisis of the existing system. Gorbachev's chances of succeeding Leonid Brezhnev in 1982 were about one in four, one in two to succeed Yury Andropov in 1983 and perhaps six:four favourite to succeed Konstantin Chernenko in March 1985. The odds decrease over time not because the country was viewed as being in a crisis but because Gorbachev was thought to be the best comrade to continue the existing system. Everyone agreed that some reform was necessary, but this was understood to be within-system or intra-systemic reform. This was tantamount to rearranging the furniture in a house, not throwing it out and bringing in new. But what would happen if the new leader realised that the country was in a systemic crisis, one which threatened the survival of the existing order? Those who elected Gorbachev in 1985 did not address this problem because they calculated the probability of this occurring as low. The other Soviet leaders who had found themselves facing a systemic crisis, Lenin and Stalin, had both been very radical in their solutions. It was predictable that Lenin and Stalin would be intra-systemic reformers, given the political and intellectual world they inhabited – the pre-1914 European world of certainty. Gorbachev might be different. To what extent was he susceptible to the influence of the post-1914 world of uncertainty? Once uncertainty is entertained, leadership can no longer provide all the answers. The other actors in the drama, the people, have to be consulted and in so doing they will influence the outcome. No one can any longer be certain what the denouement of the drama will be. In the Soviet Union and the west most analysts would have calculated the probability of Gorbachev becoming an extra-systemic reformer, going beyond the bounds of the existing system, as perhaps less than 10 per cent. In the west only Archie Brown, the British scholar, would possibly have put it higher.[1]

. . .

GORBACHEV AND HIS FAMILY

Mikhail Sergeevich Gorbachev was born into a peasant household in the village of Privolnoe in Stavropol krai, north Caucasus, on 2 March 1931. He was baptised in the village of Letnitskoe and the name he was given at birth, Viktor, was changed to Mikhail by his grandfather during the ceremony. His mother was a devout Orthodox Christian, who never learnt to read and write, and died in 1995. Mikhail Sergeevich's father's family had originally come from the Voronezh region, in Russia, and his mother's from Chernigov, in Ukraine. Mikhail Sergeevich's maternal grandfather, Pantelei, joined the Communist Party in 1928 and helped to organise the local kolkhoz, becoming its first chair. His wife, however, was a devout Orthodox believer. Pantelei was arrested in July 1937 and accused of being a member of a 'counter-revolutionary right-wing Trotskyist organisation'.[2] Neighbours began avoiding their house as if it were plague-stricken. The other boys in the village shunned Gorbachev. Anyone who associated with the family of an 'enemy of the people' was courting arrest.

Gorbachev records that 'all of this was a great shock to me and has remained engraved in my memory ever since'.[3] Even when he became first secretary of Stavropol krai and even as a secretary of the Party Central Committee (CC), he could not bring himself to ask for a transcript of the case. 'It was only after the August 1991 coup that I asked Vadim Bakatin to find the records for me.'[4] Under torture, the chair of the krai's soviet executive committee broke down and named 58 persons as co-conspirators, including Gorbachev's grandfather. The latter was found guilty of impeding harvesting

15

operations, thus causing the loss of grain, of killing livestock by ploughing up meadows so as to reduce the available fodder, and of repressing Stakhanovites (shock workers) in the kolkhoz. He was accused of being an enemy of the Communist Party and the Soviet system and of having carried out subversive acts at the behest of an anti-Soviet right-wing Trotskyist organisation.[5] The proceedings lasted 14 months and in September 1938 he was found guilty. The assistant krai prosecutor decided there was not enough evidence to charge him under article 58 of the Criminal Code, which would have meant certain death, and so he was charged under article 109 for official misconduct, which meant a jail sentence. After a purge of the secret police (the NKVD) he was released in December 1938 and was re-elected chair of the kolkhoz in 1939.[6] After his release he described the tortures to which he had been subjected. He had been blinded with a brilliant light, beaten mercilessly, had his arms broken by catching them in the door, and a wet sheepskin coat had been placed around him and he was put on a hot stove. He was soon unconscious. He never blamed the regime for his misfortune, believing that Stalin was unaware of the malpractices of the NKVD. Gorbachev relates that his grandfather died soon after leaving prison, at the age of 59.[7]

His paternal grandfather, Andrei, also fell foul of the authorities. He refused to join a collective farm during collectivisation and remained an individual peasant. In the terrible famine of 1933, a direct consequence of over-hasty collectivisation, three of his six children died of hunger (up to half of the population in Privolnoe also died). He was arrested in 1934 for not having fulfilled the sowing plan laid down by the planners for individual peasants. It mattered naught that he had no seed to sow. He was declared a saboteur and sent to fell trees in Irkutsk oblast, in Siberia. Gorbachev's father, Sergei, had to assume the role of head of the household but the family were unpersons. However, grandfather was released in 1935 before the end of his sentence because he had proved to be an exemplary worker. He then joined the local kolkhoz. The grandfather of Raisa Maksimovna Titorenko, Gorbachev's future wife, was not so fortunate. He was also a peasant, in the Altai in west Siberia, and was arrested in 1937. He was found guilty of engaging in counter-revolutionary agitation in his kolkhoz, against the Soviet system, against the Stakhanovite movement.[8] He was executed but was rehabilitated in January 1988.

Sergei Gorbachev was called up in August 1941 and Mikhail Sergeevich had to shoulder more responsibility. The winter of 1941–2 was extremely severe, the first snow fell on 8 October and Privolnoe was snowed in. There were no radios in the village and only the occasional *Pravda* got through. Mikhail Sergeevich read it aloud to the women and others of the village. In August 1942 the advancing Wehrmacht entered Privolnoe and later left a unit there. As a communist family, the Gorbachevs were in mortal danger and, getting wind of an intended massacre on 26 January 1943, Mikhail Sergeevich was hidden on a farm outside the village. Fortunately for all concerned, Privolnoe was liberated five days before this. The Germans had appointed 'Grandad Savka' Zaitsev the village elder. He resisted the appointment but the villagers convinced him to take it as it was thought he would protect the village. After liberation he was arrested and, despite the villagers writing scores of letters, he was sentenced to ten years for high treason. He died in prison as an enemy of the people.[9] In the winter and spring of 1944 famine broke out in the village. The family was saved from starvation by Gorbachev's mother taking her husband's clothes and exchanging them for maize in the Kuban. During the summer of 1944 a letter and documents arrived stating that Sergeant-Major Sergei Gorbachev had fallen in battle in the Carpathians. He had survived many perilous operations and had been decorated three times. Then another arrived from Sergei Gorbachev himself, also dated 27 August 1944. Perhaps he had written it before being killed. Another arrived, dated 31 August, stating that he was alive. He was wounded by shrapnel in Czechoslovakia and ended the war in a military hospital. He died in February 1976. Mikhail Sergeevich's worst wartime experience occurred in the spring of 1943 when, after the snows had thawed, he and other boys came upon 'decaying corpses, partly devoured by animals, skulls in rusted helmets, bleached bones, rifles protruding from the sleeves of rotting jackets'.[10] These Red Army soldiers were then buried in a mass grave. He was 14 when the war ended and he belonged to the wartime generation. 'It has burned us, leaving its mark both on our characters and on our view of the world.'[11]

17

School was an anti-climax after the dangers and privations of the war but Mikhail Sergeevich took to it, loved physics, mathematics and literature, became Komsomol secretary and became an enthusiastic amateur actor. Summer days were spent on a combined harvester alongside his father, and from the end of June to the end of August they worked away from home. At peak harvesting periods he worked 20 hours a day, an exhausting schedule for a teenager. Peasant life was very hard – was there any difference between it and serfdom?[12] Once his fellow workers played a joke on him, giving him a drink which they said was vodka but, in reality, was pure alcohol. Since then Gorbachev has had an aversion to hard liquor. The 1948 harvest turned out to be the best on record. Those who threshed 800 tonnes of grain were awarded the Order of Lenin. Mikhail Sergeevich's father was awarded the order and Mikhail was given the Order of the Red Banner of Labour at the age of 17. It was to remain his most cherished award and was indeed an extraordinary honour for one so young. In 1950 he completed his secondary school education at nearby Krasnogvardeisk, where he rented a room with other boys from his village. He was awarded a silver medal (later he would proudly say that whereas he had received a silver medal, Raisa Maksimovna had been awarded a gold medal). He had completed his ten years of schooling and was already 19, having lost two years during the war. Wishing to escape from agriculture and being impressed by the role of judges and procurators, he applied to the law faculty of Moscow State University. He was accepted without interview and given an extra grant as well (but he still had to share a room with 22 others during his first year). Gorbachev puts his good luck down to his peasant origin, the fact that he was already a candidate member of the Communist Party, and his elevated state award. There was also the point that the university was eager to recruit students who were not from the intelligentsia.

. . .

GORBACHEV AS A YOUNG MAN

Moscow was a revelation for a young man from a poor village in the provinces. The university opened up undreamed of vistas to his mind. It was to him a temple of learning. He graduated in 1955, with distinction, after the usual five years of study. This made him a member of the country's elite and when he joined the Politburo in 1978 he was the best all-round educated person there. True, Kosygin, the Prime Minister, was an able technocrat, but he lacked the general culture which a good law degree can confer. It was one of the few degrees in Russia which involved studying bourgeois countries and even Latin was on the curriculum. On reflection, Gorbachev is rather scathing about the intellectual standards of his day. 'The teaching process seemed to aim at brainwashing young minds from the first weeks of their studies, shielding them from the temptations of independent thought, analysis and comparison.'[13] At the time he was more naïve. He criticised one of his teachers and one of his fellow students wisely advised him to refrain from such behaviour until after the examinations! However, the academic got his own back and Gorbachev lost his personal grant.

In applying for full membership of the Communist Party in 1952 Gorbachev was caught in two minds about his background. How was he to explain that both his grandfathers had been imprisoned and declared enemies of the people? He acquitted himself well before the local Party committee and was promoted to full membership. Not learning from his previous brush with academics, Gorbachev complained to a teacher, in the autumn of 1952, that his lecture on Stalin's *Problems of Socialism in the USSR* merely consisted of reading from Stalin's work. This was a waste of time as far as Mikhail Sergeevich was concerned as he had already read the book. The furious lecturer reported him to the authorities and Gorbachev believes it was his worker and peasant origin which saved him. However, as deputy secretary of the faculty Komsomol committee he should have known better!

In early 1953, with the Doctors' Plot (in reality thinly veiled anti-Semitism) under way, Gorbachev encountered his friend Volodya Liberman in a very depressed state. He had been showered with insults and pushed off a tram, although he was a decorated war veteran. Mikhail Sergeevich records that he was shocked. He defended his Jewish friend in a university meeting and the persecution ended. Another university friend was Zdenek Mlynar, a Czech communist, who was to play a leading role in Czechoslovakia during the Prague Spring in 1968. He recalls that, during their discussions,

Gorbachev had a particular interest in political and legal history.[14] In 1991 one of his fellow students told Mikhail Sergeevich that he was even considered a dissident by his fellow students! Stalin's death on 5 March 1953 was felt by Gorbachev to be a tragedy for the country. Along with other students he spent the night passing through the streets before finally reaching the coffin. He had never seen Stalin before.

> Now . . . I saw him for the first time, dead and at close range . . . A stony, waxen face, devoid of any sign of life. I searched for traces of his greatness, but there was something disturbing in his appearance which created mixed feelings.[15]

Mikhail Sergeevich's world was turned upside down in 1951 by Raisa Maksimovna Titorenko, a student of philosophy (Marxism-Leninism). It was love at first sight for Mikhail, but not for Raisa. She wanted to break off the relationship, but Mikhail Sergeevich was tenacious and in June 1952 they decided to marry. He went off to work with his father and worked as never before. They sold the grain they earned and, together with their salaries, their income came to over 1,000 rubles, a fortune in those days. Now Mikhail Sergeevich and Raisa could get married. They were married on 25 September 1953 and to celebrate the occasion Mikhail Sergeevich bought his first suit. However, in the eyes of the university they could not live together. They lived in separate blocks and at 11 p.m. in Raisa's room the phone would ring and a stern voice would say: 'There is an unauthorised person in your room'. This changed in December 1953 when the Komsomol protested and they were allowed to live together. Mikhail Sergeevich's father took Raisa to his heart, but his mother gave her a very frosty reception.

Gorbachev graduated with distinction in 1955 but is now less than enthusiastic about his final paper on the advantages of socialist democracy over bourgeois democracy. Academically Raisa was ahead of him, having graduated a year earlier and then embarked on her candidate (PhD) degree. He was invited to undertake research on collective farm (kolkhoz) law but turned it down as he had already divined that it was a non-subject. However, as a Komsomol official he was a member of the commission which assigned graduates to their first jobs. He and 12 others were assigned to the USSR Procuracy, to a new department concerned with the supervision of the state security organs. Yet when he reported to the Procuracy he was coldly informed that it was impossible to employ him. Apparently a secret decree had prohibited the recruiting of law graduates as they were considered too young to take on the sensitive work of rehabilitating socialist justice. This blew Mikhail Sergeevich's career prospects apart and Raisa and he decided to head home to Stavropol and try their luck there. The meeting with Raisa's parents was rather stiff as she had failed to advise them of the wedding until after it had taken place. There was also the 'good' news that Raisa was abandoning her postgraduate studies in Moscow.

Gorbachev had worked in the procurator's office in Krasnogvardeisk raion, his home turf, during the summer of 1953, but did not enjoy the experience. In a letter to Raisa, he confessed he was 'depressed' and found his surroundings 'disgusting'. Some of this may have been due to being separated from his love, but he was also appalled by the demeanour of the local bosses. He found the 'acceptance of convention, subordination, with everything pre-determined, the open impudence of officials and the arrogance' off-putting. 'When you look at one of the local leaders you see nothing outstanding apart from his belly.'[16] These are the comments of a very self-assured young man. Despite his experiences he glided easily into a post in the Stavropol krai prosecutor's office on 5 August 1955. He had to break the law to find accommodation, paying an agent 50 rubles for three addresses. This money was classified under Soviet law as unearned income and hence illegal. One of the addresses turned out to be a shabby room, 11 square metres, one-third of it occupied by a stove. Water had to be collected from a pump and the toilet was outside. It was 250 rubles a month and the only furniture was an iron bed. Still, as he observed, beggars could not be choosers, and when Raisa finally arrived from Moscow they began their married life there.

. . .

EARLY POLITICAL LIFE

It did not take Mikhail Sergeevich long to realise that the law was not for him and he contacted some friends in the krai

Komsomol committee who welcomed him with open arms. He had to see the krai procurator and request permission to transfer. The lawyer made it quite plain that he regarded it as a retrograde career move but Gorbachev prevailed. He spent his first month's salary, 840 rubles, on a pair of sturdy boots, essential for the bad roads of the krai. His task was to enthuse youth to become model citizens and to work effectively. This involved tramping around the countryside, in which there was nowhere to purchase food or to rent a room for the night. Getting by was thus often a matter of charity or luck. Mikhail Sergeevich was appalled by the desperately low living standards he encountered. And after all, Krasnodar krai was one of the more fertile regions of Russia. People were eager to come together to listen to him as his arrival was an event to light up their lives of drudgery. The back rows would chew sunflower seeds but the rest would hang on his every word. He was learning the art of public speaking, addressing an audience which knew nothing of radio, television or books. He quickly discovered that the Komsomol was a junior branch of the Party and that success in political work was measured by economic success. If plans were fulfilled, political work was good, if not, it was bad and a scapegoat had to be found. He also learned one of the rules of Russian politics, indeed of politics worldwide: put the boot in before the other comrade does it to you. He was regarded as a smart Alec by many of his Komsomol colleagues who felt inferior when Mikhail Sergeevich paraded his university knowledge. The lesson he learned from this was that a clever man's cleverness consists of camouflaging the fact that he is clever.

Khrushchev's attack on Stalin at the 20th Party Congress shocked Gorbachev to the core. His task was to explain the speech to young people and he engaged in conversation with them instead of holding formal speeches. He encountered various reactions. The Party apparatus was bewildered and many refused to believe Khrushchev's claims. Among the young, some would not believe the information, some thought it was advisable to face the reality of the Stalin years, others wondered about the purpose of washing the Party's dirty linen in public, and some even thought that Stalin had merely punished those who had oppressed the people. 'They paid for our tears', is how they put it. This view Gorbachev found most difficult to comprehend since Stavropol krai had paid a heavy price during the Stalin years. The reality was easier for Mikhail Sergeevich to grasp since his own family had suffered unjustly. Nevertheless some doubts began to creep in about the speech. It was cleverly constructed to appeal to the emotions but it ascribed all the ills of the period to Stalin's character defects. There was no analysis of the underlying processes of the period.

Mikhail Sergeevich made an instant impression and in 1956 he was elected first secretary of the Stavropol city Komsomol committee. He introduced a discussion club, an unheard of novelty, and chaired all the meetings which discussed subjects such as taste and culture. Anyone who challenged existing nostrums was, of course, slapped down. Here he was displaying his growing self-confidence and his formal education provided him with the ammunition to win arguments. There was considerable unemployment in the town and crime was rampant. Voluntary youth groups were formed to help the authorities but Gorbachev quickly discovered that they could not always be trusted as they took the law into their own hands. Photographic displays were used to shame dirty factories and drunk officials out on the town.

In January 1957 the Gorbachevs had a daughter, Irina, who brought joy to the young household. However, they could not subsist on one income and Raisa had to return to work, rushing home to feed the child since there was no baby food available. They then moved into two rooms with a shared kitchen and toilet.

On 25 April 1958 Mikhail Sergeevich was elected second secretary of the Stavropol krai Komsomol committee and in March 1961 he became first secretary. Now he moved around the territory in a car and in his sturdy boots when the car could go no further. This afforded Gorbachev the opportunity of studying the styles of the first secretaries of the kraikom. The first one ruled by fear and got his comeuppance after the 20th Party Congress. The next, Lebedev, was a master mobiliser who would have raised the dead to bring in the harvest. But he was a yes man and devoid of initiative. In 1956 he insisted on fulfilling Moscow's order that harvesting should be in two stages: mowing, and then gathering and threshing. Since it was a wet summer it made sense to thresh immediately but the boss would not hear of it and thousands of hectares of grain went to waste. No one was held responsible. Instead the Party secretary was awarded the Order of Lenin for 'introducing successfully the two-stage harvesting method'. Mikhail Sergeevich got his first look at Khrushchev in October 1958 when he arrived to award the krai the Order of Lenin. He was not very impressed by Khrushchev's folksy ways which could degenerate into boorishness, foul language and heavy drinking. A major problem was Khrushchev's low level of culture. Lebedev licked the boots of top officials when they visited but put the boot in when one fell from grace. He tried to make Nikolai Bulganin's life a misery after he had been posted to Stavropol in the wake of his dismissal as Soviet Prime Minister. Lebedev was awarded a second Order of Lenin in 1957 and a third one in 1958. Not to be outdone by the Americans, Khrushchev launched a campaign in late 1958 to catch up with and overtake the US per capita output of meat and milk. Stavropol krai tried to compete with Ryazan oblast which delivered three years' meat in one year, 1959. Stavropol only managed two and a half years' supply. But at what a cost. Everything on four legs, including horses, was liable to be culled and the peasants' private livestock was decimated. It took years to make good the depredations. Lebedev was politically culled; he retired in 1960 'for health reasons'.

A watershed in Mikhail Sergeevich's political education was the 22nd Party Congress, in October 1961. It was his first experience of high politics at the centre and Khrushchev was in full flow. The most riveting speech was delivered by D. A. Lazurkina, a Party member before 1917, who had a special relationship with Lenin whom she carried in her heart: 'Yesterday, I consulted Lenin, as if he were alive, standing before me, and he said: "I hate being together with Stalin, who has brought so many misfortunes on the Party"'.[17] This gave a new meaning to the Order of Lenin and the delegates duly complied. Stalin was removed from the Lenin–Stalin mausoleum on Red Square and buried near the Kremlin Wall, and the mausoleum reverted to its former name, the Lenin mausoleum. Gorbachev realised that attacks on the cult of the personality (Stalin) were accompanied by praise for Khrushchev. Delegates would compete with one another to pour extravagant praise on the leader. One called Khrushchev's uneducated speech a 'powerful symphony'. Another referred to his penetrating 'insights into the fundamental processes of life'. Khrushchev loved it, much to Gorbachev's irritation. This may have been his private emotion but in public he applauded and smiled. His attitude to Khrushchev was ambivalent. On the one hand Khrushchev confronted the Stalin phenomenon head on and set in motion undercurrents which would make themselves felt two decades later. On the other hand he never attempted to get to the root of the problem and was often arbitrary in decision-making. Eventually the Party generals and officer corps (the obkom and raikom first secretaries), who had saved him in 1957, conspired to remove him in October 1964.

A stroke of luck for Mikhail Sergeevich was the appointment of Fedor Kulakov as first secretary of Stavropol kraikom in 1960. They took to one another very quickly and in March 1962 Kulakov suggested that Gorbachev move to Party work. He was made responsible for three agricultural raions and had got the job after an interview in the Central Committee Secretariat in Moscow. Gorbachev was now launched on his Party career, and the ladder of success would take him to the top, to the post of general secretary of the Party. In November 1962 Kulakov chose Gorbachev to head the department of Party organs in the krai, thus making him responsible for the appointment of Party personnel, and senior posts in industry, sovkhozes and kolkhozes. This was the nomenklatura. Besides this he was to supervise the soviets, the trade unions and the Komsomol. He began his duties in this influential post on 1 January 1963. Kulakov was a role model for Mikhail Sergeevich. His leadership style consisted in being affable with everyone but being as cunning as a fox – Gorbachev calls it 'peasant cunning'. Kulakov was involved in the plot against Khrushchev in October 1964 and was rewarded with promotion to Moscow, as CC secretary for agriculture. Mikhail Sergeevich thereby gained his first patron at the centre. Without someone to praise one's abilities in Moscow there was little likelihood of making it to the top.

Kulakov's successor in Stavropol krai was Leonid Efremov. The move for him was a demotion; he had been too close to Khrushchev and was therefore sent packing from Moscow. In 1962 Khrushchev, in an effort to make Party organisations more accountable, had split the Party apparatus into industrial and agricultural wings. In November 1964 the Brezhnev leadership decided to amalgamate the two wings and a battle royal ensued among officials to acquire one of the coveted posts. Many fell by the wayside since the new organisation was much smaller than the two previous combined. Mikhail Sergeevich, as head of Party organs of the agricultural organisation, was a key player, and participated in the no holds barred conflict over status and privilege. Efremov was a man of a different mould from Kulakov. He was well educated, had a broad political culture and was an exquisite product of the communist system. Efremov still harboured hopes of a recall to Moscow, anywhere else for him was political disaster, and he always attempted to ingratiate himself with the Moscow titans. When Leonid Brezhnev, now general secretary, was holidaying at a local Stavropol spa, Efremov would make it his business to join his entourage and attempt to make a good impression on the new Kremlin boss. Efremov regarded the 23rd Party Congress, in April 1966, as his great opportunity to make it back to the centre by praising the current leadership. He brought Gorbachev with him to Moscow, parked him in his hotel room during the duration of the Congress and phoned him after every break in proceedings with refinements to his speech, which Mikhail Sergeevich was endlessly editing. However, it was all in vain because Efremov was never called to speak at the Congress. This bitter blow forced him to accept that he was yesterday's man and afterwards he concentrated his considerable talents on Stavropol krai. Studying his mode of operation was like a permanent seminar for Mikhail Sergeevich and he learned many valuable political lessons from Efremov. On 26 September 1966 Gorbachev was elected first secretary of Stavropol city Party organisation, or gorkom. It was technically a demotion, as his previous position was higher on the nomenklatura scale and had carried a higher salary. But he had no hesitation in accepting it as it gave him more room to demonstrate his initiative. A general development plan was drawn up but the eternal problem of resources held it back.

Gorbachev discovered a basic weakness of the centrally planned economy. There was no agency to coordinate all the separate plans and to integrate them into a cohesive whole. He was frustrated by the Moscow ministries being only concerned with their own patch. The krai Party organisations also only concentrated on fulfilling Gosplan's directives. No one at the centre was interested in ideas about a more effective incentive scheme from faraway Stavropol. There were attempts to improve the situation and in February 1967 an article appeared in *Novy Mir*, the progressive journal, written by Gennady Lisichkin, advocating dramatic changes in agriculture, among which was the right of kolkhozes and sovkhozes to dispose of their produce freely. All his examples had come from a raion in Stavropol krai. Had this been adopted, farms would gradually have acquired the right to decide what to produce. In essence this would have meant the end of the state planning of agriculture. The CC apparatus in Moscow could not permit this and the raion secretary who had been implementing these radical changes, Barakov, was sacked in January 1967. Efremov then placed an article in *Selskaya Zhizn*, the CC agricultural newspaper, in September 1967, demolishing Lisichkin's arguments. Gorbachev perceived this as a classic example of the Party apparatus protecting its privileges at the expense of economic efficiency. Had farms been permitted to use their initiative, Soviet agriculture would have produced much more food under Brezhnev and saved the country billions of dollars in imports. Gorbachev commented: 'It was a hard lesson for me'.[18]

Another lesson for Gorbachev was the pervasive influence of the KGB. Zdenek Mlynar, a friend from his university days, visited him during the summer of 1967 after lecturing in Moscow on Czechoslovak thinking on political reform. He provided Mikhail Sergeevich with a detailed briefing of the situation in Czechoslovakia. Then Mlynar was appointed a CC secretary, Communist Party of Czechoslovakia (CPC), and was later to play a leading role in drafting the CPC Action Programme and the events which became known as the Prague Spring. Gorbachev was intrigued and wrote to Mlynar but received no reply. Hints by the KGB chief in the krai revealed that the reply had ended up in a KGB file. This was a revealing episode as it demonstrated that not even the first secretary of Stavropol gorkom had the right to correspond with communists abroad.[19]

During the summer of 1968 the first secretary of the Karachai-Cherkess obkom, which was part of Stavropol krai, was dismissed for adultery and leaving his wife. It was felt that cohabiting with another woman undermined the authority of the Party. The second secretary of Stavropol kraikom was appointed in his place. This left vacant the second most

27

important post in the kraikom. Mikhail Sergeevich did not think he was in the running and wanted to go off on holiday but Efremov ordered him to stay put. A few days later Gorbachev was called into Efremov's office and, not bothering to conceal his resentment, Efremov informed Gorbachev that he was going to Moscow. The latter was naïve enough to ask whom he was to see in Moscow. He was to be interviewed in the CC organisation department because 'there are plenty of people there who support you'.[20] Kulakov had evidently been spreading the word about Mikhail Sergeevich's talents. So he became second secretary of Stavropol kraikom on 5 August 1968. The fact that Efremov's nominee had been rejected by Moscow did not augur well for his future in Stavropol. Despite this insult to Efremov's authority, Gorbachev and he patched up their relationship.

The Warsaw Pact invasion of Czechoslovakia which began on 21 August 1968 was a personal blow to Mikhail Sergeevich. As Efremov was away he chaired the kraikom meeting to support the 'decisive and timely measures taken in the defence of socialist achievements in Czechoslovakia'. Privately Gorbachev was left wondering about the wisdom of the invasion.[21] The invasion had a nefarious influence on the development of critical thought in Russia. Orders came from Moscow to stamp out any deviation from orthodoxy. In early 1969 F. B. Sadykov, an assistant professor of philosophy (Marxism-Leninism) at the Stavropol agricultural institute, published a book entitled *The Unity of the People and Contradictions of Socialism*. The manuscript had gone through the usual vetting system and had been shown to the CC secretariat in Moscow. Sadykov had even published an article on the same theme in *Voprosy Filosofii*. He had been daring enough to use the term 'contradictions of socialism' and this illustrated the more relaxed political climate of the early and mid-1960s. Contradictions in Marxism are problems which arise during the development of socialism. They can either be non-antagonistic or antagonistic. The former are problems which can give rise to social unrest which does not threaten the socialist order. The latter are problems which, if not corrected, can lead to a revolutionary situation. Needless to say, Sadykov was pointing out non-antagonistic contradictions. Moscow sent orders to make an example of him. In May 1969 the kraikom attacked the 'grave errors' in Sadykov's book and he was thrown to the wolves. The krai's top ideologist demanded his expulsion from the Party, which would have ended his academic career. Gorbachev also laid into Sadykov, who afterwards left Stavropol. But Mikhail Sergeevich remembered Sadykov's suggestions and some of them were implemented under perestroika.[22] The treatment of Barakov and Sadykov left a bitter taste in Gorbachev's mouth. He states that he had 'qualms of conscience about the cruel and undeserved punishment meted out to them'.[23] It was now clear that the crushing of the 'socialism with a human face' in Czechoslovakia had almost extinguished hopes of reforming the economic system in Russia. For Gorbachev, it was the beginning of the era of stagnation.

Mikhail Sergeevich was aided by Raisa's research into the living standards of the kolkhoz peasantry in the krai and she was duly awarded her candidate of science (PhD) degree by Moscow State University in 1967. He was also academically active and acquired a diploma in agricultural economics, as an external student, at the Stavropol agricultural institute, also in 1967. He wrote his dissertation on milk production. Gorbachev was fortunate that the director of the institute was Aleksandr Nikonov, who was to influence him about ways of increasing productivity in agriculture.[24]

Efremov's desire to return to Moscow was fulfilled in early 1970 and Mikhail Sergeevich was elected first secretary of Stavropol kraikom in April 1970, a month after his 39th birthday. There was a time-honoured ritual for the new first secretary of a gorkom, obkom and kraikom to observe. The CC Secretariat collected information on the proposed new appointee, then he was interviewed by some of the CC secretaries and finally he was ushered into the presence of the 'man himself', the general secretary. The interviews with the CC secretaries were a mere formality as it was up to the boss, Brezhnev, to announce the good news. The boss prided himself on his skill with cadres, he was organisation man personified. Since he was a consensual leader he did not want officers (first secretaries) who would disobey or intrigue against him. He desired stability and sought to minimise risk-taking. Brezhnev had the skill, while uttering banalities about domestic and foreign policy, to give the impression that he was confiding in his interlocutor. Gorbachev found Brezhnev 'artless', as it was perfectly clear where his questions were leading.

The conversation lasted several hours. This was the Mark I Brezhnev, the pre-1974 general secretary, who was capable of speaking coherently for several hours.

. . .

FOREIGN VISITS

A mark of a promising Komsomol leader was an invitation to join a delegation to a socialist country. Gorbachev's first experience abroad was to the German Democratic Republic (GDR) in 1966. At the time the GDR was embarking on economic reforms which were more radical than the Kosygin reforms in the Soviet Union, so there was much to study. Mikhail Sergeevich found east Berlin 'cold and forbidding', a comment usually on the lips of visitors from the west. Their host was Erich Honecker, who was to succeed Walter Ulbricht in 1971 as Party leader, and who Gorbachev found strikingly self-assured and confident. In 1969 and 1974 Gorbachev visited Bulgaria. Agriculturally it appeared to be the Garden of Eden but the Russians, at the time, did not know the country was living beyond its means. The most painful but also educative experience was a trip to Czechoslovakia in 1969. Another member of the delegation was Egor Ligachev and this was their first meeting. The ostensible task was how to win over the youth of the country but this was a hopeless task. The open hostility communicated itself to the Soviet delegation and they realised that their Czechoslovak hosts were afraid of their own people. When visiting an enterprise in Brno, workers refused even to talk to Gorbachev and the others. Fearing assault, the Russians were guarded around the clock. There was no opportunity for Gorbachev to contact Zdenek Mlynar who was now *persona non grata* in Moscow. The visit was a chastening experience for Gorbachev but it stimulated some reflections about the domestic situation at home. Once he had become first secretary of Stavropol gorkom, he qualified for inclusion in delegations to capitalist countries. The first visit was in 1972 to Belgium which also included a quick look at the Netherlands. It was on this jaunt that he first met Anatoly Chernyaev. Later in the 1970s Gorbachev visited France, Italy and the Federal Republic of Germany. The most profound shock was the standard of living which was clearly higher than in Russia. How was this possible under capitalism? The Russians were also struck by the openness and give and take of debate on political and other issues. Their interlocutors, most of them communists, often disagreed among themselves. This led Mikhail Sergeevich to question his belief that socialist democracy was superior to bourgeois democracy. In contrast, the Russian delegation always had a single view and its members made sure no one knew what he or she was really thinking. He reflected gloomily on the old men in the Kremlin who had no interest in such affairs and who were concerned about finding ideological justification for the status quo.

A formative experience for Mikhail Sergeevich was a visit to Canada in May 1983. He discovered that although Canadian farming was highly productive, it was also heavily subsidised by the state. Just as important, he got to know Aleksandr Yakovlev, Soviet ambassador to Canada, who was later to become the father of glasnost. On his return Gorbachev returned to his argument that more state aid for the agrarian sector was needed. He decided not to talk about Canada to his audiences as it would only have depressed them.

. . .

EARLY POLICY DECISIONS AND POLITICAL ADVANCEMENT

The nature of Soviet politics required a new man to demonstrate that he was in charge by launching a few initiatives. Gorbachev was a risk-taker but risk-takers need their fair share of luck. His first move was to draft an ambitious agricultural plan for the krai. In the century before 1870, there had been droughts in 52 years. Hence water supply was of prime importance. A Stavropol canal was being constructed but Mikhail Sergeevich calculated that it would take until the millennium or even longer for it to be completed. He came up with his own ideas but the capital had to come from Moscow. The first move was to enlist the Russian Minister of Land Reclamation and Water Management, who just happened to be on holiday in the krai. Nothing could be decided without a meeting with 'himself'. Brezhnev was in Baku for an award ceremony and Gorbachev just happened to be standing beside him on the rostrum. He did not let the opportunity slip and got an interview with the boss.

Brezhnev was enthusiastic, called a special Politburo meeting and the plan was launched. It was made a Komsomol project, thus guaranteeing a supply of eager young people and resources. The canal was finished in 1978. Then the question arose about what would be grown on the irrigated land. Moscow wanted every square centimetre sown to grain but Gorbachev knew that it was advisable to allow some of the land to lie fallow (unused) each year. The silver-tongued Gorbachev could not make any impression on the men at the centre. However, luck played a part. In 1975 and 1976 there were severe droughts. In late May 1976 about half the crops were a write-off. The Russian Minister of Agriculture panicked and ordered the slaughter of sheep and cattle in the krai because of lack of fodder. Gorbachev opposed him and it was left to Kulakov, CC secretary for agriculture in Moscow, to decide. When he phoned, Mikhail Sergeevich was persuasive but Kulakov warned him that he would be held responsible if things went badly. Everyone in the krai was mobilised to collect fodder in ditches, road verges and urban lawns. Gorbachev flew to Moscow and got an emergency 60,000 tonnes of concentrated fodder. Then the rains came and the krai was saved. Buoyed up by this success, Gorbachev decided to lobby for fallow in the krai. Kulakov's response was as before: see the boss. Brezhnev was on holiday in the Crimea and as luck would have it an obkom first secretary, who was a native of Stavropol, was a member of his party. So the boss phoned and told Mikhail Sergeevich that he would back him. The Russian government opposed fallow, however, and there was also a Politburo resolution recommending the expansion of grain everywhere. Gorbachev kept his nerve. The following year, 1977, saw a bumper crop and 1978 was even better. Fortune favours the brave. Either by luck or judgement he had calculated that if 1975 and 1976 were years of drought, the probability of 1977 being an excellent year was high. Hence the time to go for fallow was 1977. Another problem for the krai was meat. About 75 per cent of its production went outside the krai and output had to be increased quickly. Gorbachev decided to take a risk and go it alone. He promoted the expansion of poultry farms and so the output of chicken rapidly increased. One of the main benefactors was Viktor Postnikov, like Gorbachev from Privolnoe, who received permission from Mikhail Sergeevich to set up a poultry farm and sell the meat in Stavropol. By 1983 he had become very success-ful, mainly due to Gorbachev keeping the government bur-eaucracy off his back.[25]

Stavropol krai was a high profile agricultural region and someone else had cast his eyes on it in order to further his political career. Fedor Kulakov needed a publicity-grabbing initiative and he found one in the perennial problem of bringing in the harvest. A proportion of it was lost annually due to failure to bring it in. The problem was urgent given the increasing expensive imports of grain from North Amer-ica, necessitated by the failure of Russian farmers to produce enough grain to feed the population and the animal stock. The raion chosen was Ipatovsky because it was flat and was sown to winter wheat which matured at the same time. A computer model of the project was refined in 1976 and it was launched in 1977. The district was divided into 54 har-vesting segments, each with combine harvesters, trucks, and 15 Party persons to underline that it was a Party initiative. Harvesting was to continue round the clock. The weather was on its best behaviour. Harvesting was completed in nine days (usually it took two or three weeks) in early July and 200,000 tonnes were delivered to the state as promised by Party officials. *Pravda* on 20 July trumpeted this success and called on the whole country to follow suit. In February 1978 Kulakov was given the title of Hero of Socialist Labour, the highest accolade in the Soviet Union. Gorbachev received the Order of the October Revolution and many others were decorated as well. The harvest in 1978 in Ipatovsky raion was even better, producing 240,000 tonnes for the state. Con-gratulations were muted as Kulakov died on 17 July 1978.[26] Gorbachev spoke at Kulakov's funeral and Russian viewers saw for the first time their future leader. But he was taken aback by the fact that Brezhnev and other members of the Politburo did not bother to interrupt their vacation to attend the funeral. It became clear to him how incredibly remote these leading comrades were from one another, indeed from the people.

The Ipatovsky method of harvesting died with Kulakov. It was a classic example of the subordination of economics to politics. The goal was not to raise the efficiency of Russian agriculture but to enhance the profile of a political actor.

The concept was sensible but was not applicable to other parts of the country. Spring sown crops mature at different times and harvesting in the rain is not advisable unless grain drying facilities are available. The concentration of so many resources in Ipatovsky raion meant that other raions were at a disadvantage. The episode is not alluded to in Gorbachev's memoirs. He reverted to his support of the link system in farming, according to which teams are paid by results and stay together from sowing until the sale of the produce. This caused him to reflect on the nature of the communist system. Why was it that initiatives from below, which clearly would have benefited society as a whole, were frowned upon by the centre? Initiatives had to come from the top and if they failed no one was held responsible. If an innovation began from below, those involved could end up in gaol. Mikhail Sergeevich concluded that it was actually impossible to do something worthwhile if one observed all the rules and regulations.

In late 1977 Gorbachev was in Moscow and got into an argument with Kulakov over credits and incentives for farms. Kulakov's ego was bruised after being informed that Aleksei Kosygin had been appointed head of the preparatory commission of an upcoming CC plenum on agriculture, and to add insult to injury he, Kulakov, was not even a member of the commission. Cunningly, he suggested Gorbachev write down all the points he had made. Mikhail Sergeevich put his heart into it and submitted a 72-page memorandum to Kulakov on 31 December 1977. Kulakov then suggested the memorandum be sent to all members of the Politburo. Gorbachev demurred but submitted a shorter version, while retaining all the main arguments, and forwarded it in May 1978. At the CC plenum on 4 July 1978 Gorbachev was given the floor for the first time at a CC plenum and spelled out the serious problems facing socialist agriculture. He favoured more autonomy for farms and operatives. Some of the ideas in the memorandum later formed part of perestroika and one can trace the influence of Nikonov in them.[27] After finishing his speech the Russian Minister of Agriculture told him he should have heeded his counsel and avoided certain topics. It turned out that Mikhail Sergeevich had been blithely unaware of the fact that there was a factional struggle within the Politburo. Gorbachev made up for this *faux pas* by lavishing praise on Brezhnev's *Malaya Zemlya*, an account of his wartime exploits. The book was ghost-written and is of doubtful literary merit. Gorbachev's speech, on this occasion, is tactfully omitted from his collected works. He, however, was becoming increasingly worried by the gulf which was developing between the rhetoric of the leadership, which emphasised successes, and the reality of a stagnating economy.

Had Kulakov been Mikhail Sergeevich's only patron in Moscow his upward mobility would have ended with Kulakov's death. The fact that he was to succeed Kulakov as CC secretary for agriculture testifies to other influential backers. They included Yury Andropov, head of the KGB from 1967 to 1982, Mikhail Suslov, the guardian of ideological orthodoxy and dismissed by some as a desiccated calculating machine, and Aleksei Kosygin, Prime Minister from 1964 to 1980. Andropov and Suslov had connections with Stavropol krai and Kosygin went there for vacations. In August 1978 Andropov proposed Gorbachev meet him at a spa in Stavropol krai. It then became clear to Gorbachev that Andropov was briefing and assessing him. The men at the centre were very interested in the young leader in Stavropol krai. Andropov listened to his usual complaint about the old cadres needing some new blood. Later Gorbachev recalled a joke which circulated at the 26th Party Congress in 1981: 'How will the 27th Party Congress be opened?' 'The delegates will stand while the Politburo members are wheeled in!'[28] Another story was that the ambition of every Politburo member was to die as general secretary. In September 1978 Brezhnev, Chernenko and Andropov arrived in Mineralny Vody and Gorbachev acted host. It was difficult keeping a conversation with Brezhnev going. At one point Brezhnev asked for Andropov's opinion of his speech. Back came the obligatory reply: 'fine, fine'. Afterwards Gorbachev asked Andropov about this and it transpired that he had misunderstood. Brezhnev had been enquiring about the way he spoke his words since by then he had considerable difficult in speaking. A Politburo member, A. P. Kirilenko, dropped in just afterwards but it became clear he had come for a row. Gorbachev judged him malevolent and incoherent. It is of interest that Suslov did not realise that Gorbachev harboured heretical thoughts about the Party management of the economy and society. He had mastered the art of pleasing almost everyone. Another enemy was Nikolai Shchelokov, the powerful Soviet Minister of the Interior, with whom he crossed swords as early as 1973. The minister and many of his police officials were corrupt and he recognised in Gorbachev someone who would not be intimidated. Under Chernenko he feared the advance of Gorbachev and told his entourage that Mikhail Sergeevich had to be destroyed.

Although Kulakov had died in July 1978 no one was appointed to succeed him before the CC plenum in November 1978. Gorbachev, as a member of the CC (he had been elected a full member at the 24th Party Congress in 1971), was in Moscow and at a party. Konstantin Chernenko's assistants desperately tried to find him and rang the flat where he was. The person who answered gave the usual Russian reply: 'wrong number'. By 1978 it was patently clear that Chernenko was Brezhnev's chosen successor. The Romans had an adage that a man of few words is a wise man. Chernenko was taciturn but Gorbachev had learned to be wary of strong, silent types. Chernenko informed him curtly that Brezhnev had selected him as the new CC secretary for agriculture. When Gorbachev enquired whether he was expected to make a speech at the plenum, Chernenko sarcastically remarked that this was not necessary since he had made one quite recently. This was promotion indeed. It was not the first time that the leadership had thought of bringing him to Moscow. In the early 1970s he was asked if he would like to head the CC propaganda department. He swiftly turned that one down. He was sounded out for the post of Soviet Minister of Agriculture and even as Procurator General, the top law post in the country. He found none of them attractive. A sleepless night followed. At the CC plenum on 27 November 1978 Gorbachev was proposed by Brezhnev as a CC secretary and it went through on the nod as did some other personnel changes. The next day, without an invitation, he called on Brezhnev. The boss had no interest in conversation, merely muttering: 'it's a pity about Kulakov, he was a good man'.[29] Gorbachev was then summoned by Suslov, who liked to keep people at arm's length and conversations short and businesslike. Gorbachev was consulted about his Stavropol successor and he recommended Vsevolod Murakhovsky. Suslov agreed and that was the end of the conversation. Then Gorbachev paid courtesy calls on the other CC secretaries and their staffs. He felt a total stranger; the officials he had worked with for years all seemed to have frozen faces. This was his initiation into the inner sanctum. It was chillingly impersonal.

It was palpably clear that Brezhnev was quite incapable of carrying out his functions as leader of the Party and state. After one incoherent Politburo session Mikhail Sergeevich voiced his concern to Andropov. The latter seized the opportunity to make clear to Gorbachev that he was extremely keen on the status quo. This view was shared by most members of the Politburo and the government as it permitted them a free hand in their domain. There was also the point that as head of the KGB, Andropov's chances of succeeding Brezhnev were slim. He needed to move into the CC Secretariat to have a real chance of becoming the next leader. As long as Suslov, head of the Secretariat, was alive there was scant chance of that happening. Hence Andropov and the other gerontocrats were placing their own careers ahead of the interests of the country, which desperately needed dynamic leadership. The seating order at Politburo meetings was strictly observed (as a CC secretary Gorbachev had the right to attend). To the right of Brezhnev would sit Suslov, to his left Kosygin, and after 1980 Tikhonov. To the left of Suslov would sit Kirilenko and a few others. Opposite Brezhnev sat Gromyko, Andropov, Ustinov, Chernenko, and then at the very end, Gorbachev. Brezhnev was less than coherent at the best of times, but when he turned his head to consult others it was impossible to hear what was being said since Gorbachev was a long way away. Sitting next to Chernenko was like sitting next to a jack in the box. He was constantly jumping up, rushing up to Brezhnev and correcting him, saying that item has been decided already or been removed from the agenda. Just as every comrade had a dedicated chair, so he was expected to concern himself only with his own policy area.

Gorbachev's first harvest in charge in Moscow, in 1979, was a disappointment. In early September he sent a memorandum to the Politburo asking for more resources and for the estimated shortfall to be imported from North America. Kosygin reacted negatively and told Mikhail Sergeevich that there was no foreign currency available and that he should be more severe and demand that farms deliver the required grain. Gorbachev's curt reply was that, if the Prime Minister thought that the Party had failed, he should order his own ministries to acquire the grain. Brezhnev sided with Gorbachev and a chastened Kosygin phoned later and requested he forward his proposals to the Politburo. Gorbachev felt bad about falling out with Kosygin, whom he respected. However, the cloud had a silver lining. Mikhail Sergeevich acquired the reputation of being a strong man and in late autumn 1979 Suslov phoned him to inform him he was to be promoted a candidate member of the Politburo. Some had even wanted to promote him to full membership but Suslov thought this unwise because of his lack of experience.

What part Gorbachev played in the decision to invade Afghanistan is debatable. As a junior member of the Politburo he was not privy to the discussions of the inner circle: Brezhnev, Gromyko, Ustinov, Andropov, Suslov and Chernenko. Gorbachev's role increased dramatically after the US declined to deliver grain already sold to Moscow as part of the sanctions imposed in the wake of the invasion. Thinking and research began which was to lead to the introduction of the Food Programme in 1982. It was an uphill task to acquire more resources for agriculture. The prevailing opinion was that agriculture was loss making, that more was spent on it than it produced. The Minister of Finance always stated that there was no extra money to invest in agriculture. A major problem was statistics. The State Committee for Statistics (Goskomstat), Gosplan, the Ministry of Finance and other bodies did not use comparable methods in computing statistics. It was also always expressed in general terms. Gorbachev began his own detailed study of the state of Soviet agriculture and was appalled by the waste, apathy and exploitation of the countryside he discovered. He spent long hours with specialists and commissioned many studies. Aleksandr Nikonov, now in Moscow, was of great assistance. Mikhail Sergeevich found that 28 per cent of national income originated in agriculture, thus refuting the argument that agriculture was the black hole of the economy. He published his findings in *Kommunist*, the official journal of the Central Committee.[30] Studies of the economy revealed that defence expenditure was rising much faster than gross domestic product. Was it possible to cut the defence budget? The chair of Gosplan, Nikolai Baibakov, hinted to Gorbachev that it might be possible. The person who could bring this up in the Politburo was Gorbachev (Baibakov was not a member). Baibakov asked if he would be willing to broach the subject. The response was an emphatic no. He and Baibakov agreed that to propose such a thing would result in instant dismissal. Defence and security was a taboo subject, the preserve of Brezhnev and Ustinov.

The Food Programme was the main problem on Gorbachev's mind at this time. The terms of trade had turned against agriculture as procurement prices had risen more slowly than industrial inputs into the agrarian sector. Annual loans were extended to keep farms afloat. If this continued the whole sector would eventually go bankrupt. Tikhonov, now Prime Minister since Kosygin's resignation in 1980, was very cool and kept insisting that the money was not available. The programme was to be coordinated by state agro-industrial committees (Gosagroproms) in the regions and the centre. Mikhail Sergeevich spent hours selling the initiative to Tikhonov and eventually the Prime Minister revealed his main objection: Gosagroprom at the centre could be used by Gorbachev to undermine Tikhonov's position as head of government. There were even rumours that Gorbachev was using the programme as a tactic to become Prime Minister himself. Again the economic merits of a project were being jeopardised by personal political considerations. Gorbachev deleted all references to the Gosagroproms and Tikhonov nodded assent. In other words, there would be no coordinating agency to drive the programme. It would be supervised by the ministries who, in turn, would have little interest in promoting its success since this would redound to Gorbachev's advantage. It was passed on 24 May 1982 and was to run to 1990.

. . .

MANOEUVRES IN THE POLITBURO

Politicians the world over mix socially in order to exchange ideas and gossip. The Soviet elite was an exception. Soon after becoming a full member of the Politburo in November 1980 Gorbachev invited Andropov and his wife over for dinner since they lived in adjoining dachas. Andropov declined and informed Mikhail Sergeevich that he could not meet privately with another member of the Politburo because the boss would hear of it and conclude that the two were conspiring against him. This is a very revealing episode and underlined the fact that Soviet politics was personal politics and that it was every comrade for himself. Every member jealously guarded his own patch and this is an explanation for the lack of communication which existed. Gorbachev may have had many bright ideas about how to improve agriculture but they could not be implemented because they would have impinged on the territory of others. Hence the Politburo did not act as a cabinet form of government. Members related directly to Brezhnev and if they displeased him they were out. Just as there was a pecking order of members of the Politburo, the same applied to their wives. Raisa was once put in her place by Kirilenko's wife pointing to her proper position, the end of the queue. This was the formal aspect of Moscow life. But there was also the informal, and Mikhail Sergeevich and Raisa feasted on the theatre, the galleries and music of the capital. Their intellectual curiosity set them apart from the other members of the ruling oligarchy.

Mikhail Suslov was second secretary under Brezhnev but never aspired to be the boss. His death on 25 January 1982 transformed relations in the Politburo. There were two main contenders for the second slot which, given Brezhnev's frailty, promised greater things. They were Konstantin Chernenko and Yury Andropov. Chernenko clung to the boss like a leech and only left him when he was asleep. Gromyko phoned Andropov and talked about the KGB chief moving into the Secretariat to become number two. Gromyko's main concern was to keep his post as Minister of Foreign Affairs. Ustinov was another Andropov fan. On 24 May 1982 Andropov was elected to the Secretariat. Andropov was not formally made chair and, hence, second secretary. Chernenko and Kirilenko continued to chair sessions. Then in July 1982 Andropov seized the initiative and rushed to the head of the table and sat down. Chernenko admitted defeat by slumping into his chair and almost disappearing from view. It turned out that the boss had phoned Andropov the night before and asked him why he was not chairing Secretariat meetings. Brezhnev had been prompted to do this by Ustinov. Andropov brought some life to the Secretariat but he played a waiting game.

There was no point in antagonising colleagues since he had his eye on the boss's chair. Politburo sessions normally lasted 15–20 minutes and discussion was minimal. Commissions were set up to cope with the business the Politburo should have been discussing. Their conclusions were presented and approved and the matter left there. Chernenko clucked around Brezhnev like an old hen. The boss liked to think of himself as the patriarch who brought only good to the country. When informed about some painful deficiency tears would well up in Brezhnev's eyes and Chernenko would mutter: 'How did he manage to slip past me?'.

Brezhnev died unexpectedly on 10 November 1982 and when Gorbachev met Andropov he did not beat about the bush. He asked Andropov if he had already seen the inner circle, Ustinov, Gromyko and Tikhonov. He nodded and this signified that Chernenko had lost and that the new boss would be one of Gorbachev's fans. During the summer of 1982 Gorbachev had drafted a memorandum on economic policy, the fruit of much consultation with specialists. He proposed a Politburo commission on economic policy and Andropov was in favour. Next came Chernenko and Brezhnev's personal assistants but they buried it because they regarded it as another attempt by Mikhail Sergeevich at empire building. Gorbachev redrafted it and forwarded it to Brezhnev. He liked it but was against another Politburo commission. Instead there should be an economics department in the CC Secretariat. Gorbachev was asked to think of names to head it. It was one of the first topics he discussed with Andropov as leader. Gorbachev wanted someone fresh, someone from outside the Secretariat. They agreed on Nikolai Ryzhkov, first deputy chair of Gosplan who had had much industrial experience. At Andropov's first CC plenum, on 22 November 1982, Ryzhkov was elected a CC secretary. The new boss wanted a close and friendly team around him and so Gorbachev and Ryzhkov came to work closely together. In December 1982 Andropov sacked Nikolai Shchelokov, the corrupt Minister of Internal Affairs. He had previously been powerless to move against the minister as he enjoyed Brezhnev's protection. Brezhnev had replaced Andropov as head of the KGB with Vitaly Fedorchuk and now the new leader made Fedorchuk Minister of Internal Affairs and appointed his own man, Viktor Chebrikov, head of the KGB. Kirilenko was also retired. He had been so far gone that Andropov had to draft his resignation note for him to copy in his own hand. Andropov began building up his own group in the Politburo. Geidar Aliev, the first secretary of the Communist Party of Azerbaijan, was elected a full member of the Politburo. Gorbachev had grave reservations about him but, as a former KGB boss of Azerbaijan, he was Andropov's man. Grigory Romanov, first secretary of the Leningrad obkom and a full member of the Politburo, whom Mikhail Sergeevich regarded as 'narrow-minded, insidious and dictatorial', was drafted in as a CC secretary to help Ustinov. The latter did not object since Romanov never came up with a sound suggestion at Politburo meetings. Egor Ligachev was brought into the leadership, at Gorbachev's suggestion, in April 1983, on being made head of the department of organisational affairs. This department was responsible for Party personnel. Ligachev was promoted a CC secretary in December 1983. As first secretary of Tomsk obkom, Ligachev had been far from Moscow and he could be relied upon to support Andropov. The other group included Tikhonov, the Prime Minister, who assumed that Andropov owed his promotion to him and acted accordingly. Then there was Vladimir Dolgikh, the CC secretary for industry. He was mortally offended when Ryzhkov was appointed to head the economics department. Brezhnev had hinted to Vladimir Shcherbitsky, the first secretary of the Communist Party of Ukraine, that he was in line for the post of general secretary. Shcherbitsky never once dropped into Andropov's office and telephone calls were difficult for Andropov.

Gorbachev and Ryzhkov were given the task of examining the possibility of increasing the prices of bread and cotton fabrics. They asked to see the state budget and were firmly rebuffed by Andropov: 'The budget is off limits to you'.[31] What an astonishing situation. Gorbachev discovered later that there was a large deficit which was met partly by using citizens' savings. How was the budget to be balanced if only the general secretary knew that it had to be balanced? Ingrained in Andropov from his KGB days was his attitude to social and economic problems. The solution was always to restore discipline. He launched anti-alcohol and discipline campaigns which backfired. He would not accept that the KGB and police seizing citizens who were queuing or in the sauna instead of being at work would undermine his authority. The anti-drinking campaign produced Andropovka, a cheap and nasty substitute for vodka which promoted the black market and the mafia.

Andropov's health began to deteriorate during the summer of 1983 and he had been undergoing dialysis treatment to cleanse his blood since February. Rumours spread that the Andropov era was coming to an end and the old guard was delighted.[32] Chernenko presided at Politburo and Secretariat meetings. Now and again Gorbachev chaired Secretariat sessions. Andropov's address to the CC plenum, on 26–27 December 1983, drafted by his aides, was awaited with interest. It concluded with the recommendation that, in his absence, Politburo meetings should be chaired by Gorbachev.[33] However, when Andropov's text was distributed to Politburo members and later to CC members, the recommendation was missing. The general department of the Secretariat, headed by a member of the old guard, had excised the key passage but could not have acted alone. It was probably Chernenko, Ustinov and Tikhonov who took the risk of opposing Andropov's wishes.[34]

When Andropov died on 9 February 1984 Gorbachev regarded Ustinov as the natural successor. He, in turn, thought Mikhail Sergeevich should be elevated to the top post. The matter was settled at the Politburo meeting, chaired by Chernenko, with Tikhonov jumping in with a point of order. The point was to nominate Chernenko, who did not object, despite the poor state of his health. No one opposed this as the tradition of the Politburo was always to avoid division. Everyone voted for Chernenko. The latter immediately proposed Gorbachev as head of the Secretariat, and thus second secretary, and to chair Politburo sessions when he was absent. Tikhonov's main objection to Gorbachev heading the Secretariat was that he only knew about agrarian affairs. It was agreed that Gorbachev would be *de facto* head of the Secretariat. Tikhonov attempted to weaken the Secretariat by courting Ligachev, but was rebuffed, and so courted Dolgikh instead, hinting that he could become Tikhonov's successor. Dolgikh trotted over to Tikhonov's group. Ustinov gave Mikhail Sergeevich unswerving support, as did Ligachev and Ryzhkov. The scheming and petty intrigue got to Gorbachev and he seized every opportunity to escape from

Moscow. The matter came to a head at the end of April when Chernenko informed Gorbachev that the work of the Secretariat would be discussed at the Politburo meeting on 3 May. Ustinov was alarmed when he heard the news but at the Politburo meeting the issue was not raised. Ustinov had convinced Chernenko not to give in to the Tikhonov faction.

In June 1984 Gorbachev led the Party delegation to the funeral of Enrico Berlinguer, the leader of the Italian communists. It made a deep impression on him as Berlinguer was mourned by all Italians. Then in December 1984 he headed a parliamentary delegation to Great Britain, where Margaret Thatcher, the British Prime Minister, immediately identified him as a new-style Russian. 'We can do business together', was her celebrated comment. One of the things she appreciated about Gorbachev was that he was the only Soviet politician with whom she could have a good argument. In order to emphasise his concern about the arms race, Gorbachev produced a diagram of the nuclear arsenals of the world, divided into a thousand squares. He pointed out to Mrs Thatcher that only one of these squares could wipe humanity off the planet. Gorbachev used his speech to both houses of parliament on 18 December to launch his new political thinking in foreign affairs and to appeal for a new era of negotiation and an end to confrontation. His expression 'Europe is our common home' was much quoted. Gorbachev made an enormous impression and the British Foreign and Commonwealth Office had already identified him as the man they wished to see in the Kremlin.[35]

Gorbachev's popularity did not please an important member of the Politburo, Andrei Gromyko. He gave Anatoly Dobrynin, the Soviet ambassador in Washington, a dressing down for reporting in detail to Moscow on American reaction to Mikhail Sergeevich's visit. Gromyko was jealous. Gorbachev cut short his visit on hearing the news of Ustinov's death. He had lost an ally in the fight against the intrigues of his detractors. Chernenko's emphysema got progressively worse and by the end of 1984 he dropped out of the picture. Gorbachev chaired the weekly meetings of the Politburo and Tikhonov would ask if he were doing so at Chernenko's request. But Gorbachev was only asked at very short notice, half an hour, thus preventing him from acquainting himself thoroughly with the agenda. Discussions sometimes took the form of a member stating that Chernenko had told him so and so during a conversation. Someone else would cut in and say what Chernenko had told him, often contradicting the first speaker. Gorbachev's cause was helped enormously by Egor Ligachev, who drummed up support among obkom and kraikom first secretaries. He also encouraged Chernenko not to give credence to everything which was whispered into his ear about Gorbachev.[36]

. . .

GORBACHEV IS ELECTED GENERAL SECRETARY

Chernenko died on 10 March 1985 and a Politburo meeting was arranged for 11 p.m. With Ustinov dead Gorbachev did not have a strong, senior supporter in the Politburo. Just before Chernenko's death, Tikhonov had approached Chebrikov, head of the KGB, to lobby against Gorbachev's nomination. Before the meeting began Gorbachev attempted to repair his fences with Gromyko. The latter had been promoted first deputy Prime Minister by Andropov and was regarded as vain and power hungry. A key question to be decided at the Politburo meeting was who was to chair the funeral commission because previously it had always been the incoming general secretary. Gorbachev was surprised to hear Viktor Grishin, a conservative and competitor, proposing him. When Mikhail Sergeevich returned home he told Raisa that he would accept the nomination if offered it. On 11 March the Politburo session opened and was chaired by Gorbachev. Gromyko was first to speak. He stated that when one thought of the post of general secretary, one thought, of course, of Mikhail Sergeevich. Such a choice would be 'absolutely correct'.[37] He then proceeded to praise his nominee to the skies. Afterwards he added a warning. 'We do not have the right to allow the world to perceive the slightest differences in our reports . . . we must act in unison . . . aware of our responsibility for our great cause.' Then Grishin spoke. 'Yesterday evening, on learning of the death of Konstantin Ustinovich, we resolved, to a certain extent, the question [of the succession] when we confirmed unanimously Mikhail Sergeevich as chair of the funeral commission. In my opinion, he measures up best to the standards we have set for the secretary general.'[38] Romanov was next to speak. 'I think he will ensure the continuity of the leadership of our Party and that he will carry out fully the duties which are placed on him.'[39] Chebrikov then stated that he had been greatly impressed by A. A. Gromyko's words about 'maintaining and reinforcing the unity of the Politburo'. He was convinced that 'Mikhail Sergeevich Gorbachev would carry out his duties with honour'.[40] Demichev then said he was sure they were making the right choice. Ligachev thought Gorbachev's promotion would 'evoke pride in our country and raise the authority of the Politburo'.[41] All the other members of the Politburo supported Gorbachev's nomination (only Shcherbitsky was absent) as did the CC secretaries. Gromyko, the master survivor, had changed sides once again. It had been hinted that he would become Soviet President. Presumably Tikhonov had attempted to put a coalition together against Gorbachev but had failed. The consensual nature of Politburo politics ensured that only one nomination was put forward. The CC plenum convened at 5 p.m. and was chaired by Gorbachev. He immediately gave the floor to Gromyko, who delivered a remarkable extempore speech, in which he lauded the new general secretary, who, of course, was elected unanimously. In his speech, Mikhail Sergeevich set out his stall. He referred to the 26th Party Congress, in 1981, to underline continuity, stressed the need for economic and social progress, based on science and technology, and high labour productivity. Democracy was to be developed, as was social consciousness. There was to be glasnost in the work of Party and state institutions. In foreign policy he proposed an end to the arms race and a reduction of nuclear stock piles. The Party was capable of uniting society and the creative forces of socialism would blossom.

· · ·

NOTES

1. Archie Brown, Professor of Politics at the University of Oxford, was the first western academic to perceive that Gorbachev was a reform-minded communist. His first published remarks about Gorbachev as a future general secretary with reformist predilections appeared in Archie Brown and Michael

Kaser (eds), *Soviet Policy for the 1980s* (London, Macmillan, 1982). His book, *The Gorbachev Factor* (Oxford, Oxford University Press, 1996), is the most scholarly study of Gorbachev and his era in any language. It is sympathetic to Gorbachev.

2. Mikhail Gorbachev, *Memoirs* (London, Doubleday, 1996), p. 24. The author was one of the editors of these memoirs and also wrote the foreword and other entries in the book. The memoirs have also appeared in Japanese and German. Michail Gorbatschow, *Erinnerungen* (Berlin, Siedler Verlag, 1995), runs to 1,216 pages. The English edition of the memoirs is based on the translation of the original Russian manuscript which is 2,355 pages long. The epilogue, written in 1996 for the English edition, runs to 66 pages. Hence the English edition, 769 pages long, is a shortened version of the Russian original. All the cuts made for the English edition were agreed with Mikhail Gorbachev. The original Russian manuscript is in the Library, School of Slavonic and East European Studies, University of London. The Russian edition of the memoirs is: Mikhail Gorbachev, *Zhizn i Reformy*, 2 vols (Moscow, Novosti, 1995).
3. Gorbachev, *Memoirs*, p. 24.
4. Ibid., p. 24.
5. Ibid., p. 25.
6. Ibid., p. 26.
7. Ibid., p. 26.
8. Ibid., p. 31.
9. Ibid., p. 31.
10. Ibid., p. 34.
11. Ibid., p. 34.
12. Ibid., p. 36.
13. Ibid., pp. 43–4.
14. Brown, *The Gorbachev Factor*, pp. 30–2.
15. Gorbachev, *Memoirs*, p. 47.
16. Raisa Gorbachev, *I Hope: Reminiscences and Reflections* (London, HarperCollins, 1991), p. 66; Gorbachev, *Memoirs*, p. 47.
17. Gorbachev, *Memoirs*, p. 69.
18. Ibid., p. 81.
19. Gerd Ruge, *Gorbachev: A Biography* (London, Chatto and Windus, 1991), p. 74; Brown, *The Gorbachev Factor*, p. 41. The correspondence between Gorbachev and Mlynar led to the KGB questioning fellow students in the Law Faculty at Moscow University about their relationship during the early 1950s.
20. Gorbachev, *Memoirs*, p. 80.
21. Ibid., p. 82.
22. Ibid., p. 83.

23. Ibid., p. 83.
24. Brown, *The Gorbachev Factor*, pp. 43–4; Gorbachev, *Memoirs*, p. 120. Nikonov had grown up in inter-war Latvia and had experienced the advantages of small-scale farming there. He was an admirer of Aleksandr Chayanov (1888–1939), a brilliant Russian agrarian economist during the 1920s, who favoured large farms but did not believe this applied to the peasant family farm, which operated according to other criteria than profit. His pre-1929 writings were in vogue, promoted by Nikonov, then president of the Lenin All-Union Agricultural Academy, during the Gorbachev years. Nikonov was the driving force behind Chayanov's rehabilitation in July 1987. Nikonov also admired the work of Nikolai Kondratieff (or Kondratiev) (1892–17 September 1938 when he was executed), a famous economist, who discovered the long cycles, named after him. He regarded private agriculture as inherently more efficient than state-run agriculture. These ideas form the basis of the proposals that farms and farmers be given more autonomy under socialism which runs through Gorbachev's years in Stavropol krai, and then afterwards as leader of the Soviet Union. Gorbachev consistently turned to Nikonov for advice when he was Party leader in Stavropol krai and this continued after Nikonov moved to Moscow in 1978, the same year Gorbachev moved there. Kondratev was rehabilitated on 16 July 1987.
25. Brown, *The Gorbachev Factor*, p. 45.
26. Zhores Medvedev, *Gorbachev* (Oxford, Basil Blackwell, 1986), pp. 81–7; Brown, *The Gorbachev Factor*, pp. 45–6.
27. Mikhail Gorbachev, *Izbrannye rechi i stati* (Moscow, Politizdat, 1987), vol. 1, pp. 180–200; Brown, *The Gorbachev Factor*, pp. 46–7.
28. Gorbachev, *Memoirs*, p. 11.
29. Ibid., p. 15.
30. M. S. Gorbachev, *Kommunist*, no. 10, 1982, pp. 6–21.
31. Gorbachev, *Memoirs*, p. 147.
32. Aleksandr Yakovlev offered an unflattering appraisal of the Andropov era. It amounted only to 'cleaning off the dirt when the levels exceeded those of the minimal standards of sanitation'. A. N. Yakovlev, *Predislovie, Obval, Posleslovie* (Moscow, Novosti, 1992), p. 102.
33. Ibid., p. 152.
34. The Andropov aide most involved was Arkady Volsky and he has offered various versions of the episode. Angus Roxburgh, *The Second Russian Revolution* (London, BBC Books, 1991), p. 17; Brown, *The Gorbachev Factor*, pp. 67–9.

35. The author organised a conference on Gorbachev and the Soviet leadership in the University of London and invited Foreign and Commonwealth Office participants. They did not appear and explained afterwards that if it were reported in the press that academics and diplomats favoured Gorbachev, this might be used by his detractors in the Kremlin against him. Someone who was good for the west could not be good for the Kremlin.

36. Yegor Ligachev, *Inside Gorbachev's Kremlin* (Boulder, CO, Westview Press, 1996), pp. 54–5.

37. Vladimir Boukovsky, *Jugement à Moscou: Un dissident dans les archives du Kremlin* (Paris, Robert Laffont, 1995), p. 264.

38. Ibid., p. 265.

39. Ibid., p. 265.

40. Ibid., pp. 265–6.

41. Ibid., p. 267.

Chapter 3

PERESTROIKA MARK I:
1985–1987

Gorbachev used the expression perestroika for the first time in March 1984 when addressing a conference on the agro-industrial complex[1] and he expanded on it at a conference on ideology in December 1984.[2] The latter conference would underline Gorbachev's role as second secretary and permit him to seize the high ground of reform. It also allowed him to address the Party officer corps over the heads of the gerontocracy in Moscow. As before, Gorbachev was willing to take the risk. (Chernenko proposed to Gorbachev on the eve of the conference that it should be cancelled.)

A group of aides began working on the draft in the autumn at a dacha and among these were Aleksandr Yakovlev (who had returned to Moscow in 1983 to become director of the Institute of World Economics and International Relations (IMEMO), USSR Academy of Sciences, through Gorbachev's good offices), Vadim Medvedev, head of the science and education department of the Secretariat, and Valery Boldin. The aides had to accept that the era of surpluses was over. There were now shortages of labour, raw materials and agricultural land. Extensive growth was no longer possible, progress had now to come through intensive growth or obtaining more from existing resources. The key resource was now labour. The idea of perestroika or restructuring the economy derived from a comparison of the Soviet and American economies. The Russians had always been chasing the Americans and had set quantitative targets, but the Americans had moved the goal posts. They, and other developed market economies, began to import oil, coal and raw materials when comparative advantage was evident. They rapidly developed new industries, chemicals, electronics and aerospace, where technical innovation was very rapid due to risk-taking. Russian industry missed out on this revolution and was pursuing outdated quantitative goals and the technological gap was alarmingly wide and growing.[3] Various solutions were proposed, based on scientific and technical innovation. Gorbachev and Ryzhkov had been instructed by Andropov to commission studies from specialists and in March 1985 about 110 major studies were ready.[4] One of those involved in drafting some of these projects, a member of the CC international department, summarised, after 1991, their rationale:

Although the various ideological scenarios, authorised or created by Gorbachev's ideologists, were radically different one from the other, they all had the same political goal: maintaining the Party élite in power. That would occur if one maintained the socialist system or if the collective property of the nomenklatura became the private property belonging to its individual members.[5]

Novikov also does not regard glasnost as the beginning of the end of Marxism-Leninism but as a return to the Marxism the Party had abandoned in 1924.

In his conference speech Gorbachev introduced the terms uskorenie (acceleration) and the 'human factor'. Would there be a role for market mechanisms? Gorbachev was briefed that commodity–money relations already existed under socialism and this term is also used in the speech. However, reformers used this term as code for a socialist market. Politically, Gorbachev was aware that most communists believed the market was unnecessary under developed socialism. The question, however, must remain open whether he really understood that there were various approaches to the market and what they entailed.[6] The speech was also notable for using the terms glasnost and democratisation. Gorbachev had an extremely retentive memory and could recite streams of statistics at will. He made a careful note of reactions in the press and among officials to his December 1984 speech. Boldin states he could still reel off those who had failed to support his ideas. This told against them later.[7]

. . .

SECURING A POLITICAL BASE

A new general secretary is elected to carry on the work of the Politburo and to protect its dominant position in the state. Unlike a US President or British Prime Minister, he may not appoint his own cabinet and launch his own initiatives. All reform has to be intra-systemic and designed to strengthen the prevailing order. If Politburo members perceived that the new boss was undermining the system, or in other words undermining their power bases, they would remove him post-haste. Gorbachev could not enact his own political preferences until he had secured a base which would ensure that he could not be dismissed overnight. His priority was to promote his own supporters and remove opponents. It could take years for a new leader to become a strong, national leader. Stalin, Khrushchev and Brezhnev all needed at least five years to become unassailable. Gorbachev achieved it in one. Yeltsin, one of his most severe critics, was lost in admiration: 'He operated with amazing finesse'.[8]

At the CC plenum on 23 April 1985 Gorbachev secured a working majority in the Politburo by proposing the election of Ligachev and Ryzhkov to full membership (without going through the usual candidate stage) and the promotion of Chebrikov from candidate to full membership. Viktor Nikonov succeeded Gorbachev as CC secretary for agriculture but did not advance to the Politburo. Gorbachev made it quite clear that Ligachev was the new second secretary and would run the Secretariat. At another CC plenum, on 1 July, Grigory Romanov, hostile to Gorbachev, was removed from the Politburo and the Secretariat. Eduard Shevardnadze, first secretary of the Communist Party of Georgia, a long-time Gorbachev confidant[9] and a candidate member, advanced to full membership of the Politburo. Two new CC secretaries were elected: Lev Zaikov, replacing Romanov, and Boris Yeltsin, for construction. On 2 July Andrei Gromyko, Grim Grom to the outside world, was moved upstairs to become Soviet President and Shevardnadze became the new foreign minister. The latter was stunned by the promotion and explained to Gorbachev that he knew nothing about foreign affairs. However, he did share Gorbachev's view of the world, which was of greater value than diplomatic expertise.

The foreign office was appalled and Gromyko was shocked by the appointment, seeing Georgy Kornienko or Anatoly Dobrynin as his natural successor. Both men remained constant critics of the new foreign minister, regarding him as an amateur among professionals. When George Shultz, the US Secretary of State, asked Dobrynin to describe the new foreign minister, the Kremlin's ambassador offered the assessment that Shevardnadze was an 'agricultural type'.[10] Shevardnadze kept Kornienko on until 1986, deferring to his knowledge until he felt he could dispense with him. Kornienko's anti-American sentiments were beginning to jar and he was packed off as Dobrynin's deputy in the international department.

On 27 September 1985 Nikolai Ryzhkov took over from Nikolai Tikhonov as Soviet Prime Minister. On 15 October Nikolai Talyzin, the new head of Gosplan, was elected a candidate member of the Politburo, thereby upgrading planning. On 24 December Boris Yeltsin replaced Viktor Grishin, nicknamed the Godfather because of his corrupt ways, as first secretary of Moscow gorkom. Two months later Yeltsin was promoted a candidate member of the Politburo (but he thought he merited full membership). At the 27th Party Congress, from February to March 1986, only one new member was elected: Lev Zaikov, CC secretary for the defence industries. The first secretaries of the Belorussian Party and Leningrad obkom, Slyunkov and Solovev, became candidate members. This was not a surprise as these posts qualified the holders for election to the Politburo. Kuznetsov, the Soviet Vice-President, and Boris Ponomarev, CC secretary and head of the international department in the CC Secretariat, were put out to grass, being already in their eighties. However, it was in the Secretariat that Gorbachev really made his mark. Only Vladimir Dolgikh, heavy industry, and Mikhail Zimyanin, culture and propaganda, survived from the Brezhnev era. Five new secretaries were appointed: Aleksandra Biryukova, consumer affairs, the family and trade unions; Anatoly Dobrynin, just back from being Moscow's man in Washington, head of the international department (this was a victory for Shevardnadze who wanted to get Gromyko's man out of the foreign office and into the Party apparatus); Vadim Medvedev, relations with communist parties in socialist states; Georgy Razumovsky, department of organisational work [cadres];

and Aleksandr Yakovlev, propaganda. In total, Gorbachev had now replaced 14 of the 23 heads of departments in the Secretariat. No previous Party leader had been able to make so many personnel changes during his first year in office. In the Russian Federation, 24 first obkom and kraikom secretaries changed, as did 23 of 78 in non-Russian republics. Four of the 14 first secretaries of republican Communist Parties were new. In government, 39 of 101 Soviet ministers were sacked. Nationwide about one-fifth of all officials of primary Party organisations lost their jobs and the number of government officials who were sacked or transferred ran into the thousands. The personnel changes testify to the consensus at the top that the Brezhnev generation had to be swept away. On paper this was a magnificent achievement, but how significant was it? One informed observer thought it was tantamount to replacing Tweedledum with Tweedledee![11] Those who succeeded had been groomed in the same political stable. Nevertheless there was reform in the air and incisive leadership was needed to give direction and purpose to change.

Gorbachev could only appeal to the new Party and state appointees to be more responsive to the aspirations of the population and to be more effective in their endeavours. However, with his own hand-picked team he could be much more demanding and hire and fire at will. Who were the men and women who helped the general secretary to formulate his ideas? Aleksandr Yakovlev, Nikolai Ryzhkov, Eduard Shevardnadze, Egor Ligachev and Boris Yeltsin played key roles in 1985–7. In his more immediate entourage there were Anatoly Chernyaev, valuable as a foreign policy adviser and also to a certain extent on domestic reform; Vadim Medvedev, head of the department for socialist countries, 1986–8; Valery Boldin, adviser on agriculture until 1987, then made head of the general department, which drafted the Politburo agenda and provided background papers; Georgy Shakhnazarov, first deputy head of the department for socialist countries, 1986–8, and then from 1988 a full-time Gorbachev aide; and Ivan Frolov, on ideology. The most important formative influence was Aleksandr Yakovlev, who had unique qualifications. Before becoming Soviet ambassador to Canada in 1973, Yakovlev had worked in the CC Secretariat. He knew the Party apparatus, brash north American capitalism and the academic world. Yakovlev was the dominant influence until 1988 and can be seen as the grandfather of perestroika and glasnost. Mikhail Sergeevich, of course, was the father. Chernyaev, Shakhnazarov and Frolov had all worked on the *World Marxist Review* in Prague and this widened their horizons. Shakhnazarov was second only to Yakovlev as an adviser and influence in the evolution of political reform in and after 1988. The disadvantage of these advisers, apart from Yakovlev, was that they had not spent any time in a western state. This would have been invaluable in considering political reform in the Soviet Union. Even more significant was that only Yakovlev had direct experience of a successful capitalist economy. Boldin was a competent economist but only in the context of a command economy. The most influential economist in the early phase of perestroika was Abel Aganbegyan, who had developed his views in the Academy of Sciences in Novosibirsk. But he had had no direct experience in industry. Tatyana Zaslavskaya, a sociologist, provided much material on what was wrong about the Party-dominated economy.

. . .

ECONOMIC AND SOCIAL PERESTROIKA

The Gorbachev leadership understood that perestroika, or the restructuring of the economy and society, would be a complex set of integrated reforms. The sequence of these reforms would depend on the balance of forces in the Politburo. In the beginning, only mild intra-systemic reform could be contemplated. When Gorbachev had secured a working majority in the Politburo he could move on to radical reform, if so desired. Gorbachev's perception in 1985[12] was that intra-systemic reform would achieve the results expected.[13] He informed the Politburo on 11 March 1985, after being elected general secretary, 'We must not change our policy. It is right, correct, authentically Leninist. We have to accelerate our rhythm, go ahead, be frank and overcome our faults and see clearly our luminous future.'[14] At the April CC plenum this became known as uskorenie (acceleration). It was only in 1987 that Gorbachev came to understand that he was confronted with a systemic crisis: the system itself was in terminal decline.

It was expected that while the economy was undergoing fundamental changes, workers would enjoy greater rewards. The engine of the economy was the machine-building sector and so it was decided to expand rapidly machine tools, instrument making, electrical engineering and electronics.[15] Abel Aganbegyan's thinking was that the Soviet economy had to grow by at least 4 per cent to compete on a global scale and at a time of rising defence expenditure.[16] As spare resources were simply not available, growth would have to be achieved by a 'considerable growth of labour productivity by introducing advanced equipment and automation'.[17] The goal set for the machine-building sector was to expand by 50–100 per cent during the Five Year Plan (1986–90). Industrial production was to rise 25 per cent, investment by 23.6 per cent and real per head income by 14 per cent.

A new approach was adopted to labour, which traditionally in Soviet industry had been treated as a cheap resource. Now industrial relations were to be transformed by the introduction of the human factor.[18] The ambitiousness of this plan is evident from the performance of the Soviet economy in the preceding years. Gorbachev wrote gloomily in 1987 that national income growth had declined almost to zero at the beginning of the 1980s.[19] Aganbegyan concluded, in 1988, that there had been no economic growth over the years 1981–5.[20] Mark Harrison concludes that GNP growth per head between 1950 and 1974 was 3.6 per cent annually, but between 1974 and 1985 was only 0.5 per cent annually. This implies that during the 1981–5 period, growth was negative.[21] However, it is important to stress that this was not the perception at the time. The fact that the Soviet economy was in crisis was not realised in 1985. Since the diagnosis of the economic ills was wrong in 1985, the medicine prescribed had little effect. Once the correct diagnosis was made in 1987, very radical medicine was prescribed, but by that time Gorbachev was concentrating on political reform and foreign policy.

The first stage of perestroika can be summed up as follows:[22]

- Uskorenie (acceleration): the concentration of investment in the machine-building sector so as to upgrade the technical base of the economy.

56

- Perestroika: restructuring the economy, transforming industrial relations.
- The human factor: the need to make more humane social and economic relations by moving away from technocratic management to involving the labour force significantly in industrial production. This is the beginning of the move away from command and control to motivation and incentives. This led on to glasnost and democratisation.
- Integral socialism:[23] an attempt to integrate the above phenomena into developed socialism (the stage which Soviet society had then reached) in order to raise it to a higher level. This was to be intra-systemic reform and was not intended to weaken the foundations of the socialist system.

Gorbachev summed up the problems facing perestroika:

> Of major importance are such fundamental problems as ways of accelerating scientific and technical progress and intensifying production; improvement of the forms of socialist ownership to guarantee increasingly close links between the immediate producer and the social means of production, strengthening the producer's feeling of being a collective owner of all social property; activation and optimisation of the system of interests, with national interest taking precedence; development of the scientific foundations and practice of planning the economy as the principal means of implementing the Party's policy; improvement of the system of distributive relations.[24]

This long, complex sentence spells out the economic mechanism the leader was searching for. He believed that state-owned enterprises, when freed from the stifling control of the central planners, would act as market agents. The discussion about cooperative property began in 1986 but it was always regarded as a side show. The search for the economic mechanism ignored two major problems: ownership and prices. The problem of ownership was not seriously considered.[25] How was demand and supply to be balanced if there was not a sweeping price reform?

Gorbachev's frustration at the lack of support for radical solutions found expression in his report to the 27th Party Congress when he stated that many wanted to 'improve things without changing anything'.[26] One of the reasons for

opposition to change was the long-standing Russian concern about egalitarianism. Gorbachev could have reflected
on a Russian joke which rejected intra-personal competition
(the envious neighbour syndrome). A peasant is ploughing
a field and unearths a bottle. When he removes the cork a
genie pops out and offers to grant him a wish.

> 'Look at Vasya's cow over there. He milks it, and makes cheese
> and butter which he then sells in the market, making a whop-
> ping profit.' 'So you want me to give you a cow like Vasya's?'.
> 'No, no, no', snorts the peasant, 'I want you to kill Vasya's
> cow!'[27]

The public perception of perestroika was that the bureaucrats were merely paying lip service to it while applying the
brakes in reality. A story going the rounds in Minsk in late
1986 neatly illustrates this. Gorbachev, Reagan and Mitterrand
meet and start discussing their problems. Mitterrand says he
has nine mistresses and one is cheating on him. He can't
work out which one. Reagan says that is a minor problem
compared to his. He has 50 bodyguards and one is a KGB
agent but can't discover who he is. Gorbachev waves all this
aside and complains that his problem is much more serious.
He has 100 ministers in his government and one of them is
implementing perestroika but he doesn't know which one.[28]

There are two main approaches to the reform of centrally
planned economies: rationalising economic reform, and the
big bang. The Kosygin reforms of 1965, the Hungarian New
Economic Mechanism of 1968, the Polish reforms of the
1970s, are examples of rationalising economic reform. Prices
are set by planners and economic activity is guided by the
centre. Ownership is of secondary importance. These reforms
resulted in some modest advances but were not sustainable.
Economists and politicians were engaged in a vain search
for the 'perfect' economic mechanism. The proponents of
this school of thought will be called rationalisers. The latter
were always trying to find a third way, between a command
economy and the market.

Those who thought a third way was a myth concluded
that the rationalisers were deluding themselves. The only
way to rationalise successfully a command economy was to
destroy it. This approach has been labelled shock therapy,
the big bang, the 500-day programme, and so on. Here it

will be referred to as the big bang, and its proponents, the big bangers. They advocated a short, sharp, shock therapy. The first time it was implemented was in Poland, beginning on 1 January 1990. A market economy has to come into existence as quickly as possible. The first stage is price reform. Price controls should be removed from as many goods as possible to cope with the problem of high inflation and chronic shortages of goods. New economic institutions have to be created, beginning with privatisation. Demonopolisation and restructuring of existing enterprises are of crucial importance. The economy, now guided by proper price signals, begins its painful transformation.

. . .

PROMOTING PERESTROIKA

Everyone wanted to see the new general secretary and shake his hand. His first visit was to the Likhachev car plant in Moscow in April 1985. Boldin claims that he advised Gorbachev to travel to the factory as ordinary workers did in order to appreciate how hard life was.[29]

Mikhail Sergeevich did not come to praise but to point out that the country was technologically backward. Since there were no surplus labour and raw materials, increases in production had to come through labour productivity. Then he visited a hospital and was shown wards with healthy looking patients sporting crew cuts. They were full of praise for the medical staff and the food but very vague about their ailments. It transpired that the KGB had turfed out the real patients and drafted in their own men! Then Mikhail Sergeevich would be invited into an ordinary worker's flat and find the table groaning with delicacies.[30]

On 15 May he made a highly successful visit to Leningrad and he was so pleased that he gave orders that his speech to Party cadres be shown complete on television.[31] He was gradually acquiring the self-confidence to speak without reliance on detailed notes. However, this revealed one of his weaknesses. He found it difficult in extempore speech to complete his sentences and often his remarks were diffuse and imprecise. He had a butterfly mind, he flitted about from subject to subject when he spoke. On the other hand, it also revealed a very quick mind.

In June he flew to Kiev and Dnepropetrovsk in Ukraine and again made an excellent impression. Here was a general secretary who was well briefed, could answer questions quickly and wittily, and who could move between two points without any support from his aides. The Ukrainian Party leadership were not so enamoured, however, as he pointed out hard home truths about industry and agriculture there. Ukraine had been like a nature reserve under Brezhnev, protected from critics.

Then came an assault on the west Siberian oil and gas industry by Mikhail Sergeevich and a posse of officials in early September. He was appalled by the rape of nature he encountered and the waste of resources. He estimated that the oil-refining rate was 58 per cent whereas the world level was about 80 per cent and that a cubic meter of timber only produced a fraction of the wood expected in the west. He also knew that the amount of energy expended per unit of output in the Soviet Union was several times that in the west. He was treated like a hero and warmed to the people, saying that all would be well with perestroika since the people were behind it. However, there was one thing on which he would not budge. The workers wanted more cooperative building in southern parts of the country where they could go on holiday and retire to. He was adamant and told them that they should live and retire in the north which was of such economic value to the country. This did not go down well with people who lived in the polar north without modern amenities. He missed an opportunity to give substance to the new policy called the human factor. Had he proposed that if they doubled output, cooperative housing would be doubled, he would have motivated them to work their fingers to the bone. Hard drink is a constant companion in the polar north and his audiences did not take kindly to his sermons on the evils of drink. The anti-alcohol campaign cut no ice in the north.[32]

Mikhail Sergeevich developed an appetite for public speeches, gatherings, interviews and press articles. A torrent of words flowed from him. The custom had been that the general secretary's speeches were approved beforehand by the Politburo but this broke down under the sheer volume of speeches and the rapidly increasing number of interviews afforded foreign visitors. Politburo and Central Committee members got used to learning about the latest initiative from the media. There was less and less time to digest the impact of one initiative before the next one was launched. Wherever Mikhail Sergeevich went, Raisa was sure to go. She cut a fine figure in the provincial backwaters. She concerned herself about the TV coverage and objected to Mikhail Sergeevich being shown from the rear. Aleksandr Yakovlev thought it irrelevant that the general secretary had been seen from the rear:

> After all, anyone who has seen him can testify that the back of his head has an exceptionally noble, handsome profile, that he is unusual in that he goes to the hairdresser every day, and that many people would be proud if the backs of their heads were shown every day on TV. So what was all the fuss about?[33]

The early years of perestroika were marked by much enthusiasm, typical of the early stages of a revolution. During this period it is common for those swept up in the process of change to believe that contradictory goals can be achieved because everyone is united in their desire for change. Inevitably interests diverge and tension surfaces, giving rise to disillusionment and anger. These began for Gorbachev in 1988. The first phase of perestroika was marked by the following:[34]

- There was a broad consensus in society about the nature of the reforms to be introduced. This obscured the fact that there were powerful interest groups opposed to all or certain aspects of reform.
- No serious study was devoted to examining whether there were interest groups which could lobby effectively to protect their interests and undermine reform. This was due to the belief that only contradictions and not antagonistic contradictions could exist. The former are blemishes on the face of socialism and can be overcome quickly but the latter give rise to social tension which can lead to a revolutionary situation.[35] Andropov, the new general secretary in 1983, conceded that there were contradictions under socialism but did not mention whether they might be antagonistic or not.[36] Chernenko firmly denied that antagonistic contradictions could surface under socialism. Gorbachev, in his December 1984 speech, declared:

61

'Under socialism, of course, they [contradictions] are non-antagonistic'.[37]

- Opposition to perestroika was expected only from some members of the top Party leadership who placed self-interest ahead of the general interest. The Gorbachev leadership accepted that such survivals of conservative thinking were also present in some sections of the population. However, they believed that articulation of the benefits of perestroika, persuasion and education would overcome these obstacles.

- Perestroika was conceived of as mass mobilisation, recalling the campaigns of the 1930s. This implied that the same values were shared by all.

- The conviction that everyone accepted the need for reforms and the nature of them deluded the leadership into believing that they could be achieved quickly and solve the problems which had been building up in society for several years.

- This led to the belief that contradictory goals could be achieved simultaneously. An example was the anti-alcohol campaign which was to overcome drunkenness[38] quickly but which resulted in large losses of revenue to the state budget at a time when there was to be greater investment in the machine-building sector. It was launched by Gorbachev in May 1985 and was based on the assumption that if the liquor was not available people would not drink. According to Nikolai Ryzhkov, the amount of vodka distilled fell by 50 per cent in a year, and wine and beer dropped two-thirds. Drinkers took to toothpaste, shoe polish and samogon (hooch). Ryzhkov estimates that the budget, over the three years 1986–8, lost 67 billion rubles (US$100 billion at the then official rate of exchange) of revenue and slid seriously into deficit at the same time. The shortage of alcohol spawned an increase in organised crime.[39] The anti-alcohol campaign was abandoned in 1988 but the damage had already been done.

- Economists did not comment on the clear contradictions in the goals of perestroika. Uskorenie was to switch resources to the machine-building sector, and at the same time it was expected that the standard of living would increase perceptibly. It is remarkable that no one pointed out these contradictions at the time.[40]

- Cooperative and individual labour activity was legalised during the first phase of perestroika. However, most top Party leaders rejected the free prices which prevailed in the cooperatives and individual activity and wished to see them brought under control. This culminated in a campaign in 1986–7 against 'unearned income' by Party functionaries. Local officials seized the opportunity to obstruct the legal transport of goods to kolkhoz markets. 'Axes and bulldozers' were used in some places to devastate peasants' early vegetables under glass and plastic sheets.[41]
- The leadership believed itself almost omnipotent and could set and achieve any desired goals.
- Perestroika Mark I was based on the assumption that the economy was not in crisis. The new measures were targeted at improving the existing economic system. Although the Party shied away from using the word market, radical economists did have a latitude and influence, unparalleled since the 1920s.
- It was thought that perestroika would result in rising living standards and there would be no unemployment as the economy was restructured. There would be no losers, everyone would be a winner. The people had decided finally and irrevocably in favour of socialism. They would not tolerate the dilution of the socialist ownership of the means of production and the social gains of socialism.

On paper, the economic reforms looked promising. However, in agriculture, the level of inefficiency was mind-boggling. Egor Gaidar calculated that 590 billion rubles (US$890 billion at the then exchange rate) had been invested in the rural sector over the years 1971–85. Yet the proportion of national income produced by agriculture in 1985 was the same as in the early 1970s.[42] Agriculture really was a black hole.[43]

.   .   .

GLASNOST

Glasnost became essential after the poor handling of the Chernobyl nuclear disaster in April 1986. The reaction of the public demonstrated that the official media enjoyed little credibility. This permitted Aleksandr Yakovlev to revitalise some parts of the media. He recruited Vitaly Korotich from Kiev to become editor of *Ogonek*, then a dull as ditch-water magazine. His brief was to shake up the effete establishment. However, Korotich regarded glasnost as tantamount to 'giving an old trollop a sponge bath and putting clean clothes on her, assuming that this would restore her virginity'.[44] In 1986 new editors were also brought in to run *Moskovskie novosti* (*Moscow News*), *Literaturnaya gazeta*, *Izvestiya*, and the influential journals *Novy mir* and *Znamya*.

On 16 December 1986 Gorbachev phoned Andrei Sakharov and invited him to return to Moscow from exile in Gorky (Nizhny Novgorod). However, on his return he was treated as a pariah (he had promised not to get involved in politics) and it was only during the summer of 1987 that the Soviet media dared quote him.

Gorbachev had had problems in deciding what to do about Sakharov. At a Politburo meeting on 29 August 1985, he reported that he had received a letter from the 'too celebrated Sakharov' in late July, requesting permission for his wife Elena Bonner to go abroad for treatment.[45] Chebrikov revealed that the main objection to allowing Sakharov to go abroad was from the Minister of the Light Machine Building Industry, which produced nuclear weapons, who feared that he would be given a laboratory to continue military research. He concluded by stating: 'His behaviour is controlled by Bonner'. Gorbachev rejoined: 'There's Zionism for you'. Gorbachev asked if it would be possible to get Sakharov to declare he would not go abroad. Chebrikov was afraid that if they gave in to Sakharov, on the eve of Gorbachev's meetings with Mitterrand and Reagan, it would be construed as weakness. Mikhail Zimyanin was the most unrestrained in his language about Bonner: 'She is a dirty viper in a petticoat, a woman who is an imperialist boot'. Gorbachev queried whether letting her go or keeping her at home would be more costly. He summarised the conclusion they had reached. They would confirm the receipt of the letter and that it had been thoroughly discussed. Bonner's desire to go abroad was acceptable but it all depended on what she intended to do abroad. In the event, Sakharov promised not to apply for an exit visa and Bonner agreed to avoid politics abroad. Throughout 1985 and 1986, Gorbachev took a close interest in Sakharov. He received, from the KGB, transcripts of Sakharov's conversations and snippets of Sakharov's memoirs. The Politburo returned to the problem in June 1986, after Gorbachev had received a letter from Sakharov, requesting the freeing of political prisoners. Chebrikov made it clear that the Sakharov problem and that of political prisoners were interlinked, one could not be resolved without the other. He thought that if Sakharov were allowed to return to Moscow, he would be prepared to abandon his 'public activities'.[46] However, in his opinion Bonner was a more formidable obstacle because she wanted to push Sakharov into confrontation with the Soviet authorities. When Sakharov returned to Moscow in December 1986, he agreed to give up all his public activities. Gorbachev had astutely neutralised the academician. However, Gorbachev found that he needed Sakharov's support and so he re-entered the political arena. For Gorbachev, Sakharov was dissident no. 1. The academician returned the compliment in January 1989 when he designated Gorbachev dissident no. 1.

Gorbachev was wooing the intelligentsia and the former dissidents. He needed allies in the battle with the Party conservatives. One of those who was irked by this trend was Egor Ligachev, who objected to attempts to denigrate the Party and Soviet achievements. Glasnost to him was to promote the virtues of the system and not to attack it. A running battle ensued between him and Aleksandr Yakovlev, and this is what Gorbachev intended.

The 27th Party Congress, from February to March 1986, was a sobering event. Great effort was put into honing Mikhail Sergeevich's report to the Congress and Raisa played a full part in the deliberations. Gorbachev began to sense that some of those he had promoted were less than enthusiastic about perestroika and the danger was that they regarded it as just another campaign. Reports by some republican leaders consisted of a tedious recitation of success and no hint of self-criticism. A letter arrived from a former fellow-student at Moscow State University informing Gorbachev that in Gorky (Nizhny Novgorod) absolutely nothing had changed.

The conclusion reached by the Politburo in April 1986 was that perestroika had run up against the 'gigantic Party and state apparatus, which stood like a dam in the path of reforms'.[47] In June 1986 Gorbachev sharply attacked Gosplan and the economic ministries. In July 1986 Gorbachev brought together local newspaper editors and chided them for their passivity. They asked him to relay this to raikom, gorkom and obkom first secretaries. 'Our newspapers, are, after all, their mouthpieces, and they do not want glasnost.'[48]

During a tour of the Far East Gorbachev was shocked by the lack of concern and accountability of local officials towards the population. Again perestroika did not move from word to deed. A Moscow raikom first secretary was reported as advising his officials to wait because in a few years things would settle down. What was to be done? By late summer he was contemplating the perestroika of the political system.

The January 1987 CC plenum declared open season on the bureaucracy with every single comrade laying into it.[49] But was it just ritual or had there been a sea change in perceptions? The first open opposition to glasnost also surfaced at the plenum. It was clear that the Party bosses would not give up their privileges without a struggle. Glasnost was breaking through. In January 1987 the jamming of the BBC ended and was soon followed by that of Deutsche Welle and Voice of America. When Margaret Thatcher visited Moscow in March 1987, she was interviewed on TV and demolished her male interviewers. She was especially critical of Soviet violations of human rights and Afghanistan. The next month George Shultz contradicted his interviewer and informed him that Afghans wanted Soviet troops out of their country.

.   .   .

THE ECONOMIC PROBLEM

Gorbachev was unaware of the true nature of the militarisation of the economy when he took over as general secretary. Discussion about the military, KGB and foreign trade were taboo in the Politburo before he came to power. Calculations, in early 1987, revealed that the military consumed 40 per cent of the state budget and not 16 per cent as previously thought. Its share of GDP was 20 per cent and not 6 per cent as imagined. Of the 25 billion rubles devoted to research and development, 20 billion went on military work. Hence the Soviet defence burden was approximately four times that of the US.

Uskorenie, with its emphasis on the machine-building sector, benefited the military-industrial complex most. Labour, energy and raw material costs per unit of output were up to 2.5 times higher than in the west. In agriculture they were ten times higher.[50] These were shocking data but they only described the problem. How was this leviathan to be turned round and encouraged to become more efficient. By early 1987, Gorbachev had realised that campaigns to improve discipline were futile. Management and labour had to be motivated to improve performance.

In early 1987 the economy began to reveal alarming signs and industrial output fell 6 per cent, compared to that of December 1986, mainly in machine building and light industry. The metallurgical and chemical industries were also in trouble. A Politburo meeting in February 1987 came to the dismal conclusion that the plans for scientific-technical progress and the modernisation of the machine-building sector were collapsing. Drastic measures had to be adopted. Work began on drafting radical economic reform documents. Inevitably there were clashes with Nikolai Ryzhkov, the Prime Minister. Prices were to respond to the market and be regulated by the state. Ryzhkov insisted that reform should not 'go beyond the framework of socialism'. Gorbachev believes this was the point when some began regarding the Prime Minister as a comrade with conservative views.[51]

Divergent views on what constituted socialism were clear here, with Gorbachev willing to go beyond the confines of the 1930s model then prevalent. During a Politburo discussion in May, Ryzhkov indicated clearly that he would uphold the powers of the government. When asked which functions the ministries would surrender under the new system, he retorted: 'None!'.[52] Party officials were to stop interfering in economic management and concentrate on making management more democratic. Ligachev, for one, did not take kindly to this and argued strongly that perestroika should not be reduced to democratisation but should strengthen socialism. Ligachev held firmly to the view that the Party should be the engine of change, regarding discipline as very important. He favoured intra-systemic change and perestroika should remain within the same socio-economic system. Ligachev was strongly opposed to private agriculture, even cooperatives, believing that kolkhozes and sovkhozes should be strengthened.

Market mechanisms were anathema to him. The parting of the ways between Gorbachev and Ligachev would clearly not be long delayed.

The July 1987 CC plenum pushed democratisation forward and decreed that the 19th Party Conference convene in June 1988. It was to become the most radical of the modern era. At the plenum, Minister of Defence Sergei Sokolov was retired and replaced by Dmitry Yazov. This was one of the consequences of the sensational flight by the young West German, Mathias Rust, from Hamburg, landing near Red Square, in May 1987. It was another dolorous occurrence and underlined the inertia and incompetence of so-called professionals.

Glasnost allowed the publication of some devastating attacks on the state of the economy and the nation. Nikolai Shmelev, a radical economist, wrote:

> At present, our economy is characterised by shortages, imbalances ... unmanageable, and ... almost unplannable ... Industry now rejects up to 80 per cent of technical decisions and inventions ... the working masses have reached a state of almost total lack of interest in ... honest labour ... Apathy, indifference, thieving ... have become mass phenomena, with simultaneous aggressive envy towards those who are capable of earning. There have appeared signs of ... physical degradation of a large part of our population, through drunkenness and idleness. Finally, there is disbelief in the officially announced objectives and purposes, in the very possibility of a more rational economic and social organisation of life. Clearly, all this cannot be quickly overcome – years, perhaps generations, will be needed.[53]

A raft of radical economic reforms hit the statute book in June and July 1987. In June the law on state enterprises and the basic provisions for the fundamental perestroika of economic management was promulgated. In July the law on the state enterprises was complemented by ten decrees on the economic system, including planning, scientific-technical progress, financial mechanisms, prices, banking, branch ministries, republican organs and social policy.[54] This, however, did not constitute a blueprint for reform, merely the first stage in the process. Ministries were to be amalgamated and committees merged with ministries. Six Union-republican ministries (a USSR ministry and one in each republic) were abolished and transformed into USSR ministries. The new legislation stated that ministries were to concentrate on perspective (long-term) planning and technical innovation and leave enterprises to manage themselves. This was supposed to reduce sharply the number of ministry officials. Gosplan lost almost half of its staff but most of them found employment in a new institute.

In mid-1987 there were over 800 republican ministries and departments in the Soviet Union and Gorbachev was determined to take the axe to them. His goal was to reduce republican officials by a half and oblast officials by a third. The result of this activity was to break or confuse the links between the centre and branch ministries and organisations throughout the country. This was one of the goals of the reforms, as was an increase in the economic independence of the republics *vis-à-vis* the centre. This developed into republican khozraschet (self-accounting) as republics gained greater control over economic activity on their territory. It was to have fateful consequences in 1991 since it fostered regionalism and nationalism.

The law on state enterprises provided for the elections of directors and all managers down to foremen, the election of works councils and a general assembly of all the workers in an enterprise. By the end of 1987, over 36,000 managers had been elected in industry and construction. However, it transpired that the nominations, and often the elections, were controlled by the local Party committee. The Party was strengthening its influence over enterprises at the expense of the ministries.[55] How long this trend would continue would depend on the progress of democratisation. The two key problems of ownership and prices were skirted around during discussions and in the legislation. Gorbachev regarded price reform (meaning price rises) as an unexploded bomb at a time when living standards were declining. He would not countenance reducing the state budget deficit by raising prices.[56]

When first introduced, in 1985, the human factor emphasised the significance of skills and abilities rather than human needs, interests and social justice.[57] Gorbachev pointed out that 'little can be changed in the economy, management and education without changing the mentality and developing a desire and ability to think and work in new ways'.[58]

Aganbegyan also stressed the need to change mind sets and to teach people to think and work in new ways. After the 27th Congress, the Party sought to enable people to develop comprehensively their individuality, and become inventive and creative at work.[59] This marks a change in the perception of the human factor, away from a narrow economic and instrumental view to the human dimension involved in scientific-technical progress. The mental and moral qualities of the individual came into play, as did honour.[60] Social psychology and the psychology of work enjoyed a renaissance after the 27th Congress, as their insights became more and more important to policy-makers. It was now perestroika from below rather than from above. Psychologists provided insights into the reasons behind popular resistance to perestroika during Perestroika Mark II (1988–9) and Perestroika Mark III (1990–1).

. . .

YELTSIN BREAKS WITH GORBACHEV

In September 1987 Boris Yeltsin, as first secretary of Moscow gorkom, invited ambassadors to meet him to discuss plans for the future development of the capital. However, Boris could not resist playing the politician and the session turned into a review of perestroika. He thought perestroika had reached its 'critical phase', involving a transition from proposals to practical measures.[61] He sensed that pressures in society were building up and that people were impatient for results. Those managers and politicians who were not up to the task should be replaced, as he had done in the capital. This contradicted the analysis being articulated by Mikhail Gorbachev who had been assuring everyone that perestroika was on track and beginning to bear fruit. Yeltsin was warning that perestroika was only just moving from word to deed and that there were storms ahead.

Some ambassadors discounted Yeltsin's talk of a crisis, but they were unaware that, in August, Yeltsin had forwarded a letter to Gorbachev, at the time on holiday on the Black Sea. In the version subsequently published in his memoirs, Yeltsin savagely attacked Ligachev's approach to perestroika in general and his interventions in Moscow Party affairs in particular. He also identified some conservative Politburo members, who opposed real change. His gloomy prediction was that the country was sliding backwards to something approaching Brezhnevite stagnation. He requested that he be permitted to resign as a candidate member of the Politburo and as first secretary of Moscow gorkom.[62]

Contradictory accounts make it difficult to divine what happened next. Gorbachev claimed that Yeltsin had agreed to discuss the matter after the celebrations of the October Revolution, on 7 November, but Yeltsin merely states that the general secretary had told him he would see him later. Without consulting Gorbachev, Yeltsin decided to present the matter at the CC plenum on 21 October. Just before the end of the meeting, Yeltsin requested the floor and repeated his accusations that the CC Secretariat had not changed its style or attitude and requested he be relieved of his duties. Gorbachev flew into a rage and accused Yeltsin of unconcealed ambition and threw the matter open to discussion.[63] Predictably members took Gorbachev's line and excoriated Boris Nikolaevich. Of the 27 who spoke, only one, Georgy Arbatov, director of the Institute for the Study of the USA and Canada, had a kind word for Yeltsin. When Yeltsin responded to the accusations and reiterated that some members of the Politburo had been insincere in their praise of perestroika and Gorbachev, the general secretary cut in and denigrated him as a political illiterate for accusing the whole Politburo of fostering a 'cult of the personality'.[64] Yeltsin, of course, had made no such accusation. Gorbachev became even more heated and made further accusations: 'What extreme egotism it must take to place personal ambitions above the interests of the Party, above our common cause!'.[65] The plenum instructed the Politburo and Moscow gorkom to act on Yeltsin's request to resign. The affair was hushed up so as not to cast a pall on the 7 November celebrations. On 3 November, Gorbachev states, Yeltsin sent him a letter requesting he be permitted to continue as first secretary of Moscow gorkom. The general secretary gave Boris Nikolaevich a piece of his mind.[66]

On 9 November Yeltsin was found covered in blood at the Moscow gorkom. Gorbachev viewed it as an attempt at suicide by using scissors to wound himself. The Moscow gorkom met on 12 November, with Gorbachev present. The next day, *Pravda* stated that Yeltsin had been relieved of his duties as Moscow Party boss and a transcript of the Moscow gorkom meeting was published. It included Yeltsin's incoherent attempts to defend himself. According to Yeltsin, Gorbachev demanded he leave his sick bed to attend the Moscow Party meeting despite being full of painkillers and drugs. Yeltsin claims that Gorbachev told him to his face that he was politically finished and would never again be permitted to play an active role in politics.

To prevent Yeltsin becoming a political martyr, he was made deputy chair of the state committee on construction, in January 1988, with the rank of a government minister. Had Yeltsin been packed off to manage a construction site on the Chinese frontier, it might have confirmed the suspicions of many among the public that perestroika was mere window-dressing. He was dropped from the Politburo at the February 1988 CC plenum. The official minutes of the October 1987 CC plenum were only published in February 1989.[67]

It is still very difficult to understand why Gorbachev flew into a fury at the plenum. Yeltsin was merely questioning the speed of perestroika and the role of the Secretariat. Unofficial versions of the plenum were published afterwards and these included attacks on Raisa's role by Yeltsin. However, there is no reference to Raisa in the official, published version. Gorbachev could have saved Yeltsin from himself, had he wished to do so. He could have stated that more time was needed to consider his points and postponed a decision to a later date. Another explanation suggests itself. Gorbachev was irritated by the starring role Yeltsin, ever the self-publicist, had carved out for himself. He was a direct competitor of the general secretary in the capital. If Moscow was a stage, then Mikhail Sergeevich wanted to be the only prima donna on it. Did personal vanity blind Gorbachev to the valuable role that Yeltsin could play in implementing perestroika? By banishing Yeltsin, Gorbachev was turning him into a political enemy at a time when the political battle for perestroika was just beginning. It was a fateful mistake.

. . .

NATIONALITIES

Lenin realised that nationality policy was a key to success in 1917. He promised a federal state, a major concession to non-Russians. Andropov warned against Great Russian chauvinism and urged Russians to be more sensitive to the feelings of non-Russians. Nevertheless Moscow boasted that the nationality problem had been solved. It had, from a Russian point of view. Non-Russians thought differently. Hence Gorbachev began by believing in the myth that nationality relations were not a problem.[68] Glasnost and democratisation were to demonstrate how wrong he was.

Since the Soviet Union was an empire, this implied that some nationalities, given a free choice, would leave the Union. Georgia was added in 1921 by military conquest. The Baltic States were incorporated in 1940 against their will. Ukraine was not given a choice because of its economic value. The 1977 Constitution afforded republics and only republics the right to secede. There were over 100 recognised nationalities with many living outside their titular areas. If the Soviet Union was an empire, so was the Russian Federation.

Gorbachev was initially blind to the fact that there was a problem. Perestroika would benefit all Soviet citizens. The first cracks began to appear after the introduction of the law on state enterprises which afforded enterprises control over wages and promoted self-financing and self-management. Republics began to argue that they were more effective at promoting perestroika than the centre. When political reform was added, in 1987, a potent mix was created: local economic and political elites began to pursue common goals – autonomy from Moscow. Added to this was the espousal of universal human values and the abandonment of the class approach in foreign policy. Human rights involved choice. How far could this go?

What was the solution to the nationality problem after 1987? Transform the Soviet Union into a democratic state? This implied that those who wanted to leave should be allowed to leave. This policy would have led to the breakup of the Soviet Union. Should the Soviet Union be dissolved and the building of a post-Soviet federal or confederal state undertaken? The attempted coup leaders in August 1991 wanted neither option. They wanted to save as much of the old Soviet Union as they could. After August 1991, Russia became the key player, followed by Ukraine. Did Russia prefer a Soviet successor state, and if so, would it be a federation or confederation? In December 1991 it, together with

Ukraine and Belorussia (Belarus), decided it did not want a successor state and put the Soviet Union to sleep. The Soviet Union went the way of most empires, it broke up. Hence the nationality issue proved to be an almost intractable problem and, together with economic failure, is the reason why the country disappeared from the world map. Given the size of the Soviet Union, there was no solution which Gorbachev could espouse which would win consensus from all nationalities. For instance, the Baltic States wanted out at any price, but Central Asia wanted to stay in at any price. Gorbachev, as a Russian, found it very difficult to understand a mentality which rejected all offers to stay within the Union. To him it was irrational behaviour. What he never grasped was that the political actors in the Baltic States regarded their behaviour as rational.

There were no serious nationality problems for Gorbachev to deal with in his first year in office. In Ukraine, Vladimir Shchcrbitsky, the party boss, continued his practice of jailing human rights activists. One who defended the rights of Ukrainian Catholics (the church was banned) got seven years in prison and five years of exile. However, the tide began to turn in late 1985. Vyacheslav Chornovil, a leading dissident, was released from a prison camp in Yakutia. Others were released in 1986.

The first real problem surfaced in Kazakhstan in December 1986 and Gorbachev failed to heed the warning. The top man in the republic, Dinmukhamed Kunaev, was a dapper dresser and cultivated the Brezhnev look, including the beetle eyebrows. He had first locked into Brezhnev when the latter was Party boss of the republic under Khrushchev. Under Brezhnev he exhibited slavish obeisance towards 'himself' and autocratically built up his own fiefdom in Kazakhstan. Kazakhstan consists of 'dzhus', or clans, so he had to apportion influence among them. When Gorbachev became leader, leading Party officials, Kazakhs and Russians, began coming to him with complaints about the state of the republic. Kunaev complained to Gorbachev that there were troublemakers in his republic and warned him about the ambitious Nursultan Nazarbaev, the Kazakh Prime Minister. Nazarbaev was a protégé of Kunaev and he had been appointed Prime Minister in 1984 at the age of 44. Kunaev wanted Nazarbaev transferred to Moscow or, even better, sent abroad to a Soviet embassy. Gorbachev decided to be brutally frank and told him about what his officials had said. Kunaev offered to resign. He suggested that his successor should be a Russian since under no circumstances did he want Nazarbaev.

The Politburo decided that the new man in Alma Ata (now Almaty) should be Gennady Kolbin, an ethnic Russian, who had served as Shevardnadze's deputy in Georgia, and came highly recommended. Kolbin was dispatched to Alma Ata, like some pro-consul, to inform the Kazakhs that he had come to take over. On reflection, Gorbachev judges this to have been a 'mistake'.[69] Kazakhs took the appointment of a Russian as an insult when it was announced on 16 December 1986. Youths gathered in Lenin Square. Kunaev claims that he was summoned to the Party building on the square, and offered to address the students, but Kolbin refused to permit this.[70] Instead, some of the Party secretaries, including Nazarbaev, went out to talk to the demonstrators. The next day, the authorities decided to act in the traditional manner: they used force. Many were injured and some killed. Thousands were arrested (over a thousand students were later expelled from the university). When the jails could hold no more, they were taken out into the freezing steppe and left there. Rioting broke out in other Kazakh cities as well. The results of this policy were not as anticipated by Moscow. Gorbachev states that the resolution adopted by the Politburo on 25 December was couched in traditional terms. There was no attempt to get to the root of the problem. The goal was to teach the Kazakhs and others a lesson.[71] That lesson was that Moscow rules. Since antagonistic contradictions could not exist in the Soviet Union, the outburst of ethnic violence and nationalism could only be the result of survivals of the past thinking and foreign influence.

Moscow's own ideology was misleading it. Kunaev was accused of maladministration and corruption and dismissed from the Politburo and Central Committee in 1987. One lesson that Moscow did draw from the Kolbin experience was that it was inadvisable to appoint a Russian or Ukrainian as Party boss of a non-Russian republic. Kolbin stayed until 1989, when Nazarbaev took over. Kazakhstan was one republic in which Mikhail Sergeevich was not the flavour of the month.

The campaign against corruption was given great publicity in neighbouring Uzbekistan. The campaign had begun under

Andropov (he had been powerless to act under Brezhnev) and targeted the Party and state leaders. The new Party boss, Inamzhon Usmankhodzhaev, adopted the tactic of collaborating with the Moscow investigators. The most famous scam was the Uzbek cotton case. This involved falsifying the cotton crop sold to the state, overstating it by about 600,000 tonnes annually. It resulted in the republic being hugely overpaid for its output. This exercise would not have worked had not everyone been bribed, including officials in Moscow. Over 18,000 Party members were expelled in Uzbekistan. The whole exercise backfired on Moscow because the Uzbeks saw it as an exercise in colonial bashing. Moscow wanted to teach the natives a lesson. Corruption to Moscow was viewed quite differently in Tashkent, indeed also in Alma Ata. It was the only way Uzbekistan or Kazakhstan could defend itself against the imperial Soviet government. The Uzbeks felt even more aggrieved when the successors to their sacked officials arrived: most of them were Russians. The latter knew little of the republic, nothing of the language, and Uzbeks engaged in the game of taking the foreigner for a ride.

There were also troubles amongst the Volga Germans and Crimean Tatars. Deported in 1941–4 for allegedly collaborating with the Germans, they were rehabilitated in 1956 but did not have their homelands restored. The Tatars actively pursued their cause and a trickle made it back to the Crimea. However, the main reason why Moscow could not officially accede to their wish was that Russians and Ukrainians had taken over their homeland. Previous petitions had not got them far, so they tried again in a large demonstration in Moscow's Red Square in July 1987. The Moscow police were very tolerant and a commission was set up to hear their case, chaired by Andrei Gromyko, now head of state. He played the diplomat but his answer was predictable: no. Moscow was wary of meeting the grievances of one ethnic group since this could lead to an avalanche of further ethnic cases. Gromyko eventually announced that all Crimean Tatars would be permitted to return to the Crimea but the Crimean Autonomous Republic would not be restored. There was discussion with Ukraine about the formation of an autonomous oblast for the Tatars within the Crimea but it ran into the sand. However, the handling of this issue demonstrates how far democratisation had developed. Gorbachev had learnt from the regime's mistakes in Kazakhstan. The state had now accepted that force could not solve political problems.

. . .

FOREIGN POLICY

Rapid industrialisation and economic growth foster outward expansion, assertion and imperialism. This occurs either during growth or shortly afterwards. Great Britain, France, Germany, Japan and the United States all followed this pattern. So did the Soviet Union. It is the only growing power not to have engaged in aggressive wars to expand its place in the sun. Instead, it was attacked by Nazi Germany in 1941 and then fought its way to Berlin to secure its position as the dominant military power in Europe in 1945. The 1970s saw the expansion of Soviet influence in Africa and other parts of the Third World. However, it overreached itself when it invaded Afghanistan in 1979. In expanding, the Soviet Union became an empire and an economic price had to be paid. Inevitably, the price became too burdensome as its economy slowed down in the second half of the 1970s. All empires expand and then contract.

Gorbachev perceived that the Soviet empire had overstretched itself and that it could no longer challenge the United States for world supremacy. His first goal was to slow down the arms race and then move to arms reduction. Foreign policy under him was that of an empire in decline. It was defensive and thus willing to abandon previously held positions. Conceptually it was much easier for Gorbachev than domestic change. It consisted of moving towards western positions and hence it was easy to divine what the Soviet Union had to do. The skill consisted in transforming Soviet foreign policy positions without giving the impression, internationally and domestically, that Moscow was caving in to Washington. His goal was to extract the highest possible price from the Americans for ending the Cold War and the arms race.

The new Cold War raged in 1983 and 1984 when NATO stated it would press ahead with deploying Pershing II and Cruise missiles in western Europe if the Soviets did not withdraw their SS20s from eastern Europe. Moscow withdrew its diplomats from arms control negotiations. However, in

September 1984 Andrei Gromyko travelled to Washington to meet President Reagan, who had been keen for a summit meeting with Chernenko throughout that year. Gorbachev's speech to the British Parliament in December 1984 was frank and innovative.

In January 1985 the Politburo decided to engage again in arms negotiations with the Americans. When Vice-President Bush attended Chernenko's funeral he handed Gorbachev a letter from the President inviting him to meet in America. Two weeks later, Gorbachev agreed in principle and suggested they meet in Moscow. In June they agreed that their first meeting would take place in Geneva in November 1985. Reagan was optimistic about negotiating with the Russians and escalated US defence spending so as to negotiate from a position of strength. This was quite something from a man who had described the Soviet Union as the 'focus of evil in the modern world'. During the spring and summer of 1985, Reagan and Gorbachev exchanged letters every few weeks. This permitted both sides to test suggestions on the other. In October Gorbachev introduced the concept of 'reasonable sufficiency' in assessing the size of armed forces. He had already dropped ideology as a factor in foreign policy formation. An important change in the presentation of foreign policy was the replacement of Grim Grom Gromyko by the smiling Georgian, Eduard Shevardnadze. It was like a breath of fresh air and helped to remove the mental blocks on the American side.

Foreign policy was the first policy area where the new thinking was evident. This included the interdependence of states: security could not be attained by military but by political means and the search for universally accepted solutions. Gorbachev had concluded that the arms race was crippling the Soviet Union and regarded conventional and nuclear arms reductions as his major task.

The Politburo drew up a negotiating position, in consultation with the Ministry of Foreign Affairs, the international department of the Central Committee, and the KGB. On substantive points there were guidelines on how far the general secretary could go. A fallback position was also worked out. On the most contentious issue, the reduction of conventional and nuclear arms, the Foreign Ministry acted as the coordinator in the early years. Then a special Politburo commission, chaired by Lev Zaikov, took over. The commission received submissions from the Foreign Ministry, the Ministry of Defence, academic institutes, Gosplan, the Council of Ministers' scientific-industrial committee, and leading specialists and academics.[72] Zaikov or Shevardnadze would brief the general secretary, sometimes joined by Yazov, the defence minister, Akhromeev, the chief of staff, Chebrikov or Kryuchkov, head of the KGB. Gorbachev would then introduce his own ideas and a final version would be submitted to the Politburo, together with the other options. Shevardnadze often lost his temper over the obtuseness of the military.

The Geneva summit was viewed as a success by both leaders. In the beginning Gorbachev regarded Reagan as not merely a conservative but a political dinosaur.[73] However, the longer they talked the more friendly they became. One of the reasons for this was that Gorbachev noticed that Reagan did not like detail. So they talked general politics and got on well. Mikhail Sergeevich says that at the end of their two-day summit, he had concluded that Ronald Reagan was also a man 'you could do business with'.[74] President Reagan wanted to get across the message that a nuclear war could not be won, so should therefore never be fought. The Russians wanted a statement that neither side would be the first to launch a nuclear war. The Americans would not accept this because this precluded a US strike if the Soviets launched a conventional attack on western Europe. Geneva saw a breakthrough. The two superpowers agreed to prevent 'any war between them, whether nuclear or conventional'.[75] They pledged not to seek military superiority. Many other agreements were signed but had been negotiated in advance. One was on local conflicts and offered a way out for both sides, without admitting military defeat. There was still the problem of Afghanistan[76] but Gorbachev made it clear that the Soviets did not intend to stay there and were seeking a political settlement. The Americans had concluded that caressing the Russian bear offered greater rewards than baiting it.

In January 1986 the goal of a nuclear-free world was spelled out, and at a conference at the Ministry of Foreign Affairs in May 1986 the new thinking in foreign policy was launched. A diplomatic merry-go-round followed with the old war horses being put out to grass and a new breed of diplomat, long on persuasion and short on ideological cant, appeared. One of those recruited was Gennady Gerasimov, editor-in-chief of *Moskovskie novosti*. He became foreign office spokesman after public relations had been handled poorly at Geneva and the ministry had offered the view that there had been no Chernobyl disaster. Gerasimov epitomised the new type: expressive, expansive and always ready with a one-liner. His dismissal in 1990 was clear evidence of a swing to the right.

What was remarkable about the new thinking was its abandonment of the class approach to foreign policy. The Soviet Union wanted to be a serious partner in the search for international security and finding solutions to political, economic and social problems world-wide. This was at a time when political reform domestically had not yet begun. Traditionally a Party leader concentrated on three criteria: enhancing the security of the country, achieving economic and social progress, and expanding communist influence abroad. Gorbachev became the first Party leader to ignore the last of these criteria. Instead, he had decided that competition between capitalism (the United States) and communism could only result in disaster for the Soviet Union. He now felt confident enough to compete in a pluralist world and to contribute to solutions which would benefit world society as a whole. In so doing, he was enhancing the security of his own country. Needless to say, Mikhail Sergeevich's abandonment of the class approach in foreign policy was fiercely resisted by orthodox communists at home. Egor Ligachev, for one, never relented in his belief that Soviet foreign policy should be class-based.

At Geneva, both leaders had invited the other to his capital for a summit and this was warmly accepted. However, American defence expenditure was still increasing and this made Gorbachev even more determined to strike an arms control deal. When Reagan proposed a summit in Washington, Gorbachev made it clear he would only come if a substantial arms control agreement would be signed. Gorbachev began to suspect that Reagan was using talk about negotiations as a political ploy to mask his lack of desire for real progress. In January 1986 Gorbachev dramatically proposed the phasing out of nuclear weapons by 2000.

Reagan, unlike most of his advisers, thought that nuclear weapons should be abolished, and was favourably impressed by Gorbachev's proposal. However, Gorbachev released details of the proposals in a letter to the press immediately it was launched. This aroused suspicion in Washington that the whole exercise was propagandistic.[77] In the letter, Gorbachev changed the Soviet negotiating position. Previously, it was that agreement had to be reached on all three nuclear arms negotiations. Now, it was possible to reach agreement on intermediate-range missiles and on-site inspection, while still negotiating on strategic and defensive weapons. In February 1986 Gorbachev referred to Afghanistan as a 'running sore'. Moscow wanted out in order to improve relations with Washington. However, arms negotiations in Geneva were getting nowhere. In early autumn Gorbachev proposed an interim meeting in a third country. This was not to take the place of a Washington summit but to draw up a list of agreements to be signed in Washington.[78] Gorbachev proposed England or Iceland,[79] a half-way house, and they agreed to meet in Reykjavik on 11–12 October 1986. The choice of location was significant. Britain was a member of NATO and Iceland was a NATO ally. Mikhail Sergeevich was willing to go more than half-way.

Getting nowhere with general issues at their first meeting at the Reykjavik summit, Gorbachev put direct questions to President Reagan. The latter shuffled his cards and some of them fell on the floor. When they were reassembled they were out of order and the President could not come up with answers. Round one to Mikhail Sergeevich. The Soviets made major concessions on arms control and on-site inspection. Elsewhere the only major shift was to accept human rights as a legitimate subject for negotiation. The two leaders came tantalisingly close to agreement. Reagan accepted Gorbachev's proposal for the elimination of nuclear weapons but would not agree that testing of the Strategic Defence Initiative (or Star Wars) be restricted to the laboratory.[80] Hence the encounter ended with no agreement. In reality, the two leaders had solved more questions than at any previous summit. Gorbachev agreed to accept equal, low levels of intermediate-range missiles and apply the quotas globally. He had also offered to cut his heavy intercontinental missiles, a major American objective, and agreed to on-site inspection.[81] Reagan could have agreed to laboratory testing of SDI without hindering the project but he was unaware of this.

81

At the press conference, Gorbachev declared that 'in spite of all its drama, Reykjavik is not a failure – it is a breakthrough, which allowed us for the first time to look over the horizon'.[82] Victory had been snatched from the jaws of defeat. Formal failure at Reykjavik resulted in a better intermediate-range nuclear forces agreement (INF) the following year, when all were eliminated. Britain and France would have resisted giving up their nuclear deterrents if Reagan's acceptance of no nuclear weapons had stood. Gorbachev learnt an important lesson at Reykjavik. He had arrived believing that Soviet–US relations could be improved through arms agreements only; he left convinced that a full agenda was needed to normalise relations, but it was going to be tough.

Gorbachev's disappointment at returning empty-handed from Reykjavik boiled over at a Politburo meeting on 22 October 1986:

> We have to change our views about policies to be adopted in the light of the new hostile behaviour of the US administration. The course of events since Reykjavik reveals that our American 'friends' do not have a positive programme and do everything to increase pressure on us. As well, they do it with extreme brutality, behaving like true bandits . . . One cannot expect the slightest constructive action or proposal from the Americans. In the present situation, we have to score propaganda points, continue our offensive of enlightenment intended for the American and international public. The leaders in Washington are afraid of that . . . We should continue to put pressure on the American administration in explaining in public our positions and to prove that the Americans are responsible for the failure to agree to limit and cut back nuclear arms.[83]

However, as Gorbachev noted later, he and Reagan were 'doomed to cooperate'.

One incident did leave a bitter taste and it threw light on Gorbachev's relations with the KGB. In August 1986 the Americans arrested Gennady Zakharov, a Soviet UN employee, on spying charges. The KGB responded by arresting Nicholas Daniloff, the Moscow correspondent of *US News and World Report*. Reagan insisted that Daniloff was innocent and be released. George Shultz and the editor of *US News* knew that the journalist had acquired secret Soviet documents and photographs and had passed them on to the US State Department.[84]

Shultz was furious to learn that the CIA had 'exposed Daniloff to the KGB', using him as a contact with a Soviet source and discussing him on an open telephone line. The Soviets had collected enough material on him to have him convicted in a US court.[85]

The CIA mishandled the case and it provided clear evidence that CIA director, William Casey, strongly opposed Shultz's efforts to improve relations with the Soviet Union.[86] During the three weeks Gorbachev took to respond, the US ordered 25 Soviet UN employees out of the country, all of whom they took to be engaged in intelligence gathering. The Soviet government was warned that if they retaliated more Soviet citizens would be sent packing. The Americans also demanded that Yury Orlov, a prominent human rights activist, be freed from prison and allowed to move to the US, together with his wife. Shultz's excellent relations[87] with Shevardnadze permitted a resolution of the case. A day after Daniloff's release Shultz announced that Zakharov would be expelled. He then stepped down from the podium and was replaced by President Reagan who announced that he had accepted Gorbachev's invitation to meet in Reykjavik.

However, after the summit Moscow ordered out five US diplomats, ignoring the previous American warning that this would result in retaliation. Washington then ordered out 55 Soviet diplomats, again perceived to be intelligence officers. Why did Gorbachev take KGB advice and order out the American diplomats after the summit? This risked souring the atmosphere at a sensitive time. It may have been pique, but it may also have been Gorbachev's unwillingness or inability to overrule the KGB. The Americans demonstrated that they could play it hard.

Gorbachev coined the expression 'Europe is our common home' in Paris in February 1986, during his first official visit to western Europe after taking office. He had chosen France mainly because of its nuclear deterrent. If he could move the French then his vision of a nuclear-free world might become reality. He found the French obdurate, but when President François Mitterrand visited Moscow in July 1986 he informed Gorbachev that he was opposed to the concept of SDI. To him, it represented an acceleration of the arms race, whereas the goal should be ways of disarming. After Reykjavik, the French reiterated their commitment to nuclear deterrence, a disappointment for Gorbachev. In April 1987, in Prague, Gorbachev spelt out his 'pan-European idea' but west Europeans hesitated because of Soviet conventional superiority. NATO countries also took their lead from the US.

When Mrs Thatcher visited Moscow in March 1987, she reiterated her commitment to nuclear deterrence and her belief that the goal of the Soviet Union was to extend communism and dominance world-wide. Gorbachev gave as good as he got (he referred to their discussions as constructive polemics)[88] and the two leaders got on famously. The British Prime Minister did have something positive to say about the Soviet Union. She warmly endorsed perestroika. Thatcher later confirmed that Gorbachev was her favourite communist politician because he was the only one with whom one could have a good argument. Thatcher was an important interlocutor as she had the ear of President Reagan. If he could win over the Prime Minister, Mikhail Sergeevich was well on the way to winning over the President.

. . .

NOTES

1. M. S. Gorbachev, *Izbrannye rechi i stati* (Moscow, Politizdat, 1987), vol. 2, pp. 20–46. In the speech he discusses changes but refers to them as merely the 'initial stages of perestroika, which is to be broadened and deepened'. Ibid., p. 38.

2. *Pravda*, 11 December 1984, excised the more innovative parts of the speech without consulting Gorbachev. However, the full version was published as M. S. Gorbachev, *Zhivoe tvorchestvo naroda* (Moscow, Politizdat, 1984). It reappears in his collected speeches, with minor changes: Gorbachev, *Izbrannye rechi i stati*, vol. 2, pp. 75–108; Archie Brown, *The Gorbachev Factor* (Oxford, Oxford University Press, 1996), pp. 78–9, 335.

3. An indication of the magnitude of the problem can be gleaned from the fact that after inspectors, in 1979 and 1980, had examined 20,000 types of machines and machine tools produced in the Soviet Union, about a third had to be withdrawn from production and fundamentally modernised. *Planovaya ekonomika*, no. 10, 1981, pp. 8–9.

4. Gorbachev stated this during a speech to a CC plenum on science and culture on 6 January 1988. The text was printed in *Literaturnaya gazeta* on 11 January 1988. Gorbachev was

defending himself against criticism that the reforms launched at the April 1985 CC plenum had not been well thought through.

5. Evgeny Novikov and Patrick Bascio, *Gorbachev and the Collapse of the Soviet Communist Party* (New York, Peter Lang Publishing, 1994); Vladimir Boukovsky, *Jugement à Moscou: Un dissident dans les archives du Kremlin* (Paris, Robert Laffont, 1995), p. 484.

6. Valery Boldin, *Ten Years That Shook the World: The Gorbachev Era as Witnessed by his Chief of Staff* (New York, Basic Books, 1994), pp. 49–51. These are hostile memoirs as befits someone who was a member of the extraordinary committee in August 1991. However, they provide insights into the functioning of the Gorbachev administration.

7. Ibid., p. 52.

8. Boris Yeltsin, *Against the Grain: An Autobiography* (New York, Summit Books, 1990), p. 140.

9. The relationship between Gorbachev and Shevardnadze was professional and little personal closeness appears to have developed. They first met at a Komsomol Congress in the late 1950s and took quickly to one another. Georgia is a short drive from Stavropol krai and the two frequently met to discuss policy. Gorbachev's Politburo dacha was at Pitsunda, a stunningly beautiful location on the Georgian Black Sea coast, and the two continued their conversations there. Shevardnadze by then was Party boss in Georgia. Both opposed the Soviet invasion of Afghanistan. Gorbachev, as CC secretary for agriculture, protected Shevardnadze's experiments in some rural areas of Georgia. Both Gorbachev and Shevardnadze used material from the numerous situation papers prepared on Andropov's instructions. Both believed that communism was reformable. They were dismayed by the level of corruption around them and, during the winter of 1984–5, at Pitsunda, Gorbachev agreed with Shevardnadze's assessment that 'everything was going to the dogs'. Carolyn McGiffert Ekedahl and Melvin A. Goodman, *The Wars of Eduard Shevardnadze* (London, Hurst, 1997), pp. 29–33.

10. Ibid., p. 106.

11. Jack F. Matlock, Jr., *Autopsy on an Empire: The American Ambassador's Account of the Collapse of the Soviet Union* (New York, Random House, 1995), p. 54. Matlock became ambassador in 1987. The only difference between Tweedledum and Tweedledee was their name.

12. Gorbachev in 1985 regarded his main task to be the perfectioning of a stagnant society and removing 'certain defects' of socialism.

13. Gorbachev's lack of perception about the impact of uskorenie is paralleled by the decision of (middle-aged) bureaucrats, for some unfathomable reason, to promote heavy metal music in 1985. Appalled by the content and popularity of the music, they tried to scupper it by depriving concerts of electricity and the bands were then driven to spreading their message on tapes. One irate correspondent wrote: 'I am very worried as a mother and as a woman that our girls are taking the risk of never being able to find a fiancé. My daughter likes discotheques, but returns from these places in tears. Imagine, boys go there to scream, to shout along with the music and to beat one another.' *Financial Times*, 9 March 1997, quoting an Itar-Tass report in 1988. This reveals that glasnost had transformed the music scene by 1988 and that these bands had become phenomenally popular by then. At a later date one of the Russian musicians explained the success of the genre thus: 'With our music, fans can scream and jump around and get all the filth and nonsense of daily life out of their systems. Only then can they go home and sleep soundly in their beds at night.'

14. Boukovsky, *Jugement à Moscou*, p. 478.

15. Mechanical engineering was traditionally strong but electrical engineering and electronics had lagged behind and this was to remain a major weakness.

16. Abel Aganbegyan, 'Na novom etape ekonomicheskogo stroitelstva', *EKO*, no. 8, 1985; and, 'Generalny kurs ekonomicheskoi politiki', *EKO*, no. 11, 1985. Defence expenditure in the late 1970s was growing at double the rate of national income growth.

17. Gorbachev, *Izbrannye rechi i stati*, vol. 2, p. 147.

18. Tatyana Zaslavskaya, 'Chelovechesky faktor razvitiya ekonomiki i sotsialnaya spravedlivost', *Kommunist*, no. 13, 1985. As *Kommunist* was published by the CC Secretariat, she was speaking for the Party leadership. She introduced two expressions, human factor and social justice, which were to be given wide currency by Gorbachev. Investment in the machine building sector was to grow by 80 per cent.

19. Mikhail Gorbachev, *Perestroika: New Thinking for Our Country and the World* (London, Collins, 1987), p. 19. In November 1988 he even thought national income was decreasing in the early 1980s. In his *Memoirs* Gorbachev states that economic growth had 'virtually stopped by the beginning of the 1980s' (London, Doubleday, 1996), p. 216.

20. Abel Aganbegyan, *The Challenge of Perestroika* (London, Hutchinson, 1988), p. 3.

21. Mark Harrison, *Accounting for War: Soviet Production, Employment, and the Defence Burden, 1940–1945* (Cambridge, Cambridge University Press, 1996), p. 302.
22. Vladimir Mau, *The Political History of Economic Reform in Russia, 1985–1994* (London, Centre for Research into Communist Economies, 1996), pp. 17–24.
23. The draft programme, published in *Pravda*, 7 March 1986, referred to the current stage of the development of socialism as integral socialism. However, this phrase was dropped from the final version which spoke of the era of reforms. The term, integral socialism, was borrowed from Lenin but the authors had not grasped the real meaning of it. Lenin used the term to describe the integration of the German military economic machine of that time and Soviet government. V. I. Lenin, *Polnoe Sobranie Sochinenii* (Moscow, Gosizpollit, 1963), vol. 36, p. 300; Mau, *Political History*, p. 119.
24. Gorbachev, *Izbrannye rechi i stati*, vol. 2, p. 81.
25. The first book for almost two decades which examined whether cooperative property, quoting Lenin, might not be more efficient than state-owned property was by A. S. Tsipko, *Nekotorye filosofskie aspekty teorii sotsializma* (Moscow, Nauka, 1983). Tsipko was not an economist but a specialist on ideology and later blamed Lenin for choosing the wrong route for Russia in 1917. Tsipko became a vigorous advocate of a market economy. In 1983, however, he was harshly criticised for his then modest views.
26. A revised version of the Party programme, introduced in 1961, was adopted at the 27th Congress and it was, as to be expected, enthusiastic about the future. One of the challenges to be achieved was to provide every family with a flat or house by 2000. However, no one had calculated what this rash promise would cost. A moment's reflection would have led to the realisation that the state could not foot the bill. This did not matter because, as usual, the promise was forgotten soon after it was made.
27. Quoted in Dusko Doder and Louise Branson, *Gorbachev: Heretic in the Kremlin* (London, Macdonald, 1990), p. 80.
28. Ibid., p. 167.
29. Boldin, *Ten Years That Shook the World*, pp. 69–70. Gorbachev arrived by Politburo limousine. Yeltsin, when he became first secretary of Moscow gorkom, did travel by public transport and this added greatly to his popularity.
30. Ibid., p. 69. Boldin says that he later informed Raisa about the show that was always put on for their visit. She was unconcerned and said it was quite natural to tidy up

and put on a good show when visitors arrived at one's home.

31. Gorbachev, *Memoirs*, p. 201 states that Ligachev (then his right-hand man) and Zimyanin (chief ideologist) first proposed that the speech be televised and, on hearing this, he agreed.

32. A secret paragraph in the Party–state decree on alcoholism regulated the annual decrease in alcohol production. It was typical of the era that this was regarded as a state secret.

33. Boldin, *Ten Years That Shook the World*, p. 110, reporting Yakovlev's crisp comments. Boldin also claims that Gorbachev changed his tie every day, and often his shirt as well. Another example of personal vanity was the elimination of the birth mark on his forehead in official photographs. It was left on when Gorbachev became well known. The British comedian Bob Monkhouse once quipped: 'Is Gorbachev an imperialist?' 'Of course.' 'Why?' 'He has a map of the world on his forehead!'

34. Mau, *Political History*, pp. 40–4.

35. See Jonathan C. Valdez, *Internationalism and the Ideology of Soviet Influence in Eastern Europe* (Cambridge, Cambridge University Press, 1993), pp. 134–55 for a penetrating analysis of contradictions.

36. Yury Andropov, 'Ucheniye Karla Marksa i nekotorye voprosy sotsialisticheskogo stroitelstva v SSSR', *Voprosy Filosofii*, no. 4, 1983, pp. 3–16.

37. Gorbachev, *Zhivoe tvorchestvo naroda*, p. 13.

38. The magnitude of the task can be gleaned from the fact that Ligachev informed the CC, in April 1985, shortly before the campaign had been launched, that in 1984 199,000 Party members and 370,000 Komsomol members had been reprimanded by the authorities for alcohol abuse. Stephen White, *Russia Goes Dry: Alcohol, State and Society* (Cambridge, Cambridge University Press, 1996), p. 67. Those keenest on the anti-alcohol campaign were Ligachev, a teetotaller, and Mikhail Solomentsev, a reformed alcoholic. As a cynic remarked, this was akin to putting a virgin in control of a brothel. One of the byproducts of the campaign was Gorbachevka, a vodka which apparently made one blather uncontrollably about perestroika!

39. Matlock, *Autopsy on an Empire*, p. 58, quoting an interview with Ryzhkov.

40. The failure of perestroika to improve living standards led to conflict within the leadership and, at the October 1987 CC plenum, Boris Yeltsin sharply criticised Gorbachev on this and other matters. The two parted company and Yeltsin was

sacked as first secretary of Moscow Party gorkom the following month.

41. *Voprosy ekonomiki*, no. 7, 1987 gives numerous details of this practice. Alec Nove, *An Economic History of the USSR 1917– 1991*, 3rd edn (London, Penguin, 1992), p. 397. Unearned income was derived from trade and continued to be banned. The law on individual activity, November 1986, legalised family and individual enterprise activity. Officially, in 1989, those involved only numbered 300,000. The breakthrough for co-operatives came in May 1988, with the passing of the law on cooperatives. They could employ an unlimited number of non-members on a contractual basis. Hence they developed quickly into private companies. The law on leaseholds, 1989, and the law on land, 1990, extended non-state economic activity.
42. *Pravda*, 25 July 1990.
43. One estimate of the cost of importing grain and other food and consumer goods from the west during the 1970s was US$180 billion. E. Shevardnadze, *Moi vybor, V zashchitu demo-kratii i svobody* (Moscow, Novosti, 1992), p. 107.
44. From his unpublished memoir, *Zerkalo*, as recorded in Matlock, *Autopsy on an Empire*, p. 59. His comment was made later.
45. Boukovsky, *Jugement à Moscou*, p. 276.
46. Ibid., p. 279.
47. Gorbachev, *Memoirs*, p. 188.
48. Ibid., p. 194.
49. Brown, *The Gorbachev Factor*, p. 123, regards the January 1987 CC plenum as the beginning of serious political reform.
50. Gorbachev, *Memoirs*, p. 215.
51. Ibid., p. 227.
52. Ibid., p. 230.
53. N. Shmelev, *Novy mir*, no. 6, 1987, pp. 144–5.
54. Anders Åslund, *Gorbachev's Struggle for Economic Reform: The Soviet Reform Process, 1985–88* (London, Pinter, 1989), p. 111.
55. Ibid., p. 120.
56. Gorbachev, *Memoirs*, p. 230. He was aware that the nettle had to be grasped sometime but the Politburo decided that retail price reform should be postponed indefinitely. This was tantamount to lighting a slow-burning fuse.
57. Richard E. Rawles, 'Soviet psychology, perestroika, and the human factor: 1985–1991' in V. A. Koltsova et al., *Post-Soviet Perspectives on Russian Psychology* (Westport, CT, Greenwood Press, 1996), p. 103.
58. Gorbachev, *Izbrannye rechi*, vol. 2, pp. 98–130.
59. *Kommunist*, no. 7, 1986, pp. 50–9.

60. Rawles, 'Soviet psychology', p. 107.
61. Matlock, *Autopsy on an Empire*, p. 114.
62. Yeltsin, *Against the Grain*, pp. 178–81.
63. Gorbachev, *Memoirs*, p. 244, states that 'those who pointed to his overgrown ambition and lust for power were right'. On p. 245, Gorbachev claims that the 'main conclusion one should draw . . . is that Yeltsin even then was not a real reformer'. If Gorbachev believed this at the time, it was a tragic misjudgement.
64. Matlock, *Autopsy on an Empire*, p. 115. The expression 'cult of the personality' was a coded term for Stalinism.
65. Ibid., p. 115. The following day George Shultz, Secretary of State, met Gorbachev but he appeared distracted. Shultz commented to Matlock that Gorbachev reminded him of a boxer who had never been knocked down, one who was confident and self-assured. That day, he reacted like a man who had hit the canvas for the first time. Ibid., p. 115.
66. Gorbachev, *Memoirs*, p. 246.
67. *Izvestiya TsK KPSS*, no. 2, 1989, pp. 209–87.
68. At the 27th Party Congress, on 6 March 1986, it was proudly stated: 'The nationalities question, inherited from the past, has been successfully solved in the Soviet Union'.
69. Gorbachev, *Memoirs*, p. 331.
70. Dinmukhamed Kunaev, *O moem vremeni* (Alma Ata, RGZhl Deuir, MP Yntymak, 1992); Matlock, *Autopsy on an Empire*, p. 161.
71. Gorbachev, *Memoirs*, p. 331.
72. Ibid., p. 404.
73. Ibid., p. 406.
74. Ibid., p. 405.
75. Matlock, *Autopsy on an Empire*, p. 92.
76. The war in Afghanistan was costing the Soviet Union between 3 billion and 4 billion rubles annually (about US$4–6 billion at the then rate of exchange). N. I. Ryzhkov, *Perestroika, Istoriya predatelstv* (Moscow, Novosti, 1992), p. 232.
77. Matlock, *Autopsy on an Empire*, p. 94.
78. Ibid., p. 95.
79. Gorbachev, *Memoirs*, p. 414.
80. Matlock, *Autopsy on an Empire*, p. 96.
81. Ibid., p. 97.
82. Gorbachev, *Memoirs*, p. 419.
83. Boukovsky, *Jugement à Moscou*, pp. 482–3.
84. George P. Shultz, *Turmoil and Triumph: My Years as Secretary of State* (New York, Charles Scribner's Sons, 1993), p. 738.
85. Ibid., p. 738.

86. Casey was aware that the CIA was leaking secrets but did not know that Aldrich Ames, an experienced CIA officer, had offered his services to the KGB. Ames provided Moscow with very valuable information during the whole Gorbachev era, enabling the KGB to eliminate many CIA sources in the Soviet Union and also counter US agents. Kryuchkov, therefore, had much evidence to place on Gorbachev's desk about CIA spying. Presumably Shevardnadze was not privy to this information.

87. Shultz found Shevardnadze warm, sincere and friendly. Shultz organised a boating trip on the Potomac, serenaded the Georgian with 'Georgia on my mind', and arranged for the Yale Russian choir to sing Georgian folk songs to Shevardnadze's delegation. In Moscow, during tense and difficult negotiations, Shultz had three Russian speakers from the US embassy give a rendering of 'Georgia on my mind'. It dissolved the tension. Ekedahl and Goodman, *Wars of Eduard Shevardnadze,* pp. 106–7.

88. Boukovsky, *Jugement à Moscou,* p. 435.

Chapter 4

PERESTROIKA MARK II:
1987–1989

Economic results in 1987 turned out to be worse than in 1986. Industry was finding it difficult to adjust to cost accounting, self-financing and self-management. Gorbachev believes this was the time when alienation between the central and local Party bodies set in.[1] Most local Party organisations were unable or unwilling to adjust to the new framework of work required under glasnost and democratisation. A new type of Party was needed, one which could seize the initiative and respond creatively to the new environment. Previously Party officials had concentrated on eliminating risk. The more secure the local Party committee felt, the more risk averse it became. And it had become very secure under Brezhnev. Also periods of stability and calm (the Brezhnev era, for example) do not stimulate new ideas. Now Gorbachev expected it to perform a totally different role and to become an agent of change at the local level. Not surprisingly, most officials resented this as they felt inadequate. Gorbachev realised that change was not keeping pace with public expectations and this could lead to the Party being left behind.

The 70th anniversary of the October Revolution afforded Gorbachev the opportunity to engage in revisionism. He could reinterpret the course of events since 1917 so as to promote perestroika. His speech on 2 November 1987 disappointed many as too conservative. However, one must remember the constraints under which Gorbachev was labouring. The speech was watered down in its condemnation of Stalin after opposition in the Politburo.

In January 1988 Gorbachev responded to the widespread criticism of bureaucratic privileges through a government decree cutting back drastically on the number of officials who would be entitled to a black Volga and chauffeur. On 1 July 1988 over 400,000 bureaucrats were to lose this much-sought-after privilege. The Volgas were to be sold to the public or turned into taxis. Also on 1 July, Soviet citizens with hard currency could no longer spend it in the hard currency shops in Moscow.[2]

Glasnost led to a flood of material being published, much of it critical of the Party and its record.[3] Ligachev was the most vociferous opponent of this 'muck-raking' and called for an end to be put to it. He was often joined by Mikhail Solomentsev, Viktor Chebrikov, Dmitry Yazov and eventually by Nikolai Ryzhkov. At the February 1988 CC plenum, Gorbachev turned Party values on their head. The most important values were not those that had been taught for decades: the primacy of the Party, state property and the planned economy. He asserted that the leading role of the Party had 'not been given by anyone from above or for all time'.[4] Man was now the centre of the socialist universe and this was to give rise to universal human values. Not surprisingly, this caused indignation among conservative ideologues and they rushed to defend the *status quo ante*. In other words, they sensed that their comfortable lifestyles were under threat.

On 13 March 1988 Gorbachev flew off to Yugoslavia, and Yakovlev to Mongolia. Ligachev was left in sole charge of the CC Secretariat which still supervised the press. When Gorbachev was handed that day's newspapers, he was advised by Georgy Shakhnazarov, his aide, to pay particular attention to an article by Nina Andreeva, entitled 'I cannot forgo my principles', in *Sovetskaya Rossiya*. The newspaper was well known for its close ties to conservatives. It was a full frontal assault on perestroika and caused the blood of the reformers to run cold. A letter from a chemistry teacher filled a whole page and the language was that of the Stalinist era. She defended Stalin and used anti-Semitic barbs, taken verbatim, from Andrei Zhdanov's speeches during the anti-cosmopolitan campaign of 1948.

Ligachev denied being behind its publication but conceded he was pleased by some of the sentiments expressed in it. These included the attacks on muck-raking history which cast the Stalin period in a bad light. To Gorbachev the letter could not have been penned by an ordinary Party member since it contained information only accessible to a narrow circle. The Leningrad Party was particularly zealous in ordering study of it. No rebuttal appeared until Gorbachev got back from Yugoslavia on 18 March. He soon discovered that several Politburo members, including Ligachev, Vorotni-kov, Gromyko and Solomentsev, sided with Andreeva.

He called a Politburo meeting on 24 March and found that Viktor Chebrikov, head of the KGB, and Anatoly Luky-anov also sided with the conservatives. The fact that Lukyanov, a fellow student at Moscow State University, had gone over to the opposition, came as a shock to Gorbachev. To Gorba-chev the article was an anti-perestroika platform. What irritated him was that the letter had been promoted by Party officials as authoritative. Yakovlev, Ryzhkov (partly because he resented Ligachev's attempts in the Party Secretariat to interfere in government affairs), Shevardnadze and Medvedev attacked the letter's sentiments.

Viktor Afanasev, the editor of *Pravda,* and his staff set about composing a reply but Gorbachev rejected it as far too tame. On 5 April *Pravda* published an unsigned article (mainly drafted by Yakovlev) tearing Andreeva's letter apart but without mentioning her name so as to underline the attack on conservative thinking.[5] Gorbachev and Yakovlev viewed the letter as the first shot in a campaign to force per-estroika back to its pre-1987 form. Gorbachev told the American ambassador in 1992 that he did not enjoy the option of moving faster in 1988 and 1989. 'They opposed me every step of the way. I managed to get formal approval for *partial* reforms in 1987. Then what happened? I turned my back, and they hit me with Nina Andreeva!'[6] Ligachev was shunted out of ideology and Yakovlev took over sole responsibility. Inevitably, a split was looming.

Tactically Gorbachev had two options when it became clear that many leading Party officials were lukewarm about change. He could attempt to remove these from the Central Committee or he could devise a mechanism for circumvent-ing their opposition. He chose the former option. A Party Congress was not due until 1991, so he came up with the idea of a Party Conference. When he floated the proposal to hold the Conference, at the January 1987 CC plenum, it was not approved, but he got his way at the June plenum. However, he lost an important battle when it was decided that new members could only be elected at a Party Congress.

The Conference could only promote from candidate to full membership. With Yakovlev in charge of ideology in the Secretariat, full vent could be given to radical thinking. The Conference was a risk as most members opposed reform. It could have been cancelled if the conservatives had revolted. The main reason why this did not occur was that Party discipline still held and the authority of the general secretary was supreme. Members were conditioned to accept decisions proposed by the Party leader but it was quite a different story when it came to implementing them.

Draft theses or proposals were presented to a CC plenum on 23 May and they sailed smoothly through. When they were published in *Pravda* on 27 May, they caused a sensation. They marked the transition from Soviet-style socialism to something akin to west European social democracy. This remarkable document proposed free, multi-candidate elections to soviets, secret ballots, guaranteed freedom of the press, speech and assembly and promised legal protection for them. Judges were to be independent. Social justice was to be a guiding principle. Gorbachev had attempted to go further. He had advocated political pluralism and amending the Soviet Constitution to legalise a multi-party system. The Politburo had rejected this, with only Yakovlev, Shevardnadze and Vorotnikov voting in favour. Only in 1990 would the Party agree to end its political monopoly.[7]

. . .

THE 19TH PARTY CONFERENCE

In his opening speech, on 28 June, Gorbachev surprised the delegates by proposing that the same person could hold the leading Party position and the leading government position throughout the country, from local soviets right up to head of state. Reformers were taken aback. Gorbachev, on the one hand, favoured restricting Party interference in the state, but, on the other, was handing them power through the soviets. This could be read as strengthening the institution which was most opposed to perestroika.

However, it could be read another way. Since there were to be free elections to local soviets, Party officials had to win them before they could consolidate their power. Gorbachev put his faith in the people. They would choose those who wanted to implement perestroika. This was a brilliant tactical move by the general secretary. There was no way he could order Party officials to hand over power to the soviets. In this way he could effect a quiet revolution since it did not occur to most Party officials that they could lose these elections. His opening address was a careful blend of the orthodox with splices of radical thinking. He praised the leading and guiding role of the Party and Marxism-Leninism as the scientific foundation of the Party's work. However, he also added that the free competition of intellects was a fundamental tenet of perestroika.

The leadership sat facing the delegates and some speakers used the Party 'dinosaurs' as target practice. One who came in for rough treatment was Andrei Gromyko, but others included Solomentsev, Afanasev, the editor of *Pravda*, and Arbatov. 'Today, comrade Gromyko is behind the times . . . he has completed his work.'[8] This unprecedented behaviour contained seeds of danger for Gorbachev. If Party leaders were no longer a protected species, he would, sooner or later, be dragged into the firing line. He sensed a conservative Party opposition forming at the Conference. A rift was developing in the Party and an increasingly critical attitude to perestroika was becoming evident. This was later to develop into direct sabotage by a large number of Party secretaries and those in the central Party apparatus.[9]

For ordinary citizens and foreigners – the proceedings were televised – the most dramatic confrontation at the Conference was that between Ligachev and Yeltsin. On the final day of the Conference, Yeltsin, just before the midday break, left his seat in the balcony and moved like an actor centre stage. He was not down as a speaker but he demanded and was given the podium by Gorbachev. In a carefully prepared speech, he decided to become a populist and launched into a bitter attack on the Party and perestroika. He honed in on corruption in the Party and accused Mikhail Solomentsev, chair of the Party Control Commission and responsible for the behaviour of Party members, of investigating petty offences and ignoring glaring corruption at the top. His righteous indignation was then turned on Party privileges. Then he alluded to the events of the October 1987 plenum, which had not yet been published, so as to give his side of the case. Sarcastically, he remarked that it was the Party's custom to rehabilitate comrades after 50 years. He would like to be rehabilitated while he was still alive. Yeltsin asked the Conference to annul the decision of the CC plenum. His request was debated after lunch.

As speaker after speaker laid into Boris Nikolaevich, it was plain that they had spent the break chewing over which insults they should spit out. Ligachev had spent lunch writing out his barbs and he read them with the skill of a practised orator. Everything Boris had done was wrong, even when he had been Party boss of Sverdlovsk oblast. In a ringing voice, he exclaimed: 'Boris, you are wrong!'. He used the intimate second personal singular, *ty*, instead of the formal second person plural. This signalled condescension and was very offensive. It was as if Ligachev had been scolding his pet dog. Ligachev took great exception to Yeltsin's charges of Party privilege. He waxed lyrical about how hard life had been in Siberia and the only privilege he had enjoyed was to work his fingers to the bone. The delegates sided with Ligachev at the Conference, but the people sided with Yeltsin. They knew how the fat cats lived. Wags then coined the expression: 'Egor, you are wrong!'.

Gorbachev's leadership skills were fully displayed at the Conference. Probably only he could have got a conservative Conference to adopt resolutions which emasculated the Party apparatus and to accept almost free elections to the Congress of People's Deputies, in 1989. The tactics he adopted were to split the opposition, make concessions which turned out to be less radical than they appeared, and to use his authority as general secretary. The Conference, indeed the Politburo and Central Committee, would agree to almost any compromise to avoid a split. As chair, Gorbachev ruthlessly used his position to ensure that votes went his way. The Conference was Mikhail Sergeevich's Rubicon. He had left the old Soviet Union behind and was now fashioning a new, restructured society. His commitment to perestroika convinced some of his critics, including Anatoly Sobchak, later to be mayor of Leningrad, and Sergei Stankevich, to join the Party. This revealed that these reformers perceived the Party as the vanguard of reform.

The Conference underlined the goal of separating Party and state. However, the Party was to retain its monopoly on power. Gorbachev was promoting the pluralism of opinions but all these opinions had to be socialist. What about opposition from conservatives in the Politburo? Were there antagonistic contradictions which could lead to a split? No, there were only 'temporary interests'.[10]

Gorbachev was very skilled in handling delicate matters in the Politburo. The general rule was that the disagreeable tasks were handed to the conservatives and the agreeable tasks to the reformers. One instance was the renaming of the icebreaker L. Brezhnev. The existing one was to revert to its former name, the Arktika. A new one was to be called the L. Brezhnev. It was decided that the ceremony would take place without the television cameras. Ligachev and Zaikov were put in charge of the operation. Another instance was a request by Svetlana Alliluyeva, Stalin's daughter. Someone had to interview her to discover exactly what was in her mind. Gorbachev did not want the job:

> If I have to do it, I shall have to judge Stalin, Stalingrad and all that. I come from a family in which my uncle had his health ruined. My mother is from a very poor family with five children. I received a medal for writing an essay on 'Stalin is our martial glory, Stalin is the life force of our youth'. Perhaps comrade Solomentsev should conduct the interview.

Gromyko then proposed E. K. Ligachev. Gorbachev finally commented. 'Let comrade Ligachev conduct the interview'.[11]

. . .

OPPOSITION FORMS

While the reformers were lining up behind Mikhail Sergeevich, his opponents were organising their own campaign. The Democratic Union (Demsoyuz), set up in May 1988, was the first opposition party to the Communist Party of the Soviet Union. It mustered about 2,000 members and its leading light was Valeriya Novodvorskaya, born in 1950. In 1968 she had set up an underground student organisation whose objective was to overthrow the Soviet state. She was first arrested in December 1969 and was sentenced for dissident activities in 1978, 1985 and 1986. She graduated in French, under a false identity. During her last incarceration, she spent three months in a closed psychiatric hospital. Under Gorbachev she was arrested 17 times and each time she went on hunger strike.

Many other political parties and organisations came into being in 1989.[12] The Russian Christian Democratic movement spawned the Russian Christian Democratic Union and the Christian Democratic Union of Russia, which were conservative Christian. The Liberal Democratic Party of Russia and three Constitutional Democratic parties (the Constitutional Democratic Party, the Party of Constitutional Democrats – the main difference between them was their interpretation of the legacy of the Constitutional Democratic Party (the Kadets) – and the Union of Constitutional Democrats) were broadly conservative. The Democratic Party of Russia, led by Nikolai Travkin, was set up in May 1990, and began as a liberal party but gradually moved to the conservative wing of politics. The Republican Party of the Russian Federation came into being in November 1990 and claimed 30,000 members. Democratic Russia (DemRossiya), the standard bearer of liberal democratic ideas, appeared in October 1990. There were two social democratic parties (the main one was the Social Democratic Party of Russia, founded in May 1990) and there was the Anarcho-Syndicalist Confederation and the Anarcho-Communist Revolutionary Union. Conservative nationalist parties appeared in the autumn of 1990, such as the Russian National Democratic Party. The monarchists, advocating the return of a Romanov Tsar, also set up their own party.

Gradually two main political groups emerged: the communists and the democrats. The former, led by Gorbachev, advocated the renewal of socialism, preference for the development of socialist property, collective forms of social relations, self-management and the activation of the human factor. The democrats wanted the privatisation of state property, a market economy, a full parliamentary system and guarantees for human rights.

When Gorbachev went off on holiday on 1 August, Ligachev, now in charge in the Kremlin, grasped the opportunity to present his understanding of perestroika. He spelled out his opposition to a market economy and stoutly defended the 'class nature of international relations'. The latter starkly contradicted a speech by Eduard Shevardnadze, delivered at a conference of diplomats and specialists, in July. In it Shevardnadze had stated that 'we are fully justified in refusing to see in peaceful coexistence a special form of the class struggle . . . The struggle of two opposing systems is no longer the decisive tendency of the contemporary era.'[13] Here was the definitive statement, in the Party's own newspaper, that the Soviet Union had abandoned the central tenet of Marxism-Leninism.

Yakovlev, in a speech in Vilnius expressed in dense syntax and almost Jesuitical sophistication, replied for the reformers. He placed the common interests of mankind above those of any country or ethnic group.[14] No wonder there was confusion. Ligachev, in Gorbachev's opinion, was reverting to 'pre-perestroika' positions.[15] There was a possible solution. The Party should be removed entirely from the management of the economy and should only concern itself with intra-Party affairs. Thus Gorbachev could circumvent Party opposition of economic reform.

. . .

CHANGES IN THE PARTY

Gorbachev decided to set up transitional bodies until the soviets and the government agencies had gained strength and experience. In a memorandum to the Politburo of 24 August 1988, Gorbachev recommended that the number of departments of the CC Secretariat be reduced from 20 to nine. Only two economic ones were to be left: agriculture, and a new socio-economic department. Government members of the Politburo were enthusiastic about this. As in pluralist countries, the government ministries were to be supervised by the legislature. The department for relations with communist and workers' parties of socialist countries was downgraded and became a part of the international department. This significant move signalled that socialist countries were no longer to be treated as stepchildren but as sovereign states. Valentin Falin, a German specialist, took over from Anatoly Dobrynin, who had been systematically sidelined by Shevardnadze, as head of the enlarged Secretariat international department. Andrei Gromyko and Anatoly Dobrynin were put out to grass at the same time, October 1988.

In September Gorbachev went further and the Secretariat was reorganised into six commissions. The chair of each commission became responsible for that policy area in the

Party. Vadim Medvedev was made chair of ideology and the main benefit of this was that Ligachev was no longer responsible for this sensitive area. Medvedev was not as radical as Yakovlev, however, Yakovlev was appointed chair of international affairs, and here he was in his element. Ligachev became chair of agriculture. This meant sacrificing the rural sector because no moves towards the market would be made under Ligachev. Georgy Razumovsky took on personnel policy, and Nikolai Slyunkov took on social and economic policy. Viktor Chebrikov was moved from the KGB to chair the legal commission. Its task was to supervise the Ministry of Internal Affairs, the Ministry of Defence and the KGB. It would have been difficult to find someone less suited to the task in the post-19th Conference world than Chebrikov. Gorbachev placed a lot of faith in the KGB and he may also have been wary of alienating such a person.

Gorbachev's relationship with the KGB is revealing as he never perceived it could operate against him. He was used to getting personal reports from Chebrikov. On 19 February 1986 the KGB chief reported on the activities of his organisation in 1985:

> KGB organs have stepped up their struggle against ideological diversions and class enemies. The Chekists have participated everywhere in the work of Party organs to eliminate various negative processes and phenomena, and have improved their preventive activities . . . In Moscow, Leningrad, in the Union capitals and in other towns, acts of ideological sabotage, perpetrated by several hundred emissaries and functionaries of foreign anti-Soviet organisations, nationalists, Zionists and clerics, have been discovered and eliminated. Three hundred of them have been expelled and 322 have been refused entry to the Soviet Union. In Ukraine, the Baltic republics and elsewhere, 25 illegal nationalist groups were discovered and liquidated while they were still embryonic . . . 1,275 authors and distributors of anonymous, illegal, anti-Soviet, slanderous documents, of which 97 have appeared before the courts . . . Preventive measures have been taken against 15,271 persons.[16]

On 25 September 1986 Gorbachev asked Chebrikov, at a Politburo meeting, how many political prisoners there were, according to the western definition. He replied that there were 240. They had been sentenced for espionage, crossing the Soviet frontier illegally, distributing hostile tracts, hard currency dealing, etc. Since some had renounced their activities, it would be possible to release about a third, then a half of them. Two had been executed for spying. Gorbachev reported that one of them, an American agent, had had 2 million rubles on him. Chebrikov stated that he had passed important military secrets to the Americans.[17]

The Politburo was very concerned about the impact of the death of a prisoner, Tolya Marchenko, who had refused food for three months before dying. His death was reported to the leadership on 4 February 1987. There was a need to reduce the number of political prisoners so as to soften the image of the Soviet Union in the west. On 15 January 1987 the KGB reported that there were 288 persons in custody, of whom 114 had been sentenced for anti-Soviet agitation propaganda (article 70 of the RSFSR criminal code), 119 for slandering the Soviet political and social system (article 190–1) and 55 for other offences. A tactic adopted was to encourage prisoners to sign statements stating they renounced their illegal activities. Some 51 had done so and had been amnestied.[18] On 1 May 1987 there were still 98 persons sentenced under these articles.[19] The draft criminal code, published in December 1988, dropped the offences contained in articles 70 and 190–1 of the RSFSR criminal code and those of the other republics. Those sentenced and who refused to recant remained in prison. All political prisoners were freed by President Yeltsin in February 1992.

The new KGB chief was Vladimir Kryuchkov, a worse appointment than Chebrikov. In his defence, Gorbachev states that Kryuchkov had been for 'many years a close ally' of Andropov.[20] What he overlooked was that the Soviet Union he was fashioning would have caused Andropov to turn in his grave. Setting up the commissions was an astute move as no one paid any attention to their deliberations. Political decision-making had moved elsewhere. There was, however, a serious drawback to the marginalising of the Secretariat. It had been responsible for supervising the implementation of Politburo resolutions. No body took its place. Gorbachev would need to establish a new institution to ensure that top decisions were implemented.

A CC plenum, on 30 September, allowed some of the deadwood in the leadership to be cleared. Andrei Gromyko had been dozing off at meetings, waking up and making quite inappropriate remarks. Petr Demichev, first deputy chair of the Presidium of the USSR Supreme Soviet (deputy head of state), was long overdue for his pension. Anatoly Lukyanov replaced him and repaid Gorbachev by becoming a plotter in August 1991. Mikhail Solomentsev gave way to Boris Pugo as chair of the Party Control Commission. Gorbachev refers to Pugo as a 'man of integrity'.[21] This was bad judgement as Pugo was one of the conspirators in August 1991. Vitaly Vorotnikov was shunted off to become chair of the Presidium of the RSFSR Supreme Soviet, or Russian head of state (merely an honorific title at that time). Who was to take over from Gromyko as head of state? Mikhail Sergeevich himself, recommended by Ligachev. Hence, Gorbachev judged it wise not to discard Ligachev, even though he was out of temper with the course of reform. The risk was that he could have headed a conservative, pre-perestroika opposition. There was a potentially large constituency. Gorbachev estimated that there were 18 million bureaucrats, administering about 127 million workers. Of the bureaucrats, 2.5 million were in ministries and agencies and the rest were in enterprises. This was administration gone mad. For every seven workers, there was someone to tell them what to do.[22]

Ever mindful that the CC was conservative and potentially dangerous to his ambitions, Gorbachev had attempted to remove the 'dead souls' or deadwood at the 19th Conference but had failed.[23] After the January 1987 CC plenum, Party secretaries had to stand in contested elections and many of them were swept away. The Party bosses with all the resources of the local media at their disposal were being rejected by the membership. This is the point when Gorbachev thinks the authority of the Party declined as members ceased being afraid of it.[24] Officials were now judged according to their performance and not according to their position in the hierarchy. The Party membership was becoming alienated from the Party bureaucracy. This spread to the general public and became visible during the elections to the Congress of People's Deputies in March 1989. People were losing their fear of the Party but, more significantly, they were losing their fear of the KGB. Glasnost had loosened their tongues and the hitherto protected species, the general secretary, was no longer inviolable.

This transformed politics. Officials were judged by results, not by promises. As economic problems mounted in 1989, the establishment came in for harsher and harsher criticism. This was a new experience for Party and state officials who had previously demanded and obtained acquiescence. Now they had to defend themselves against an avalanche of complaints, some justified, some not, but they acquitted themselves poorly. They had to learn democratic politics on the hoof and they complained often and bitterly to Gorbachev about the injustice of it all. A wave of talented polemicists emerged and the nomenklatura was no match for them. The polemicists, and others, seized the opportunity eagerly to seek revenge on their former tormentors.

Gorbachev finally cleared the dead souls out of the CC in April 1989 when 74 full members and 24 candidate members offered their resignation. He estimated that of the 303 full members, elected at the 27th Party Congress, 84 had retired, as had 27 of the 157 candidate members.[25] Thus he made an almost clean sweep. Retirement was sweetened by promises of pensions, dachas, medical services, cars, and so on. However, some of these promises were not kept.

Among the dinosaurs who departed were Andrei Gromyko, Nikolai Tikhonov and Boris Ponomarev. Among those who moved up from candidate to full membership were Evgeny Velikhov, the scientist, and Valentin Falin, the head of the international department of the Secretariat. However, as was normal for a CC plenum, no new members were elected. That would have to wait for a Party Congress. Not that there was a phalanx of aspiring perestroika implementers waiting in the wings. Gorbachev mournfully came to the conclusion that contested Party elections normally produced clones, not new blood. Even after more elections, the result was the same: clones. They had all been groomed in the same stable, the Stalinist stable, and had been trained to carry out orders rather than to innovate and be accountable to the population.

. . .

THE CONGRESS OF PEOPLE'S DEPUTIES AND THE SUPREME SOVIET

Elections to the Congress took place on 26 March 1989, and were a watershed. They were the first contested national elections organised by the Bolsheviks. The concept of the Congress went back to the early years of the revolution. The Congress was to have 2,250 deputies: 750 from social organisations, 750 representing territorial constituencies, and 750 representing nationality constituencies. Hence, one-third were to be indirectly elected. Of the social organisations, 100 seats were set aside for the Party, the Academy of Sciences was allotted seats, as was the Cinematographers' Union, and so on. Gorbachev decided that only 100 names would be on the Party list. He feared that if there were, say, 200 names, all the radicals, including himself, would be defeated.

The Congress was then to elect a new Supreme Soviet, consisting of two houses, the Soviet of the Union and the Soviet of Nationalities, each with 271 deputies. This was a replica of the former Supreme Soviet but it had been directly elected. It is interesting that the combined number of the two houses is roughly equivalent to that in the House of Representatives and Senate in the United States.

The Party apparatus was very confident that it could handle nominations in such a way as to ensure cosmetic democracy. The Party would ensure that its man or woman won. All the mavericks would be excluded. Maverick number one was Boris Yeltsin. He took the precaution of getting himself nominated in a rural constituency in Sverdlovsk oblast, his home turf. He gave the Party commission no advance warning and simply turned up unexpectedly. However, his eyes were set on higher things. He wanted to be on the ballot paper in national territorial district number one, Moscow. There were ten candidates left on 22 February when the final decision was to be taken about who would appear on the ballot paper. The Party had decided they were to be Yury Brakov, manager of the ZIL car plant, and Georgy Grechko, a well-known cosmonaut. So sure were the authorities of themselves that they arranged for the proceedings to be televised live on local Moscow TV. Boris Nikolaevich was heading for a spectacular fall.

Yeltsin was castigated by delegates and told to withdraw. He fielded the most hostile questions at the podium. However, he knew something that no one else knew, that Grechko intended to withdraw his nomination. Grechko told Yeltsin of this and Boris Nikolaevich persuaded him not to make this public until after the votes had been counted. Then he could resign, leaving the Party no time to prime another candidate. After twelve hours, the delegates were ready to vote. Predictably Brakov came first, Grechko second, and despite the clamour, Yeltsin third. Then Grechko dramatically announced that he was withdrawing. The Party was in a quandary. If it accepted Yeltsin it was a humiliating defeat, if it declared that another candidate was to take the vacant spot, it would make a mockery of the nomination process. It swallowed hard and put Yeltsin on the ballot paper.[26]

On 26 March Yeltsin received an astonishing 89.4 per cent of the votes, with Brakov trailing hopelessly at 6.9 per cent. Gorbachev worked behind the scenes to impede Boris Nikolaevich but significantly did not attempt to sabotage the result. The stunning victory demonstrated that the votes had been fairly counted and this represented a victory for burgeoning democracy. The people's champion was back on the national political stage. Public interest was extremely high with an 89.8 per cent turnout.

There were other spectacular falls for Party favourites. The greatest was the defeat of Yury Solovev, first secretary of Leningrad obkom, and a candidate member of the Politburo to boot. He had ensured that his name was the only one on the ballot sheet. Surely he could not lose. He did, because of the rule that to win on the first ballot a candidate had to obtain at least 50 per cent plus one vote. In Russian elections one can vote against a candidate or against all candidates by striking out their names. Not only did Solovev lose the election, he had also to resign as Party boss in Leningrad oblast. This rule had been accepted by the Party, blithely unaware that it could become reality. As a Russian observed, it takes a special talent to lose an election where there is no opposition, but this talent was in liberal supply in the upper echelons of the Party.

Radicals did especially well in Moscow and Leningrad and among those elected were future stars such as Sergei Stankevich, a 35-year-old specialist on American history, Anatoly Sobchak, a skilled lawyer and later to be mayor of Leningrad, Yury Afanasev, a historian, and Nikolai Shmelev, an economic scourge of the establishment. Oleg Bogomolov, a talented reform economist, won in Moscow despite the Party playing a host of dirty tricks on him. He quipped afterwards: 'I had no idea it was such an advantage to stand against the

Party'.[27] Andrei Sakharov and Roald Sagdeev, a famous space scientist, were elected as members of the Academy of Sciences' delegation. The first time round, the Academy Party committee had filled the list with old hacks. Such had been the commotion that they were forced to accept those members which academicians wanted. The Cinematographers' Union, known for its radicalism, predictably returned only pro-reform candidates. Gavriil Popov, the editor of the leading economics journal *Voprosy Ekonomiki* and vigorously pro-market, and Tatyana Zaslavskaya, the leading sociologist, were also returned for social organisations. One woman who won in direct elections in Evevan, Armenia, was Galina Starovoitova, a leading specialist in nationalities and later to be a leading light of the Democratic Russia movement. Otherwise women did not do very well, with the Congress much more heavily male than the old Supreme Soviet. The scene was set for the first no-holds-barred debate in Soviet history.

Had the Party won or lost? Gorbachev claimed it had won since about 87 per cent of deputies were communists. Ryzhkov challenged this assessment, pointing out that 30 important regional Party leaders had been defeated and many Party members had won despite the Party campaigning for more establishment figures. Significantly, the Party had done badly in leading industrial cities and scientific and cultural centres. This was a bad omen for the Party. The warning was quite explicit: if the Party did not engage in perestroika and reform itself in line with changes in society, it would cease to be a vanguard party and find itself trying to lead from the rear. Politics had again become legitimate, the first time since 1920–1. The Party would now have to compete with other persuasions for public support. The Bolsheviks had won in 1917 by being more radical than their opponents. The risk was now that others would win popular support by being more radical than the Party.

Gorbachev came to the Congress to dominate it. During his speech recommending himself as chair or speaker, he said: 'I know everything. Maybe I even know more than you.' He called for some discipline. 'Reform is bursting forth, the political process is bursting forth . . . it is time for consolidation for the sake of our supreme interest.'[28] On the nationalities, he issued a stern warning: 'If we begin separating our peoples and ethnic groups now . . . if we start redrawing our country, it will be the road to disaster, I assure you'. It was the Nagorno-Karabakh problem which was uppermost in his mind. Some delegations had come to do battle with the new President. 'Our delegation travelled to the Congress rather aggressively inclined against Moscow and even Mikhail Gorbachev personally', Brazauskas later revealed.[29] They all voted for him as speaker, however.

Gorbachev's attitude to the election of a speaker at the beginning of the Congress reflected poorly on his grasp of democratic politics – the need to demonstrate that one was willing to countenance opposition. Andrei Sakharov proposed that the vote for speaker of the Supreme Soviet (and head of state) be delayed until all issues could be debated, rather than as the first item on the agenda. It was inevitable that Gorbachev would be elected but he called for a vote and the Congress took its cue from Gorbachev – it voted down the proposal. Gorbachev encouraged Party officials to accept multi-candidate elections but he was unwilling to allow anyone to stand against him for speaker. Gennady Burbulis, later to be a prominent member of Yeltsin's Russian government, proposed Yeltsin but he refused to stand. Aleksandr Obolensky, an engineer from Murmansk, was so keen to get on the ballot paper that he nominated himself. The deputies voted again as Gorbachev would have wished but about one-third were in favour of Obolensky's nomination. Mikhail Sergeevich lost an opportunity to play the democratic politician and had he intimated that he was in favour of a contested election, Obolensky would have been added. When it did come to the decision, Gorbachev got 95.6 per cent of the vote, with only 87 voting against. This led a keen observer, the American ambassador, to conclude that Mikhail Sergeevich would have made a poor chess player.[30]

If he revealed faulty judgement here, he was a wizard at back-stage negotiations at the Congress. He was a master at cutting a deal. This could, however, not protect him from criticism from the floor. Day after day (the Congress ran from 25 May to 9 June) he was subjected to sharp criticism from delegates, many of them conservative communists, and the whole population was privy to it as proceedings were shown on television in the evening and into the early hours. These communists objected to the opportunities being afforded Sakharov and the radicals to express their views and that their comments were not being rebutted effectively. The radicals complained that they were not being given enough air time. Mikhail Sergeevich was caught in the crossfire and was certain to lose whatever he decided. One delegate asked if it were true that a dacha was being built for him in the Crimea at state expense. Many of them told him that he should not be, simultaneously, speaker and general secretary of the Party.

A sensitive issue at the Congress which revealed how contentious nationality affairs were, concerned the killing of unarmed demonstrators in Tbilisi, Georgia, on 9 April 1989. Sakharov criticised the role of the Soviet Army, commanded by General Igor Rodionov (Russian Minister of Defence July 1996–May 1997). For this he was vilified by many deputies who took an attack on the army to be tantamount to a challenge to their virility. Other speakers wanted to know who in Moscow had ordered the assault in Tbilisi (Gorbachev was absent at the time). Gorbachev's authority was bound to suffer. His popularity at the end of 1988 had been very high. In an opinion poll on leading politicians, he received 55 per cent and Yeltsin 4 per cent. However, this began to slip in 1989 as criticism mounted. It was now possible for a nobody to berate the general secretary and get away with it. Until 1989 he had appeared a strong, national leader, but now he began to look vulnerable.

Elections to the new Supreme Soviet took place at the Congress and it was to convene when the Congress had concluded its deliberations. Whereas Congress deputies had other jobs, Supreme Soviet members were to become professional politicians, with the Supreme Soviet meeting about 40 weeks a year. Given the composition of the Congress, it was unlikely that many radicals would make it through to the new body. Russia was granted 11 members for the Soviet of Nationalities. Yeltsin was number 12 on the list. The Congress had rejected the deputy with the largest majority in Russia. The situation was saved by Aleksei Kazannik, a lawyer from Omsk, who was number 11 and ceded his place to Boris Nikolaevich, stating that he could not face his voters if he turned out to be the one who was responsible for Yeltsin's elimination.[31] Gorbachev, the lawyer who had forgotten most of his law, consulted Lukyanov, the lawyer, and found nothing in the rule book to prevent it. Gorbachev chaired the early Supreme

Soviet sessions but then gave way, due to pressure of business, to Anatoly Lukyanov, his nominee as deputy speaker.

According to the Constitution, Prime Minister Ryzhkov had to present his ministerial nominations for confirmation before the Supreme Soviet. Deputies took an almost masochistic delight in rejecting nomination after nomination. Well-known ministers were verbally flogged and cast aside.

The resultant government reflected the belief that there was no crisis in the offing. It was a mixture of economic interests (the military-industrial complex, the fuel, energy and agrarian lobbies), reform-minded bureaucrats (such as Valentin Pavlov, who was later to be Gorbachev's Prime Minister), and reform economists (such as Leonid Abalkin). The balance of power within the government indicated that it would not move to radical reform. It would continue its search for improvements of the economic mechanism. The market meant the planned or regulated market. It would attempt incremental reform, step by step. In a stable political environment this would have been quite reasonable. However, the country was heading towards a systemic crisis, one in which political, economic and social crises emerged simultaneously. This government did not possess the skills to cope with such a situation.[32] Gone was its feeling of omnipotence. This affected the Party to an even greater extent. It now became hesitant, looking over its shoulder at the new parliament, which was in its initial phase, that of euphoria.

In elections to the Congress the radicals had done particularly well in Moscow, Leningrad, Sverdlovsk (now Ekaterinburg, and Yeltsin's home base), parts of the Caucasus, and the Baltic States. They had done badly in elections to the Supreme Soviet. How were they to maintain the momentum? The natural leader was Yeltsin. He was no intellectual but he was hugely popular in Moscow.

The intellectuals cast aside their doubts about the reform credentials of Boris Nikolaevich and began planning a pro-reform group in parliament. As a minister Yeltsin had been assigned a suite in the Moskva Hotel, just off Red Square. Most non-Moscow deputies stayed there. Yeltsin's suite became the natural meeting place for drafting proposals and discussing tactics. Almost all of them were communists and still forbidden to form factions. Should they attempt to set up a party to challenge the ruling Party? Under no circumstances, since the average Russian's reaction would be: 'Another party, God forbid, isn't one bad enough?'.

On 19 July Yeltsin informed the Supreme Soviet that a coordinating body had been set up to organise an Inter-Regional Group of deputies and that a founding congress would follow by the end of July. The group declared its aims to be the 'acceleration of perestroika'. Since it would be in the minority, it would become an opposition and propose alternative legislation. This underlined that these deputies had broken the taboo about being officially an opposition. Also, the first overtly pro-perestroika group had formed.

How was this minority to punch above its weight in politics? They adopted tactics which had been brilliantly successful elsewhere – the mass demonstration. They proceeded to organise demonstrations in Moscow and elsewhere which caught the public imagination and received coverage on television. This refuted the conservative charge that the proposals of the radicals had little support among the population. Members of the Inter-Regional Group did not consider themselves in opposition to Gorbachev, rather as a force to assist him to push perestroika further. Dining at the American ambassador's residence, Yeltsin expressed himself content with the progress made. About a quarter of the objectives had been achieved. He made no disparaging remarks about Mikhail Sergeevich, the only barbs were directed at Raisa.[33] The ambassador judged Yeltsin a critical supporter of Gorbachev, not a competitor. The intense political rivalry, which was to descend into personal hatred, was to come later.[34]

.   .   .

CHANGES IN POLITICS

The radical nature of the demands at the Congress of People's Deputies and the Supreme Soviet and the formation of opposition parties and movements changed the political landscape. For the first time the initiative began to slip from Mikhail Sergeevich's fingers. At a CC plenum in July 1989 he conceded that there were still many who thought that all that was necessary was the propagation of age-old verities: 'socialism, the interests of the people, democracy, glasnost, and the Party as the generator of ideas and the organising force of society'.[35] The Party and the instruments of coercion, the police and the military, could retain power but perestroika from below and glasnost were gradually chipping away at the legitimacy of the existing order. Gorbachev felt the decline in Party authority acutely. How was perestroika to be implemented, if not by the Party? Inevitably, his personal authority declined with that of the Party. Nikolai Ryzhkov thought that, 'as things went from bad to worse, he lost his vision and therefore his strength and authority in the country'.[36] He wrestled with the administrative-command system and could not resolve the problems it threw up. The Party was splitting. The only thing he was left with was parliament, where he was speaker, and also head of state. The planned economy was dissolving but nothing was taking its place. Brilliant at escaping from tight corners, he would need to be like Houdini to avoid the gathering storm.

A fundamental error in drafting amendments to the Constitution to cater for the Congress of People's Deputies and the Supreme Soviet had not yet surfaced. This was the failure to understand the need to make a clear distinction between the legislature and the executive, or in other words, the separation of powers. It was overlooked that the Congress had been granted the power to issue instructions to the executive, the government, if a two-thirds majority were achieved. This was to have disastrous consequences for economic policy, especially the battle to contain inflation. This fatal weakness also applied to the Russian Congress of People's Deputies and, since the conflict between the legislature and executive could not be resolved, resulted in the tragic events of October 1993.

The extent to which Gorbachev's brand of socialism was becoming old-hat can be gleaned from the subscription figures of national newspapers. *Pravda*, under the editorship of Ivan Frolov, Gorbachev's man, fell from 9.5 million to 6.5 million copies between early 1989 and early 1990.[37] The much more radical *Argumenty i Fakty*, renowned for its factual reporting of Soviet reality, was selling about 33 million copies by early 1990. A turning point was reached in 1988 when Vladislav Starkov, the editor, interviewed the American ambassador. He dared to ask a very sensitive question. 'Did we [the Soviets] really bug the US embassy?' 'Yes, you did, and I have seen the evidence.'[38] This was an explosive revelation for Russian readers. Gorbachev's sensitivity about his popularity rating became clear in October 1989 when *Argumenty i Fakty* summarised the results of readers' letters. It revealed that the most radical deputies in the Congress of People's Deputies were the most popular. The pecking order was Andrei Sakharov, Gavriil Popov, Boris Yeltsin and Yury Afanasev. Starkov, Ivan Laptev, the editor of *Izvestiya,* and Afanasev himself were given a dressing down by Gorbachev on 13 October 1989, and accused of undermining perestroika.

The next day, Vadim Medvedev, who had taken over the press brief from Yakovlev, demanded that Starkov resign and offered him the job of editing *World Marxist Review,* in Prague, or the Supreme Soviet bulletin. Starkov referred the matter to his board and they supported him by 47 votes to 2. Judging by past experience, Gorbachev should have got his way. However, the journalists were testing glasnost to the limit. Would Gorbachev revert to pre-perestroika ways and banish Starkov or would he back off? He backed off. Starkov responded in the next edition of his paper by publishing, for the first time, the results of a poll on the standing of national politicians. Gorbachev was approved by 66 per cent of respondents. Mikhail Sergeevich had committed a cardinal error. He transformed Starkov, an advocate of perestroika, into a personal enemy and the editor never forgave Mikhail Sergeevich for trying to fire him for writing the truth.[39] After this, editors stepped up their campaign for legislation to protect the freedom of the press. This appears to have been a watershed for Mikhail Sergeevich and the press. The love affair was over.

Opinion polls were back in vogue under perestroika and the All-Union Centre for the Study of Public Opinion of Socio-Economic Problems was set up in 1988. Tatyana Zaslavskaya was its first director. The people could now express their views and this was glasnost from below. Gorbachev assumed that they would bring good tidings but by 1989 they were recording deeply felt pessimism about perestroika. *Ogonek* revealed in late 1989 that only one person in eight believed that perestroika would improve their living standards in the near future. Almost three-quarters did not think that it would make much difference.[40] Opinion polls starkly emphasised the growing divisions in Soviet society, especially the gulf between Russians and non-Russians about the future of the Union. One of the most dramatic consequences of the revelations about the history of the Stalin era was the decision, taken in 1988, to destroy all the existing history textbooks. History examinations were cancelled for that year and the task of adding some warts to the record of the past began.[41]

As a former lawyer, Gorbachev appreciated the need for a law-governed state (*Rechtsstaat*). It would help to make officials accountable and combat corruption. He believed that the KGB was capable of supervising the transition as Andropov had reformed it sufficiently to take on this task. A special parliamentary commission was established to supervise the KGB and military. Evidence of how powerful the instruments of coercion were was demonstrated in mid-1988 when the Ministry of the Interior (MVD), headed by Yury Vlasov, on its own initiative, set up a special anti-riot squad to deal with political demonstrations. The new draft criminal code ended internal exile and reduced the number of crimes for which the death penalty applied.[42] An awesome range of legislation was placed before the Congress of People's Deputies and the Supreme Soviet in the autumn of 1989. It included legislation on the freedom of the press, freedom of conscience (religious belief) and many bills on economic matters, such as cooperatives, joint ventures with foreign companies and the founding of new commercial banks.

. . .

ECONOMIC PROBLEMS

Before Gorbachev became leader, he was blithely unaware of the true state of the budget. He, like everyone else, believed it to be in surplus. But it was not. In the late Brezhnev era deficits were overcome by resorting to the printing press and using the savings of the population, without their knowledge, of course. In 1985 the deficit was 37 billion rubles. In 1986 this increased to 47.9 billion, to 57.1 billion in 1987, to 90.1 billion in 1988 (19.1 per cent of the budget), and was about 100 billion in 1989 (19.5 per cent).[43] This mismanagement of the economy, Herculean in scale, was finally officially admitted in 1988. Why had this come about? Budget revenue had fallen due to the anti-alcohol campaign, the drop in world oil prices and the reduction of imported consumer goods which were retailed at higher prices. Budget expenditure rose because of increasing subsidies, especially on food (farm prices rose but retail prices only increased in 1991), the high, unexpected cost of cleaning up after Chernobyl and the Armenian earthquake of December 1988, and the military bill kept on rising inexorably. The rising money supply (the currency in circulation in 1987 increased by 7.8 per cent, in 1988 by 13.6 per cent and in 1989 by 19.5 per cent[44]) produced the inevitable: rising inflation, a shortage of goods and declining living standards. Budget deficits are normal occurrences in developed market economies. There they were solved by borrowing on the money markets. Moscow did not have this option as there was no money market there.

A memorandum was forwarded to the Politburo on this problem by Otto Latsis and Egor Gaidar in late 1988. The Politburo discussed it in December 1988 and again in early 1989. In the 1989 budget the planners cut social and cultural expenditure, consisting of science and education, social welfare and security and health. However, the Congress of People's Deputies objected in the strongest possible terms to this, arguing that this was inadmissible at a time when living standards were declining. The planners, in the 1990 budget, compensated for the cuts in 1989 by raising expenditure to a level above that of 1988. This underlined the new-found power of the Congress. In reality, the Congress was exacerbating the monetary and fiscal position but few deputies understood this.

One of the few deputies who comprehended the gravity of the situation and spelled out the social price of reform was Nikolai Shmelev. He proposed measures to cut the budget deficit and gradually introduce the market. A painful price would have to be paid for this; one of the consequences would be an increase in hard currency debt. He was a prophet but the Congress was a wilderness. Deputies reacted angrily to his proposals. Among those who were sharply critical was Nikolai Ryzhkov, the Prime Minister. However, he was long on criticism but short on alternative solutions. The Congress did mark a breakthorough on this front. Hitherto the fiction had been peddled that perestroika would result in everyone being a winner. Now, for the first time, the view was articulated that there would be losers and that the process would be painful.

The law on state enterprises (there were about 46,000 enterprises) had handed control over finance to the enterprise. Wages, hitherto tightly controlled by the centre, increased rapidly and the manager devoted considerable energy to finding sources to pay his workforce. The investment fund, for one, was raided. The situation was exacerbated by the reluctance of the leadership to embrace price reform. The enterprise increased the prices of its goods, used some of this revenue to pay wages and even more to begin a construction project. It calculated that, once begun, the state would have to continue financing it.

Egor Gaidar calculated that the centre froze 24,000 investment projects in 1989, but at the same time 146,000 new projects were begun. This turned on its head the centre's policy of concentrating investment in projects which could be completed.[45] Without price reform which balanced demand and supply, a market economy could not come into being. At the same time the centre's ability to influence the economy was declining as the mechanisms of control were being gradually dismantled. The economy still functioned in 1988 and 1989, as if through inertia, but the economic train was heading for the buffers.

Workers quickly grasped the essentials of democratisation. It permitted them to organise, to strike and to improve their position *vis-à-vis* management and the government. Officially the Soviet economy in 1989 lost 7.3 million worker-days to strikes, almost all due to miners' strikes and nationalist unrest in Georgia, Armenia and Azerbaijan.[46] In 1990 the number of days lost increased 2.5 times. The first mass strikes under perestroika (there was a *de facto* general strike in Armenia in 1988 but it was political, protesting against the situation in Nagorno-Karabakh) were by miners in the summer of 1989. They began as economic strikes, against low and declining living standards, poor accommodation, lack of medical supplies and so on. These demands could not be resolved by the local Party or trade union branch. Only national government could satisfy such demands.

The law on state enterprises granted enterprises control over the wage fund and they were to become self-financing and self-managing. This strengthened workers' resolve to gain more of the pie. They were aided by the labour shortage which did not permit management to sack strikers and replace them with more compliant operatives. The July 1989 strike affected four of the five main coal-mining regions, involved about 400,000 miners and lasted two weeks. An independent trade union, the Independent Union of Mineworkers, sprang up but, unlike its predecessors, was not brutally suppressed. It began in the Kuzbass, in western Siberia, and then spread. M. I. Shchadov, Minister of the Coal Industry, arrived to negotiate. The miners demanded that Gorbachev and Ryzhkov join the talks. Slyunkov was sent instead. The strike committees then added political demands: transfer of power to the soviets, direct and secret elections of chairs of the Supreme Soviet and local soviets, the abolition of article 6 of the Constitution guaranteeing the Party a political monopoly, the abolition of privileges for all those in official positions, and the drafting of a new Soviet Constitution.[47]

They also demanded that every miner become a free economic agent and that mines be permitted to market their own coal. The government gave in and signed an agreement running to almost 400 paragraphs. It was signed live on television by Ryzhkov since the miners did not trust the government to keep its word. This led Ryzhkov to reflect on the disastrous drop in the authority of the Party.[48] He feared that it could become irrelevant. To combat this he proposed that the Secretariat and Politburo be reformed and Gorbachev's workload be lessened so that he could concentrate on restructuring the Party. The miners had revealed that government was weak and ineffective. Strikes again became legal according to the new law of 9 October 1989. They were not to take place in service industries, railways, transport, communications, energy and defence. But how was this law to be enforced? An added difficulty for the government was the naïve belief of workers that a move to the market would benefit all of them.

A major problem for the leadership was how to activate the human factor. In 1987 Gavriil Popov, co-chair of the Inter-Regional Group of deputies and later mayor of Moscow, pointed out that the 'political avant-gardism of some walked hand and hand with the passivity of others – backwards'[49] and he chided those who waited for someone else to implement perestroika. He judged that resistance to perestroika was not subsiding. A psychologist who addressed the problem of social inertia was Igor Kon. He regarded the first task as getting rid of the 'idealised, radiant image of New Soviet Man' and concentrating on social inertia. He found the reasons for this phenomenon in the depersonalised nature of Soviet public life and de-individualisation. Such phenomena were often accompanied by feelings of personal helplessness and social apathy, which contributed to the passive personality. Passivity, mediocrity and dullness were cultivated deliberately by the Soviet authorities, at the expense of initiative and enterprise, qualities which were required under perestroika.

Kon was very critical of the Soviet educational system, which concentrated on the passive transmission of information to students. He regarded the key question of perestroika to be the extent to which a feeling of social responsibility was present in people. The only way to foster this was to increase democracy and self-management.[50] He identified four syndromes: the teenage syndrome (in which young people exhibited maximalism and intolerance – which was also present in many adults), the authoritarian syndrome, the envious neighbour syndrome, and the learned helplessness syndrome. The last syndrome affected those who had no moral or social strength left to begin a new beginning with perestroika.[51] Another psychologist, A. I. Kitov, found four causes of opposition to perestroika: inert thinking, dogmatism, conservatism, and defensive thinking.[52] The average person simply blamed Gorbachev for all their troubles. This was summed up by a popular ditty.

> Sausage prices twice as high
> Where's the vodka for us to buy?
> All we do is sit at home
> Watching Gorby drone and drone.

Another caustic comment was: 'How do you translate perestroika into English?' 'Easy. Science fiction.' A cartoon shows an enterprise director dictating a telegram to Moscow: 'We have successfully implemented perestroika. Await further instructions.'

. . .

NATIONALITIES

The most bloody conflict which erupted under perestroika occurred in the southern Caucasus and involved Christian Armenia and Muslim Azerbaijan. It rumbled on for several years and defied resolution. Nagorno-Karabakh, claimed by Armenia, had been made part of Azerbaijan by Stalin in 1923. Another enclave, Nakhichevan, was also made part of Azerbaijan. Over time, Nakhichevan acquired a predominantly Azeri population. By the 1980s, in Nagorno-Karabakh about 85 per cent of the population were Armenian. It was separated from Armenia by a thin strip of territory. Over the years Armenia had complained to Moscow about the situation but to no avail. Glasnost permitted Armenians again to articulate their aspirations and during the winter of 1987–8 rallies were held in Armenia and Nagorno-Karabakh to demand the return of Nagorno-Karabakh to Armenia.

Armenians in Nagorno-Karabakh sent delegations to Moscow on three occasions during the winter to press their case. Unfortunately for Gorbachev, they gained the impression that their request would be granted. This appears to have been the fault of Abel Aganbegyan, an ethnic Armenian and a leading economic reformer in Moscow. In February 1988 the Nagorno-Karabakh soviet voted in favour of merging with Armenia. The Supreme Soviet in Moscow rejected this and the Communist Parties in Azerbaijan and Armenia were instructed to restore order. The Politburo sent Ligachev and Razumovsky to Baku and Yakovlev and Dolgikh to Erevan to elucidate the problem. The Armenians kept on pressing their case but gained the impression that Gorbachev favoured Azerbaijan. Azeris came to believe that he would side with them. Demonstrations continued in Nagorno-Karabakh and Armenia, and Moscow underestimated the seriousness of the situation.

When unfounded rumours spread that Azeris had been killed by Armenians, Azeris attacked Armenians in the Azerbaijani town of Sumgait on 27 February. When the violence subsided, 26 Armenians and six Azeris were dead. Fearing further attacks, Armenians in Azerbaijan began leaving and this led to the Armenian authorities taking direct action to force Azeris to move back to Azerbaijan. Party leaders in the two republics were changed on 21 May and Moscow did not commit the error of parachuting Russians in to take charge. The men chosen, Abdulrakhman Vezirov in Azerbaijan, and Suren Arutyunyan (Harutiunian in Armenian) in Armenia, were outsiders without direct links to the Party establishments in the two republics. Gorbachev began to see the conflict as a 'mine under perestroika'.[53] At a Politburo meeting in June 1988, he stated that 'some people in the higher levels of power in the republics were fanning the flames and igniting passions'.[54]

On 15 June 1988 the Armenian Supreme Soviet voted to annex Nagorno-Karabakh. In July 1988 the airport at Erevan was blockaded, the Nagorno-Karabakh soviet passed another resolution withdrawing from Azerbaijan, and in Baku the Supreme Soviet declared this null and void. What advice did the Politburo give Gorbachev? Gromyko, when presented with such a problem, always recommended the same thing: 'The army will appear on the streets and order will be restored immediately'. Yakovlev proposed that Nagorno-Karabakh be run from Moscow. Shevardnadze thought that Nagorno-Karabakh should be made an autonomous republic. Ligachev was fired up: 'We must bring in the troops, dismantle factories, dismiss the Party organisations and soviet executive committees and establish order'.[55] No wonder Gorbachev was confused. His Politburo was hopelessly divided on the issue. It is significant that some senior members of the Politburo still advocated the use of force[56] despite Gorbachev reiterating time and again that force could not be used to solve domestic problems.

A special commission was set up within the Soviet of Nationalities in Moscow and it recommended direct rule from the centre. In July Arkady Volsky was sent to Nagorno-Karabakh as a special envoy, but he could not work a miracle. In December Gorbachev met deputies from Azerbaijan and Armenia. He told them the naked truth: 'We are on the brink of disaster'.[57]

In December 1988 Andrei Sakharov and his wife, Elena Bonner, went to Erevan, the capital of Armenia, Baku, the capital of Azerbaijan, and Stepanakert, the capital of Nagorno-Karabakh, with Moscow's official blessing, to mediate. They failed abjectly to find a common language and gloomily concluded that the views of the two sides were unbridgeable.

Then nature struck and a devastating earthquake visited Armenia. The solution of an autonomous republic for Nagorno-Karabakh and Nakhichevan was almost achieved but was torpedoed by Armenia. The growing Armenian nationalist movement fed off Nagorno-Karabakh and Erevan voted again to incorporate the enclave. Had they been given the necessary leeway, Party leaders might have arrived at a solution. Since Gorbachev was unwilling to use force, Armenian nationalists were encouraged to push for annexation. Gorbachev was mindful of the fact that ethnic problems were surfacing in Central Asia, the Baltic republics, Ukraine and Moldova. He could not countenance any territorial changes. Had Armenia or Azerbaijan begun to demand independence from the Soviet Union, it would have added urgency to Moscow's efforts to find a solution. Moscow's conduct of the affair can be judged disastrously passive.

If the southern Caucasus was not thinking of secession, some in Estonia, Latvia and Lithuania were. The official Soviet view was that the Baltic States had joined the Soviet Union voluntarily and here again Moscow was fooling itself. Western governments never accepted the legality of the transfer and this nourished the hopes of nationalists that one day their lands would again be free. On 23 August 1987, the 48th anniversary of the Molotov–Ribbentrop pact which had handed over the Baltic States to Moscow, Estonians, Latvians and Lithuanians decided to test the limits of glasnost by organising demonstrations in protest against the pact. The authorities did not intervene. Resentment was greatest in Estonia where it was feared that Russians could soon become the majority in the republic. In January 1988 the programme for an independence party was issued in Tallinn. It advocated the restoration of Estonian as the dominant language instead of Russian and Estonians to leading positions of power. Environmental problems had to be addressed. The market economy should replace the planned economy and Estonian diplomatic missions abroad should be re-established. Independence was regarded as the aim but not an immediate goal.[58]

As political organisations could not call themselves parties, since they would have been regarded as opposition parties to the Communist Party, it was decided to form popular fronts. Astutely, these were defined as movements in support of perestroika. This gave the impression they were rooting for Mikhail Sergeevich. Estonia took the lead and in April 1988 a popular front in support of perestroika was founded. In June, in Lithuania, Sajudis (meaning movement) was set up. Then Latvia followed suit. Founding congresses were held and by October all had adopted programmes modelled on the Estonian programme for an independence party. Significantly, many Party members joined these popular fronts.

The inability of Party officials to react tactically to the rising tide of nationalism is illustrated by the inactivity of the Communist Party of Lithuania. Ringaudas Songaila, elected Party boss in October 1987, had not made a public speech by the spring of 1988. That was left to the CC secretary for ideology, Lionginas Sepetys. In a frank interview in *Moskovskie novosti*, published on 24 April 1988, he thought that since the 'national question had been solved in principle, it had been solved in fact'. The Soviet system had actually fostered the emergence of 'extremism' among nationalists by not 'telling the truth and concealing facts'. Remarkably, he then claimed that 'national pride' was the most important aspect of the 'international world view'. A few months later he spoke of Lithuania emerging from 'asphyxia'.[59]

A major problem for the Party leadership in Lithuania was the absence of firm orders from Moscow. The Nina Andreeva letter inspired confidence that Moscow was imposing order, but the later attack on it sowed confusion and discord. Despite the attack on Andreeva in *Pravda* on 5 April, a hard-hitting article appeared on 14 April, maintaining that the tens of thousands of Lithuanians deported under Stalin had deserved everything they got. On 20 April a philosopher, unconnected to the nationalists, denounced the falsification of history and referred to Lithuania as the 'last bastion of Stalinism in the Baltic'.[60] As if wishing to pour oil on nationalist flames, the Party newspaper, *Tiesa*, published another article on 30 April defending the deportations. Observers regard these events as the turning point in Lithuania. When the list of delegates to the 19th Party Conference was announced, on 28 May, it met with derision. It was simply a list of Party hacks and the old guard. This promoted the emergence of the movement for perestroika in Lithuania, Sajudis. Its leaders expressed support for Gorbachev and the general secretary was also pleased by its stance.

There have been claims that it was set up on the initiative of the KGB in an effort to take over the nationalist movement. However, the Lithuanian KGB chief later lamented: 'Although we had our agents in its structures, we, frankly, missed out on the beginning of the formation of Sajudis'.[61] It mustered 20,000 protesters to see the Party delegates off on 24 June and 100,000 to greet them on their return on 9 July. The flags and anthem of their once independent states were displayed and played.

A turning point was the visit to Vilnius by Aleksandr Yakovlev on 11–14 August 1988. He spent most of his time with representatives of Sajudis and openly clashed with Nikolai Mitkin, the Lithuanian Party second secretary, over developments in Moscow and Lithuania. Mitkin revealed how out of touch he was by complaining to Yakovlev that Sajudis sympathised with the sentiments expressed in *Moskovskie novosti*.[62] Yakovlev publicly instructed the Party to accept Sajudis. 'Perestroika', he claimed, had 'begun as an intellectual explosion' and the intelligentsia was the 'expression of the self-consciousness of the people'. What Yakovlev said on other matters took Sajudis's breath away. He maintained that Lenin had defined defence and foreign policy as the only concerns which needed to be directed by the central government.[63]

Ligachev was left in charge of the Politburo as Gorbachev was on holiday in the Crimea. In early September he was alarmed by a report from Chebrikov on the situation in Lithuania. Yakovlev offered a different assessment. 'There's nothing special going on. Just the normal processes of perestroika.'[64] At a special Politburo meeting Yakovlev again presented his case. There were complications, but they had arisen because the centre had 'dictated much that [had] damaged the republic'. However 'Russians were flooding in' and that was leading to 'clashes'. He suggested halting migration, but the 'situation in Lithuania' was not 'critical'. The republic would overcome these things during 'the course of perestroika'.[65] Ligachev was incandescent in his anger at Yakovlev. 'A social and class-based analysis of processes in Lithuania was replaced by an analysis that manipulated and concealed.'[66] He and other conservatives in the Politburo appeared to believe that Yakovlev should have gone to Lithuania as Dr Death and strangled Sajudis in its cradle. That would have solved the Lithuanian question.

Yakovlev did, however, make it clear to the Lithuanians that the restoration of foreign missions was out of the question. This was hardly an important point. His relaxed attitude misled many into believing that Gorbachev also shared his views about the future of the region. When Gorbachev returned to Moscow, Yakovlev confided to him that the best solution would be to grant the region autonomy within a Soviet confederation. This was flatly rejected by Gorbachev and the other members of the Politburo.[67]

Gorbachev did not sense the gathering storm and at a CC plenum, in September 1988, regarded national sentiment as of secondary importance in the range of problems facing the government. When asked, in May 1992, which question had taken him most by surprise, he answered, the 'national question'. He had only recognised the seriousness of the problem in the autumn of 1990, when the republics had held back tax payments.[68] Gorbachev, in common with many other Russians, thought the nationalities' problem had been solved. In September 1992 Arkady Volsky, to excuse the nomenklatura's embarrassment, argued that Soviet scholars had claimed genetic proof for the existence of a new being, Soviet man and woman.[69]

In December 1988 Yakovlev conceded: 'We have ethnic problems'. Moscow regarded these as existing within republics, with itself as the peacemaker. It did not conceive of these becoming a republic-wide phenomenon and hence a potential contradiction between a republic and the centre. When the centre judged that the Lithuanians were promoting inter-ethnic conflict, in 1989, it encouraged other nationalities, Russians and Poles, to stand up for themselves and complain about the behaviour and ambitions of the Lithuanians. The key role was played by the KGB. It was central to the founding of 'international fronts' in the republics which were becoming 'obstinate in their relations with the centre'.[70]

The Balts learned from Russian democrats the power of protest demonstrations. These became almost a way of life and helped to radicalise public opinion. The demonstrations of 23 August 1988, marking the anniversary of the Molotov-Ribbentrop pact, were a major event attracting 150,000 in Vilnius and many thousands in Riga and Tallinn. A major point was the secret protocol which had handed Lithuania over to the Soviet Union. Only a few Party conservatives still claimed it was a myth.

Gorbachev was in a quandary over developments in the Baltic republics. He welcomed support for perestroika, but the growing nationalism was anathema to it. He was alarmed at the ammunition it was providing Ligachev and the conservatives who were demanding a crackdown. All three Party leaders were changed between June and October 1988 and replaced by comrades judged capable of working with the burgeoning nationalist movement. Their task was to take over the leadership of the reform movement in the republics. The comrade chosen by the Lithuanian Party was Algirdas Brazauskas, hitherto unknown to Gorbachev. By then the Lithuanian Party was conducting its affairs in Lithuanian and the Lithuanian tricolour was flying over the Gediminas tower in Vilnius. Brazauskas attended the founding congress of Sajudis on 22–24 October and brought warm wishes from Gorbachev. Brazauskas made himself one of the most popular figures at the congress by announcing the return of Vilnius Cathedral to the Roman Catholic Church. He released political prisoners and appeared on the same platform with Sajudis leaders.

The September 1988 CC plenum saw Gorbachev becoming President, Kryuchkov replacing Chebrikov as head of the KGB, Boris Pugo becoming head of the Party Control Commission, Ligachev moving from ideology to agrarian affairs and Yakovlev moving from ideology to international affairs. Vadim Medvedev took over ideology. These changes were viewed with apprehension in the Baltic. Lithuania had lost a colleague at the centre. Yakovlev had no desire to move over to international affairs and enquired of Chernyaev if Gorbachev intended to 'part with the most ardent supporter of perestroika?'. Chernyaev, in his own words, naïvely replied that Mikhail Sergeevich was not influenced by personal differences. He only replaced those who had no 'objective' role in the reform process.[71] Yakovlev had to adjust to the more conservative attitude. In an interview, he criticised the Balts for pursuing 'many ideas' which were 'out of touch with reality'. He referred to Sajudis leaders as 'performers and musicians and people of this sort'.[72] In private, Yakovlev did not hold these views, but it is instructive that he felt the need to protect his back against conservatives. On 28 September troops from Minsk forcibly broke up a Freedom League rally, led by Vytautas Landsbergis. This only brought the Freedom League and Sajudis closer together.

Further evidence that Gorbachev was rethinking the decentralising tendencies, so evident at the 19th Party Conference, appeared in October when the draft amendments to the Soviet Constitution providing for the Congress of People's Deputies were published. The Balts discovered to their chagrin that the new USSR Supreme Soviet was to have the right to decide such issues. It was also to be authorised to declare null and void legislation passed in the various republics which contravened Soviet laws. Instead of cooling the situation, the draft laws acted like a red rag to a bull in the Baltic region. The popular fronts, of course, condemned it and millions signed protests. A crushing blow for Gorbachev was that the three republican Supreme Soviets, the parliaments, also condemned the attempt to annul the right of a republic, enshrined in the Constitution, to secede. This alarming development revealed that a majority of communists had gone over to the nationalist side as the parliaments had been elected in pre-perestroika days.

Moscow sent senior officials to the Baltic republics over the period 11–14 November 1988. When he arrived in Vilnius on 11 November Nikolai Slyunkov cut a totally different figure from Yakovlev. He tried to pull the wool over Lithuanian eyes by insisting that the constitutional changes would extend the rights of the Union republics. He angered Lithuanians by referring to their republic as a krai or territory. Brazauskas decided to oppose a constitutional amendment affording primacy to Lithuanian law. Nevertheless parliament adopted the legislation.

On 16 November the Estonian Supreme Soviet went even further and passed a declaration on sovereignty which stated that Soviet laws which conflicted with Estonian legislation would be annulled. Gorbachev had to put his foot down and he convened the Presidium of the USSR Supreme Soviet which annulled the Estonian declaration. In an hour-long monologue, Gorbachev sharply attacked Baltic deputies for the confusion in their republics. He went further and launched a sharp attack on private property, close to the heart of Estonians. He stated that 'private property . . . is the basis of the exploitation of man by man and our revolution was completed in order to liquidate it and to transfer property to the people'. An 'attempt to restore it' would be 'retrogressive and a very serious mistake'.[73] This was not the language of a man who was contemplating introducing a market economy. Other republics also protested against the draft constitutional amendment and it had to be delayed. His mishandling of the amendment increased the vote of the opposition in the Congress of People's Deputies' elections in March 1989. He maintained that the amendments were only the first stage of reform but the Balts perceived them as the last word. They refused to listen to this explanation.[74]

The elections to the Congress of People's Deputies permitted the popular fronts in the Baltic republics to publish their election manifestos. The Estonians, for example, demanded the implementation of the resolutions of their Supreme Soviet on sovereignty, the movement to a market economy and private property (the Soviet Constitution only envisaged personal property), and the creation of new institutions based on the popular will.[75] How was the Party to cope with such demands? Gorbachev gloomily commented that the Party was 'simply unable to operate under conditions of democracy. The Party leaders, who were accustomed to dealing with economic affairs, became confused when they had to engage in democratic politics.'[76] This was a polite way of saying that the Parties in the Baltic republics had become irrelevant. In 1989 the Parties had already lost power in these republics. The cancer set in when the informal organisations were set up. They were declared to be opposition movements. It would then be up to the KGB to deal with them. Gorbachev lamented the fact that valuable time was lost 'in the vain hope that the new organisations would just vanish, go away like a bad dream'.[77]

The popular fronts won the elections to the Congress of People's Deputies and this sealed the fate of the Parties. In Vilnius, Algirdas Brazauskas scored a personal triumph but the Party was routed. Ironically, most Sajudis deputies were Party members. The popular fronts' mushrooming success can be gauged from the rapid expansion of their membership. In mid-1989 the Estonian Popular Front counted 60,000 members, the Latvian 115,000 members and Sajudis 180,000 members. The success of the popular fronts in the Baltic republics encouraged other republics to imitate them. For example, a popular front emerged in Georgia and Rukh in Ukraine.

On 22 August 1989 the Lithuanian Supreme Soviet declared that the incorporation of Lithuania into the Soviet Union in 1940 was illegal. The following day, the 50th anniversary of the pact, a human chain stretched from Gediminas hill in Vilnius to the Tompea tower in Tallinn, called the Baltic Way. On 26 August the CPSU Central Committee condemned events in Lithuania, Latvia and Estonia in the sharpest terms yet. 'Nationalist, extremist groups' had taken over national affairs. The 'fate of the Baltic peoples is in danger . . . The consequences could be disastrous.' The working class and peasants were called on to defend the 'new revolution and perestroika' and Party members were to lead the way.[78] The three Baltic Parties met to consider their response. However, the ideology secretaries of the Estonian and Lithuanian Parties publicly condemned the document. The popular fronts were even more rude. All waited for a counter-blast from Moscow but none came. Gorbachev was away from Moscow but had apparently confirmed the statement.

Vadim Medvedev, ideology secretary, later claimed that he had signed the document without reading it. On 4 September Brazauskas informed a press conference in Vilnius of a recent telephone conversation with Gorbachev. The general secretary had a message for Sajudis. If things continued to develop in such an extreme direction, 'I shall not be your friend'.[79] As the months passed, and the centre did not follow up its threat with action, it lost authority.[80] The CC plenum on nationalities, in September 1989, proposed a stronger Soviet federation which had to set up institutions which 'respected national and international values and interests', while respecting their 'sovereignty'. Brazauskas's speech, warning the Party to move faster than changes in society, was listened to in total silence.[81]

The Baltic dilemma was discussed by the Politburo, with the Baltic Party leaders present, on 16 November. Ligachev was, as ever, blunt. What was there to discuss with the Baltic leaders? They had already conceded that their laws took precedence over Soviet laws. The Politburo singled out Lithuania as the worst offender. It was 'trampling on the freedoms' of its citizens. It went as far as declaring that the Communist

Party of Lithuania was the 'agent of a foreign power'.[82] This astonishing statement was followed, not by the dissolution of the Lithuanian Party, but by a visit to Vilnius by Vadim Medvedev. His task was to convert the Lithuanians to orthodox Marxism-Leninism. Talk of independence from the CPSU, Medvedev warned, was bringing Moscow to the end of its patience. Brazauskas made clear that the Lithuanian Party could only become a party of the whole Lithuanian people if it cut its links with Moscow. Like characters in a Chekhov drama, Medvedev and the Lithuanians talked but did not communicate. Moscow then encouraged the Belarusians to claim Vilnius oblast and declared that it had the right to detach Klaipeda from Lithuania. Gorbachev then added up Soviet investment in Lithuania and warned Vilnius it would have to repay everything, in US dollars no less, if Lithuania went independent. Significantly, however, he did not threaten the use of force. Against the opposition of Ryzhkov and the conservatives, he accepted economic autonomy for the Baltic republics, from 1 January 1990.

Belarus, Moldova and Ukraine did not experience the violence which occurred in the Baltic and Transcaucasia. The most radical regions were those annexed by the Soviet Union in 1939–40. This applied to Moldova, the western parts of Ukraine and Belarus. In all three regions language emerged as an important issue for the cultural elites. In Moldova they wanted to return to the Latin alphabet since Moldovan was virtually Romanian written in Cyrillic. A democratic movement for perestroika was set up in Kishenev (now Chisinau). Lviv, in western Ukraine, became a hotbed of activity, driven by such former dissidents as Vyacheslav Chornovil. He published an open letter to Gorbachev in 1987 and the *Ukrainian Herald* and the Ukrainian Helsinki Group (renamed the Ukrainian Helsinki Union in 1988) were relaunched. Chornovil fell out with Levko Lukianenko, who returned as leader of the Union in January 1989. In 1988 the police regularly broke up meetings and demonstrations, but that changed in 1989 as a nation-wide organisation came into being. In Belarus, intellectuals came together in an association called Adradzhennye (rebirth) to promote the Belarusian language. When mass graves of Stalin's victims were discovered, it further undermined the legitimacy of the Party. The authorities broke up demonstrations and were

129

reluctant to register groups and a national front. Belarusians could legitimately point out that such activities were legitimate in the Baltic republics, so why not in Belarus?

In early April 1989 the situation in Georgia became more tense as new parties and movements demonstrated. On 7 April Dzhumber Patiashvili, Party boss in Georgia, requested that extraordinary measures be taken to contain extremist elements and declared that events were getting out of hand.[83] He asked for Ministry of the Interior and Ministry of Defence troops to be sent to Tbilisi and a curfew to be imposed. A Politburo meeting, hastily called, and chaired by Ligachev, agreed to Patiashvili's request. Ligachev was going on holiday on 8 April and Chebrikov was in charge. It was he who briefed Gorbachev and Shevardnadze on their return from London late on 7 April. They were informed that troops had been dispatched to Georgia to protect 'important facilities'. Gorbachev then reiterated that the conflict be resolved by political means. He requested Shevardnadze and Razumovsky to fly to Tbilisi to assess the situation on the spot. The Georgian first secretary, however, informed Shevardnadze on the telephone that the situation had normalised and that there was no need to come to Tbilisi. Shevardnadze took the fateful decision not to board the plane waiting to take him to Tbilisi. Then during the night of 8–9 April, troops, using sharpened spades and poison gas, charged the unarmed demonstrators, killing nineteen and injuring several hundred. Most of the dead were young women asphyxiated by inhaling poison gas. The local police tried to restrain the troops but without success. Shevardnadze, in Tbilisi, condemned the behaviour of the military as quite unacceptable in a society implementing perestroika and glasnost. But he was too late to influence the tragic events.

Five days later, the Georgian Party leader, President and Prime Minister were all sacked. But the damage had been done. Who had given the order to attack the demonstrators? Was it taken in Moscow or by the Georgian Party? No clear answer ever emerged. Irrespective of who was responsible, Gorbachev was blamed by nationalists and democrats everywhere. He has reiterated that he had no knowledge of the decision and this appears to be accurate.[84] If the military and the KGB acted to restore order without consulting Gorbachev, it reveals that he was no longer in full control of the instruments of coercion. The murders in Tbilisi did irreparable harm and Gorbachev concludes that they had an 'adverse effect on all our attempts to bring harmony to relations between nationalities in our country for a long time'.[85] The President's authority was also irreparably undermined. The massacre paved the way for the election of Zviad Gamsakhurdia, a virulent Georgian nationalist, as head of an anti-communist Georgian government in 1990. He was elected President of Georgia in May 1992. Georgia under Gamsakhurdia gradually sank into civil war.[86]

Ethnic violence visited Central Asia in June, in the Fergana valley, in Uzbekistan. Uzbeks took bloody revenge on Meskhetian Turks, deported there by Stalin from Georgia because he feared they might prove disloyal to the Soviet Union. No clear reason for the riots has ever emerged but it may have been over control of local markets. Also in June, in Novy Uzen, in western Kazakhstan, Kazakhs attacked Chechens and others from the north Caucasus. Here again, the main reason may have been economic. The Soviet authorities reacted quite differently to these events, compared to their behaviour in Tbilisi. They did not intervene and allowed the riots to run their course. This led some local observers to conclude that Moscow was not concerned about the loss of life among Muslims. Afterwards the Meskhetian Turks were removed to Krasnodar krai and other parts of Russia.

The year 1989 was a turning point in the attitude of many Soviet citizens to the regime. Glasnost had unearthed such a plethora of crimes that the foundations of the system had been undermined. In November the truth about the massacre of Polish officers at Katyn was admitted officially. It was the NKVD who had murdered them and not the Germans, as had been claimed for 48 years. Another important breakthrough was the resolution by the Congress of People's Deputies in December stating that the secret protocol, added to the Molotov–Ribbentrop pact in August 1939, was invalid *ab initio*. When the truth emerged about the Chernobyl disaster, it reflected poorly on the Ukrainian and Belarusian Parties. An accurate map of radiation levels was published for the first time in 1989 and it revealed that persons in some of the most seriously affected areas had neither been warned nor evacuated. To compound this folly, radiation dosimeters, distributed to the population as part of civil defence, were collected by the authorities to prevent citizens from measuring the radiation levels.[87] Later, when asked when he had first decided on independence for Ukraine, President Leonid Kravchuk replied: 'in 1989'. The concrete evidence of atrocities, and their magnitude, only became clear to him in that year. His conclusion was that only independence would protect Ukraine from such crimes in the future.[88]

What was the Party's response to the rapidly mounting problems in nationality affairs? 'The nationalities policy of the Party under modern conditions' was published on 17 August 1989. Policy had to be renewed radically, the rights of all the national areas were to be increased, all peoples were to be equal and guarantees provided, and national cultures and languages were to be permitted to flourish. For the first time the question of signing a new Union treaty was raised. The role of Russia was to be given greater emphasis. This became Party policy in September but it was too little too late. The Party had missed the boat.

. . .

EASTERN EUROPE

In his speech to the United Nations in December 1988, Gorbachev presented his understanding of universal human values. Among these was the right of all peoples to choose their governments, and he underlined there were no exceptions to this. Did this only apply to those in bourgeois states or did it also include those in socialist states? After all, Soviet foreign policy supported the right of national self-determination abroad but not at home. After Chernenko's funeral in March 1985, Gorbachev met the leaders of the east European states. He explained to them that the Brezhnev doctrine (the right of the Soviet Union to intervene in the domestic affairs of socialist states, if it deemed that socialism was under threat) was dead and that henceforth they could choose their leaders and their own policies. He made it clear that the Soviet Army would not intervene in domestic affairs in socialist states. He reiterated this at the meeting of the Warsaw Pact, in April 1985, to extend the alliance for another 20 years.[89]

This was a radically different stance from the one he had adopted as late as April 1984. At a Politburo meeting on 26 April 1984, which discussed a report on meetings between Ustinov, Gromyko and Jaruzelski, Gorbachev stated:

> The report of the meetings . . . reveals that the latter is trying to present the situation in a better light than it is. I think we have once again to discover what Jaruzelski's real goals are. One should try to find out if he wants eventually a pluralist government in Poland. At the same time, it is clear that the situation of the Polish United Workers' Party is deteriorating, especially relations between state power and the working class . . . During our meeting with Jaruzelski, the policy of the CPSU Politburo should be pushed hard.[90]

Moscow was aware that the situation in Poland was critical and that the Polish United Workers' Party had almost lost control of the situation. The Politburo did not think that the Polish leadership was firm enough in its opposition to the 'counter-revolutionary' Solidarity.[91]

Most leaders found the new hands-off policy hard to comprehend as their regimes depended on the presence of the Soviet military to ensure they stayed in power. Gorbachev appears to have been convinced that the peoples of eastern Europe had made their choice, for socialism. Reform within the region would therefore be socialist and thereby strengthen socialism. Soviet embassies in socialist states were staffed with mainly Party officials as these states were not classified as foreign, but fraternal. They and the security forces reported to Moscow what Moscow wanted to hear. Everything in the garden was lovely. If there were a few weeds they would soon be pulled up. If trouble appeared to be brewing, the Soviet ambassador would phone Moscow and state that he had just had a talk with Honecker, Husak, or some other leader, and had been assured that everything was fine.[92] Information to the contrary was only western propaganda.

This does not mean that the Russians were blind to the realities of the economic weaknesses of the east European states. A case in point is Poland. In 1981 Jaruzelski asked for US$700 million to service Poland's hard currency debt. Moscow did not oblige but that year delivered 13 million tonnes of petrol at 90 rubles a tonne. The world market price was 170 rubles a tonne. In the difficult days before martial law was imposed on Poland, the Soviet Union did its best to ease the food situation by sending 30,000 tonnes of meat to Warsaw. It took a lot of searching to find the meat and the Politburo discussed the meat question on several occasions. Then on 10 December 1981, three days before the onset of martial law, Nikolai Baibakov, head of Gosplan, reported to the Politburo on his visit to Warsaw:

> As you know, according to the instructions of the Politburo and the request of our Polish comrades, we had to deliver 30,000 tonnes of meat to them. 16,000 tonnes of this has already crossed the frontier. It should be pointed out that . . . the meat has been delivered in dirty wagons, wagons which had previously carried ore, and had not been cleaned, and that it looked rather pathetic. Sabotage occurred during the unloading of this meat at Polish stations. The Poles expressed themselves in the most inappropriate manner about the Soviet Union and its inhabitants, they refused to unload the wagons, etc. It would be impossible to count the number of insults which showered down on us.[93]

One estimate of the cost of Poland to the Soviet exchequer in 1981 was US$2.934 billion dollars.[94] Presumably it did not diminish over the succeeding years. The question of Soviet military intervention may have been discussed by Marshal Kulikov, commander-in-chief of the Warsaw Pact forces. However, the Politburo was against the use of military force. The Soviet Union had invested too much in the struggle for peace to throw it all away by invading Poland. Andropov and Suslov make this quite clear. In a note to all Soviet ambassadors, it was stressed that 'world opinion would not understand us' if force were used.[95] Poland was to be left to its own devices, with the Soviet Union only providing economic and political support. It would appear that Moscow was willing to contemplate Solidarity taking over in Poland in 1981. Afterwards Moscow attempted to influence Jaruzelski's policies by trying to ensure that the Polish leader took its advice in return for all the economic aid he was getting.[96] Gorbachev's decision, as leader, not to use force in eastern Europe merely followed the Politburo's decision in 1981 not to use the military. It would appear that the disastrous intervention in

Afghanistan in December 1979 had paralysed Moscow's will to intervene militarily elsewhere.

Gorbachev can be forgiven for misunderstanding the real situation in the region as he was fêted everywhere he went. When the true state of affairs emerged in 1989, the Soviet foreign ministry was profoundly shocked. The impact on the Party must have been even greater. East European leaders were alarmed by perestroika, glasnost and democratisation and warned Mikhail Sergeevich of the consequences of weakening the ruling Party. Gorbachev was in a quandary. His foreign policy relationship with the United States was at a delicate stage in 1989. If he sanctioned the use of force in eastern Europe, it could terminate hopes of ending the Cold War. It appears he was not aware of the consequences of his words and deeds in eastern Europe. A prime example is the German Democratic Republic or east Germany.

Erich Honecker, leader of the ruling Party, the SED, had been in power since 1971 and much regretted the demise of Brezhnev. He was immensely proud of the GDR's achievements and could see no valid reason why he should adjust to perestroika. After the January 1987 Party plenum, which accelerated democratisation, Honecker simply stated that perestroika did not suit the GDR. The plenum speeches were banned in east Germany but *Pravda* could be bought on the black market.[97] Afterwards all Soviet news was censored. This was self-defeating as east Germans could follow events in Moscow on west German television. Honecker had got to the stage where he simply ignored information he found uncomfortable. Gorbachev found him a frustrating interlocutor as it was impossible to engage him intellectually. Erich simply made speeches about how wonderful everything was.

Gorbachev, initially, did not want to attend the 40th anniversary celebrations of the GDR in October 1989. However, he realised that his absence would be perceived as a Party insult to the SED. Nevertheless, if he went he would be placing the seal of approval on the Honecker regime. He had no intention of toppling Honecker, that would be up to the SED leadership. At the march past of the youth movement in east Berlin, which included many from other GDR cities, there were many cries for reform. Mieczyslaw Rakowski, the Polish leader, leaned over to Gorbachev and said:

Mikhail Sergeevich, you do not understand what they are shouting but I do. They are saying: Gorbachev save us! But this is the Party aktiv who are appealing to you. This is the end.[98]

Honecker was standing stony faced right beside Gorbachev at this time. Other young people also called on Gorbachev to save them later the same evening. On the streets of east Berlin Mikhail Sergeevich commented that history punishes those who are left behind. He also warned the GDR leadership about this. He reported all this to the Politburo when he returned to Moscow and thought that the regime was on its last legs. His comments helped to topple Honecker but his replacement, Egon Krenz, was a pathetic apology for a communist leader. Krenz's hangdog look and rings under his eyes were gifts to cartoonists. More and more GDR citizens left for west Germany through Czechoslovakia and Hungary (Honecker appealed to Gorbachev to force them to observe treaty obligations which would have prevented this) and pressure built up in Berlin to breach the Wall. Günter Schabowski, a senior official, phoned Gorbachev to warn him that if east Berliners attempted to break down the Wall to west Berlin, the east German regime would not stop them.[99] When the Wall finally came down on 9 November 1989, it was the result of a misunderstanding between two GDR authorities.

During his visit to Moscow in March 1989, Károly Grósz, the Hungarian Party leader, explained why Hungary had introduced a multi-party system. There was not even a murmur of protest as it was regarded as a domestic Hungarian affair. In July 1989 the communists in Poland were defeated in elections and the way was open for the first non-communist Prime Minister of Poland to take office. Also in July, Gorbachev addressed the Council of Europe and stated: 'Any interference in domestic affairs of any kind, any attempts to limit the sovereignty of states, both of friends and allies, no matter whose it is, is impermissible'.[100] The Soviet goal appears to have been to provoke reform in eastern Europe, confident that these states had made their choice for socialism. Reform was very slow to emerge, however. Shevardnadze revealed at the 28th Party Congress, in July 1990, that Soviet ambassadors had reported from eastern Europe that 'tragic events' were imminent if serious reform were not initiated.[101] Gorbachev had no option but to let events take their course.

. . .

FOREIGN POLICY

Despite the espousal of universal human values, the Soviet Union continued to fund Communist Parties around the globe until 1990. On 14 February 1990 the CC Secretariat acceded to the request of the Communist Parties of Argentina and Chile to train five Argentinian members and four Chilean members in the technical skills of Party security, for up to three months. The international department was to look after them and the KGB was to be responsible for their training and special equipment.[102] A hilarious episode, at least to the outsider, was the case of Luis Corvalán, the former leader of the Communist Party of Chile, who had been living illegally in Chile since 1983, 'with a different face', while conducting the communist struggle against General Pinochet. Corvalán asked the CC to help him to become legal again. There was no need to stay in hiding since Pinochet had called elections and lost them. However, there was a problem. Corvalán had undergone plastic surgery so as to go unrecognised in Chile. He needed to return clandestinely to the Soviet Union, have plastic surgery to restore his original face, and obtain a legal passport. The Communist Party of Chile asked the CC to arrange for comrade Corvalán to be eased into a western country where he could go to the Chilean embassy to obtain a valid passport. While waiting, he had to leave Chile unrecognised, so he needed another new face to leave![103] A less engaging decision was taken by the CC Secretariat on 18 January 1989. The Ministry of Defence was to receive, in 1990, twenty Libyan terrorists for 'special military training'.[104] In April 1989 a report revealed the extent of the training of comrades from non-socialist countries:

> The leadership of several fraternal parties in non-socialist countries every year request the CC to accept their activists for special training. During the last ten years, over 500 full time Party officials from 40 communist and workers' parties (including members of their Politburos and CC) have received instruction. According to the decision of the CC, the international department has been responsible for welcoming and looking after them, and the KGB for providing their training.[105]

Reagan and Gorbachev were due to meet again at the Washington summit in December 1997. President Reagan had four objectives in his relations with Gorbachev: arms reduction, withdrawing from military confrontation in third countries, building respect for human rights, and raising the iron curtain.[106] Gradually the Soviet side came to see that progress on these issues would be of mutual benefit. If progress were made on one issue, it would not be because the Soviet Union had given in to the United States, but because both sides would benefit. Zero-sum diplomacy was nearing its end. The breakthrough came, in late 1987, and when Gorbachev arrived for his first visit to the United States in December, he and Reagan signed a treaty which eliminated a whole class of nuclear weapons, those carried by intermediate-range ballistic missiles (the INF treaty). It was the first agreement on arms signed by the two sides since 1979. The visit was a watershed for Gorbachev's perception of the US. On the last day, 10 December, on his way to the White House he suddenly instructed his driver to stop. He got out and shook hands with the crowd. He was enthusiastically received and was exhilarated by the warmth and emotion he encountered. At lunch he informed everyone that his reception had made a deep impression on him.[107] He had clearly been briefed by the KGB to expect reticent, undemonstrative crowds.

Psychologically this came at a vital moment for him. At home, he was having difficulty in competing with Boris Yeltsin as the people's champion. Also there was a rising tide of opposition to perestroika from within the leadership and the country. As things began to get more difficult at home, they blossomed abroad. Gorbymania can be said to have been born in Washington in December 1987. He was adored and he loved it. In future, when he was feeling battered at home, all he had to do to recover was to go abroad and bask in public acclaim. Abroad the doubters were being silenced. At home they were on the increase. The Washington summit established a partnership with the US and progress towards ending the Cold War accelerated.

In February 1988 Gorbachev announced that the Soviet Union would withdraw its forces from Afghanistan.[108] An agreement on this was signed in April. In May 1988 President Reagan travelled to Moscow for his last summit with Gorbachev. They exchanged, on 1 June, the instruments of ratification which implemented the INF treaty. The two superpowers agreed to apprise one another of nuclear missile launches. They made progress towards reducing strategic nuclear arms. Reagan addressed the Soviet public and strongly underlined the mutual benefits of democracy, freedom and human rights. In June it became easier for Soviet citizens to travel abroad and emigration and private travel mushroomed. In July Shevardnadze convened a conference of Soviet diplomats to elaborate a policy based on universal human values. Gorbachev began regularly to visit western Europe and receive foreign statesmen. In December 1988, at the United Nations, Gorbachev announced that the Soviet Union would reduce its armed forces by 500,000 within two years without reciprocal moves by the US or its allies. The remarkable thing about this speech was that neither Gorbachev nor Shevardnadze had consulted the defence ministry before announcing the cuts. In protest, Marshal Akhromeev, chief of the general staff, announced his resignation the same day. Akhromeev agreed with many of the disarmament proposals but drew the line at any conventional cuts without reciprocation.

Gorbachev expounded his vision of universal human values, stated that they were to be the basis of Soviet foreign policy, and acknowledged that freedom of choice was a universal principle. There were to be no exceptions. Afterwards he met President Reagan and President-elect George Bush on Governors Island. He had to cut short his visit after news of the Armenian earthquake reached him. This also meant he could not visit Cuba. The impetus in Soviet–American relations was then lost as President George Bush took his time to reappraise his foreign policy options. Bush felt that the Reagan presidency had been too ready to deal with Moscow. In May 1989 Marlon Fitzwater, the White House spokesman, dismissed Gorbachev as a 'drugstore cowboy'. George Bush's change of mind occurred during his extended tour of eastern and western Europe in July 1989. Everyone advised him to meet Mikhail Gorbachev as there were momentous events in the offing.

The turning point in the relationship between James Baker, US Secretary of State, and Eduard Shevardnadze occurred in September 1989 when Shevardnadze accepted Baker's invitation to accompany him to his ranch at Jackson Hole,

Wyoming. Before leaving Moscow Shevardnadze had been sharply critical of the US administration's reluctance to pursue arms negotiations. Shevardnadze stayed two weeks and forged as close a relationship with Baker as he had enjoyed with Shultz. On arrival the Governor of Wyoming presented Shevardnadze with a Stetson cowboy hat. When asked what size the hat should be, the Soviet embassy in Washington was stumped. The Americans came up with the answer of how big Shevardnadze's head was! The Soviet foreign minister cut quite a figure in his ten gallon hat, cowboy boots and three-piece suit. In order to bring home to Baker the seriousness of the economic crisis, Shevardnadze had brought along Nikolai Shmelev, a pro-market economist. The foreign minister was desperate for a partnership with the US to promote reform at home. Without gaining anything in return, he conceded that Moscow was willing to sign a START treaty without a separate agreement to limit space-based weapons. IIe confessed that the giant radar station at Krasnoyarsk was a violation of the ABM treaty and promised it would be dismantled.

On his return to Moscow he made other concessions, including giving in to Washington's insistence that it have 880 submarine-launched cruise missiles (SLCM). Akhromeev and Kornienko, among others, berated him for not gaining reciprocity with the US on this issue.[109] The only morsel of comfort Shevardnadze received in return was Bush's willingness to go beyond the Soviet proposal to eliminate 80 per cent of chemical weapons and eliminate them completely.

The first Gorbachev–Bush summit, in Malta, took place in December 1989. It did not produce many tangible agreements but was a major step forward in Soviet–American relations.[110] Marshal Akhromeev, while on a visit to America in July 1989, was given a note from President Bush which extended an invitation to Gorbachev to meet in December. However, it was not revealed at the time and only a few officials knew of it. The Bush administration was having difficulty in agreeing on its stance on arms control. Shevardnadze, in November 1989, in a confidential personal memorandum, advised Gorbachev that it was of critical importance to get Bush's 'public commitment to the reform programme' and warned him that the US President was an 'indecisive leader'.[111]

By the time Bush arrived, on 1 December, he had made up his mind about perestroika. It was a good idea and all reasonable people should support it. He had come in for some sharp criticism at home and abroad for being so slow to seize the initiative and arrived in Malta with a whole raft of proposals about economic cooperation. In order to prevent Gorbachev complaining about the long delay, he decided to present them to him at their first meeting. The Americans had warned Gorbachev about trying to outsmart Bush by launching a series of new initiatives, as in Reykjavik. Gorbachev took the advice.

Bush was proposing an economic partnership. As regards the market economy, President Bush and James Baker were struck by his lack of understanding.[112] He kept on saying that much property in a market economy was held collectively, for example joint stock companies. Either he was woefully ignorant of the stock exchange or he was subtly hinting that he had changed his view about the Soviet economy. Hitherto he had always insisted that state-owned enterprises were superior to any other form of ownership. The concept of private property always stuck in his throat. Gorbachev was revealing that he was prepared to accept that enterprises could change into cooperatives. Although no formal agreements were signed, there were informal agreements on eastern Europe, Germany and the Baltic republics. Eastern Europe did not present a problem because Gorbachev and Shevardnadze had previously stated many times that force would not be used to prevent the peoples of the region deciding their own future. Gorbachev told Bush that he hoped the Warsaw Pact would continue. Bush informed Mikhail Sergeevich that as long as force was not used the United States would not take advantage of the situation to embarrass the Soviet Union. On German unification, Gorbachev stated that unification was a 'serious business and required a cautious approach. There was no need to push events.'[113]

On the Baltic republics, Gorbachev was less forthcoming, stating that he wished to avoid force since this would end perestroika. He was willing to consider any form of association for the Baltic republics, short of outright secession. Again the United States would not make life more difficult for Gorbachev in the region, providing force were not used. Rumours circulated later that a deal had been struck. The United

States would keep out of eastern Europe and the Baltic republics if the Soviet Union agreed to the unification of Germany. No such agreement was reached, to the relief of the region. On arms, it was agreed that the objective should be to sign a conventional forces in Europe (CFE) treaty in 1990. A strategic arms reduction treaty (START) might be ready for the next summit, proposed for Washington, in the summer of 1990.

There were also sharp disagreements. Bush criticised Soviet delivery of arms to Latin America and the behaviour of their ally, Cuba. Gorbachev countered by saying that the Soviets had agreed not to supply weapons to Nicaragua and had kept their promise. On Cuba, the best way to clear up the differences was to meet Fidel Castro face to face. Before the summit the Cuban leader had asked Gorbachev to help normalise relations with the United States.[114] The Soviets were willing to set up a dialogue. Bush coldly rejected the offer and expressed incomprehension about the continuing Soviet trade with Cuba. After all, Cuba had condemned perestroika. Another sore point was Bush's assertion that western values were prevailing. Gorbachev did not like the expression 'western values' as it implied the Soviet Union was capitulating to the west. He preferred universal democratic values. The two sides agreed to use the term 'democratic values'. Malta was a watershed in Soviet–US relations. Gorbachev assured Bush: 'We do not consider you an enemy any more'. Shevardnadze added that the two superpowers had 'buried the Cold War at the bottom of the Mediterranean'.[115]

In October 1985 Gorbachev chose France for his first visit to western Europe because it was a nuclear power but also because it had floated ideas about pan-European integration in the past. East–west relations at the time were rather frigid. Gorbachev used the term 'reasonable sufficiency', in terms of defence, for the first time and rejected ideology as the basis of foreign policy. Reflecting on Europe, he came up with a new expression, 'Europe is our common home'. He proposed the elimination of nuclear weapons by 2000 but this went down like a lead balloon in France. Western Europe was too conscious of Soviet conventional superiority. When Mitterrand visited Moscow to reciprocate Gorbachev's trip to Paris, the French President informed Gorbachev that he was opposed to the Strategic Defence Initiative (SDI or Star Wars), regarding it as accelerating the arms race. He had seen President Reagan just before coming to Moscow and thought that the President's arguments in favour of SDI to be 'mystical' rather than rational.[116] However, the French took the hardest line against the elimination of tactical nuclear weapons and began complaining that disarmament was starting at the wrong end. It should begin in the Soviet Union. The French parliament even voted to upgrade their armed forces. Far from being discouraged, Gorbachev, in Czechoslovakia in April 1987, waxed eloquent about the virtues of disarmament and the concept of a common European home. In meetings with many west European statesmen in Moscow, Gorbachev made clear that he was not trying to drive a wedge between Europe and north America. Indeed, the United States and Canada were included in the common European home! Mrs Thatcher visited Moscow in March 1987 and the two leaders continued their spirited polemics. The British Prime Minister believed in plain speaking: 'We believe in nuclear deterrence and we do not consider the elimination of nuclear weapons practicable'.[117] She would not budge from her argument that nuclear weapons were the only way to ensure the security of Great Britain in the event of a conventional war in Europe. Mikhail Sergeevich protested at length but made no progress. In December 1987 there was an opportunity to continue the dialogue, at Brize Norton, en route to the Washington summit to sign the INF treaty. They went at it again like hammer and tongs, and Geoffrey Howe, British Foreign Secretary, later commented to Gorbachev: 'Your talks with Mrs Thatcher are simply breath-taking. You work like two Stakhanovites [shock workers] to fulfil your plans at an unprecedented pace and thoroughly discuss every topic.'[118]

Gorbachev's first extended official visit to Great Britain took place in April 1989 and he entered 10 Downing Street for the first time. Thatcher was intensely interested in perestroika and questioned the Soviet leader closely about its progress. In response to Gorbachev's doubts about the reception perestroika was receiving in the west, the British Prime Minister swept all negative comments aside and assured him that all in the west were enthusiastic about it.[119]

Gorbachev chose to visit France and Great Britain before the Federal Republic of Germany. They, of course, were nuclear powers. Then, in June 1989, it was time to go to the economically most powerful state in western Europe. Indeed the Germans had been getting nervous about their relations with Moscow. When Gorbachev met Kohl after Chernenko's funeral, he enquired of the Chancellor: 'Kyda driftyet Federalnaya Respublika?' (where is the Federal Republic drifting?). The deputy German foreign minister, who spoke Russian, was struck by the use of the verb driftovat, to drift, especially as this word was not to be found in any Russian dictionary.

Kohl was the first foreign statesman to hear such neologisms and they became a feature of Gorbachev's speech. He loved to pepper his remarks with newly acquired English expressions. They had come straight out of some Moscow think-tank.[120] Kohl was very impressed by Mikhail Sergeevich's communicative skills and likened him to Josef Goebbels. The latter was a brilliant and skilful Nazi propagandist and Gorbachev was mortified by the comparison.[121] Not surprisingly, this soured relations between the two leaders. Chancellor Kohl used a different approach to that deployed by Thatcher. He did not attempt to convert Mikhail Sergeevich to his way of thinking but agreed to disagree on some points. Nuclear disarmament was high on the agenda and he left optimistic that a breakthrough could be achieved in Europe.

Everywhere he went, Mikhail Sergeevich was fêted as if he were the first man from Mars. In July he was off again to Paris and informed President Mitterrand that the postwar period had come to an end. A good omen was the decision to reduce the French military budget. At the Sorbonne, Gorbachev told French intellectuals: 'Lack of spirituality and anti-intellectualism are terrible dangers. Pure intellect that is deprived of a moral basis is just as dangerous a threat in today's world.'[122] Then he went to Strasbourg to address the Council of Europe. He was in Helsinki in October. Next it was off to Italy in November 1989. The reception he experienced in Milan was the most emotional of his career. On 1 December another first was registered, the first visit by a Soviet head of state to the Vatican, for an audience with Pope John Paul II. Gorbachev informed the Pope that a law on the freedom of conscience was being drafted. He also told him that, after reflection, he had come to the conclusion that democracy was not enough:

We also need morality. Democracy can bring good and evil . . . For us, it is essential that morality should become firmly established in society – such universal, eternal values as goodness, mercy, mutual aid. We start from the principle that the faith of believers must be respected.[123]

. . .

NOTES

1. Mikhail Gorbachev, *Memoirs* (London, Doubleday, 1996), p. 241.
2. Dusko Doder and Louise Branson, *Gorbachev: Heretic in the Kremlin* (London, Macdonald, 1990), p. 297.
3. In July 1987 Gorbachev told a group of editors that glasnost was a mutual learning process. 'We do not have a cultural tradition of discussion and polemics, where one respects the views of one's opponent. We are an emotional people . . . I do not pretend to know the absolute truth; we have to search for truth together.' Quoted in Doder and Branson, *Gorbachev*, p. 77.
4. Gorbachev, *Memoirs*, p. 251.
5. Archie Brown, *The Gorbachev Factor* (Oxford, Oxford University Press, 1996), pp. 172–5.
6. Jack F. Matlock, Jr., *Autopsy on an Empire: The American Ambassador's Account of the Collapse of the Soviet Union* (New York, Random House, 1995), p. 120.
7. The source of this information is Arkady Volsky. Matlock, *Autopsy on an Empire*, p. 122.
8. Gorbachev, *Memoirs*, p. 257.
9. Ibid., pp. 257–9.
10. Roy Medvedev and Giulietto Chiesa, *Time of Change: An Insider's View of Russia's Transformation* (New York, Pantheon, 1989), p. 182; Alfred Erich Senn, *Gorbachev's Failure in Lithuania* (New York, St Martin's Press, 1995), p. 9.
11. Vladimir Boukovsky, *Jugement à Moscou: Un dissident dans les archives du Kremlin* (Paris, Robert Laffont, 1995), p. 268.
12. Michael Urban with Vyacheslav Igrunov and Sergei Mitrokhin, *The Rebirth of Politics in Russia* (Cambridge, Cambridge University Press, 1997), pp. 201–33, is an informative account of the emergence of political parties and movements.
13. *Pravda*, 26 July 1988.
14. *Pravda*, 13 August 1988.
15. Gorbachev, *Memoirs*, p. 262.
16. Boukovsky, *Jugement à Moscou*, pp. 269–70.

17. Ibid., pp. 270–1.
18. Ibid., pp. 273–4.
19. Ibid., p. 274.
20. Gorbachev, *Memoirs*, p. 267.
21. Ibid., p. 266.
22. Ibid., p. 264. One estimate of the bureaucrats' annual salary was 40 billion rubles (about US$60 billion at the then rate of exchange) or about 10 per cent of the state budget, before their perks were taken into consideration. Alexander A. Danilov et al., *The History of Russia: The Twentieth Century* (New York, The Heron Press, 1996), p. 327.
23. He had, however, cut back the CC apparatus which had numbered about 3,000. The goal was to reduce it to less than half this number.
24. Gorbachev, *Memoirs*, p. 283.
25. Ibid., p. 283.
26. Matlock, *Autopsy on an Empire*, pp. 207–11.
27. Ibid., p. 210.
28. M. S. Gorbachev, *Izbrannye rechi i stati* (Moscow, Politizdat, 1987), vol. 7, p. 551.
29. Algirdas Brazauskas, *Lietuviskos skyrybos* (Vilnius, Politika, 1992), p. 62; Senn, *Gorbachev's Failure*, p. 62.
30. Matlock, *Autopsy on an Empire*, p. 206.
31. Ibid., p. 217.
32. Vladimir Mau, *The Political History of Economic Reform in Russia, 1985–1994* (London, Centre for Research into Communist Economies, 1996), pp. 52–3.
33. Criticisms of Raisa were common at meetings. After the Reykjavik summit, a Party speaker was asked: 'Did she pay for her own ticket?'. A barbed joke going the rounds at the time was about Raisa and Mikhail Sergeevich in bed. She asks him: 'Tell me, Misha, what does it feel like to sleep with the wife of the leader of the Soviet Union?' Often, attacks on Raisa were coded attacks on Mikhail Sergeevich. It was not possible to criticise him personally in public before 1989.
34. Matlock, *Autopsy on an Empire*, pp. 222–4.
35. Speech at 18 July 1989 CC meeting (Moscow, Politizdat, 1989), p. 109.
36. N. I. Ryzhkov, *Perestroika, Istoriya predatelstv* (Moscow, Novosti, 1992), p. 345.
37. Richard Sakwa, *Gorbachev and His Reforms 1985–1990* (London, Philip Allan, 1990), p. 68.
38. Matlock, *Autopsy on an Empire*, p. 264.
39. Ibid., pp. 264–5. In 1992, Starkov warned the ambassador: 'If you give Gorbachev credit for glasnost, you will insult all

of us who had to fight to get it. The Party Central Committee was always on our backs, right up to August 1991. Gorbachev did not give us glasnost. We took it.'

40. *Ogonek*, no. 44, 1989, p. 5; Sakwa, *Gorbachev and His Reforms*, p. 70.
41. One of the products of this endeavour was the undertaking by professors at the Moscow State Pedagogical University to write the history of Russia from its origins to the present day. One of the fruits of this scholarship to appear in English translation is Danilov et al., *The History of Russia*. This is an excellent volume with some new research material in it. It is worth reflecting on the fact that these distinguished scholars wrote Marxist history before 1988 and the same distinguished scholars wrote non-Marxist history after 1988.
42. *Izvestiya*, 17 December 1988; Sakwa, *Gorbachev and His Reforms*, p. 132.
43. Alec Nove, *An Economic History of the USSR 1917–1991*, 3rd edn (London, Penguin, 1992), p. 404. In March 1989, Boris Gostev, the Minister of Finance, declared that the government needed to borrow 63.8 billion rubles. The deficit of 100 billion rubles in 1989 was equivalent to 11.7 per cent of Gross National Product (*Izvestiya*, 30 March 1989).
44. Ibid., p. 406.
45. *Kommunist*, no. 2, 1990, p. 27.
46. Donald Filtzer, *Soviet Workers and the Collapse of Perestroika: The Soviet Labour Process and Gorbachev's Reforms, 1985–1991* (Cambridge, Cambridge University Press, 1994), p. 94.
47. Ibid., p. 98.
48. *Pravda*, 21 July 1989.
49. Richard E. Rawles, 'Soviet psychology, perestroika, and the human factor: 1985–1991' in V. A. Koltsova et al., *Post-Soviet Perspectives on Russian Psychology* (Westport, CT, Greenwood Press, 1996), p. 109; the article by Popov was reprinted in V. Mezhenkov and E. Skelley (eds), *Soviet Scene 1988* (London, Collets, 1988), pp. 171–6.
50. Rawles, 'Soviet psychology', pp. 109–11; Kon's article 'The psychology of social inertia' is in *Social Sciences*, vol. 20, no. 1, 1989, pp. 60–74.
51. Rawles, 'Soviet psychology', p. 111.
52. A. I. Kitov, *Lichnost i perestroika* (Moscow, Profizdat, 1990); Rawles, 'Soviet psychology', p. 111.
53. Gorbachev, *Memoirs*, p. 336.
54. Ibid., p. 336. This conceded that Moscow no longer exercised full authority in the two republics.
55. Ibid., p. 337.

56. Gorbachev renounced the use of force, officially, at the United Nations in December 1988.
57. Gorbachev, *Memoirs*, p. 339.
58. Matlock, *Autopsy on an Empire*, p. 169.
59. *Sovetskaya Kultura*, 1 September 1988; Senn, *Gorbachev's Failure*, p. 16.
60. Senn, *Gorbachev's Failure*, p. 17.
61. Interview in *Lietuvos rytas*, 9 April 1993; Senn, *Gorbachev's Failure*, p. 18.
62. Senn, *Gorbachev's Failure*, p. 23.
63. This was Lenin Phase I, in his pre-1918 commune state days. Yakovlev was ignoring Lenin Phase II, post 1920–1, when he favoured a strong, centralised state.
64. Yegor Ligachev, *Inside Gorbachev's Kremlin* (Boulder, CO, Westview Press, 1996), p. 137.
65. Ibid., p. 138.
66. Ibid., p. 140.
67. Matlock, *Autopsy on an Empire*, p. 171, in a personal interview with Yakovlev.
68. Senn, *Gorbachev's Failure*, p. 26.
69. Ibid., p. 27. Gorbachev and the leadership referred to the nationalities problem as 'inter-ethnic problems' (*mezhnatsionalnye problemy*).
70. Vadim Bakatin, *Izbavlenie ot KGB* (Moscow, Novosti, 1992), p. 49; Senn, *Gorbachev's Failure*, p. 30.
71. Anatoli Tschernajew, *Die letzten Jahre einer Weltmacht: Der Kreml von innen* (Stuttgart, Deutsche Verlags-Anstalt, 1993), pp. 206–7.
72. Senn, *Gorbachev's Failure*, pp. 39–40.
73. M. S. Gorbachev, *Izbrannye rechi i stati* (Moscow, Izdateltsvo politicheskoi literatury, 1990), vol. 7, p. 142.
74. Gorbachev, *Memoirs*, p. 341.
75. The Estonian Constitution was amended to recognise private property. The land, air, minerals, natural resources, and principal means of production were also declared to be the property of Estonia. These are the property of the Soviet people in the USSR Constitution (1977).
76. Gorbachev, *Memoirs*, p. 341.
77. Ibid., p. 342.
78. *Pravda*, 26 August 1989.
79. *Sovetskaya Litva*, 6 September 1989.
80. As it had become an embarrassment no one in the CC apparatus in Moscow would admit to drafting it. To the Balts it appeared that the Party's right hand did not know what the left hand was doing.

81. Senn, *Gorbachev's Failure*, p. 70.
82. Ibid., p. 72.
83. Brown, *The Gorbachev Factor*, p. 266.
84. The commission of the Congress of People's Deputies, set up to investigate the affair, exonerated Gorbachev. However, it complained that it was repeatedly frustrated by the military when seeking precise information.
85. Gorbachev, *Memoirs*, p. 342.
86. Gamsakhurdia was overthrown in 1992 and Eduard Shevardnadze took over, with Russian help.
87. Matlock, *Autopsy on an Empire*, p. 287.
88. Ibid., p. 287.
89. Anatoly Sergeevich Chernyaev, during a seminar at the School of Slavonic and East European Studies, University of London, on 20 October 1994; Gorbachev, *Memoirs*, pp. 464–6.
90. Boukovsky, *Jugement à Moscou*, p. 497.
91. Ibid., p. 449. The Politburo resolution of 23 April 1981 and the report of the Politburo commission of 16 April 1981.
92. The exception to this was Romania where the leader Nicolae Ceausescu and Gorbachev did not get on. Romania, to Gorbachev, was like an oriental despotism. Mikhail Sergeevich regarded Ceausescu in a class of his own when it came to vanity and self-confidence. 'An absolute leader for decades, he always wore an arrogant smirk, treating others with apparent contempt, everyone from retainers to equal partners.' Gorbachev, *Memoirs*, p. 475.
93. Boukovsky, *Jugement à Moscou*, pp. 459–60.
94. Ibid., p. 460.
95. Ibid., p. 455. The Politburo meeting of 10 December 1981.
96. Jaruzelski enjoyed good relations with Brezhnev. It is interesting that the Soviet leader addressed the Polish leader in the familiar second person singular but Jaruzelski always used the formal second person plural when addressing Brezhnev. Critics would regard this as evidence of a master–servant relationship.
97. Romania totally ignored the plenum and Ceausescu warned the Soviet ambassador that the Soviet Party was travelling down a dangerous road. The Bulgarians stated that they had no need of such a plenum but Todor Zhivkov, the Party leader, changed course shortly afterwards and attempted radical personnel and policy changes. His aim was to demonstrate that Bulgaria could implement perestroika more successfully than the Soviet Union. The Hungarian and Polish Parties were best disposed towards the January plenum.

98. Michail Gorbatschow, *Erinnerungen* (Berlin, Siedler Verlag, 1995), p. 934. Honecker blamed his sacking as Party leader on Gorbachev-sanctioned intrigues in the apparatus of the Central Committee of the SED.
99. Chernyaev (same as note 71).
100. FBIS-SOV-89-129, 7 July 1989, p. 29; Jonathan C. Valdez, *Internationalism and the Ideology of Soviet Influence in Eastern Europe* (Cambridge, Cambridge University Press, 1993), p. 120.
101. *Pravda*, 4 July 1990; Valdez, *Internationalism*, p. 121.
102. Boukovsky, *Jugement à Moscou*, p. 494.
103. Ibid., pp. 494–5. The CC international department note about this is dated 17 July 1989.
104. Ibid., p. 495.
105. Ibid., p. 495. The note by Valentin Falin, Nikolai Kruchina and Vladimir Kryuchkov was dated 31 March 1989. Kruchina committed suicide, by jumping from a window, after the failure of the August 1991 coup. He was rumoured to have been involved in illegal currency deals.
106. Matlock, *Autopsy on an Empire*, p. 149.
107. Ibid., p. 151.
108. Ibid., p. 149. A major reason why it took Moscow so long to get out of Afghanistan (Gorbachev had declared in March 1985 that the Soviet Union had to get out) was because it was trying to negotiate an agreement with Washington which would permit Najibullah's government to stay in place. The Soviets wanted the Americans to stop supplying arms to the mujahidin the moment they left Afghanistan but the Americans refused.
109. Carolyn McGiffert Ekedahl and Melvin A. Goodman, *The Wars of Eduard Shevardnadze* (London, Hurst, 1997), pp. 119–21.
110. There are extensive excerpts from the notes Gorbachev took at the summit in Michail Gorbatschow, *Gipfelgespräche: Geheime Protokolle aus meiner Amtszeit* (Berlin, Rowolt, 1993).
111. Anatoly Dobrynin, *In Confidence: Moscow's Ambassador to America's Six Cold War Presidents* (New York, Random House, 1995), p. 634.
112. Matlock, *Autopsy on an Empire*, p. 272.
113. Gorbachev, *Memoirs*, p. 514.
114. Ibid., p. 513.
115. Michael Beschloss and Strobe Talbott, *At the Highest Levels: The Inside Story of the End of the Cold War* (Boston, Little, Brown, 1993), p. 165; Ekedahl and Goodman, *Wars of Eduard Shevardnadze*, p. 123.
116. Gorbachev, *Memoirs*, p. 430.
117. Ibid., p. 435.

118. Ibid., p. 436.
119. After London, Gorbachev went off to Beijing to heal the Sino-Soviet rift. Both sides agreed to desist from polemics and not to interfere in one another's domestic affairs. However, the visit embarrassed the Chinese leadership. Gorbachev was given a rapturous welcome with the Chinese hoping his visit would promote democracy in their own country. The tragedy of Tiananmen square occurred shortly afterwards, in June 1989. During 1989, Gorbachev also visited Cuba and the German Democratic Republic and received a stream of western statesmen in the Kremlin. The year 1989 was an *annus mirabilis* in foreign policy but an *annus horribilis* in domestic policy.
120. Doder and Branson, *Gorbachev*, p. 67. Gorbachev could not refrain from using them to domestic Russian audiences. He liked the word consensus, but this was quite unintelligible to the average Russian.
121. Kohl had in mind Goebbels's instinctive gift of rousing an audience and leading it in the direction he wanted. Kohl was thinking of Goebbels's oratorical skills and not the content of his speeches. Gorbachev, like any non-German, thought he was referring to the content of his speeches. When George Bush returned to Washington after the funeral, he commented that Gorbachev was an 'impressive idea salesman'. Doder and Branson, *Gorbachev*, p. 68. He used direct speech. Whereas the average Soviet politician would talk about the masses, the working class and so on, Mikhail Sergeevich merely said: 'I think'. Richard Nixon later commented: 'Gorbachev was born with a master's degree in public relations'.
122. Gorbachev, *Memoirs*, p. 506.
123. Ibid., p. 509. He was confessing that morality was almost absent from Soviet society.

Chapter 5

PERESTROIKA MARK III:
1990–1991

An indication of what was in Gorbachev's mind was provided by an article in *Pravda* in November 1989. It was headed 'The socialist idea and revolutionary perestroika' and was signed 'M. Gorbachev', indicating it was his personal credo. He made it clear he had changed his mind about many things:

> Whereas, at first, we thought it was basically a question only of correcting individual deformations in our social organism, of perfecting the system which had been developed, we are now saying that we must radically remodel our entire social system, from the economic foundation to the superstructure ... reform of property relations, the economic mechanism, and the political system.[1]

He wished to move on from the command-administrative economy but did not wish to embrace capitalism. A 'humane, free and rational society' would come about by workers running their own enterprises and peasants running the land. The aim was a civil society where democracy and freedom would reign. Significantly, he pointed out that real democracy was the end goal and could only be achieved under socialism. But in the meanwhile formal democracy was important. This accepted that the formal democracy of capitalist states was a step in the right direction. Also important was the separation of powers, of the legislature, executive and legal system. He conceded that the Party lagged behind society in the race to democracy. This suggested he was moving towards western social democracy, although there is no indication that he was contemplating anything like the market economy and private property. Of course, as leader of the Party, he could not openly accept such heretical ideas.

Gorbachev continued his search for an economic mechanism which would solve all his problems. A one-party system was expedient during the 'present, complex stage' but the Party had to embrace the pluralism of ideas and become more open.[2] What would happen if the Party refused to catch up with society? No answer was provided, but Gorbachev had told Berliners that history punished those who lagged behind. Gorbachev was more daring during his New Year's message on 31 December 1989. He omitted references to Lenin, communism and the Party.[3]

The winter of 1989–90 was one of discontent. The collapse of communism in eastern Europe, culminating in the execution of Nicolae and Elena Ceaucescu, the Romanian ruling family, in December 1989, excited hope and despair. Those pressing for autonomy and independence were encouraged, while members of the Soviet ruling class found their blood running cold. The deteriorating economic situation fuelled resentment, and glasnost was stripping the Party of its legitimacy. The Party was becoming a major problem for Gorbachev. The Inter-Regional Group of deputies, almost all communists (the notable exception was Andrei Sakharov), in the Congress of People's Deputies was becoming bolder and more radical. The elections to the republican Supreme Soviets (only Russia followed the Soviet pattern in having an outer and inner parliament, a Congress of People's Deputies and a Supreme Soviet) took place in early 1990. They favoured radicals and conservative communists were rejected.

This encouraged the Inter-Regional Group to believe that the future belonged to it. Opinion polls in autumn 1989 had revealed that the more radical a deputy was, the more popular he or she became in the eyes of the public. The Inter-Regional Group wanted article 6 of the 1977 Constitution amended. This article guaranteed the Party a monopoly of political power. This would then legalise factions in the Party, something which had been banned since the 10th Congress, in 1921. They favoured more decentralisation of economic activity but Prime Minister Ryzhkov was attempting to impose more central direction. The deputies also favoured the private ownership of land and businesses. This amounted virtually to promoting a Soviet confederation, with Moscow only having the powers which the republics conferred on it.[4]

Gorbachev opposed all these initiatives. He was particularly sensitive about article 6, but also genuinely believed that private property was a retrograde step. He used his position from the chair to curtail or avoid a full-scale debate on these subjects. This created the impression he was protecting the prerogatives of the ruling class. There was a head-on confrontation between him and Andrei Sakharov on 12 December 1989. The latter proposed that a debate be permitted to consider private property of land and enterprises, and article 6 of the Constitution, and that the Constitution be correspondingly amended. These items could be added to the day's agenda. Gorbachev reacted as if stung by a wasp and sent Sakharov packing from the rostrum before he had had an opportunity to argue his case. Gorbachev insulted the aged academician and when it was shown on national television the same evening it was Sakharov who won a moral victory. Two days later he was dead from a heart attack. Many radicals linked the two events, believing his humiliation had precipitated his death. Gorbachev did not want any debate on article 6, he argued that the matter should be resolved in a new Constitution.

On 13 December Nikolai Ryzhkov presented to the deputies his carefully elaborated two-stage plan to move to market relations. Each stage was to last three years. Gavriil Popov, a co-chair of the Inter-Regional Group, ridiculed Ryzhkov's grasp of economics:

> The past five years have shown that the concept of perestroika from 'above' does not work, that a new approach is needed. The centre must be prepared not to rush in to save a drowning enterprise, but to hand over the salvage operation to others who are nearer ... that is the republics and the local soviets. And, above all, the people who are actually drowning. Especially since our enterprises are often 'drowning' not because they do not know how to swim but because the centre binds them hand and foot, puts a millstone around their neck, and then offers advice about how to keep above water.[5]

Popov pointed out that a market economy cannot be introduced in fits and starts, just like a car needs an engine, made up of interacting parts, to move forward. He believed that five fundamental laws were needed: on ownership, land, enterprises, economic independence of the republics, and local self-management. The Congress of People's Deputies, nonetheless, passed Ryzhkov's version of market relations by a large majority. They were determined to keep trying to rationalise the economy. The reformers were disillusioned and a Ukrainian deputy expressed bitterness at the injustice of a republic working very hard and finding that the centre took 95 per cent of its output and only left it with 5 per cent.[6] There was, however, an exception: the Baltic republics. On 1 January 1990 they went over to economic self-accounting or, put simply, they achieved economic autonomy.

. . .

NATIONALITIES

The test case for Gorbachev's nationalities policy was Lithuania. At the Malta summit, President Bush had made clear that the US would not complicate matters for the Soviet leader, providing he did not use force. Representatives from the Baltic republics had met the US ambassador to Moscow before the summit and had been assured that Moscow and Washington were not going to strike a deal on the Baltic. On 7 December the Lithuanian Supreme Soviet amended article 6 of the Lithuanian Constitution, which conferred the monopoly of power on the Party. The Communist Party of Lithuania convened a Congress on 20 December and at noon that day Gorbachev phoned Brazauskas, 'in a particularly angry voice', to enquire if the resolution on separating the Lithuanian Party from the CPSU had been passed. 'Do you know where all this can lead?', the general secretary asked.[7] Alarmed that this could mean troops dispersing the Congress, Brazauskas rushed back to the session and recommended that the Party separate. It duly declared itself independent. The pro-Moscow faction broke away, about one-sixth of the delegates, and formed their own party, the Communist Party of Lithuania, loyal to the Moscow programme.

Brazauskas's party now became the independent Communist Party of Lithuania. At the Congress of People's Deputies on 21 December Gorbachev sarcastically addressed the Lithuanian delegation as 'comrades, communists, non-party Bolsheviks'. When Landsbergis began to speak, Gorbachev

155

maliciously enquired: 'non-party Bolshevik?'. Landsbergis replied: 'Yes', having not heard the word Bolshevik. The two then traded insults. Afterwards, the general secretary, with a sad mien, sighed: 'Algirdas, what have you done to the Communist Party?'.[8] It was as if Mikhail Sergeevich had lost a family friend. There was a sweetener for the Lithuanians. On 24 December the Congress finally accepted the Yakovlev commission report on the Molotov–Ribbentrop pact, secret protocol and all.[9]

On the negative side, the Congress saw the first head-on confrontation between Gorbachev and Shevardnadze. The Sobchak commission reported to the Congress on the Tbilisi massacre, exonerated Gorbachev and Shevardnadze and blamed the military, commanded by General Igor Rodionov. The military took umbrage at this and responded vigorously in its defence. Shevardnadze then requested to be allowed to counter some of the military's claims but Gorbachev would not permit him to speak. This made Shevardnadze furious because he thought there had been an agreement for the report to be presented without discussion. On 24 December Shevardnadze advised Gorbachev he would resign in protest but the President refused to listen and the foreign minister backed down.[10] Gorbachev's decision to take the military's side was the first clear evidence that the Gorbachev–Shevardnadze partnership was in danger of disintegration. It also revealed Gorbachev's lack of sensitivity on nationality issues.

At the CC plenum on 25 December abuse was showered on Brazauskas. Vadim Medvedev saw the Lithuanian Party Congress as the merging of the Party and Sajudis. To Ligachev, the Party had become the 'tool to achieve the nationalist goals of Sajudis'. Nursultan Nazarbaev, first secretary of the Communist Party of Kazakhstan, thought the Communist Party of Lithuania was aiming at depriving the CPSU of its role as the 'political avant-garde of Soviet society'. However, he hastened to propose the restructuring of the Politburo to represent the nationalities of the Soviet Union. Gorbachev interrupted other speakers while they were criticising Brazauskas. Once he added that the Lithuanian leader was a 'Trojan horse'. One perceptive critic referred to Brazauskas as all the more dangerous since he was a 'sensible man, a man of authority'.[11] The CC conservatives had a field day, jeering and catcalling at will. Perestroika was being brought into question.

Afterwards, Gorbachev criticised the supporters of perestroika for not speaking up. Chernyaev explained that they took their lead from him. If he sat there and accepted the criticism, there was nothing his supporters could do. Gorbachev had allowed Ligachev to lead at the CC plenum on 9 December and he had attacked perestroika. Yakovlev had reported that the general secretary, afterwards, had commended Ligachev for again 'defending the Party'. This behaviour had confused Gorbachev's supporters. Chernyaev told Gorbachev that as long as he praised Ligachev in public, although he knew him to be his enemy, there could be no perestroika in the Party.[12] Yakovlev told Gorbachev that he should not have tolerated the personal criticism to which he had been subjected. He should have got up and left and another 100 would have followed him out. Among the leaders, Yakovlev thought Medvedev, Shevardnadze, Slyunkov and Kryuchkov would have followed Mikhail Sergeevich. Yakovlev thought that Gorbachev should abandon the Party nomenklatura since perestroika could not succeed with them on board.

The plenum made clear that Gorbachev would not countenance a federal Party, as Yakovlev and others were advising. Even though the overwhelming majority of Party members in Lithuania favoured a federal Party, Gorbachev saw this as the road to ruin. This course, he argued, would mean 'dismemberment of the USSR, and that would be an historical dead end for all the peoples of the Soviet Union'.[13]

The situation in Lithuania was getting serious and Gorbachev felt that he could work his magic by appealing to the population over the heads of the Communist Party. On 4 January he met Brazauskas's Party bureau in Moscow, at his invitation. Yakovlev predicted that Lithuania could set in train a domino effect which could call into question the very existence of the Soviet Union. Gorbachev warned them against thoughts of independence but also pleaded with them to understand his predicament. When he arrived in Vilnius on 11 January 1990, he received an elaborate welcome from Sajudis which appealed to the population to show respect to the 'leader of a neighbouring country' and a 'friendly neighbour'. He criticised Brazauskas for this later but the Lithuanian replied that he could not answer for Sajudis. Mikhail

Sergeevich solved the tricky problem of there being two Lithuanian Parties. He was accompanied around the republic by the leaders of both. He was taken aback by the vigour of the responses of the Lithuanian public which impressed on him that national feelings were the deepest of all. He tried to wean Lithuanians away from their desire to be independent. He hoped that political and economic reform would 'outpace the secessionist process. Having experienced the real benefits of a federation, people would no longer be obsessed by the idea of full independence, and the problem would be resolved to everyone's advantage.'[14] He did, however, announce two major concessions. A law was being drafted to clarify the procedures to secede from the Soviet Union. He was also contemplating a multi-party state. No incident clouded his visit and the Lithuanians thought that the main achievement of the visit was that nothing had changed. On 16 January Brazauskas was elected speaker of the Lithuanian Supreme Soviet, or head of state. He was preparing the way to meet Gorbachev as President to President. Lithuania was following the Soviet pattern. Power was moving from the Party to the Supreme Soviet.

The CC plenum met on 5–7 February and heard Gorbachev's account of his visit to Lithuania. He conceded that 'at present separatist tendencies dominate in the republic'. Nevertheless, the two wings of the Party in Lithuania should seek common solutions to the pressing problems. Both Parties were to be invited to send delegates to the 28th Party Congress in Moscow. The mood of the plenum, however, was dominated by conservatives. They pointed to the 'Ceaucescu syndrome' and expressed fear that one day they could find themselves hanging from lamp posts. If this started in Lithuania, where would it end? The pro-Moscow Lithuanian Party concentrated its fire on Yakovlev, blaming him for starting the rot in Lithuania. Gorbachev, in the end, sided with the conservatives and censured Brazauskas's Party. He backed the pro-Moscow Party, but it had practically no following in Lithuania. It was the parting of the ways for Gorbachev and Lithuania. He was never to regain the initiative in the republic.

The tension between Azerbaijan and Armenia over Nagorno-Karabakh intensified during 1989 and Moscow decided to hand the problem of the enclave over to the republics. The special administration, under Arkady Volsky, ended on

28 November 1989, when the USSR Supreme Soviet voted to return Nagorno-Karabakh to Azerbaijani control. Tension rose in Stepanakert, the capital, and on 1 December the Armenian Supreme Soviet voted to integrate Nagorno-Karabakh. Azerbaijan replied by blockading Armenia, since almost all goods to Armenia had to cross Azerbaijani territory. The Azerbaijani National Front, now legal, organised huge protest demonstrations. On 13 January 1990 the bloodiest riots of the Soviet era hit Baku. Armenians were slaughtered wherever they could be found. The National Front took over and the Party leader moved to Moscow. On 18 January the National Front declared a state of emergency and communist power began to crumble. On 19 January the front seized government and Party buildings.

The same day, Moscow declared martial law and Soviet troops moved into Baku to restore communist power. On 21 January the Azerbaijani Supreme Soviet voted to hold a referendum about secession from the Soviet Union if Soviet troops stayed. Over 200 may have been killed in Baku during the crackdown. The episode could only fuel Azeri desires for independence. The involvement of the military in Baku provoked demonstrations in Russia. They were not protesting against the crackdown but about sons and relatives being sent into a dangerous cauldron. However, a precedent had been set: blood could be spilt to keep the empire together. Gorbachev's own conclusion was that the authorities 'cannot avoid the use of force in extreme circumstances'.[15] A bonus for Gorbachev was the muted American response to the Baku killings. Washington had accepted that it was an inter-ethnic conflict.

. . .

GORBACHEV, THE RADICALS AND THE CONSERVATIVES

Over 400 radicals in the Party came together on 20–21 January 1990 to establish the CPSU democratic platform. Many of them were from the Inter-Regional Group of deputies. They favoured a multi-party system, the end of the Party monopoly, democratic centralism and the election of officials by secret ballots. There were those who believed that it was better to stay in the Party, such as Yeltsin, so as to change the organisation from within. However, others, such as Gavriil Popov, favoured splitting from the Party if it did not become more democratic. Aleksandr Yakovlev did not participate but it was assumed that the group had his blessing.

The intense battle behind the scenes surfaced in the pages of *Le Monde*. Its Moscow correspondent had got hold of a policy document, drafted by Gorbachev advisers, who supported the democratic platform. They advocated a complete break with the Party conservatives who were now the greatest barrier to perestroika. Furthermore, the latter were beginning to forge alliances with chauvinist and patriotic elements in society. To promote perestroika, Gorbachev had to ally himself with the radicals and no longer occupy the middle ground between the two factions.[16] This heightened the suspicions of the conservatives, such as Ligachev, that Gorbachev had abandoned the class struggle and was betraying the country. Gorbachev was revealing a great talent to get out of tight corners and Bill Keller, the respected *New York Times* correspondent, graphically summed up his skills as the CC plenum of 5 February opened:

> Now Mr. Gorbachev, the Houdini of politicians, is back on the stage, ready for his next act. He had slipped out of two perilously tight spots [Lithuania and Azerbaijan] and again confounded the credulous spectators who believe, each time the master is wrapped in chains and dropped into the river, that they are witnessing his final stunt.[17]

Gorbachev worked one of his miracles at the plenum. He got the conservative majority to accept a presidential system, included in the new Party programme to be presented to the 28th Party Congress in July 1990. He adopted various tactics to achieve this. First there was the element of surprise. The issue had not been debated in the Party or press before the plenum. He banked on getting it through before factions could form against him. He did not provide too much detail. However, he also made concessions to the conservatives. He opposed federalism and defended the centralised Party apparatus. There would be no private ownership of land. And, of course, he went on at length about promoting socialism. He must have realised that he could not exert strong presidential power if the Party clung on to its central role. If he were to be President, he would eventually have to give up his Party role. That could only occur when he had reduced the Party to a talking shop. He had apparently concluded that if he were to become more radical he had to secure his own base. As general secretary and speaker of the Congress of People's Deputies, he could be removed at a moment's notice. As President, he would be secure for five years. In the short term, in order to get the Party to accept a presidential system, he was willing to compromise. However, the concessions he made exacerbated the already alarming economic situation and once again put off decisive economic reform.

The plenum also accepted that article 6 of the 1977 Constitution should be revised at the next session of the Congress of People's Deputies. In his memoirs, Gorbachev refers to it as the 'accursed article 6'.[18] In principle, the decision to abandon the monopoly of the Party had been taken at the 19th Party Conference and this implied a multi-party system and a political opposition. But when were these fundamental changes to be introduced? The conservatives in the leadership, headed by Ligachev, did not want to give up the leading role of the Party. Gorbachev's rudeness to Sakharov in December 1989 was apparently related to a failure of the radicals, Gorbachev, Medvedev, Shevardnadze and Yakovlev, to push a revision through the Politburo.[19] Gorbachev had his own timetable for reform but it depended on his tactical skill in outmanoeuvring the conservatives. On the other hand, society had moved ahead of the Party and was pushing for more radical change. Gorbachev's difficulties arose from attempting to manage change, to satisfy two constituencies which were moving further and further way from one another. There was also the point that he was better at tactical planning (short-term) than strategic planning (long-term). As yet, he had no clear strategic vision of where he was going. One of his weaknesses was an inability to foresee the consequences of his actions.

Gorbachev's extraordinary sensitivity to personal criticism surfaced when pro-democracy groups called for a demonstration in Moscow on 25 February. A previous demonstration on 4 February had been largely in his favour but Vladimir Kryuchkov, skilfully exploiting Gorbachev's dislike of criticism, had distorted some of the remarks to give them an anti-Gorbachev flavour.[20] Kryuchkov put it about that the marchers on 25 February[21] intended to storm the Kremlin. Ryzhkov went on television to advise people to stay at home to avoid being caught up in possible violence. A compromise was reached and a crowd of over 100,000 gathered in Gorky Park and then moved to Smolensk square, well away from the centre. Troops were on stand-by in case anyone tried to approach the centre. The whole episode angered some democrats who became suspicious about Gorbachev's motives in becoming President. The demonstration was mishandled by the future President and gave the impression that he had no faith in democracy. At the Supreme Soviet session two days later, Sergei Stankevich and Anatoly Sobchak called for more debate before the amendment to the Constitution went through. Gorbachev was accused of seeking too much power. This hurt him and his incoherent remarks reflected his perplexed state of mind. When it came to a vote, there was a large majority in favour of the amendment.

. . .

LITHUANIA AGAIN

Elections to the Lithuanian Supreme Soviet or Council[22] took place on 25 February 1990 and the second round was completed for the Council to convene on 10 March. Sajudis-supported candidates (Sajudis was not technically a political party) scored an overwhelming victory and over two-thirds of deputies had pledged to push for independence. The pro-Moscow party took over Party property and Gorbachev warned Brazauskas that secession would cost Lithuania 21 billion rubles or US$33 billion in hard currency since Moscow would not accept payment in rubles. Lithuania might also lose Vilnius and Klaipeda and be returned to its 1939 borders.

Sajudis leaders, headed by Vytautas Landsbergis, requested and were granted a meeting with the US ambassador on the morning of 7 March. However, Shevardnadze requested an urgent meeting beforehand. He had prepared his notes in Georgian. It was serious. With a solemn expression, he explained that the coming weekend, 10–12 March, would be 'decisive' for the Soviet Union. Gorbachev's plan to establish a presidency and a federation of sovereign states was running into strong opposition. The internal situation was so explosive, especially regarding the military, that a wrong move could precipitate a civil war and 'bring a military dictatorship to power'. If the new Lithuanian parliament declared independence before the Congress of People's Deputies adopted a presidential system, 'civil war could result'. If the Lithuanians declared independence after Gorbachev became executive President, he could handle it. Shevardnadze then asked the ambassador to postpone his meeting with Sajudis. This was to avoid suspicions that the United States was 'manipulating' Lithuania so as to break up the Soviet Union. This might precipitate military action against the Lithuanians. The ambassador told Shevardnadze that he could not postpone the meeting.

Landsbergis stated that the delegation had come to inform the ambassador that the Supreme Council would convene over the weekend and would probably declare independence. The Lithuanians had two questions: how would the United States react to the declaration of independence, and had a deal been struck between Washington and Moscow on nationalities' affairs? The ambassador explained that the United States would only recognise a government which controlled its own territory. Since this was not the case, Washington would not recognise Lithuania. On the nationalities' issue, there was no understanding between the two governments. The Lithuanians wanted to declare independence before Gorbachev became President. Why? 'We simply don't trust him', Landsbergis replied, 'He wants the power so that he can crush us!' The ambassador countered by saying that Gorbachev already had the power to crush them.[23]

The ambassador saw Shevardnadze the following day. He suggested that President Bush could contact Landsbergis to advise waiting another week before declaring independence. However, Gorbachev had to give his word that he would not use force against Lithuania. Nothing ever came of this. On leaving, Shevardnadze shocked his visitor by saying: 'Jack, I'll tell you one thing. If I see a dictatorship coming, I'm going to resign. I'll not be part of a government with blood on its hands.'[24] The Lithuanian Supreme Council declared independence on 11 March, five years to the day after Gorbachev had been elected general secretary. Washington reaffirmed the 'Baltic peoples' inalienable right to peaceful self-determination' and urged the Soviet government to 'enter into immediate constructive negotiations with the government of Lithuania'.[25] Vytautas Landsbergis was elected chair or speaker and hence head of state. Algirdas Brazauskas was runner-up. The official name became the Republic of Lithuania and the deputies proclaimed the 're-establishment of the independent Lithuanian state'. Kazimiera Prunskiene became Prime Minister on 17 March and Brazauskas was made first deputy. His gamble to split with the conservatives had paid off and he was later to succeed Landsbergis as President of independent Lithuania.

.   .   .

FIRST PRESIDENT

The election of Gorbachev, on 13 March 1990 at the Congress of People's Deputies, as the first executive President of the Soviet Union was a foregone conclusion. He had been endorsed at a CC plenum the day before. The rising tension between Gorbachev and the radicals or democrats became clear from the speech by Yury Afanasev, speaking for the Inter-Regional Group. He revealed that the group would vote against the introduction of a presidential system unless certain conditions had been met. They wanted presidential elections to follow a Union treaty, the introduction of a multi-party system, the election of a new legislature, and a popularly elected President. The President should not play a major role in any political party.

It was clear that the radicals feared Gorbachev would use his new power against them. Afanasev deliberately insulted Gorbachev. He claimed that the purpose of the presidency was to 'legalise the extraordinary power of a certain person, at this moment Mikhail Sergeevich Gorbachev'.[26] Other deputies defended Gorbachev, stating that he had attained absolute personal power five years previously. The other conditions might be desirable but there was simply no time to engage in presidential elections. Another deputy was fearful of the amount of power being concentrated in Gorbachev's hands. It represented a threat to the 'process of democratisation ... There is the danger of a return to dictatorship, discipline is falling sharply ... no one listens to anyone.'[27]

Nursultan Nazarbaev, first Party secretary in Kazakhstan, proposed something which had not occurred to Gorbachev.

He wanted a presidential system introduced in the republics, to 'eliminate contradictions between the notion of the presidency and the desire of the republics to broaden their autonomy'.[28] With one deft speech, Nazarbaev was cutting back the growing power of the centre. When it came to the vote, by roll call, 1,817 voted in favour of a presidency, 133 against and 61 abstained. There were three names on the ballot for President, but Nikolai Ryzhkov[29] and Vadim Bakatin withdrew, leaving Gorbachev unopposed. He was elected President, in a secret ballot, with 1,329 voting for, 495 against and 313 abstaining or submitting invalid votes. This represented 59.1 per cent of the deputies and well above the 50 per cent plus one vote needed. However, it revealed how much had changed since the vote, in May 1989, when he had been elected chair (speaker) of the Supreme Soviet by 2,123 votes (95.6 per cent) to 87.

Another issue at the Congress was whether the 'person elected to the post of President of the USSR may hold any other political or state post'. Both the Inter-Regional Group and the conservatives were against and the motion to amend article 127 (the powers of the President) failed as 1,303 voted against and 607 in favour. A constitutional amendment needed a two-thirds majority of all deputies. The conservatives had just failed to achieve their objective.

Opinion was divided over whether Gorbachev had committed a major error in not being popularly elected. Yeltsin, for one, hammered away at this point. Being directly elected would have increased Gorbachev's legitimacy. However, on sober reflection, he may have concluded that he would not win. In order to be elected President, a candidate required a majority in a majority of republics. Given the animosity against Mikhail Sergeevich in the Baltic and Transcaucasia, it was unlikely that he would carry a majority of republics. The temptation would be to concede too much to the republics in order to win. The Constitution wished to prevent Russians electing a Russian as Soviet President who would then impose his will on non-Russians.

The President nominated the Council of Ministers and submitted it for the approval of the Supreme Soviet. He chaired the Defence Council. A Presidential Council, representing various constituencies, was to be appointed. It can be viewed as an ersatz Politburo. Such was the balance of interests, when it was appointed, that it was guaranteed to be ineffective. From a protocol point of view, it took over from the Politburo. Its members received foreign dignitaries on national holidays. Also a Council of the Federation was to come into being, representing the republics. These two councils were consultative, with the President exercising executive power. Here was the separation of powers. There were major weaknesses, however. Ryzhkov was nervous lest the government be downgraded. Some of Gorbachev's advisers counselled him against getting involved in the management of the economy – a fatal error. No strong executive body was set up to implement the President's decisions. The Party was to stay out of state affairs. The soviets were still largely legislative bodies and had not yet taken on an executive role. A major oversight was the failure to establish a strong, independent judiciary. The constitutional commission gave little guidance as its judgments were like those of Solomon, finding for both sides. The eventual result was, in the absence of clear, central executive power, intermediate bodies, such as the republics and the rapidly growing mafia, stepping in to fill the vacuum.

. . .

BACK TO THE BALTIC

At the Congress, the Lithuanians attended as observers and did not vote for a President. They appealed to the Congress to smooth the way for independence negotiations. The Estonians, likewise, would not vote for a President and formally requested Gorbachev to begin negotiations on independence. He put his foot down. 'There can be no question of any negotiations with Lithuania, or with Estonia or Latvia.'[30] The Congress's riposte was to annul the Lithuanian Supreme Council's declaration of independence. Moscow encouraged the minorities in Lithuania to demonstrate for their rights and against secession. Glasnost went out of the window as the Moscow media only presented the centre's point of view.

On 23 March all diplomats were ordered out of Lithuania within 12 hours (the US had two monitoring events there) and journalists were informed that visits there would not be approved. The war of nerves had begun. The Americans encouraged dialogue but Landsbergis would only negotiate as a sovereign state and Moscow would only negotiate if the situation on the eve of the declaration of independence were restored. Whereas Washington had turned a blind eye to the killings in Baku, bloodletting in Lithuania would end developing cooperation between the superpowers.

The long-awaited law on secession was finally passed and signed by President Gorbachev on 3 April. The goal was to make secession such a long, complicated process that it would be practically constitutionally impossible. First there had to be a referendum, with a two-thirds majority, then negotiations would begin. The Congress of People's Deputies would then decide the length of the period of transition (it could be up to five years), and finally Congress would legislate to permit a republic to secede. Gorbachev was going to keep the empire together at any costs.

On 13 April, Good Friday, Gorbachev delivered his final ultimatum:

> If within two days, the Supreme Soviet and the Council of Ministers of the Lithuanian SSR do not revoke their aforementioned decisions, orders will be given to suspend delivery to the Lithuanian SSR from other Union republics of the type of production that is sold on the foreign market for foreign currency.[31]

The blockade began on 18 April. The first to be cut was oil, and natural gas deliveries were reduced 80 per cent. A long list of goods, including coffee and sugar, were not to be delivered and Gorbachev turned down a Lithuanian offer of hard currency for them. The man put in charge of seeing the economy through the crisis was Brazauskas. He was an excellent choice because he had contacts everywhere in the Soviet Union. Since Lithuania was a net exporter of food, there was no food crisis. What could have crippled the republic was the closing down of the atomic power station at Ignalina. Moscow did close it down for repairs but Brazauskas threatened to cut off electricity to Kaliningrad oblast, which received 60 per cent of its power from Ignalina, and the power station was soon back on stream. Most users in Kaliningrad oblast were military. The blockade was an embarrassment to President Bush who did not wish to act against Gorbachev. The latter thought that economic pressure and the never-ending military manoeuvres in the republic would bring the Lithuanians to heel.

167

Far from intimidating the Balts, Moscow's pressure on Lithuania had the opposite effect. On 30 March the Estonian Supreme Soviet, now dominated by the National Front in the recent elections, declared Soviet rule illegal from its inception and a 'period of transition' to the 'restoration of the prewar Republic of Estonia'.[32] On 19 April Gorbachev met delegations from Estonia and Latvia separately, hoping to dissuade them from following Lithuania's example. They were promised autonomy in a new federation. This was predictably unappealing and in late April Latvia declared its accession in 1940 invalid.

On 16 May Lithuania declared itself prepared 'temporarily' to suspend the actions which had flowed from its declaration of independence. Landsbergis and Prunskiene met Gorbachev and he indicated that he might accept a compromise. Whereas Prunskiene was willing to explore possible developments through negotiations, Landsbergis was unbending. Prunskiene was very critical of his 'uncompromising' stance.[33]

When Secretary of State James Baker visited Moscow in late May to prepare the ground for the Washington summit, Lithuania was high on the agenda. Baker, when meeting Shevardnadze, made the point that the legal status of the three Baltic republics was different from that of the rest of the Soviet Union. Shevardnadze retorted that the peoples of the Caucasus felt just as passionately about their enforced incorporation in the Soviet Union, as also did many in Central Asia. He made clear that, although Gorbachev and he sincerely wanted better relations with the United States, if it came to a choice between keeping the Union together and better relations with America, the former would take precedence. Civil war would immediately follow if just one republic were allowed to secede from the Union. Baker then met Kazimiera Prunskiene, whom he found a more skilled negotiator than Landsbergis, who was wont to restrict himself to slogans and set positions. Prunskiene wanted to know whether a Lithuanian suspension of its declaration of independence would indicate that it was submitting voluntarily to Soviet jurisdiction? Baker assured her that whatever the Lithuanians did, Washington would continue with its nonrecognition of the Baltic republics as part of the Soviet Union. The Soviets' need for a trade agreement with the US increased in proportion to the decline of their economy. Washington was able to use this to apply pressure for an end to economic sanctions. As part of the deal, the Americans had stated that they would not sign a trade treaty until Moscow passed a law allowing free emigration.

Gorbachev was threshing about in search of a way out of his Lithuanian morass, aware that Russia might pose a greater threat than Lithuania. Despite doing his best to scupper Yeltsin's chances of being elected chair of the Russian Federation's Supreme Soviet, Boris Nikolaevich became speaker, and thereby head of the republic, on 29 May. That was the day Gorbachev flew off for summit meetings in Canada and the United States. For the first time, Gorbachev's summitry had been overshadowed by domestic events.

At the summit (30 May–4 June) Bush had not yet made up his mind about signing the trade agreement. Shevardnadze was very despondent when he was told that Bush would probably not sign the deal. In the end Gorbachev persuaded Bush to sign but he had made two concessions. The Soviet Union was to pass a law on emigration and Gorbachev was to lift economic sanctions against Lithuania, before the trade bill went to Congress. The Lithuanian understanding was private and was not made public at the time.[34]

On 1 June Yeltsin met Landsbergis to discuss cooperation between the two governments and was critical of the blockade. Before going to Washington, Gorbachev had accused Yeltsin of wanting to break up the Soviet Union. At the summit he told George Bush that Yeltsin was a 'destroyer'. The Lithuanians were divided on how to deal with Moscow. Landsbergis wanted a tough stance but Prunskiene favoured concessions, even a limited retreat. She was aware of the horrendous economic cost the republic might have to pay for independence. Of the two men in Moscow, she wanted to negotiate with Gorbachev. Yeltsin was too much of a risk. On 12 June Landsbergis met Gorbachev and on 13 June Ryzhkov, and was promised an increase in natural gas supplies. The deadlock was broken by introducing the word moratorium. The declaration of independence would be suspended not annulled.

The Lithuanian Supreme Council accepted a 100-day moratorium on 29 June and Gorbachev immediately lifted the blockade. The whole episode had been an embarrassing defeat for Gorbachev and had exacerbated an already difficult economic situation. Lithuanian exports to other parts of the Soviet Union had also been suspended. Vadim Bakatin's explanation for the lack of flexibility in Gorbachev's handling of the problem was that the President 'received a false impression of a lack of mass support for the governments of Latvia, Lithuania and Estonia'.[35] There was also the unrelenting pressure from the conservatives and the military to force the Balts into line. Moscow and the Balts remained far apart. The centre wished to negotiate with the three republics on the basis of the law on secession and the new Union treaty. However, Vilnius, Riga and Tallinn argued that independence was already a fact and all they needed to do was to negotiate its implementation.

. . .

RUSSIA AWAKES

Elections to the Russian Federation (RSFSR) Congress of People's Deputies took place in March and April 1990, but the democrats, gathered under the umbrella of Democratic Russia (DemRossiya), were in the minority. This was partly due to their inability to agree among themselves. This had allowed the Party candidate, often a member of the apparatus or an enterprise director, to win in many constituencies, almost by default. Some of the democrats were members of both the Soviet and Russian parliaments. It transpired that 86.7 per cent of deputies were Party members. This was not as significant as it appears since almost all radicals, at that time, had remained in the Party. However, about a quarter of deputies were from Party, soviet and social organisations. Women were underrepresented: only 5.3 per cent of deputies were female. A striking factor was the level of education of deputies: 92.7 per cent had enjoyed further education.

Boris Yeltsin scored a spectacular victory in Moscow. Gorbachev states that he 'underestimated the phenomenon of the election of Yeltsin in Moscow and believed that this would not spread throughout Russia'.[36] The DemRossiya movement won majorities in Moscow, Leningrad, Sverdlovsk (Yeltsin's home base) and other major cities. When the Congress opened on 16 May, it became quickly evident that the democrats were in the minority, but counted for about 40 per cent.

The conservatives also had about 40 per cent. The key to success in the Congress would be the ability to win over the floating deputy. The vote for the chair or speaker of the Supreme Soviet would be crucial. Yeltsin had to attract votes from middle of the road communist deputies.

Gorbachev declared his hand and came out strongly in support of Aleksandr Vlasov, but he was a poor speaker and appeared to lack the dynamism for the job. Gorbachev feared the election of Yeltsin would increase confrontation between Russia and the Union. 'I already knew that this man was by nature a destroyer.'[37] On the first ballot, Yeltsin obtained more than Vlasov but short of a majority. Vlasov and some others withdrew for the second ballot and Yeltsin outpolled Ivan Polozkov, later to be the conservative leader of the Russian Communist Party. Again Yeltsin was short of a majority. Polozkov dropped out and Vlasov came back in. At the third time of asking, Yeltsin won with a wafer-thin majority. He immediately declared that he would not associate himself with any party or faction, but would represent all the peoples of the Russian Federation. This decision was to cause him problems later. Yeltsin was already eyeing a Russian presidency but that would require a two-thirds majority of all deputies to amend the Russian Constitution of 1978. This was quite out of the question in the summer of 1990.

Yeltsin's election as speaker of the Supreme Soviet, and therefore head of the Russian Federation, provided him, for the first time, with a political base independent of Gorbachev. Russia now could influence the evolution of the Union and even become the decisive factor. The republic, however, faced formidable problems in defining itself. Was Russia coterminous with the Soviet Union? On the other hand, was Russia simply the largest republic of the Soviet Union? This conflict between what became known as 'nation-builders', those who thought Russia was coterminous with the Russian Federation, and the 'empire-savers', those who believed that Russia was the Soviet Union, was to tear DemRossiya apart. Was Russia a nation state? Who were the Russians? After all, there were about 25 million living outside the Russian Federation. Russia had no separate Communist Party, the USSR Academy of Sciences supervised Russian scientific and intellectual life, the USSR Ministry of Culture administered Russian museums, theatres, etc. Whereas all other republics had the above institutions, Russia was administered by the Union. Some Russian economists thought that the Russian Federation, accounting for about three-quarters of the Soviet GDP, was being exploited by the other republics. If Russia could gain control of its economy, everyone would be better off.

It was inevitable that the question of sovereignty would come up. Already the Baltic republics and Azerbaijan had declared themselves sovereign. But what was sovereignty? According to article 76 of the Soviet Constitution a 'Union republic is a sovereign Soviet socialist state which has united with other Soviet republics in the Union of Soviet Socialist Republics'. Hence all republics were already sovereign. In reality, however, this had been cosmetic sovereignty. Now the republics wanted real sovereignty.

The most important decision taken by the new Russian parliament was the declaration of sovereignty on 12 June 1990. This placed Russian Federation law above that of the Union, and accelerated the war of laws. Russian institutions were to act in the interests of the republic and were not to be subordinate to Union institutions. Many communists voted for this declaration which began the process of unravelling the Union. Many of the same communists supported the abortive coup of August 1991 to keep the Union together. Clearly, they had not understood the implications of the declaration. Vladimir Kryuchkov, on reflection, however, was very clear in his own mind about the impact of the declaration. The 'decisive phase in the destruction of the Union began in the summer of 1990 after the RSFSR Congress of People's Deputies passed the Russian declaration of sovereignty and the primacy of Russian over Union laws'.[38] Gorbachev is also emphatic: 'I am certain that, had it not been for this fatal step, the Union could have been preserved'.[39] On the other hand, he concedes that 'some of the principles and provisions recorded in the declaration of state sovereignty of Russia could have formed the basis of a new Union Treaty'.[40] So what went wrong?

Gorbachev and Yeltsin held fundamentally opposing views on the new Union federation. Gorbachev wanted to strengthen central institutions and any residual power would then flow to the republics. He talked of a strong centre but the republics countered by proposing a strong centre and strong republics. Concerned about strong central institutions, he logically refused to countenance a federal Party and the passing of economic power to the republics. Yeltsin, on the other hand, favoured strong republics which would then decide among themselves which powers they were willing to delegate to the centre. Gorbachev's model saw him playing a decisive role in the life of the new federation. Yeltsin's model saw Gorbachev as a weak President, only able to act with the consent of the republics. Yeltsin was tilting towards a confederation, rather than a federation. The above picture only emerged over time and was not clear during the summer of 1990. Gorbachev was bitter about the 'parade of sovereignties' which he regarded as destructive. The 'sovereignisation' of Russia scuttled the 'search for a new formula for relations with the Baltic republics in a reformed Union'.[41]

However, every republic, logically, had to declare itself sovereign in order to participate as an equal partner in discussions about a new Union. Uzbekistan and Moldova declared sovereignty in June, Ukraine and Belarus in July, Turkmenistan, Armenia and Tajikistan in July, and Kazakhstan and Kyrgyzstan by late October. Hence by then all 15 republics had either declared sovereignty or independence. Autonomous republics within the Russian Federation followed. The Karelian autonomous republic declared sovereignty in August 1990, soon followed by nine other autonomous republics. Many also upgraded themselves from autonomous to full republics of the Soviet Union. They were seeking control over their natural resources, economic assets, the right to keep taxes and even the right to secede. The sovereignty fever did not stop there and affected autonomous oblasts, within a krai in the Russian Federation. Gorbachev's tragedy was that he could only see the negative side of the constitutional struggle, instead of grasping that it opened up a route to a new Union.

Gorbachev's reaction to the success of the democrats in the Russian elections was striking. Instead of welcoming them, he appeared to perceive them as a growing threat to his authority. Radicals put together a democratic platform for the upcoming 28th Party Congress. Just as elections of Congress delegates were beginning, *Pravda* carried a CC statement condemning the democratic platform and its sponsors.[42] It accused them of attempting to transform the Party into a 'shapeless association with total freedom for factions and groups'. Was it possible for such people to stay in the Party? It then instructed Party organisations to move against those who 'organise factional groups'. This was inviting organisations to purge the Party of radicals. This appeared an extraordinary thing to be doing just before a crucial Congress when Gorbachev would need all the support he could muster. Some, such as Yury Afanasev, immediately handed in their Party card. Others, such as Yeltsin, decided to wait and see.

Two other events also provided food for thought. Gorbachev chose Anatoly Lukyanov as his successor as speaker of the USSR Supreme Soviet, instead of a radical. Lukyanov, lukewarm about perestroika, was a dull speaker who came across poorly on television. He backed Aleksandr Vlasov as speaker of the Russian Supreme Soviet. Vlasov, vapid, monotonous and bereft of ideas, was turned down by communists who saw him as too weak to defend the interests of Russia. Had Gorbachev chosen a more dynamic candidate, he almost certainly would have won. By backing Vlasov, Gorbachev made it easier for Yeltsin to win. Was a trend emerging? Was Gorbachev more concerned about preventing the rise of the radicals, especially those with a popular following, who could challenge his authority, rather than the promotion of perestroika? Lukyanov and Vlasov lacked a public following, they were apparatus men. Was this the main reason for choosing them? Anyone with a hint of charisma was perceived as a potential threat.

With democrats talking about Russian sovereignty and even independence, it was only a matter of time before Party members increased pressure for a separate Russian Communist Party. 'Why should all the republics have their own Communist Parties and their own Central Committees, but not Russia?', became an oft repeated question at Party meetings. Egor Ligachev began to argue that the public mood favoured a separate Party. Gorbachev had attempted to head off the formation of a Communist Party of the Russian Federation, a Russian Party, at the December 1989 CC plenum. A Russian Bureau had been set up, chaired by himself, and including other senior officials such as Vitaly Vorotnikov, Aleksandr Vlasov, Russian Federation Prime Minister, Yury Prokofev, first secretary of Moscow gorkom, and Boris Gidaspov, first secretary of Leningrad obkom. All of these can be classified as conservatives. The Bureau, however, never made an impact, and Gorbachev blames himself for this. He simply lacked the time to devote much attention to a Russian Bureau.[43] This increased pressure for a separate Party, not least from the conservatives and those officials who had lost their position during the contraction of the CPSU central apparatus.

By the spring of 1990, over 65 per cent of Party members in the Russian Federation favoured a separate organisation.[44] Gorbachev felt uneasy about the Russian Party but allowed things to drift. The question arose about delegates to the conference of Russian communists, to convene on 19 June, two weeks ahead of the 28th Party Congress. Due to the lack of time for new elections, it was decided to empower delegates from the Russian Federation, who had been elected as delegates to the 28th Congress. Since Russian communists made up 62 per cent of the CPSU, it would be a dress rehearsal for the Congress. The conference immediately decided to transform itself into the founding Congress of the Russian Party. There was a conservative majority and this led to representatives of the democratic and Marxist platforms in the CPSU being given the opportunity to present their case. There was no danger that they would sway the Congress. The obkom first secretaries had coordinated their approach, behind Ivan Polozkov, first secretary of Krasnodar kraikom. Some of the criticisms were *ad hominem* remarks, targeted at the general secretary. The first secretary of Kemerovo obkom, Melnikov, with close links to Ligachev, complained that the Party leadership was living in a different world. Then the sting was in the tail:

> With the deliberate assistance of the general secretary's closest associates, we are bit by bit creeping into a new cult of individual personality . . . I am obliged, in the spirit of Party comradeship, to caution him and shield him in the name of our common cause and the great final purpose, from this disease, which unfortunately is chronic for us.[45]

Melnikov then revealed that the Kuzbass Party conference, on 1 June, had passed overwhelmingly a motion of no confidence in the CC and Politburo, and had demanded the resignation of all their members.

All was not yet lost. It all depended on who was elected first secretary of the Russian Party. Gorbachev thought of Valentin Kuptsov, a member of the CC Secretariat and Russian Bureau. There was also Oleg Shenin, who was later to join the attempted coup. But, of course, the leading candidate was Ivan Polozkov, an open opponent of perestroika. Gorbachev realised too late that Polozhkov was the leading contender and desperately tried to prevent his election. At 2 a.m. on the day the vote was taken, Gorbachev summoned Ivan Antonovich, deputy head of the CC's Academy of Social Sciences. The general secretary was so tired, the colour had drained from his face. Apparently he had not slept for days. He told Antonovich that everything possible had to be done to prevent Polozkov's election. But it was too late. His support train had gathered momentum and there was simply not enough time to prime a pro-reform candidate.[46] Gorbachev regarded Ligachev as the decisive force behind Polozkov's election.[47] The refusal of the delegates to elect Kuptsov, after he had been expressly endorsed by Gorbachev, was the first time a general secretary's will had been flouted since the removal of Khrushchev in October 1964. This was an ominous message on the eve of the 28th Congress. Kuptsov, however, was a poor choice by Gorbachev. In 1997 he is a leading member of the Communist Party of the Russian Federation. The election of Polozkov, a dry, monotonous bureaucrat, precipitated a rush out of Party ranks. There was even a bright side to the refusal of Party officials in the Russian Federation to face reality. It would move Gorbachev to break finally with the Party as a reform institution.

In June 1990 the American ambassador decided to pay a courtesy visit on Ruslan Khasbulatov, Yeltsin's chosen deputy as speaker of the Russian Supreme Soviet. The handsome Chechen, formidably fluent in Russian but the pitch of his voice revealing that he was not a native speaker, was known to be volatile. As befits someone who was deported to Central Asia in 1944, along with his family and nation, he could be rude and crude. Remarkably, he had clawed his way up the educational ladder and had graduated from the prestigious Plekhanov Institute of Economics in Moscow. His postgraduate work had been on the Canadian economy, where he was concerned about how an economy functioned in a federal state. When he met the ambassador he deployed all his native Chechen charm. What he said took the envoy's breath away. He informed him that Russia would soon be the successor state to the Soviet Union. The Union would resemble a loose confederation, which would not need a constitution, since it would not really be a state. There would be a short Union treaty because the Union would have few powers. Only republics would have the authority to tax, with an agreed amount being passed to the centre. Economic decision-making would, naturally, rest with the republics. Russia wanted to move in the direction of a market economy, privatisation would be a primary objective, but the central bureaucracy hampered this.

As regards foreign policy, Gorbachev could continue but Russia would require its representatives in Soviet embassies around the globe. It intended to conduct its own foreign economic relations. Eventually Soviet embassies would become Russian embassies, as Russia would be the successor state. Conventional military forces would be under the command of the republics; nuclear weapons, perhaps, under the centre. There would be a senate of ten representatives from each republic, at the centre, and it could rule. Russia was willing to assume the lion's share of Soviet hard currency debt, say, 75 per cent.[55]

This was an astonishing scenario, especially since Yeltsin lost no opportunity in public to swear allegiance to the federal or confederal goal. Here was his deputy telling the United States that Russia's aim was to be a successor state, with only a very loose relationship with the other ex-republics. Gorbachev, the President standing in their way, was to be destroyed. It is tempting to see Yeltsin pursuing a double-track policy from the summer of 1990 onwards: negotiating a new Union treaty but trying to break up the Union. Since the goal sketched by Khasbulatov was remarkably close to what actually did happen in December 1991, it was obviously his preferred option. Had it not been for the attempted coup in August 1991, this option might not have come to fruition. Presumably, there was another option, a half-way house, en route to the destruction of the Union. The above thinking had been fuelled by the frustration experienced at seeing Gorbachev refusing to move to a real market economy. The Baltic republics, Georgia and, possibly, Moldova wanted to take the same exit. The key to the future would be Ukraine.

If it chose the market and independence, the Union was doomed.

. . .

THE 28ᵀᴴ PARTY CONGRESS[48]

From Gorbachev's point of view the Congress of 2–14 July 1990 was a draw. No split, engineered by the conservatives, occurred and he was re-elected general secretary. His preferred candidate, Vladimir Ivashko, first secretary of the Communist Party of Ukraine, became deputy general secretary. Ligachev, who had mounted a determined battle to get the position, was defeated and sidelined. The reason why Gorbachev chose Ivashko was that as he himself was from Russia, he thought the number two should hail from Ukraine. This was not a very happy appointment. Ivashko made the cardinal error of leaving Kiev at a time when nationalism was on the rise. Leonid Kravchuk took full advantage of his absence. Ivashko went over to the plotters in August 1991.

The new 24-person (including one woman, G. V. Semenova) Politburo revealed it had been completely revamped. All those holding state offices, such as Shevardnadze and Ryzhkov, no longer qualified for election. Other lions of perestroika, such as Aleksandr Yakovlev, also departed. All first secretaries of republican Parties now qualified for membership (candidate membership was abolished), *ex officio*. Yury Prokofev, first secretary of Moscow gorkom, still made it. There were some CC secretaries as well. Many of the names in this motley body were unknown to the general public. Electing first secretaries of republican Parties ensured that it was, on balance, a conservative institution. Such a large body was unlikely to take any radical decisions and it became an elite Party club. Of course, one lost one's membership when one ceased to be a republican Party boss.

The general secretary did, however, commit some egregious mistakes. The worst one was to make Oleg Shenin the Politburo member responsible for supervising the CC organisational department, the body which services the Politburo. 'Because of some strange aberration of vision I took him to be a sincere advocate of reform. Perhaps this was due to his ability to mimic, to skilfully play the part of a progressive, an innovator, while remaining an incorrigible retrogradist at heart.'[49] Mikhail Sergeevich was always on the lookout for pro-perestroika talent to promote to the CC. He states that while moving back and forward from the Congress and the commissions, charged with drafting resolutions, he met 'many interesting people and added some to the central slate, thus advancing them into the leadership organs of the CPSU'.[50] This appears a remarkably haphazard way to select his new team! It also reveals the level of disorganisation which had set in by the summer of 1990.

During most of the Congress, the conservatives were angry. They were angry about the Soviet Union giving away eastern Europe, about approaching German unification, about kow-towing to the Americans, about the mess the country was in. There was a lot of *ad hominem* abuse for Gorbachev and Shevardnadze. Gorbachev skilfully managed the proceedings and eventually got his way. His old magic surfaced from time to time. One communist remarked that Mikhail Sergeevich was absolutely convinced that he could persuade anyone of anything. Perhaps this was a fault. He scored a resounding victory over Ligachev. He gave the floor to one delegate who wanted to speak against Ligachev holding the position of deputy secretary:

Mikhail Sergeevich, you need a young, energetic, sober minded assistant. Egor Kuzmich [Ligachev] is seventy years old, he has become irritable, and is no longer self-critical, and therefore it is better to send him into retirement, with ceremony, honour and respect.[51]

Whether by accident or design, the microphones were left on during a break in the Congress when Gorbachev, behind the scenes, was fixing the vote against Ligachev.

Yeltsin was nominated for the CC but stated that he did not wish to be considered since he was speaker of the Russian Supreme Soviet and the country was going over to a multi-party system. Gorbachev did not disguise his pleasure at seeing the back of Boris Nikolaevich. After all the elections were over and before delegates dispersed, Gorbachev engaged in an extempore monologue. It was Mikhail Sergeevich at his worst. He spoke for about half an hour and reduced the audience to puzzled silence. His peroration was like a poor university essay: no focus, no big idea, no clear analysis and no convincing conclusion. Then he decided to answer some written questions which had been placed on his desk. His old magic returned and it was Mikhail Sergee-vich at his best: sharp, witty, focused, humane, persuasive. Why did he perform like Jekyll and Hyde? In the first speech, he had no script and his old weakness, not completing his sentences, took over. In the second, he had a focus and was brilliant.

. . .

TOWARDS A MARKET ECONOMY

Utter confusion reigned on what constituted a market and how a market economy could be brought into being. Gorba-chev laboured under the disability of having a limited grasp of economics and no grasp of market economics. Often it was a dialogue of the deaf because the interlocutors under-stood market in quite differing senses. The function of gov-ernment in a market economy varies over time. Until the 1960s, Keynesian economics was very influential. John Maynard Keynes argued that leaving everything to market forces could lead to a downward spiral in demand and that unemploy-ment could remain at permanently high levels. The govern-ment could actively stimulate demand by spending money on public works and lowering interest rates. Then monetarism, guided by Milton Freedman, took over. This rejected manage-ment of demand by fiscal policy – stimulating demand by cutting taxes or increasing public spending to stimulate eco-nomic growth. It favoured the control of the money supply and thereby combating inflation was put top of the agenda.

Hence, when the Soviet Union began thinking about a market economy, monetarism was the dominant ideology. This was not very helpful in a country in which there were no money markets and commercial banking was only in its infancy. Industry was dominated by the military-industrial complex, in which many enterprises were monopolies. Was there to be a gradual movement to the market, through pro-gressive deregulation, or a jump into the economic deep end? Ryzhkov, and those who wanted to retain central con-trol, favoured the first option.[52] Yavlinsky, Shatalin, Gaidar and the other radicals promoted the second option. After all, they were monetarists and big bangers. Logically, they placed their faith in the unrestrained dynamism of the market. The big bangers bewitched Gorbachev with their talk of a vibrant Soviet economy in a relatively short time. Part of Mikhail Sergeevich's problem was that the language of monetary economics was English and hence he was bombarded with Russian equivalents, none of which were in common currency at the time. Arguably, had Keynesian thinking been the dominant economic fashion in the late 1980s, Gorbachev and the establishment might have found it easier to accept a market economy. There would then have been an important interventionist role for government to play. The big bang rejected state management of the economy.

The election of republican Supreme Soviets, and the government they empowered, increased demands by republics for control of their economic activities. Since they were legitimate governments, they could argue with more confidence that the centre should transfer responsibilities to them. In theory, the Baltic republics enjoyed economic autonomy, but in reality they did not. The Moscow ministries refused to cede any of their powers. The Balts quickly realised that autonomy only meant something in a market environment. They began going over to the market by initiating privatisation.

A major problem for the nomenklatura was property. They strongly opposed the private ownership of land. Since ownership of economic assets was a very contentious issue and could lead to civil war, it was best not to attempt privatisation. Here the nomenklatura can be divided into the ideological nomenklatura, those who had made their careers in the Party apparatus, such as Gorbachev, Ligachev and Yeltsin, and the economic nomenklatura, those who were managers of enterprises or collective and state farms, such as Ryzhkov. Gorbachev's reforms had almost destroyed the power of the ideological nomenklatura but had enhanced the power of the economic nomenklatura. They had filled the void left by the Party officials excluded now from economic management.[53] It was natural for Ryzhkov and enterprise managers and farm leaders to favour strong central control of the economy. Ryzhkov became associated with the regulated market economy – the economic nomenklatura did the regulating. However, he never defined what had to be regulated. In market economies natural monopolies, such as electricity and water, are regulated but a whole market economy cannot be regulated. Since the economic nomenklatura had no under-standing of a market economy, they found the arguments in favour of monetarism, controlling money supply and inflation and no direct government intervention, quite alien. Placing faith in such doctrines to ensure economic success must have sounded to them like twentieth-century witchcraft.

Ryzhkov, a dapper dresser, quiet spoken and resembling a top American executive, as head of government, had to compete with the Congress of People's Deputies. The unclear separation of powers in the Constitution made it difficult to locate the institution which was the final decision-maker. As regards legislation, the Congress of People's Deputies, the government and the President all passed decrees. Everyone accepted there should be retail price reform but no one, neither the Congress, nor the government, nor Gorbachev, was willing to suffer the opprobrium for introducing it. In May 1990 Ryzhkov took the extraordinary step of going on television and debating with the population the desirability of introducing retail price rises. Not surprisingly, all he achieved was the panic buying of everything of value. He cleared the shops in record time and thereby increased shortages. He was proposing higher prices in six months' time but everyone took this to mean tomorrow. If this was an example of Ryzhkov's grasp of the market, then it is not surprising that this handsome, well-meaning man reaped the whirlwind. Perhaps he was simply playing the populist. However, there was a member of the top team who was quite clear in his own mind about the impact of a market economy: Vladimir Kryuchkov. He told the 27th Party Congress, in July 1990, that it would be a 'ruinous mistake to throw the country into the arms of the elemental forces of the market'.[54]

The proposals of Ryzhkov and his government were un-satisfactory, the more so since the economy was in decline. Ryzhkov based his reforms on the experience of eastern Europe, especially Hungary. His approach can be referred to as rationalising economic reform. The essence of it is gradualism with the state determining prices. Terms such as a regulated market and a socialist market were used to give the impression that the market was being espoused. Unfortunately for Ryzhkov, Abalkin and other supporters of this type of reform, it had failed everywhere it was practised.

The government's clear failure to address the malaise of the economy predisposed Gorbachev to toy with the big bang. However, to all except academic economists, the market was a potential monster and simply frightened them. The economic nomenklatura buttonholed him every day with warnings that a market would bring chaos, even civil war. He took the usual course. If in doubt, set up a working group. It included Academicians Shatalin (chair) and Abalkin, Petrakov, Grigory Yavlinsky, Boris Fedorov, other economists, and representatives of the republican governments. They all gathered outside Moscow on 6 August and set to work. As a framework, they accepted a draft programme which Yavlinsky and others had been working on for months. It had been popularly dubbed the 500-day plan. Why 500 days? Think of a number between 1 and 10 and add two noughts! It was only of symbolic significance since no government can ever introduce a market economy in 18 months. By 21 August the draft Shatalin programme was ready. This group demonstrated that they understood the basics of a market economy. Privatisation was stressed, as was private property. Republics were to be responsible for the necessary legislation to promote economic activity on their territory. The centre was to look after all-Union property and those powers delegated by the republics. However, the group could not resist the temptation to make the package irresistible. They promised that the state would bear the cost of moving to the market and the average person would only receive benefits. The market would mean that everyone would live better straight away, not in the nebulous future. This, of course, was nonsense.

From Gorbachev's point of view, the Shatalin–Yavlinsky programme had several drawbacks. The major one was that the programme could have come from Mars. It did not analyse the reasons for the failure of perestroika over the previous few years and suggest the way ahead. The group had also found it impossible to work with the Ryzhkov–Abalkin government. Gorbachev then called a joint meeting of the Presidential Council and the Council of the Federation, plus many specialists and politicians.[56] The leaders of the republics were enthusiastically in favour, as it stripped the centre of its power to direct the economy. Privatisation would transfer almost all economic assets on their territory to them. On prices, the 500-day programme wanted to go over to free prices at the beginning of 1991, whereas the Ryzhkov–Abalkin proposal was to introduce gradual price reform.

The 500-day programme was a joint Soviet–Russian effort and Yeltsin stated that a common policy was being implemented. However, Russia knew it could not implement a pro-market policy on its own. An economic union, embracing all republics, was needed. The programme avoided a crucial question? Which institution was to implement it? Clearly this had to be the Soviet government. However, it would be a radically different government from the present one. Ryzhkov, of course, was furious and Gorbachev decided not to provoke a governmental crisis, against the advice of some of his closest advisers. Logically, Ryzhkov had to go but Gorbachev refused to face this problem at the time. He comforted himself with the thought that Ryzhkov was now in favour of a market economy. Here, as before, he was deluding himself.

The adoption of the programme was fudged as it was decided to encourage the two groups, the big bangers or monetarists, and the Ryzhkov–Abalkin team, to arrive at a consensus to present to the Supreme Soviet. Yeltsin made it quite clear that he did not favour this and that his government would proceed to implement the Shatalin–Yavlinsky programme. On 3 September the 500-day programme was distributed for discussion and this put pressure on Gorbachev. There was a wide gulf between the Shatalin–Yavlinsky programme and the Ryzhkov proposal. The former involved little state intervention but the latter was heavily interventionist. In the former the Union government would be weak, in the latter it would be a strong, central force. In the former, taxes would be collected locally and the republics would decide what amount would be forwarded to the centre. In the latter, the centre would impose federal taxes, collected by itself.

What role was to be played by the centre? It was inevitable that Gorbachev would choose a strong centre. Hence problems over political power sank the move to the Shatalin–Yavlinsky programme. Politics sabotaged economics. On 4 September Yeltsin informed a group of American senators and the US ambassador, that he would not accept any reconciliation of the two programmes. He thought the USSR Council of Ministers was beyond its sell-by date and should give way to a smaller Presidential Council. Russia and other republics wished to move ahead with economic reform and refused to be blocked by the central Soviet bureaucracy. Only functions such as defence, communications, energy distribution, rail and air transport were to be left with the central government.[57]

Gorbachev prevaricated and brought the two groups together on 4 September, under the direction of Abel Aganbegyan, to find a compromise. Yeltsin, graphically, called the proposal to merge the big bang and rationalising the command economy, akin to attempting to 'cross a hedgehog and a grass snake'. Even Chernyaev, a non-economist, thought that even a 'layman, at first glance, would recognise that the two programmes could not be merged'.[58] To begin with, Abalkin was reluctant to get involved and then Shatalin went off to the US for medical treatment. The big bangers had little to say about government but Abalkin and the rationalisers had. Abalkin favoured reorganising the government and the Presidential Council to embrace a greater range of economic and social interests. Vadim Medvedev and Valentin Pavlov, later to take over from Ryzhkov as Prime Minister, came up with the suggestion that all executive power should be concentrated in the hands of the President. The government would then play a minor role. Since Shatalin had absented himself, Gorbachev chose Abalkin to write the final draft. Predictably, it was almost a carbon copy of the government's programme. Since that would not do, Petrakov and Aganbegyan were then drawn into the redrafting and Gorbachev devoted over 40 hours of his time to it. When Aganbegyan was later challenged by economists about being associated with a document which was economically illiterate, his lame excuse was that he agreed with very little of the draft.

On 11 September the Russian Supreme Soviet adopted Yeltsin's motion to approve the Shatalin–Yavlinsky programme in principle. The vote was quite startling: 213 for and one against, with four abstentions. This meant that the communists, many of them belonging to the economic nomenklatura, had voted for the big bang. They clearly had only a vague grasp of what this meant. However, the reason they overwhelmingly endorsed the programme was, presumably, that it transferred control of the Russian economy to Russia. Then the debate about implementing a market economy could begin. The Russian Council of Ministers was to draft detailed proposals for implementation within a month. Opinion polls in Russia and the rest of the Soviet Union began to reveal majority support for a market economy. Again, it was clear that they had no grasp of monetarism.

Gorbachev wrung special powers out of a doubting Supreme Soviet in late September. Now he could issue decrees on and promote a market economy throughout the Union, if he so desired.

The economic nomenklatura closed ranks at the CC plenum, on 8–9 October, and savaged the big bangers. Institutional conflict also surfaced at the plenum. CC members wanted to know why they were discussing the economic reform, after it had been discussed in the Supreme Soviet. The attitudes of a significant number of deputies from the Party apparatus in the Supreme Soviet coincided with those in the CC. They had formed the Soyuz (union) group, basically conservative, and Anatoly Lukyanov, chair of the Supreme Soviet, sympathised with their views. CC members complained that Gorbachev had ceased consulting the Politburo and preferred his own apparatus, the Presidential Council, the Council of the Federation and direct contacts with Yeltsin. Ryzhkov, who had welcomed less Party interference in economic management, found that he had allies in the ideological Party nomenklatura, who were as opposed to the big bangers as he was. Together they were forming a band around Gorbachev.

Yeltsin kept up the pressure on the centre. In a biting speech in the Russian Supreme Soviet on 16 October, he promoted the 500-day programme and accused the Soviet parliament of attempting to limit the sovereignty of the republics, slowing down the transition to a market economy and preserving the command-administrative system. The leadership began to split wide open. Ryzhkov saw the reasons for economic decline in the weakness and indecisiveness of the centre. Yakovlev thought the trouble stemmed from slowness in moving to a market economy. There was also the problem of declining production and increasing social programmes, to compensate those who suffered most. This could only lead to raging inflation. A market economy would eventually come into being, not because it was willed from the centre, but because of the collapse of the command-administrative system. Russia carried on signing economic agreements with other republics and tried to wean away Union-controlled enterprises and farms. Unilaterally, Russia increased procurement prices for meat. This was partly in answer to increases in the Baltic republics which had resulted in meat moving north. There was, clearly, no longer such a phenomenon as the Soviet economy.

Andranik Migranyan, a noted publicist, caustically summed up the situation in September 1990:

> The President and the Supreme Soviet are attempting to marketise and democratise the Soviet Union, a state that no longer exists. The final collapse of the political centre means that there is little prospect of any reform programme being implemented by it ... What is falling apart is not just the empire, but the ideology which held it apart.[59]

Migranyan makes two profound points. First, in reality the Soviet Union no longer existed since power had flowed away from the centre. Second, the ideology, the glue which kept it together, had lost its cohesiveness. Take away the ideology and the legitimacy of the system went with it. The Constitution was very vague about the relationship of the centre and the republics. This was because the Party had overall power. The republics were experiencing power, and liking it. The centre would have to offer something very attractive to wean them back. Time was not on Gorbachev's side.

The inability of the Ryzhkov government to deal with the economic crisis and to agree on reform testifies to its weakness. Yury Semenov, USSR Minister of Power and Electrification in the government, concluded, in 1990, that the 'Ryzhkov government lacked the will and determination to take a tougher line before the onslaught of the Supreme Soviet and the President, who had already begun to hesitate, and had become scared'.[60]

. . .

GORBACHEV MOVES TO THE RIGHT

On 7 November, during the festivities marking the October Revolution, an incident occurred on Red Square which profoundly shocked Gorbachev. A man with a shotgun attempted to assassinate him and was prevented by guards who ensured that the bullets went harmlessly into the air. On 13 November when he met over 1,000 military personnel elected to various representative bodies, he was the butt of considerable hostility. They simply blamed him for all the ills of the country.

The Supreme Soviet, on 14 November, led by the Soyuz group, engaged in Gorbachev and government bashing and again accused him of sidelining parliament in favour of his own institutions. On 16 November Gorbachev addressed the deputies but was subjected to a torrent of abuse. Afterwards, several republican leaders, but not Yeltsin, urged him to strengthen presidential power. This was the only way to bring order to the very confused situation. On 17 November the Council of the Federation met to discuss Yeltsin's biting speech of 16 October. Ryzhkov was in a panic:

> No one listens to us. When we request someone, no one comes. Decrees are ignored. The country has gone off the rails. The whole mass media are against us and work for the opposition . . . Even the Party.[61]

Gorbachev, finally, came to the conclusion that Ryzhkov was yesterday's man.

On 18 November Gorbachev addressed the Supreme Soviet and laid before it eight points. They were vague and would need fleshing out. The message, however, was clear. Gorbachev was downgrading parliament and taking more executive power. The Presidential Council was to be dissolved and replaced by a National Security Council. There would be a Vice-President. A Cabinet of Ministers would replace the Council of Ministers. The Council of the Federation would become a consultative body for centre–republican relations.[62] Gorbachev told George Bush on 19 November: 'We are going to introduce important organisational changes. I mean the office of President, the presidential system, in which executive power will be directly subordinated to the President.'[63]

On 24 November the draft Union treaty was finally published, but of course it did not give the republics what they wanted. All the key issues were fudged. The draft spoke of joint control in many areas of policy but the republics suspected that this meant the centre would dominate the relationship. The two key republics were Russia and Ukraine. Yeltsin and the democrats found the draft unacceptable. In Kiev, Leonid Kravchuk, speaker of the Ukrainian Supreme Soviet, informed the American ambassador that Ukraine would not sign a treaty until it had adopted a new constitution, expected in mid-1991, at the earliest. There would also be a referendum, based on the new constitution.[64] Presumably the referendum would be about independence. Yeltsin then signed a bilateral agreement between Russia and Ukraine. Hence Russia and Ukraine were set on a course which aimed at the ending of the existing Union. It would be replaced with a loose confederation. Azerbaijan took the same line. Armenia and Georgia were eyeing independence and would then contemplate their relations with the other Union republics. Moldova might go the same way as Ukraine. The Baltic republics also desired to be free of Moscow's tutelage. That only left Belarus and the Central Asian republics. They would probably settle for a close association with the centre but wanted greater control over their natural resources and economic assets. The problem for Gorbachev was that these republics were among the least developed in the Union. Russia held the key. Whatever it decided would have a decisive influence on the future shape of the Union. Yeltsin's tactic was to keep negotiating, as was Kravchuk's, but never reach agreement. Khasbulatov's scenario of summer 1990 appeared to be becoming reality.

Relations between Gorbachev and the democrats from the Inter-Regional Group went from bad to worse after they published an appeal for action by Gorbachev on 16 November.[65] They wanted him to move to a market economy, give real sovereignty to republics, private land to farmers, the ending of Party influence over the military and local government, a new pro-reform government and a partnership between Gorbachev and Yeltsin. What infuriated Gorbachev most were calls by some of these deputies for him to resign if he did not wish to implement a market economy.[66] It appeared he was burning his bridges with the democrats.

He regarded them now as part of the opposition, not as potential allies.

From mid-November, Gorbachev gave greater rein to the right and warnings were issued that force might be used under certain circumstances. On 1 December Gorbachev replaced the democratically disposed Minister of the Interior, Vadim Bakatin, with Boris Pugo, a hard man from Latvia who had been KGB and Party leader there. Bakatin and Kryuchkov had clashed often over the right to demonstrate. The former believed that anyone had the right providing he or she stayed within the law. The latter was against all such manifestations. Bakatin had also refused to take orders from Party officials, arguing that the militia should defend the law and the state. Bakatin was not dropped into oblivion and was later appointed to the new Security Council. His sacking was a source of great satisfaction for a whole range of conservatives, from the Party to the military, where Colonels Viktor Alksnis and Nikolai Petrushenko had been making waves. General Boris Gromov, formerly commander-in-chief of the Soviet forces in Afghanistan, became first deputy Minister of the Interior. The stage was being set to use force to keep the Union together. Also on 1 December, Gorbachev signed a decree nullifying all legislation on defence and security by republican parliaments. Pugo quickly made clear that he would defend the existing Soviet Constitution. On 11 December Kryuchkov returned to one of his hobbyhorses: that all the trouble was emanating from abroad and all those seeking to weaken the Union were their agents.

On 17 December, at the opening of the 4th Congress of People's Deputies, a deputy rose to propose that the first item on the agenda should be a vote of no confidence in the President. Most of the 400 votes in favour, not enough to place it on the agenda, came from the Inter-Regional Group and the Soyuz faction. Yeltsin and most of the Russian democrats voted against. It was an ominous warning to Gorbachev. However, he did get the Congress to pass a motion calling for a referendum on a future Union, on 17 March 1991.

The confusion over the separation of powers, the urgent need to clarify the rights of the legislative and executive branches, dragged on during November and December. This paralysed initiative on the economic front, at a time when urgent action was needed. The government was going to be refashioned; eventually a Cabinet of Ministers, subordinate to the President, replaced the Council of Ministers, subordinate to parliament. Since Ryzhkov was almost certain to be rejected by the Council of the Federation, whose approval was now needed by the amended Constitution, a new Prime Minister had to be found. Ryzhkov's massive heart attack, on 25 December, added urgency. Eventually Gorbachev chose Valentin Pavlov, despite the fact that Pavlov had, as Minister of Finance since 1989, been responsible for a rapid increase in the money supply which, in turn, had fuelled inflation. He quickly acquired the sobriquet 'hedgehog-swine' because of his crew-cut and corpulence. Ryzhkov had warned Gorbachev that Pavlov liked a tipple. He was regarded as impulsive and easily swayed. He informed the American ambassador, on 11 January, that the ruble overhang – excess purchasing power – was about 25 billion rubles when every economist knew it was 100 billion or more. He then told the envoy that he had set the black market rate for the dollar. He was conceding that the Ministry of Finance was working the black market. The Ministry got about 40 rubles to the dollar, at a time when the official rate was 5 rubles 60 kopeks.[67] Pavlov regarded this trade as an excellent way of taking rubles out of circulation. Needless to say, trading in dollars on the black market was still a criminal offence.

Since Ryzhkov had recommended him, he was a state interventionist. Gorbachev let slip the opportunity to appoint a big banger. The Council of the Federation would have loved one, but the Supreme Soviet would have turned him down flat. Events were to prove that Pavlov was a disastrous choice. The new Prime Minister and his first deputies were approved by the Supreme Soviet on 14 January 1991. Within a few week other ministers had been approved. It was to be the first, and last, government to hold office that had been put together by the President and Council of the Federation and approved by the Supreme Soviet. Pavlov and his new cabinet had long been irritated by the results of the freedom of the press law. Gorbachev discussed with them the possibility of his suspending the press law.[68]

Why did Gorbachev surrender the initiative in the autumn of 1990 by declining to endorse the Shatalin–Yavlinsky programme? First of all, he lacked understanding of what a market economy entailed. It is based on private initiative, private property, with the state providing the framework for creative endeavour. This would have meant disfranchising the economic nomenklatura. The market would have meant that economic power, and hence political power, would have passed to the republics. Had Gorbachev sided with the big bangers, he would have abdicated power and played only a coordinating role at the centre. He loved power too much to agree voluntarily to such a course. Then there were the insistent calls for strong government from the conservatives, especially the colonels, a vociferous group of military men in the Congress of People's Deputies. They claimed that the market would precipitate the break up of the Union and civil war. Gorbachev hesitated, shuffled back and forth, prevaricated, tried to sail a middle course, and floundered. The main reason for his predicament was lack of clarity in his own mind about where the Union should be going. He seemed persuaded that he could find a middle way between the big bangers and the rationalisers. He simply refused to listen to those who told him there was no middle way. Either he had to go back to the command-administrative system or move forward to the market. His obstinacy cost him dear.

On 26 December Gennady Yanaev became Vice-President. Deputies were reluctant to endorse Gorbachev's choice but the President insisted: 'I want to have a person whom I trust completely at my side during this most difficult turning point in life'.[69] Time would reveal that he was a bad choice. However, he fitted into the new team that Gorbachev was fashioning. He had travelled the world as a Komsomol and trade union official, but had no public profile. He was of a nervous disposition and was a poor speaker. His conversation usually recounted the views of others. It is tempting to see him as another of Gorbachev's appointments who lacked charisma. As such they would not detract attention from the President. Another voice which was becoming more and more influential was Anatoly Lukyanov. As speaker of the Supreme Soviet, he appeared to be a major influence in the Soyuz group, dedicated to keeping the Union together, come what may. The concept of a neutral speaker was alien to him. Gorbachev trusted him. When Evgeny Primakov began to report on a meeting between Lukyanov and the Inter-Regional Group, Mikhail Sergeevich interrupted him: 'Wait until Lukyanov reports to me on this meeting. He always reports the truth.'[70]

With new advisers claiming Gorbachev's ear, old ones were dropped. The lion of perestroika, Aleksandr Yakovlev, was the most prominent. When the Presidential Council was dissolved, there was no place for him in the Security Council, set up in March 1991. He continued as an adviser, with an office in the Kremlin, but who was listening to him? He finally resigned in July 1991, when the Party's Central Control Commission began exclusion proceedings against him. Justifiably, he could feel aggrieved that Gorbachev had not protected him. Fans of the Shatalin–Yavlinsky programme were no longer in vogue.

The volatile, emotional Shevardnadze had had a very close relationship with Gorbachev but had been feeling exposed to criticism during the autumn. He felt that Gorbachev should have given him more backing. He was targeted as the comrade who had 'lost' eastern Europe, who had permitted the reunification of Germany, thus nullifying Soviet gains in 1945, who had conceded too much to the American imperialists, who had given in to the Americans and deserted Saddam Hussein, a Soviet ally, in the Gulf War, and so on. In 1990 Marshal Akhromeev had informed Yuly Vorontsov, Soviet permanent representative at the UN, that the military 'one day will hang him [Shevardnadze]' for submitting to the United States.[71] The military did have a point. Out of office, the American ambassador conceded that Washington had achieved '120 per cent of what it wanted in negotiations' with Shevardnadze.[72] Even Valentin Falin, a leading Soviet specialist on Germany, and then in the CC Secretariat, had savaged him over the terms of German reunification, knowing full well that the decision-maker had been Gorbachev.[73] Lukyanov, as speaker of parliament, lost no opportunity to present the foreign minister in the worst possible light. Shevardnadze knew how to be dramatic, when addressing the Congress of People's Deputies on 20 December 1990:

> Comrade democrats . . . you have run away. Reformers have taken cover. A dictatorship is coming. I am being completely responsible in stating this. No one knows what kind of dictatorship it will be and who will come or what the regime will be like.

I want to make the following statement: I am resigning . . . Let this be my contribution, if you like, my protest, against the onset of dictatorship.[74]

Gorbachev was embarrassed and annoyed at the resignation, the more so that he had not been advised of it beforehand. This was quite deliberate as Shevardnadze feared he might be obliged to change his mind once again if he told Gorbachev beforehand. There had been rumours for about a year that Shevardnadze would be moved to another responsible post but, given the lurch to the right by Gorbachev, he could only resign. Gorbachev had thought of Shevardnadze as Vice-President but that post was mainly decorative. Nevertheless, Gorbachev may have feared that a man of Shevardnadze's panache and charm could prove an embarrassment as his number two.

The growing influence of Evgeny Primakov also irked Shevardnadze. After visiting Saddam Hussein, Primakov flew to Washington to slow down war preparations against Iraq. Shevardnadze took pleasure from the fact that his advice to the Americans to cold-shoulder Primakov had been followed. A major reason for deciding to leave Gorbachev's team was his discovery in Houston, Texas, during a meeting with Baker that the Soviet military had been circumventing the terms of the CFE treaty. It was all the more embarrassing for Shevardnadze because he was unaware of the fudge. Among other things, the Soviets had moved over 16,000 tanks from eastern Europe east of the Urals (not covered by the treaty) to avoid having them destroyed. It was painful for Shevardnadze to have his ongoing conflict with the military exposed so blatantly. To the foreign minister's chagrin, Gorbachev defended the policy of the military in a speech to the Supreme Soviet. This may have been the last straw. Gorbachev was changing his arms policy, siding with the military and leaving Shevardnadze in the lurch.

Shevardnadze was also very concerned about the fact that Gorbachev was consorting with the instruments of coercion and, he believed, they would cast him aside in due course. He had no hard evidence of a plot. He sensed the coming violence and wanted no part of it. Shevardnadze's departure was a greater blow to Gorbachev than he realised. He was loyal and straight, as was Yakovlev. The President had lost two men who could tell him the truth. Their replacements were comrades of quite a different mould.

. . .

GERMANY BECOMES ONE

When West German President Richard von Weizsäcker visited Moscow in June 1987, he broached the question of German reunification very tactfully. Gorbachev made clear to him that the subject was something for the distant future, indeed it was 'premature and even harmful to raise the issue'.[75] Gorbachev's visit to east Berlin in October 1989 brought home to him the critical situation there. On 24 October 1989 Egon Krenz, the new Party general secretary, set in train a candid overview of the economic situation in the GDR. The report, submitted to the SED Politburo on 31 October 1989, made dismal reading. Labour productivity in the GDR was at least 40 per cent below that of the Federal Republic. The GDR was on the verge of financial collapse.[76]

On 1 November Krenz met Gorbachev in the Kremlin. The Soviet leader made clear to Krenz that he already knew the mess the east German economy was in. Krenz conceded that if east German living standards had to rely exclusively on east German economic performance, they 'would have to be cut immediately by 30 per cent. But such a move would be politically unacceptable.'[77] The Soviet Union could provide little aid, Gorbachev explained, since many Soviet republics which 'primarily supply raw materials were demanding a redistribution of national income from those republics where finished products were concentrated. They were threatening to cease raw material supplies if the proportions were not adjusted.'[78]

Since there was to be no Soviet economic aid, Krenz then asked Gorbachev to tell him frankly 'what place the Soviet union had set aside for the Federal Republic and the GDR in his all-European house'. Krenz pathetically pointed out that the GDR was the child of the Soviet Union, and 'paternity for the child had to be accepted'. Gorbachev explained that the Soviet Union was developing closer links with the

Federal Republic and the GDR, but the Federal Republic was 'expecting the Soviet Union to offer its support for unification'. He advised east Berlin to 'foster and constantly strengthen relations with the Federal Republic'. In other words, go cap in hand to Bonn, in the hope of getting credits which would halt the collapse of the GDR.

However, he told Krenz that German unification was not on the international agenda. The collapse of the Berlin Wall on 9 November 1989, however, accelerated events.[79] Chancellor Helmut Kohl, without consulting his foreign minister, Hans-Dietrich Genscher, the United States, Britain or France,[80] launched a ten-point programme for German unification. When Genscher visited Moscow in early December, the meeting was 'tense and unpleasant for both of us'.[81] Genscher was forced to defend a document with which he was ill at ease. When Hans Modrow, the new east German Prime Minister, visited Moscow on 30 January 1990, he did not hide the gravity of the situation: 'The majority of the people in the GDR no longer support the idea of two German states, and it seems that it is impossible to preserve the republic'.[82] This was not a surprise to Gorbachev as he and his advisers had reached a similar conclusion a few days earlier. The Soviet Union should take the initiative and set up a group of six, the four victorious powers and the two German states. However, this was the second best option. Gorbachev had tried and failed to convince the allies that a four-power grouping should decide. Washington insisted that Moscow deal directly with Bonn. Marshal Akhromeev should prepare the withdrawal of Soviet troops from the GDR.

When James Baker arrived in Moscow on 9 February, he was at pains to point out that 'neither the President nor I intend to derive any advantage from the developments'.[83] The following day, Gorbachev met Kohl and pleased him by saying that it was up to the Germans to decide things for themselves. Gorbachev favoured a neutral Germany but Kohl would have none of it. In February Bonn proposed a monetary union. Modrow learnt of it from the press! The Federal Republic had written off the GDR government and was courting the political parties, ahead of parliamentary elections in March. The Alliance for Germany, backed by Kohl's own CDU, won the elections. The new government, in April 1990, called for the unification of the country according to article 23 of the Federal Constitution. In other words, east Germany would be immediately swallowed up by west Germany. When Kohl arrived in Moscow in mid-July, he was very confident about what he wanted. He had struck up a warm relationship with Gorbachev, after an inauspicious start, and was much more demanding than his foreign minister, Genscher.

However, the achievement of German reunification, on 3 October 1990, owed even more to the man in the White House. Germany becoming one again can be regarded as the coincidence of three factors: the Gorbachev revolution in the Soviet Union, the collapse of the GDR economy which drove many east Germans west, and George Bush's determination to make German unity one of the crowing achievements of his presidency. Gorbachev gave him everything he wanted. On the issue of whether united Germany should be a member of NATO, pressure by Bush and Baker eventually resulted in Gorbachev conceding the point, orally, to the consternation of his officials. In his memoirs, he claims that the idea to allow Germans to decide their own security arrangements – it was a foregone conclusion they would go for NATO – originated with him, and not with Bush. He claims he made it at a meeting with Bush in May 1990. The White House sees it the other way round.

One of the reasons for acceptance by Moscow of a united Germany in NATO was Gorbachev's close understanding with Kohl. A graphic example of this was the meeting at Archys, in the north Caucasus, in July 1990. Here, in formal and informal meetings, the two leaders agreed many of the details of unification.[84] Without informing Shevardnadze, who had done all the spade work on Soviet–German relations, Gorbachev abandoned all claims as an occupying power and any restrictions on German sovereignty, including the future Germany's right to be a member of NATO. Shevardnadze knew that the ire of the military and the conservatives at the 'loss' of the GDR would descend on his head. Gorbachev also failed to discuss German unification in the Politburo. Forgetting his domestic travails for a moment, Mikhail Sergeevich could comfort himself with the thought, that as a co-father of German unification, he would always be immensely popular in Germany.

. . .

MURDER IN VILNIUS[85]

When the Lithuanian government met Gorbachev in October 1990, they sensed that the climate had cooled. In November, on Soviet television, members of the pro-Moscow Party claimed that the Lithuanian government had drawn up a list of Party members who were to be executed. For understandable reasons, they did not have the original copy of this document. In December this black propaganda led to the claim that Lithuania was claiming the territory of other republics. Gorbachev's close relationship with Bush and Kohl frustrated Lithuanian attempts to break out of their international isolation. In November Colonel Viktor Alksnis, known as the black colonel because he liked wearing that colour, gave Gorbachev 30 days to restore order. 'I do not want this to sound like a threat to you, but this will simply be achieved.' He wanted committees of national salvation to save the Soviet Union as a 'united and indivisible state'.[86]

On 7 January 1991 Soviet paratroops entered all three Baltic republics, ostensibly to search for deserters and draft dodgers. The Lithuanian government had increased food prices sharply and this was causing considerable tension. On 8 January Prime Minister Kazimiera Prunskiene left for Moscow to discuss the troop movements. On 7 January a demonstration against price rises by over 5,000 members of Edinstvo,[87] the Russian nationalist movement, called on the government to resign. They began breaking down the door to the Supreme Council building, broke windows but were repelled by fire hoses. The deputies hastily rescinded the price rises. Landsbergis called on all Lithuanians to protect the republic. When they poured into parliament, they pushed out the Russians. Gorbachev would not discuss troop movements with Prunskiene but instead told her, 'Go back and take care of the situation and restore order, so that I do not have to do it myself'.[88] When she got back to Vilnius, she found that parliament had amended the Constitution so that now only a simple majority was enough to remove her. Landsbergis, the nationalist, had finally prevailed in his long campaign against the liberal, flexible Prime Minister. She resigned without attempting to defend herself. Also on 7 January, Burokevicius, boss of the pro-Moscow party, met several

top officials, including Kryuchkov, Pugo and Yazov. Burokevicius argued that the time was ripe for the introduction of
presidential rule in his republic. Colonel General Achalov,
deputy Minister of Defence, and Yazov's top man for emergency situations, was sent to Lithuania with his men.
On 8 January Edinstvo called for a demonstration at 16.00
hours, the following day. At noon, Soviet personnel carriers
entered the area where the demonstration was to take place,
and parked. During the afternoon Soviet paratroops landed
at Vilnius airport. A Lithuanian counter-demonstration
gathered nearby, in front of parliament, only separated by
Lithuanian militiamen. When the Russian Orthodox arch-
bishop, in Vilnius, appealed to the Russians to avoid violence,
they dispersed. The military left as well.

At 14.30 on 10 January, a telegram from Gorbachev arrived,
stating that he had received appeals from 'public organisations, industrial collectives and persons of all nationalities'
for the introduction of presidential rule. The Lithuanian
parliament would be responsible for everything that was to
follow if did not 'immediately restore the USSR Constitution
and the Constitution of the Lithuanian SSR, in their entirety,
and revoke the unconstitutional acts adopted previously'.[89]
On radio, the deputy speaker of parliament declared that
the hour of decision was approaching. It was either independence or eternal slavery.

Moscow began to act without waiting for a reply to the
Gorbachev ultimatum. During the evening, Vilnius airport was
closed by a Russian strike. Troops and vehicles moved around
the city during the night. Rival demonstrations gathered
during the morning of 11 January. The first blood flowed at
noon when the military attacked the Press House. Seven persons were taken to hospital, two of whom had been shot.
Those inside had expected Russian workers and were only
armed with fire hoses. The violence led to the Russian demonstrators melting away and they did not return to protest
against the Lithuanian government. Lithuanians gathered
in front of the Press House to see and argue with the tank
crews and soldiers. Others went off to the television tower.
Eventually about 5,000 formed a ring around the tower.
Landsbergis tried twice to contact Gorbachev by telephone
but was told he was unavailable, he was eating. During the
afternoon, the pro-Moscow Party announced the formation

of the Lithuanian committee for national salvation, which, in turn, stated it was assuming 'all power in Lithuania'. Some 65 members of Kryuchkov's crack Alpha unit[90] arrived at Vilnius airport at 23.00.

On 12 January the Council of the Federation, in Moscow, decided to send three persons to assist in resolving the crisis by political means. Soviet military officials denied they were planning to use force. Things appeared to be returning to normal. Strangely, the Federation delegation did not travel directly to Vilnius but flew to Minsk for an overnight stay. At 01.00 on Sunday 13 January, tanks rolled through Vilnius. The Alpha unit was to take the radio and television centre and the television tower.

At 01.47 Landsbergis appeared on television and said if blood flowed it would be on Gorbachev's hands. He had again tried to phone him, this time he was sleeping. Soviet troops attacked, led by the Alpha unit, and by 14.20 had taken the radio and television centre, and television tower. The radio announced that the committee for the salvation of Lithuania had taken power. An attack on parliament was expected but never came, to the relief of the deputies inside and the huge number of demonstrators outside. The violence had left 13 dead, and 165 injured, of whom 26 were seriously hurt. The citizens were informed that the committee was in power and that a commandant was in charge of the city. Presumably, the next step would be the proclamation of presidential rule.

The Federation delegation finally arrived. The world quickly learned of the violence, it had been recorded by television cameras. Yeltsin immediately flew to Tallinn[91] to meet the leaders of the three Baltic republics. He called on Russian (RSFSR) troops not to obey orders to act against 'legally established state bodies, and the peaceful civilian population which is defending its democratic achievements'. This, in short, was a call to mutiny. He joined Baltic Presidents in an appeal to the United Nations. Then Yeltsin signed an agreement, by which Russia recognised the sovereignty of the Baltic republics and agreed to develop relations according to international law, or in other words as sovereign states, not as Soviet republics. Yeltsin was aware that had the attack in Vilnius succeeded, the next major target would have been Russia and himself. He was attempting to bring home to

Russian (RSFSR) officers and men that their first loyalty was to him, not to President Gorbachev.

A member of the Federation delegation, Levon Ter-Petrosyan, later President of Armenia, openly criticised the Soviet government's unconstitutional acts in Lithuania. The delegation moved to parliament and managed to arrange a deal. The government would call on the demonstrators to go home and the military would take its patrols off the streets. Kryuchkov did not give up. He recalled a Lithuanian diplomat from Mozambique, a former Lithuanian Prime Minister, and he arrived in Moscow on 12 January. The next day, Kryuchkov, Oleg Shenin and Yury Maslyukov offered him the post of Lithuanian Prime Minister in a government serving under presidential rule. Yazov also supported this move. The diplomat flew secretly to Vilnius, apprised the situation, and on his return to Moscow told Kryuchkov and company that he wished to return to Mozambique.

The whole operation was a disaster. The failure to take parliament, presumably because of the presence of a large foreign press contingent and so many unarmed civilians who were willing to die in its defence, was of crucial importance. No new government could be installed until it had been occupied. In a statement to foreign ambassadors on the afternoon of 13 January, Gorbachev stated he did not know who had given the order to attack the television tower. This remarkable admission implied that he had lost control of his security forces. If this were true, would he condemn the action and call for the perpetrators to be brought to justice? He never condemned the violence, except to state that it had been provoked by the Lithuanians. On 14 January, addressing the Supreme Soviet, he stated that the first he knew of the operation was at 03.00 hours on 13 January, i.e. after the television tower had been taken. Yazov maintained that the city commandant had sanctioned the use of force. Krychkov told Gorbachev that neither he nor Yazov had 'ordered the use of force'.[92] Ter-Petrosyan reasoned that Gorbachev went along with the conservatives, sent the telegram, and then, realising it was going to fail, pulled out. Another explanation would be that Gorbachev, in sending the telegram on 10 January, further prepared the ground for the crackdown. Did he not realise that it would probably lead to bloodshed? Yakovlev and others advised Gorbachev that the optimal course would be for him to go to Vilnius, meet Landsbergis, and condemn the murders. He did not heed their counsel.

As is usual, the various agencies began to blame one another. The Party blamed the clumsy military for falling into Landsbergis's trap. Later, Gorbachev ridiculed the idea that the city commandant had acted on his own. The orders must have come from the Ministry of Defence and the General Staff. Why did the military not attack the Russian parliament in August 1991? Because they had 'learned a lesson' in Vilnius, concluded Gorbachev.[93] The Alpha unit commander, in explaining why his unit had not attacked the White House in August 1991, later stated: 'Vilnius was the last straw and our patience ran out . . . Honestly, had it not been for Vilnius we would not have refused to storm the White House.'[94]

A journalist compared the Soviet Union to a dying octopus, blindly milling around, unaware that its tentacles were being cut off, one by one.[95] Further embarrassment was heaped on Gorbachev at the funerals of the victims, in Vilnius. The Russian Orthodox metropolitan, in Lithuania, expressed shame, as a Russian, for the crimes committed by Russians and stated that the Moscow media had distorted the events. He concluded by declaring: 'Lithuania will be free'.[96] This demonstrated that not all Russians in Lithuania supported the activities of the pro-Moscow committee.[97]

When the Alpha unit left Vilnius on 13 January, it moved to Riga. The same day, a Latvian Party CC plenum backed workers' demands for the dissolution of the Supreme Soviet and all local soviets in Latvia, to dismiss the government and hold new elections. An All-Latvian committee of national salvation, headed by Alfreds Rubiks, the Party boss, was ready to assume power if this ultimatum were not heeded. On 20 January OMON troops[98] attacked the Latvian Ministry of Internal Affairs building, killing four persons. They then withdrew. When Ivars Godmanis, Latvian Prime Minister, telephoned Boris Pugo, the latter claimed that he had not authorised the attack. This turned out to be true. An OMON officer had acted on his own initiative.[99]

The tragedies of Vilnius and Riga were body blows to Gorbachev's legitimacy. He was fortunate that the US and NATO were involved in the Gulf War and needed him on their side. President Bush had telephoned him on 11 January expressing US concern. The west did not react to Landsbergis's appeals for recognition The bloodshed increased the determination of the Balts to break free. Some in the rest of the Soviet Union began wondering if keeping them in the Union against their will was worth the candle. Even Kryuchkov appeared to be having second thoughts. 'Nobody is against Lithuania's right to withdraw from the Soviet Union if the republic's population deems it necessary.'[100] However, they had to hold a referendum first. Gorbachev had, in turn, deployed persuasion and violence. Both had failed. His Baltic policy was now bankrupt.

Another example of Gorbachev's policy hampering rather than helping to defuse ethnic tension was Georgia. Growing tension in South Ossetia led to some of their leaders talking of union with North Ossetia, in the Russian Federation. Eventually President Zviad Gamsakhurdia sent in the Georgian army. On 7 January Gorbachev ordered the Georgian army to withdraw under pain of Soviet military intervention. This simply exacerbated the situation, especially as no Moscow troops were ever dispatched. Gorbachev may have been listening to the hard men around him who were encouraging him to assert his authority. However, in issuing threats on which he did not act, he was undermining his own authority.

. . .

DISILLUSIONMENT AND STABILISATION

The high hopes of the democrats, in autumn 1990, for a Gorbachev–Yeltsin coalition to push for democracy and a market economy, were dashed, among bitter recriminations, in January 1991. DemRossiya, like a spurned lover, lashed Gorbachev as the man who had become a dictator. It feared the victorious march of the conservative nomenklatura. The most savage criticism, however, came from rejected big bangers. Stanislav Shatalin expressed his dismay and made it known that he no longer considered himself a member of the Gorbachev team. On 19 January it was Nikolai Petrakov who came out with the vitriol:

A regime in its death throes has made a last-ditch stand: economic reform has been blocked, censorship of the media reinstated, brazen demagogy revived, and an open war on the republics declared ... The events in Lithuania can be classified unambiguously as criminal ... While opposing the onslaught of dictatorship and totalitarianism, we are pinning our hopes on the leadership of the Union republics.[101]

Among others who signed the Petrakov broadside were Popov, Yury Ryzhkov (later Russian ambassador to Paris), Shatalin and Zaslavskaya. On 20 January a huge demonstration in Moscow called on Gorbachev, Yazov and Pugo to resign, for the withdrawal of Soviet troops from Lithuania and the trial of those responsible for the use of force in Lithuania. Yeltsin did not attend but sent a message. One of those who did not leave Gorbachev's team at this time was Anatoly Chernyaev. The Vilnius events had deeply affected him, the more so since Gorbachev did not appear to appreciate the damage they were doing his cause. He penned a bitter, reproachful letter of resignation.[102] In it, he told Gorbachev to listen to the millions of ordinary people, not the views of those selected by his aides. He made a telling point. A key element of the new political thinking had now been lost: trust. 'Now no one will trust you, irrespective of what you did in the past.' The letter was typed up by his assistant, who strongly opposed his decision to resign. She locked it away for a week and by then Chernyaev had come round to her way of thinking.[103] He decided to stay in Gorbachev's team.

Pavlov came up with a stabilisation programme which contained sensible elements but could not be implemented in the political climate of 1991. In order for harsh stabilisation measures to be accepted and implemented, the population had to be convinced of their need and, more importantly, their success. Pavlov's standing was not high. He had earlier imposed a 5 per cent value added tax on retail sales, in an attempt to increase revenue and reduce the ruble overhang. It was, predictably, extremely unpopular at a time of declining living standards. Pressure from various lobbies ensured that certain interest groups were compensated for the tax and it was not a success.

His first major policy initiative as Prime Minister was to attack the ruble overhang problem. He decreed that all 50 and 100 ruble notes had to be exchanged for new ones.

Only a certain quantity could be exchanged. Since many savings were kept in the proverbial mattresses, this caused consternation among the public. Pavlov was restricting money supply at the people's expense. He put it about that the reform was aimed at eliminating the profits of the black marketeers. Of course, the wide boys had heard of the reform and had exchanged their money beforehand. It was also quite easy to bribe bank officials. Since the first explanation met with popular disbelief, Pavlov reached into his bag of tricks and came up with another, even more far-fetched explanation. The reform had been to thwart the plans of Swiss, Austrian and Canadian banks (he judged it politic not to accuse US banks) to cause chaos by flooding the Soviet market with 8 billion rubles. When the exchange rate plummeted, the banks could buy up large amounts of Soviet assets on the cheap.[104] If his reputation among western economists was low before this gaffe, it was now at derision level. The US Department pointed out that Pavlov had printed more rubles than that held by western banks. Even the KGB stated it had no knowledge of such a plot.

Despite the currency fiascos, Pavlov did have a recognisable stabilisation programme. Economic resources were to be concentrated in the state's hands and technological breakthroughs achieved on that basis. Capital goods production should again have priority over consumer goods. The cooperative sector was relegated to a minor role. He did not mince his words. The economy was on the brink of collapse and, if the stabilisation programme were not implemented, the situation would be reminiscent of the worst days of war communism. At long last, a Prime Minister grasped the nettle of wholesale and retail price reform. Once again, however, interest groups were so powerful that he had to compensate them. Enterprises, for example, were permitted to dip into development funds to reimburse workers for the price rises. This surely was the road to ruin. Gorbachev also signed a decree permitting direct interference by the Ministry of Internal Affairs and the KGB in the economic affairs of enterprises (including joint ventures) throughout the Union. This reduced interest in foreign direct investment and also trade with the Soviet Union.

The most serious challenge to Pavlov's stabilisation programme came from the miners. As elsewhere in industry, living and working conditions had been declining. They wanted rapid improvements in both. However, stabilisation implied attempting to balance the budget. The 1991 budget envisaged revenues of 55 billion rubles in the first quarter. Actual revenue was 19.9 billion rubles and expenditure 47 billion. The republics were simply failing to transfer federal taxes to the centre. Republics, such as Russia, were already running large budget deficits themselves. The price of beef had risen from 2 to 7 rubles a kilo, that of pork from 1 ruble 90 kopeks to 5 rubles 30 kopeks, and children's clothes were up to five times more expensive.

A warning strike was called for 1 March in Ukraine, mainly in the Donbass, with a mixed menu of political and economic demands. Karaganda miners in Kazakhstan joined in. Strikes in the Kuzbass, in west Siberia, and Vorkuta, in the Arctic north, had been gathering momentum. By mid-March about one-third of the pits were out and a half by 1 April. Pavlov tried to act the strong man and threatened to prosecute the strikers. However, at the end of March the Soviet authorities began to negotiate with miners' representatives.

The event which led to the resolution of the conflict was the signing of the Nine Plus One accord. Yeltsin arrived in the Kuzbass and on 1 May 1991 signed an agreement transferring all Russian mines to Russian jurisdiction and promising them economic independence.[105] The large pay rises demanded were not conceded, except in Kazakhstan. The miners' attempt to remove Gorbachev had failed because Yeltsin was not interested in causing chaos at the top of the Soviet establishment. Russian miners resolved, politically, to support Yeltsin and accept his promise of a better future. The attempt by the miners to extend their strike into a national strike also failed. However, the strike had demonstrated that the Soviet government had little legitimacy and that, in Russia, only Yeltsin could negotiate a deal.

In order to put pressure on the republics, Gorbachev came up with the idea of a referendum on the future of the Union. The Congress of People's Deputies approved it in December 1990, but Gorbachev ignored advice that he was blundering into a minefield. He had to frame the question in such a way as to make it almost impossible to say no. The best way to do this was to make it extremely complex and insert some sweeteners: 'Do you think it essential to preserve the Union of Soviet Socialist Republics as a renewed federation of equal sovereign republics, in which human rights and liberties will be fully guaranteed for all nationalities?'. This begged several questions. The nature of the renewed federation had not yet been agreed. By using the word republics and not states, did this imply it would not be a confederation? What did sovereignty entail? The experience of Lithuania boded ill for guarantees of human rights and liberties. When it came to be held on 17 March, it was predictable that several republics would refuse to hold it. These were the three Baltic republics, and then Georgia, Armenia and Moldova. In Kazakhstan a different question was posed: 'Do you think it essential to preserve the Union of Soviet Socialist Republics as a Union of equal sovereign states?'. There was no mention of a renewed federation and rights and liberties had vanished. Significantly, states had replaced republics. In Ukraine, an additional question was posed: 'Should Ukraine be a member of a Union of sovereign states?'. However, the biggest winner was the Russian Federation. The Russian parliament had consistently refused to amend the Russian Constitution to permit the election of an executive President. Russians were invited to answer an additional question: 'Are you in favour of a directly elected executive President?'.

Gorbachev campaigned vigorously for his referendum and Yeltsin, in Russia, for his. Gorbachev got his vote, 76 per cent were in favour of the Union. But which Union? In Russia, 71 per cent of voters were in favour, but, more importantly, almost as many for a President. The Baltic republics held their own referenda on independence and obtained majorities. For instance, in Lithuania, 94 per cent voted for independence. The Georgian Supreme Soviet, on 9 April, voted for the restoration of state sovereignty and independence. When Armenia voted in September, the outcome was a foregone conclusion.

The referendum had backfired. It made negotiating a Union treaty more difficult but it also catapulted Yeltsin forward in his race with Gorbachev. The Russian leader had called for Gorbachev to resign on 19 February, on national television, and the Russian intelligentsia was switching from Gorbachev to Yeltsin. Gorbachev, in Minsk, on 27 February, revealed how rattled he was. He accused democrats of using neo-Bolshevik tactics – demonstrations and strikes – to de-stabilise the government and prepare the ground for a seizure of power. Did Gorbachev seriously believe that democrats were planning a coup? Surely this flew in the face of all the norms of democratic politics? Again, he was having difficulty in distinguishing between legitimate, democratic opposition and the politics of the conservatives, which aimed at restoring order and central power. As before he was extremely sensitive to criticism, taking it all *ad hominem*. He regarded the strictures of his former allies as tantamount to betrayal. He did not appear to perceive that his policies were at fault.

When Gorbachev saw James Baker in Moscow in mid-March, he mentioned that he had received a report from one of Yeltsin's associates. This stated that Yeltsin had enquired of the US ambassador what American reaction would be if he came to power by unconstitutional means. The ambassador explained to Mikhail Sergeevich that the report was a fabrication.[106] How could Yeltsin come to power with Kryuchkov still head of the KGB and Yazov head of the military? Gorbachev accepted the denial but it revealed that the KGB was fabricating evidence against Yeltsin and feeding it to Gorbachev. Presumably, it was doing the same on a range of other issues. Was Gorbachev's faith in KGB reporting the reason for his attack on democrats and the extraordinary claim that they were thinking of a coup? Mikhail Sergeevich could not claim that he had one-sided information. He just did not believe what his critics said.

Serious tension was emerging between central and local authorities. An example of this was Gorbachev's decree of 29 January 1991, introducing joint military and militia patrols, as of 1 February. Local authorities opposed it since they had not requested it, but it was imposed over their opposition. It raised the important question: who was responsible for law and order in a community, the centre or the local community? In Russia, it was seen as an attempt to impose the will of the centre and restrict Russian power. The patrols had little effect and the constitutional committee criticised the decree as defective. Another, more menacing example was the demonstration in Moscow on 28 March, called by democrats in support of Yeltsin.

The Russian Congress of People's Deputies was due that day to review Yeltsin's competence as speaker. The Moscow authorities permitted the demonstration. Gorbachev reacted by issuing a decree subordinating the city of Moscow and Moscow oblast militia to the Ministry of Internal Affairs and also brought troops into Moscow to help the police protect the centre of the city. Evidently, the KGB had fabricated a report, claiming that the democrats were going to attempt to take the Kremlin by storm. Protests by the Russian government and the Moscow city authorities were to no avail. Most deputies were angry at Gorbachev's attempt to dictate to Russian authorities and voted to annul the President's decree and demand the withdrawal of the troops. When Gorbachev stated they would remain until the morrow, the Congress voted to suspend business until the following day. The demonstration was held on 28 March and there was no violence. If Gorbachev's aim had been to cow the Russian parliament and weaken Yeltsin, it had the opposite effect. Many communists voted for Yeltsin because they saw Gorbachev's action as an attempt to weaken Russia.

Things began to turn in Yeltsin's favour at the Congress. Aleksandr Rutskoi, an Afghan veteran, and later to be Yeltsin's Vice-President, formed the communists for democracy faction and brought these communists into Yeltsin's camp. Yeltsin asked parliament to grant him the extraordinary powers in the Russian Federation which Gorbachev had been given in the Soviet Union. He achieved this objective on 4 April and also his biggest prize: a date was set for presidential elections, 12 June. He then attended the Easter service, conducted by the Patriarch Aleksi II. This was a powerful symbol of the reconciliation of temporal and spiritual power in Russia.[107]

Gorbachev's desperate need for republican support for measures to stabilise the economy forced him to make concessions to achieve a new Union treaty. Without such agreement, there would be no viable all-Union economic policy. Nine republican leaders (the three Baltic republics, Armenia, Georgia and Moldova were not represented) and Gorbachev met on 23 April, at a government dacha at Novo-Ogarevo, outside Moscow, to thresh out final details. Previous drafts of the treaty had proved unacceptable to most republics because of two main problems. First, was the new formation to be a Union of sovereign republics or a Union of sovereign states? The former, favoured by Gorbachev, presaged a federation; the latter, a looser grouping, presaged a confederation, desired by most republics. The second problem was the question of economic power. Were most Union assets to be under the control or joint control of the centre? The republics wanted economic assets and decision-making to flow to them. Gorbachev wanted heavy state intervention from the centre. A major reason for Gorbachev's reluctance to concede economic decision-making to the republics was that the military-industrial complex would be the great loser. It was unlikely that the republics would allocate much budget revenue to the defence sector.

The big players in the Union stakes began to coordinate their approach to the Union treaty. On 18 April Russia, Ukraine, Belarus, Kazakhstan and Uzbekistan convened in Kiev to agree on a common position. They also rejected Gorbachev's suggestion that the autonomous republics, most of which were in the Russian Federation, such as Tatarstan and Sakha-Yakutia, be given Union republican status. Mikhail Sergeevich had come up with this ploy in an attempt to outbid Yeltsin for the loyalty of these regions. The agreement reached on 23 April offered the hope that a final deal could be struck. Gorbachev began calling it the One Plus Nine agreement but the republics quickly insisted it become known as the Nine Plus One agreement. Those which signed the treaty would be in a special position. This implied that those which declined to do so would, *de facto*, have seceded and would have to negotiate an agreement with the new Union.

The draft treaty signalled a U-turn by Gorbachev. He was now returning to the position he held in October 1990. He now espoused a loose confederation and, in so doing, the big bang. The time had come to dump his conservative allies. A fillip for Gorbachev was that the Supreme Soviet accepted the Nine Plus One agreement.

How would the CC plenum, on 24–25 April, react? Surely, as the agreement meant the end of the all-Union Party, it would savage Gorbachev and perhaps remove him as Party leader. On the first day, despite vicious criticism, motions critical of Gorbachev failed. On the second day, things changed and Gorbachev became enraged and shouted that he could only do his job if he had the support of members. Otherwise he would go. His deputy, Ivashko, then intervened and called for a pause. Seventy-two members came to Gorbachev and declared that, if he went, they went too. The Politburo then met and the terrible truth dawned on its members. If Gorbachev went it could mean the end of the Party. The state might then seize Party assets, as in Armenia. The plenum then closed ranks and kept Gorbachev. It transpired later that there had been a conspiracy to remove Gorbachev at the plenum. A member had organised a campaign of telegrams to the CC before the plenum demanding that order be established in the economy. The aim was to convince the plenum to sack Gorbachev and to establish an emergency committee to save the country, similar to the one set up in August 1991. The case against Gorbachev would be overwhelming since only speakers who opposed the general secretary would be allowed to address the session. Then the committee would attempt to recreate Party power, as it had been enjoyed in March 1985.[108] These conservatives simply did not give up but fought to the bitter end, as August 1991 was to show.

Should Gorbachev have seized the opportunity at the plenum to go? Had he done so, he would have taken the Party democrats with him, and therefore split the Party. The conservatives would have been forced to establish their own Party but Gorbachev could decree that all Party property pass to the democrats. By staying Party leader, Gorbachev was inviting the conservatives to try again to put the clock back. He appears to have reasoned that he was better off as Party leader until the Union treaty was signed. Then it would break up into republican Parties. Perhaps he could even persuade them to accept democracy and a market economy! The Party conservatives suffered from one major drawback. They had no obvious leader to succeed Gorbachev. Yeltsin was playing a waiting game. By signing the Novo-Ogarevo accord, he was ensuring that Gorbachev stayed in office. A weak Gorbachev suited him until he could launch his challenge to destroy him.

.   .   .

RUSSIA ELECTS A PRESIDENT

The law on the election of a Russian President and Vice-President laid down that it was for five years. Each would be required to suspend his membership of political parties and

211

social organisations. The President could be removed from office for violating the Russian Constitution, Russian law and the oath of office, by a two-thirds majority of all elected members of the Russian Congress of People's Deputies. The Constitutional Court, to be established, was to judge the legality of the decision. This provision was to have moment-ous consequences for President Yeltsin and Russia over the next two years. Since this requirement was the same for USSR President Gorbachev, it was not perceived how desta-bilising it could be in a time of dangerous transition.

In order to be elected, the President had to obtain a minimum of 50 per cent plus one vote, in the first round. If no one obtained this in the first round, the top two would run off in the second round. The victor would be the one who obtained more votes. The constitutional lawyers wished to ensure that the first, directly elected President of Russia be perceived to be legitimate. He had to be the choice of the majority of voters. Yeltsin chose as his running mate, Aleksandr Rutskoi. As a distinguished airforce officer, he would attract some military votes. Yeltsin had not enamoured himself to the military over Lithuania and the promotion of a loose Union of sovereign states. The duties of the Vice-President, following US practice, were vague. Rutskoi had no political pedigree so did not appear to constitute a danger to Yeltsin. DemRossiya was very disappointed that one of its members was not on the ticket. Presumably, Yeltsin wished to avoid being put under pressure by his democratic number two.

Yeltsin won on the first round, with 57.3 per cent of the vote. He did extremely well in the larger cities but poorly in the countryside, where the communists still held sway. Nikolai Ryzhkov, back from his heart attack, came in second, with over 16 per cent. The dark horse was Vladimir Zhirinovsky, who collected over 6 million votes, over 7 per cent of the vote. Next came Lieutenant-General Albert Makashov, a super-patriot, who had stunned Gorbachev at the 28th Party Congress by attacking perestroika and glasnost and demand-ing the general secretary return to Leninist norms. Then came Amangeldy Tuleev, from Kemerovo, in the Kuzbass, and last of all, Vadim Bakatin. The latter deserved better because of his record as a liberal Minister of the Interior but, presumably, it was his close connection to Gorbachev that Russians found off-putting.

When Yeltsin took the oath of office, in a grand ceremony on 10 July 1991, Gorbachev was present. Yeltsin took his oath on the Russian Constitution and the Russian declaration of state sovereignty. He proclaimed the beginning of a new era for Russia. Significantly, he received the blessing of Patriarch Aleksi II, the first Russian leader to do so since Tsar Nicholas II was crowned in Moscow in May 1896. Yeltsin was twice blessed, by the church and by the people, as Russia's first popularly elected leader. Gorbachev could only admire his opponent's natural gift for populism and symbolism.

. . .

FOREIGN RELATIONS

Saddam Hussein's invasion of Kuwait on 1 August 1990, and its incorporation in Iraq, was a severe test for the developing Soviet–American relationship. There were also the universal human values on which Gorbachev was placing such great store. Gorbachev was in a quandary. Iraq was an ally and there were thousands of Soviet troops in Iraq. James Baker and Shevardnadze met at Vnukovo 2 airport. They agreed on a statement, condemning the Iraqi aggression, as a precursor for other joint votes in the UN. Gorbachev and Bush met in Helsinki on 9 September and talked most of the day. The Soviet leader wanted assurances on two points: that military pressure would be applied to force Saddam out of Kuwait without war, and that US forces would leave Kuwait when it was liberated.[109] Gorbachev broached the subject of financial support for the Soviet economy. Indirectly, he was hinting that Kuwait and the economy were linked.

Cooperation over the unification of Germany further cemented the relationship between Moscow and Washington. Events in Lithuania almost caused a fissure. The war against Saddam took precedence in Washington but Bush reiterated time and again that the use of force in the Baltic would jeopardise Gorbachev's desire for economic assistance and undermine their friendship. Gorbachev assured Bush he was mindful of these things but the Soviet Union was on the brink of civil war. However, he kept his promise, made to Bush in Helsinki, that he would cooperate with the United States in putting a stop to Iraqi aggression. The Gorbachev–Bush relationship bloomed in 1991. They talked

213

by telephone almost every week and the foreign ministers met several times a month.

President Bush was due in Moscow in February 1991 for a summit, but tension in the Baltic made it impossible to keep the appointment. Also, the Soviet military were not observing the terms of the Conventional Forces in Europe (CFE) Treaty, signed in Paris in November 1990, which had helped to reduce Soviet superiority. Since Gorbachev could not or would not force his military to observe the treaty, General Mikhail Moiseev, chief of the general staff, was dispatched to Washington to clear up the misunderstandings.

When the US ambassador met Gorbachev on 7 May 1991, the Soviet leader treated him to a plaintive monologue about his fears that President Bush was reassessing their relationship.[110] The President was quite frank in revealing his own sense of insecurity. Mikhail Sergeevich was feeling unloved. He needed Bush and he needed money. The ambassador had requested that his posting come to an end, for personal reasons. Gorbachev enquired: 'Maybe you think this ship will sink?'.[111] The next day, when he met Rupert Murdoch, the media magnate, he was feeling even more exposed. He told Murdoch that Bush was risking a new cold war. This stung George Bush into action and he eloquently assured Mikhail Sergeevich that the thought of cooling their relationship had never entered his head. Progress was made on the CFE treaty so that Bush could, eventually, send it to the Senate for ratification. Eventually, on 11 June, Gorbachev was informed that the Americans had acceded to his request for US$1.5 billion credit guarantees in order to buy much-needed grain.

The Soviet budget deficit was climbing inexorably and there were no money markets in the Soviet Union to provide loans. The only source of finance was the capitalist world. Gorbachev began dreaming that the west would provide him with the money to keep afloat, say, something like US$100 billion. This was at a time when the Soviet Union's hard currency debt was approaching US$100 billion. Gorbachev told every foreign statesman he met that the Gulf War had cost up to US$100 billion. The money had been found. Why could a comparable sum not be found to support perestroika, an undertaking ten or one hundred times more important than war in the Gulf?[112] The rich man's club was the G7, and its next meeting was in London in July. Could the Soviet Union not join?[113] He had first to secure an invitation. The Americans told him he needed a financial plan, one which presented a transition to a market economy. A document, drawn up by Prime Minister Pavlov, would only evoke derisive laughter. Someone with more market pedigree had to be found. The ideal man was Grigory Yavlinsky. In May Yavlinsky attended a cabinet meeting and Gorbachev was very dismissive of Pavlov's stabilisation programme. He informed the ministers that every foreign head of state he had met had told him the programme would not work. 'Even the American ambassador tells me it's no good, and he knows the country pretty well.'[114] The next week Yavlinsky was off to Harvard to consult with Graham Allison. The objective was to draft a programme which combined Yavlinsky's economics with Allison's politics. Yavlinsky called the programme 'the window of opportunity' and Allison labelled it 'the grand bargain'. The west would supply money if the Soviet Union moved to democracy and partnership.[115]

Gorbachev decided to pull out all the stops to promote his bid for big money. So he invited Lady Thatcher to the Soviet Union at the end of May. When she returned from the Gorbachevs' dacha, she was very enthusiastic. She instructed the American ambassador:

> Please get a message to my friend George. We've got to help Mikhail. Of course, you Americans can't and shouldn't have to do it all yourselves, but George will have to lead the effort, just as he did with Kuwait. Just a few years back, Ron and I would have given the world to get what has already happened here . . . History will not forgive us if we fail to rally to his support.[116]

Who could resist such an appeal? Especially since she had divined that his political situation was really desperate. When the ambassador pointed out some of the practical difficulties in drafting such a programme, such as Gorbachev's failure to adopt market-oriented polices, she glared at him and responded: 'You're talking like a diplomat. Just finding excuses for doing nothing. Why can't you think like a statesman?'[117]

On 17 June Valentin Pavlov, addressing the Supreme Soviet, began discussing the possibility of introducing a state of emergency in the whole country or in certain sectors of the economy. Lukyanov, in the chair, raised no objection. Pavlov was requesting that parliament confer on him some extraordinary powers, hitherto the prerogative of the President, mainly in economic policy.[118] He would also have the right of legislative initiative. This would put paid to the sovereignty of Russia and other republics. Kryuchkov, Yazov and Pugo expressed enthusiastic support for the Prime Minister's initiative.[119] When other deputies enquired whether he had cleared the matter with the President, he replied tamely that he had not.

On 20 June Gavriil Popov, the newly elected mayor of Moscow, paid a courtesy call on the American ambassador, to say farewell, as the envoy was returning to Washington in August. When they were seated, Popov began writing on a sheet of paper and then handed it to the ambassador. The message was dramatic: 'A coup is being organised to remove Gorbachev. We must get word to Boris Nikolaevich [Yeltsin].'[120] The envoy scribbled in reply: 'I'll send a message. But who is behind this?' Popov wrote down their names: Pavlov, Kryuchkov, Yazov, Lukyanov. Then conversation resumed for another ten or fifteen minutes. The note had been necessary since the KGB bugging devices would have picked up any oral communication. The message was sent to Washington and President Bush was to inform Yeltsin. He could reveal the source as Popov but not to anyone else. How was the ambassador to tell the President that a plot was under way to remove him? Would Gorbachev take it as an insult? He found the words to communicate to him that President Bush had information about an attempt to remove him, even that week. However, it was based on rumour, not hard information. Gorbachev leaned back and chuckled:

> Tell President Bush I am touched. Thank him for his concern. He has done what a friend should do. But tell him not to worry. I have everything in hand. You'll see tomorrow.[121]

He said that times, of course, were unsettled. Pavlov, a competent economist, was an inexperienced politician and had already conceded that he had acted rashly on 17 June. Political reconciliation was in the air. The Union treaty would soon be signed and even Yeltsin might cooperate. There were those in parliament, especially in the Soyuz faction, who might have been talking about overthrowing the government.[122]

The Americans decided not to tell Gorbachev the names of the conspirators. However, when James Baker met Aleksandr Bessmertnykh, the foreign minister, in Berlin on 20 June, he gave him the names, but not the source, and asked him to convey the information urgently to Gorbachev. Baker should have known that all Soviet communications were monitored by the KGB. Hence the message would not have reached Gorbachev, since the KGB chief was named as one of the conspirators. Bessmertnykh told Baker he could not send such a message. At least he was honest, and discreet. He suggested that the message should be delivered to Gorbachev by the American ambassador. When President Bush finally reported to Gorbachev[123] on Yeltsin's Washington visit, he blurted out that Popov had been the source. This breached an agreement by the ambassador and the White House staff that the source should not be mentioned, except to Yeltsin. It also revealed to the KGB who had blown the whistle on them.

The next time Gorbachev met Popov, he shook his finger at him and asked: 'Why are you telling tales to the Americans?'.[124] When the same group moved against Gorbachev in August, Popov's name was near the top of the list for arrest. Bessmertnykh returned to Moscow the following day, 21 June, and told Gorbachev what Baker had said in Berlin and asked if the ambassador had reported to him. The President replied that he had and that he had given 'those officials' a good telling off. He enquired whether Baker had mentioned a time and the foreign minister replied in the negative but it could 'happen any day now'. Bessmertnykh thought Gorbachev had worked out those involved in the plot, but in retrospect it appeared he had been thinking of the Soyuz leaders who had criticised him in the Supreme Soviet.[125]

On 21 June Gorbachev appeared before the Supreme Soviet and, without difficulty, reasserted his authority. What would Gorbachev do? Presumably sack the four plotters. He had merely restricted himself to a statement that he had not agreed to the démarche! Gorbachev's insouciance,[126] or downright recklessness, is remarkably reminiscent of the coup against Nikita Khrushchev in October 1964.[127] In that case, Khrushchev's son recounted the names of the conspirators to him. Khrushchev then asked one of them if he were conspiring against him! The inevitable denial satisfied him.

The American ambassador became concerned when he discovered that Moscow was asking that Vladimir Shcherbakov, first deputy Prime Minister, and Pavlov's number two, and Evgeny Primakov, be received by President Bush and James Baker. This was ominous as Grigory Yavlinsky was the principal source of Soviet economic proposals for the G7 summit. The ambassador informed Primakov, now in charge of foreign economic relations in the Security Council, that Bush and Baker were interested in what Yavlinsky had to say. If Shcherbakov were there to add support, then everything would be fine. However, if Shcherbakov were going to take precedence and try to sell Pavlov's stabilisation programme, the whole venture would fail. Primakov replied that Gorbachev would not accept any programme which his government had not approved. Economic reform would have to be agreed and implemented by Pavlov and his cabinet. When the meeting took place, on 31 May, Bush concluded that Gorbachev did not have a viable market programme. He began wondering whether Gorbachev would be wasting his time coming to London for the G7 meeting. Kohl and Mitterrand stepped in and Gorbachev received his invitation, from Prime Minister John Major, in mid-June.

Yavlinsky was told that Baker would use a specific phrase, in a speech to be delivered in Berlin, to signal that Bush had accepted the programme. He duly did so. Gorbachev turned the report over to Vadim Medvedev to prepare for his London visit. On 6 July, on the eve of Gorbachev's visit to London, the US ambassador had an urgent message for him from Bush. He found the President in a remarkably relaxed mood at a dacha outside Moscow. Something struck him. The officials with him, preparing for the London summit, did not include any prominent reform economists, not even Yavlinsky.[128] Gorbachev had not taken on board the warning that his programme, to succeed, had to map out the route to a market economy.

The G7 listened politely to him, but when he addressed business and the press afterwards, his invitation to invest in the Soviet Union only evoked a lukewarm response. Investing in the Soviet Union was still too risky, mainly because Moscow did not understand what a market economy entailed. Gorbachev was offered associate membership of the International Monetary Fund and the World Bank and technical assistance. He ignored this insult and applied for full membership on 23 July 1991. Despite misgivings, it was eventually granted. He had to return to Moscow without any hard cash.[129] The London fiasco was his first major foreign policy defeat since Soviet–American relations had become friendly. It resulted mainly from his inability to grasp market economics.

Gorbachev made matters worse when he met Bush in London on 17 July. Still offended at being turned away without any money, he had a go at Bush:

> I think the President of the United States is a serious person. He thinks through his political decisions and they are not reached on the spur of the moment. As a result of these decisions, we have achieved much in security policy. However, I have also the impression that my friend, the President of the United States, has yet to provide a final answer to an important question. How does the United States expect the Soviet Union to develop? As long as there is no answer to this question, certain important problems about our relationship cannot be resolved. And time is running out. And I ask: what does George Bush want from me? When my G7 colleagues tell me later, that you like what I am doing, and that you want to support me, but for the time being I can stew in my own juice, I must reply that we are all stewing in that juice. It is strange that US$100 billion could be produced for a regional conflict. Money can also be found for other programmes. But this is about changing the Soviet Union, to give it a totally new quality, to make it part of the world economy so that it will no longer be a disruptive force and a possible source of threats. There has never been a task of such dimensions.[130]

This attack wounded Bush and he replied, in an offhand manner, that it was his fault that he had not made himself clearer:

> We want you to become a democratic state, with a market economy, integrated into the western world ... and the federation between the centre and the republics can be resolved successfully ... We do not welcome an economic catastrophe in the Soviet Union ... We do not feel *Schadenfreude* when we contemplate your economic problems ... the destruction of the Soviet Union is not in our interests.[131]

Chernyaev could not understand why Gorbachev had posed the questions, especially since the answers provided by Bush were already well known. Possibly, it was that Kryuchkov's reports that the US government was working against him had struck a chord after the failure of the G7 meeting. Again, it may have been that he felt that he was not being given his worth for all the efforts he had put into developing the new relationship.[132] Bush was also at a loss to understand Gorbachev. When he got back to Washington, he remarked: 'It's funny. He's always been his own best salesman, but not this time. I wonder if he isn't kind of out of touch.'[133]

. . .

TAKING LEAVE OF SOCIALISM

Gorbachev was awarded the Nobel Peace Prize in October 1990. He decided not to collect the award himself in December, and a deputy foreign minister accepted it on his behalf. The events in Vilnius in January 1991 turned many foreign observers against Gorbachev and led to demands that the committee reconsider its decision. Some Soviet citizens were just as wounding. One congratulated the President on the award of the 'imperialist prize'. He found time to travel to Oslo in June 1991 and deliver the traditional speech expected of laureates. It was remarkable for the fact that he spoke as a post-Leninist. He had liberated himself from the official ideology of the Party, Marxism-Leninism.

Even more remarkable was the draft programme of the Party, entitled 'Socialism, democracy, progress'.[134] The socialist choice, a phrase oft-quoted by Gorbachev, was dropped from the final draft. The Party was no longer the Party of the working class, but of all those in employment. The class basis of the Party had finally been abandoned. The ideology of the Party was now 'humane, democratic socialism', which emerged from Marxism but also from other 'concepts of domestic and humanistic thinking'. The new ideology was left vague, to develop over time. Much was made of the Party's commitment to the rule of law, democratic institutions, the separation of powers and the new Union of sovereign states. Communism was mentioned in passing but no one thought it was feasible in the near future.

The last CC plenum adopted, reluctantly, the new programme. The new Party had been born but it would be more accurate to say stillborn. On 20 July, shortly before the plenum convened, Yeltsin signed a decree banning political activity by any party in state institutions, on the territory of the Russian Federation. These included the KGB, the military and the militia. If implemented, this would paralyse the Party in Russia. Gorbachev refused to issue a decree countermanding Yeltsin's order, despite many Party members lobbying strongly for one. He stated that he would only act if the constitutional committee judged Yeltsin's action to be unconstitutional. The CC plenum condemned Yeltsin's decree but it had no legal force. Gorbachev appeared, finally, to have abandoned the Party.

The democrats, despite feuding as usual among themselves, did manage to establish an embryonic democratic alternative to the Party, the movement for democratic reforms. Many democratic luminaries belonged to it and, significantly, Gorbachev did not pour vitriol on it. As it was geared to attracting democratic-inclined Party members, it could, conceivably, serve as a vehicle for the President if he broke his formal links with the Party at its upcoming Congress, expected in the autumn of 1991. It was generally felt that the Party would disintegrate and split into factions at the Congress. Gavriil Popov thought it would take the democrats another three to five years before they could assume power.[135] To Popov, someone like Vladimir Zhirinovsky, however, posed the greatest danger. Economic misery would make his party very attractive, not only to civilians but also to the military and police. This was a prescient analysis, in the summer of 1991.

.   .   .

BUSH IN THE SOVIET UNION

George Bush arrived in Moscow for his first summit as President on 29 July 1991.[136] It was to be the fourth, and last, Bush–Gorbachev meeting. The Strategic Arms Reduction Treaty (START I) was ready for signature after ten years of negotiations. The CFE treaty had been sent to the Senate for ratification. Moscow had finally passed a bill incorporating the right to emigrate. The trade agreement, signed in 1990, was before Congress. It granted the Soviet Union most favoured nation status. The current, tense situation in the country occupied both Presidents. Bush encouraged Gorbachev to be more conciliatory towards the Baltic republics and to move more rapidly towards a market economy. There was a tentative agreement on a Middle East peace conference. An embarrassing episode occurred on 31 July at the Novo-Ogarevo dacha while Gorbachev and Bush were engaged in negotiations. A note was passed to Bush that six Lithuanian customs officials had been murdered during the night. Gorbachev was put out, especially since Bush's question about the incident was the first he had heard of it. It later transpired that the incident had been perpetrated by members of the Riga OMON unit. It was assumed that the incident had been staged to disrupt the summit. It also demonstrated that Bush had better sources about what was happening in the Soviet Union. Also, Gorbachev was not in control of his own police force.

The growing reputation of the republican leaders was taken into account at a summit, for the first time. Gorbachev invited Yeltsin and Nursultan Nazarbaev, the leader of Kazakhstan, to participate in a working lunch with him and Bush and to join the Soviet negotiating team for some sessions. Yeltsin replied that he preferred to receive President Bush in his office, President to President, rather than meet him with others. Bush intended to visit Kiev after the summit, call officially on Yeltsin and invite several republican leaders to his official dinner. Yeltsin received Bush in the Kremlin, in the same office Gorbachev had occupied as speaker of the Supreme Soviet. Yeltsin went so far as to keep Bush waiting ten minutes and the meeting lasted longer than scheduled. The Americans were not impressed. At the state dinner, hosted by the Gorbachevs, Yeltsin sent his wife ahead and waited until Barbara Bush entered. He then tried to escort her to the top table as if he were the host. At the return dinner, hosted by the Bushes, there were no diplomatic gaffes. Nazarbaev went to the table where Yeltsin and Ter-Petrosyan, the Armenian leader, were seated and invited them to go with him to the top table to offer a toast to Gorbachev and Bush.

Bush liked the idea of visiting a republican capital after the Moscow summit. Kiev would be a suitable venue since it had escaped the turmoil of the Caucasus. The Baltic republics were out of the question and Central Asia had hardly begun its transition to democracy. The Soviet Ministry of Foreign Affairs raised no objections. The Americans were astonished, on 21 July, when the Soviet chargé d'affaires in

Washington brought a message from President Gorbachev's office. It stated that, in the light of tensions there, it was inadvisable for President Bush to visit Kiev. Instead, the President was invited to spend time with Gorbachev in Stavropol krai. There was the danger of a scandal which would overshadow the gains at the summit. The Americans would be obliged to inform the Ukrainians that Gorbachev did not want Bush to go to Kiev. After discussing the negative side-effects of the decision on the open telephone, to ensure the KGB got the message, the President's office relented and gave the go ahead. Presumably, Gorbachev had been so annoyed that Bush wanted to go Kiev that he failed, once again, to think through the consequences of a veto.

In Kiev, President Bush would meet privately with Leonid Kravchuk, speaker of parliament. No Soviet official would be present. All speeches and toasts were to be in Ukrainian and English. No Russian was to be used. Bush pointed out to the Ukrainians that independence was not the same as democracy and freedom. An independent state could be oppressive. The first goal should be democracy because when there was freedom of choice, independence could be chosen. However, all this fell on deaf ears. The Ukrainians were concerned, first and foremost, with independence.

. . .

THE UNION TREATY READY

In June the Ukrainian Supreme Soviet passed a resolution that the republic should take over all enterprises on Ukrainian territory, run from Moscow. It was also difficult to determine whether Russia would sign or not. Gorbachev had to cobble together the best agreement he could negotiate. By the summer of 1991, the initiative had passed to the republics. The President desperately needed an agreement to obtain international aid to stiffen the stabilisation programme.

Ominous for Gorbachev was the fact that an alliance had come into being in the republics. The economic nomenklatura and nationalists had come together to demand control over the republican economies. However, on 26 June the Ukrainian parliament voted overwhelmingly to accept the draft Union treaty. It was then sent to parliamentary commissions which were to report in September. Ukraine would then state its conditions for entry into the new Union. On 2 August Gorbachev announced on television that the treaty would be ready for signing on 20 August, and that the Russian Federation, Kazakhstan and Uzbekistan would sign that day. Gorbachev called the new formation, a 'new, genuinely voluntary Union (or association[137]) of sovereign states'. Many democrats urged Yeltsin not to sign, but when he met Nazarbaev in Almaty on 18 August, they seemed to have agreed to carry on with the signing.

. . .

NOTES

1. *Pravda*, 26 November 1989.
2. Jack F. Matlock, Jr., *Autopsy on an Empire: The American Ambassador's Account of the Collapse of the Soviet Union* (New York, Random House, 1995), pp. 288–91.
3. The Orthodox New Year, a week later, was celebrated, on television, by a three-hour mass from a cathedral in Leningrad.
4. Matlock, *Autopsy on an Empire*, p. 274.
5. FBIS-SOV-89, Daily Report: Soviet Union, 19 December 1989, p. 37.
6. Ibid., 29 December 1989, pp. 38–9.
7. Alfred Erich Senn, *Gorbachev's Failure in Lithuania* (New York, St Martin's Press, 1995), p. 77.
8. Ibid., p. 78.
9. Another breakthrough, in November, had been the admission of NKVD culpability for the murder of Polish prisoners-of-war in the Katyn forest near Smolensk in 1940. Gorbachev handed over the relevant Soviet documents to Jaruzelski on 13 April 1990. A TASS statement expressed the Soviet Union's sincere regret for the Katyn tragedy, one of the most heinous crimes of the Stalin era. The documents directly implicating those involved were only discovered in a special file in December 1991. A memorandum recommended that all the internees be executed and was signed by Stalin, Molotov and Voroshilov. The memorandum had been drafted by Beria. Gorbachev then handed it over to Yeltsin for transmission to the Poles. Mikhail Gorbachev, *Memoirs* (London, Doubleday, 1996), pp. 480–1.
10. Carolyn McGiffert Ekedahl and Melvin A. Goodman, *The Wars of Eduard Shevardnadze* (London, Hurst, 1997), p. 247.
11. Senn, *Gorbachev's Failure*, pp. 79–81.

12. Anatoli Tschernajew, *Die letzten Jahre einer Weltmacht: Der Kreml von innen* (Stuttgart, Deutsche Verlags-Anstalt, 1993), pp. 274–5.
13. *Pravda*, 26 December 1989. He accepted the logic of a federal Party in a federal state in 1991, but by then it was too late. During his speech, Gorbachev took umbrage at Lithuanian contacts with the US embassy in Moscow, accusing them of attempting to 'internationalise' the question. In the world of universal human values, this was strange criticism. The US ambassador met regularly groups from all three Baltic republics. Matlock, *Autopsy on an Empire*, passim.
14. Gorbachev, *Memoirs*, p. 573.
15. Ibid., pp. 343–4; Matlock, *Autopsy on an Empire*, pp. 300–4.
16. *Le Monde*, 31 January 1990; Matlock, *Autopsy on an Empire*, pp. 307–10.
17. *New York Times*, 5 February 1990.
18. Gorbachev, *Memoirs*, p. 314.
19. Matlock, *Autopsy on an Empire*, 314; Gorbachev, *Memoirs*, p. 317.
20. Ibid., p. 319; the information comes from an interview with Vadim Bakatin on 6 October 1992.
21. The 73rd anniversary of the Petrograd strike which led, two days later, to the February revolution. Gorbachev may, quite falsely, have drawn a parallel between these two dates.
22. The Lithuanians, Latvians and Estonians preferred Council as a foreign language translation.
23. Matlock, *Autopsy on an Empire*, pp. 322–7.
24. Ibid., p. 329.
25. Senn, *Gorbachev's Failure*, p. 94.
26. Gorbachev, *Memoirs*, p. 320.
27. Ibid., p. 321.
28. Ibid., p. 319.
29. In an interview with the former US ambassador on 14 March 1992, Ryzhkov stated that he had withdrawn out of loyalty to Gorbachev, something he regretted later, and claimed that he would have won the election had he stood. Matlock, *Autopsy on an Empire*, p. 789.
30. Matlock, *Autopsy on an Empire*, p. 337.
31. Senn, *Gorbachev's Failure*, p. 101.
32. Matlock, *Autopsy on an Empire*, p. 357.
33. Kazimiera Prunskiene, *Leben für Litauen* (Berlin, Ullstein, 1992), p. 191; Senn, *Gorbachev's Failure*, p. 108.
34. Matlock, *Autopsy on an Empire*, p. 381.
35. Vadim Bakatin, *Izbavlenie ot KGB* (Moscow, Novosti, 1992), p. 45.

36. Gorbachev, *Memoirs*, p. 346. A major reason for underestimating the political support enjoyed by Yeltsin was the increasingly bitter personal rivalry between the two politicians.
37. Ibid., p. 346.
38. *Pravda*, 11 July 1992.
39. Gorbachev, *Memoirs*, p. 347.
40. Ibid., pp. 346–7.
41. Ibid., p. 347.
42. *Pravda*, 11 April 1990.
43. Gorbachev, *Memoirs*, p. 353.
44. Matlock, *Autopsy on an Empire*, p. 376. The information comes from Ivan Antonovich, deputy head of the CC's Academy of Social Sciences, which conducted unpublished opinion polls within the Party.
45. Gorbachev, *Memoirs*, p. 357.
46. Matlock, *Autopsy on an Empire*, p. 377.
47. Gorbachev, *Memoirs*, p. 358.
48. For the first time in decades, no foreign delegations were invited. There was nothing at the Congress about the world communist movement and the new Party statutes omitted the statement that the CPSU was a part of this movement.
49. Gorbachev, *Memoirs*, p. 369. This is another example of poor personal judgement by Gorbachev.
50. Ibid., p. 367.
51. Ibid., p. 369.
52. In early 1990, the chair of the state commission on economic reform, Abalkin, and the chair of Gosplan, Maslyukov, drafted a memorandum on resolving the economic crisis. They presented two variants to Ryzhkov on 17 February 1990: reverting to the command-administrative system or 'accelerating the transition to a planned-market economy'. L. Abalkin, *Neispolzovanny shans* (Moscow, Politizdat, 1991), p. 123. There was a general consensus that going into reverse was no longer a feasible option. It is instructive that they used the expression 'planned-market economy', a contradiction in terms. It may have been chosen to make it politically palatable to Ryzhkov and the leadership. No serious case was made for reversion to the old system in the Politburo. It was accepted that the country had to move forward towards a market economy. However, there was no agreement on what measures should be taken to move to a market economy. Gorbachev could simply not make up his mind. An excellent overview of the policy conflict of the Gorbachev leadership is Michael Ellman and Vladimir Kontorovich, 'The collapse of the Soviet system and the

Memoir literature', *Europe-Asia Studies*, vol. 49, no. 2, 1997, pp. 259–79.

53. Matlock, *Autopsy on an Empire*, p. 791.
54. *Pravda*, 5 July 1990.
55. Matlock, *Autopsy on an Empire*, pp. 403–5. Since this interview had taken place in an official building, presumably it had been recorded by the KGB. Kryuchkov, one surmises, then passed it on to Gorbachev.
56. Gorbachev once ruefully commented that if one put 25 specialists in a room, one got 30 opinions!
57. Matlock, *Autopsy on an Empire*, p. 416.
58. Tschernajew, *Die letzten Jahre einer Weltmacht*, p. 317.
59. *Izvestiya*, 20 September 1990.
60. Mikhail Nenashev, *Poslednee Pravitelstvo SSSR* (Moscow, Krom, 1993), p. 184.
61. Tschernajew, *Die letzten Jahre einer Weltmacht*, p. 323.
62. *Pravda*, 18 November 1990.
63. Tschernajew, *Die letzten Jahre einer Weltmacht*, p. 327.
64. Matlock, *Autopsy on an Empire*, p. 427.
65. *Moskovskie novosti*, 18 November 1990.
66. Tschernajew, *Die letzten Jahre einer Weltmacht*, p. 333.
67. Matlock, *Autopsy on an Empire*, pp. 464–5.
68. *Moskovskie novosti*, no. 4, 27 January–3 February 1991.
69. FBIS-SOV-90, 27 December, pp. 12–13.
70. Tschernajew, *Die letzten Jahre einer Weltmacht*, p. 333.
71. Ekedahl and Goodman, *Wars of Eduard Shevardnadze*, p. 95.
72. Ibid., p. 101.
73. Valentin Falin, *Politische Erinnerungen* (Munich, Droemer Knauer, 1993), p. 496. He writes that when he heard the terms of the agreement, he resigned and immediately addressed parliament. 'It only took me three to five minutes to provoke deputies into making the strongest possible objections.' Falin regarded a divided Germany as the Soviet Union's trophy for winning the Second World War. Elsewhere in the memoirs, he thrusts his knife into Shevardnadze at every opportunity. See for example pp. 39–42, 419–20, 471, 483–4. Falin was rather lugubrious, but capable of wit and biting sarcasm, and a formidably learned German specialist. As befell all Soviet officials, his colleagues made snide remarks about him, especially about his pretty, young wife. All in all, he was very good company.
74. Matlock, *Autopsy on an Empire*, p. 429.
75. Gorbachev, *Memoirs*, p. 518.
76. Manfred Wilke, 'Hard facts', *German Comments*, no. 42, April 1996, pp. 24–5. So dire was the situation that the

Politburo resolved not to inform members of the SED Central Committee of the report. GDR negotiators began to ask the west Germans for up to DM3 billion annually, just to keep going. The end was near.

77. Ibid., p. 26.
78. Ibid., p. 26.
79. The author was attending a conference in the Reichstag on '40 Years of Divided Germany', when the Wall went down, signalling the beginning of the end of a divided Germany. Gorbachev was one of the heroes of the hour. Participants realised that that memorable day was one of the results of his new political thinking.
80. When President François Mitterrand first read the ten points, he flew into a rage, and uttered: 'I'll never forget this!' Mitterrand claimed that Germany would not unite since Prussians (many in east Germany) would not tolerate being bossed around by Bavarians. Chancellor Kohl was a Rhinelander and Genscher hailed from Halle! Margaret Thatcher was livid. 'Stop him [Kohl]! He wants everything.' As an unkind critic said, her mental picture of Germans and Germany was Luftwaffe bombers over Grantham.
81. Gorbachev, *Memoirs*, p. 527.
82. Ibid., p. 528.
83. Ibid., p. 528.
84. The best book on the diplomacy of German unification is Philip Zelikow and Condoleeza Rice, *Germany Unified and Europe Transformed* (Harvard, MA, Harvard University Press, 1995). This concentrates on American input. Jacques Attali, *Verbatim III, 1988–1991* (Paris, Fayard, 1995), is by a Mitterrand adviser. The memoirs are quite indiscreet and recount the deal done by Mitterrand and Kohl. Mitterrand would go along with German unification if Kohl accepted a united Europe. James A. Baker III, with Thomas Defrank, *The Politics of Diplomacy: Revolution, War, and Peace* (New York, Putnam's, 1995), does not contain any revelations about these events but includes a glowing testimony of the qualities of Eduard Shevardnadze as foreign minister. Hans-Dietrich Genscher, *Erinnerungen* (Berlin, Siedler Verlag, 1995), gives the impression that Genscher was the key decision-maker. Kohl and the others just agreed to Genscher's proposals! Attali, for one, reveals that Genscher contemplated a neutral Germany and was willing to take Germany out of NATO to reach agreement. Genscher had not sensed, as Kohl did, that the time for refined statements, offending no one and pleasing everyone, was over and that straight-talking would bring

greater rewards. Kohl and Gorbachev had many heated arguments, one of the reasons for their later closeness. Margaret Thatcher, *The Downing Street Years* (New York, Harper-Collins, 1993), is bitter on German unification. She was left out in the cold after Mitterrand and Kohl had struck their deal. Bush was strongly in favour and Gorbachev had no choice but to make the best of a bad situation. Gorbachev's relationship with Bush was of paramount importance, and next to that, that with Kohl. Had Gorbachev wanted to halt German unification, he would have found a willing ally in Thatcher.

85. This section is partly based on Senn, *Gorbachev's Failure*, pp. 127–41.
86. *Krasnaya Zvezda*, 27 November 1990; Senn, *Gorbachev's Failure*, p. 124.
87. This organisation, founded in May 1989, attracted those Russians who felt affinity with Moscow and the Soviet Union: for example, Russian members of local soviets, army personnel, retired army officers and workers in large military-related enterprises. They did not want the Union to fall apart and blamed Lithuanians for the mess they were in. They only constituted a small proportion of Russians in Lithuania. They can be classified as *homo sovieticus*. The confusion which reigned among pro-Soviet Russians found strange outlets. In Klaipeda, they proclaimed the Soviet Republic of Klaipeda, which was immediately disowned by the Soviet authorities. The majority of Russians in Lithuania regarded themselves as Lithuanian Russians, or Russians who belonged to the Russian cultural community in Lithuania. They had little sympathy for the conservatives in Moscow. Then there were the Russian speakers, minorities, such as Belarusians, Ukrainians, Jews and others, who had moved to Lithuania since 1945. They were confused and felt marginalised. Some of them supported Edinstvo. Many Russians, Poles and Jews supported Sajudis and there were Polish and Russian language editions of the Sajudis newspaper. The subtleties of the loyalties of the Russian-speaking community in Lithuania were lost on the Moscow conservatives and this is a major reason for their failure to mobilise them in their cause. Some of the Polish minority favoured autonomy within Lithuania. On 7 September 1989 the Salcininkai Polish autonomous oblast was proclaimed. On 16 September 1989 the Vilnius oblast soviet declared autonomy within Lithuania. On 21 September 1989 the Lithuanian Supreme Council Presidium annulled the decisions of the two authorities but took

cognisance of the fact that minorities issues had assumed greater significance. In the independence referendum, in February 1991, 50 per cent in Salcininkai voted for independence, and in Vilnius oblast, 56 per cent.

88. Senn, *Gorbachev's Failure*, p. 128.
89. Ibid., p. 130. Gorbachev had signed a decree and it was sent to Vilnius as a telegram.
90. The same unit, on 24 December 1979, had attacked the presidential palace in Kabul and killed President Hafizullah Amin.
91. The Soviet air commander was General Dzhokhar Dudaev, later to be President of Chechnya. He had refused permission for extra Soviet troops to land in Estonia. Hence there was no violence in Tallinn.
92. Gorbachev, *Memoirs*, p. 579. Gorbachev adds that he still trusted Yazov at that time. Chernyaev calls the speeches by Pugo and Yazov, at the Supreme Soviet session, 'stupid, cheeky and a pack of lies'. Tschernajew, *Die letzten Jahre einer Weltmacht*, p. 344.
93. *Izvestiya*, 15 October 1991.
94. *Rossiiskaya gazeta*, 11 July 1992.
95. *Nezavisimaya gazeta*, 15 January 1991.
96. Matlock, *Autopsy on an Empire*, p. 462. Burokevicius, the pro-Moscow party leader, and others, fled to the Russian Federation. Landsbergis asked for their extradition and this was reported on 2 January 1992. They were extradited by Belarus to Lithuania on 15 January 1994 and charged with anti-state activities and complicity in the deaths of 13 independence activists. The pro-Moscow Party went underground and operated clandestinely.
97. Some pro-Soviet Russians, disheartened by the rise in Lithuanian nationalism, began to leave Lithuania. In 1990 there was a net outflow of 6,221 but in 1991 this dropped to 5,504. In 1992 there was a net outflow of 13,672. These are official figures.
98. The black berets, elite Ministry of the Interior troops. OMON stands for specially designated militia units (otryady militsii osobennogo naznacheniya).
99. Matlock, *Autopsy on an Empire*, p. 462.
100. FBIS-SOV-91-018, 28 January 1991, p. 51.
101. *Nezavisimaya gazeta*, 19 January 1991.
102. *Tschernajew, Die letzten Jahre einer Weltmacht*, pp. 344–8. He uses the formal, second person plural, form of address.
103. Archie Brown, *The Gorbachev Factor* (Oxford, Oxford University Press, 1996), p. 281.

104. *Trud,* 12 February 1991.
105. Donald Filtzer, *Soviet Workers and the Collapse of Perestroika: The Soviet Labour Process and Gorbachev's Reforms, 1985–1991* (Cambridge, Cambridge University Press, 1994), p. 106.
106. Matlock, *Autopsy on an Empire,* pp. 489–92.
107. Later, he informed the US ambassador that at the time he had no religious beliefs. However, he came to believe in God and the value of prayer after his life had been spared during the August 1991 attempted coup. Matlock, *Autopsy on an Empire,* p. 795.
108. Valentin Stepankov and Evgeny Lisov, *Kremlevsky zagovor* (Moscow, Izdatelstvo Ogonek, 1992), pp. 76–7; Matlock, *Autopsy on an Empire,* p. 516.
109. Matlock, *Autopsy on an Empire,* p. 411.
110. Ibid., pp. 525–7.
111. Ibid., p. 526.
112. Tschernajew, *Die letzten Jahre einer Weltmacht,* p. 373.
113. Kohl told Gorbachev that if he attended the London meeting as an observer, he would become a full member at the 1992 meeting in Munich. Ibid., p. 373.
114. Matlock, *Autopsy on an Empire,* p. 534.
115. Ibid., p. 536.
116. Ibid., p. 537.
117. Ibid., p. 538. Thatcher's faith in Mikhail Gorbachev was only shaken after both had left office. Vladimir Bukovsky showed her, in 1992, the copy of a document, bearing Gorbachev's signature, which pledged US$1 million to the National Union of Mineworkers, led by Arthur Scargill, during the bitter miners' strike against Thatcher's government. 'She went white when I showed her that paper. Gorbachev had specifically denied to her that any such funds had been given by the Soviets to help the British miners.' *Times Magazine,* 24 May 1997. It is uncertain whether the funds ever reached the NUM.
118. *Pravda,* 18 June 1991.
119. *Nezavisimaya gazeta,* 20 June 1991.
120. Matlock, *Autopsy on an Empire,* p. 541; Gavriil Popov, *Izvestiya,* 2 February 1993.
121. Matlock, *Autopsy on an Empire,* p. 543.
122. Matlock states that there are several inaccuracies in the report of the conversation as reproduced in Chernyaev's book. Chernyaev was so astonished at the information that he made few notes. Matlock, *Autopsy on an Empire,* p. 797; Tschernajew, *Die letzten Jahre einer Weltmacht,* pp. 379–80. Gorbachev told the ambassador that Primakov had phoned him the evening

before and warned him that he was too much trusting of the KGB and his security personnel. He told Primakov to relax and not to spread such panic stories.

123. Bush had attempted to telephone Gorbachev earlier but had not got through on the red telephone, the hot line. Gorbachev was annoyed and Boldin gave orders that the secretaries had to go. Gorbachev's response was: 'At last, one of them still calls me Leonid Ilich [Brezhnev]!'.
124. Matlock, *Autopsy on an Empire*, p. 545.
125. Stepankov and Lisov, *Kremlevsky zagovor*, p. 79; Matlock, *Autopsy on an Empire*, p. 546.
126. Some authors wonder if Gorbachev was part of this attempt to restore law and order by decoupling his presidential office from that of the cabinet. The latter, given extraordinary powers, would have taken drastic measures to save the Soviet state. Michael Urban with Vyacheslav Igrunov and Sergei Mitrokhin, *The Rebirth of Politics in Russia* (Cambridge, Cambridge University Press, 1997), p. 247; Yu. Burtin, *Demokraticheskaya Rossiya*, 3 November 1991.
127. Martin McCauley, *The Khrushchev Era 1953–1964* (London, Longman, 1995), pp. 77–80.
128. Matlock, *Autopsy on an Empire*, p. 550.
129. The Russian government did not take kindly to what Yavlinsky was trying to do. It saw him attempting to help Gorbachev and Pavlov out of the economic hole they had dug for themselves. Large foreign credits for Gorbachev might prolong the Union, especially if Gorbachev could use the credits as bait.
130. Tschernajew, *Die letzten Jahre einer Weltmacht*, pp. 382–3.
131. Ibid., p. 383.
132. Ibid., p. 384.
133. Michael R. Beschloss and Strobe Talbott, *At the Highest Levels: The Inside Story of the End of the Cold War* (Boston, Little, Brown, 1993), p. 407; Matlock, *Autopsy on an Empire*, p. 554.
134. *Pravda*, 8 August 1991.
135. Matlock, *Autopsy on an Empire*, p. 560.
136. Ibid., pp. 562–71, 798.
137. Whereas in the 17 March referendum about a future Union, he had used the word *soyuz*, he now said *obedinenie*, association. The latter suggests a much looser formation than the former.

Chapter 6

THE ATTEMPTED COUP
AND AFTER[1]

Gorbachev hammered out the final details of the Union treaty with Yeltsin and Nazarbaev at Novo-Ogarevo on 29 July. Yeltsin appeared satisfied with the compromise on federal taxes. Article 9 of the treaty stated that there would be fixed percentages, to be agreed by the member states. Control over federal spending would be exercised by the signatory states.[2] This ensured that the centre would be weak. The treaty was to be signed on 20 August. Yeltsin also demanded changes in the cabinet of ministers. He wanted Pavlov, Kryuchkov and Pugo to go, and Gorbachev did not object. The interlocutors thought that they were in a bug-free environment but unfortunately the KGB had the room wired. A transcript of their talk was later found in Boldin's safe.[3]

When Gorbachev and his family flew off to Foros, their holiday dacha in the Crimea, on 4 August, Kryuchkov got to work. He sent a small team of KGB officers to a safe house, outside Moscow, to work out a plan for a state of emergency. On 8 August they reported there was no pressing need to introduce a state of emergency. Kryuchkov silenced them by saying that it could not be introduced after the treaty was signed.[4] The following week, Kryuchkov sent another team to refine further plans for a state of emergency. On 16 August the paperwork was ready and the decree, establishing the state committee on the state of emergency and removing Gorbachev, was in front of him. Officers were immediately sent to the Crimea to cut Gorbachev off from the outside world.

. . .

THE COUP

The time had now come to invite others into the spider's web. On 17 August Kryuchkov invited Pavlov, Yazov, Boldin, Oleg Baklanov (the CC secretary who supervised the defence sector) and Oleg Shenin to a luxurious KGB residence, known as the ABC complex. Then they all had a steam bath. Afterwards Kryuchkov gave Pavlov some news: he was going to be sacked. He complained that he had a thankless task, the country was going to the dogs and no one obeyed orders any more. Only a state of emergency could stop the rot. Kryuchkov agreed with him and said that Gorbachev simply did not want to listen to the truth. He always changed the subject when Kryuchkov broached the need for emergency measures. The KGB chief then presented his proposal. Set up an emergency committee, send a delegation to Gorbachev to lobby his support, and if he refused, cut him off in the Crimea and tell the people that he was unfit. Yanaev would take over as acting President and Lukyanov, as speaker of the Supreme Soviet, would ensure that parliament accepted it.

Kryuchkov informed the conspirators that one important person was still unaware of what was afoot: Boris Pugo. Shenin was confident that Pugo would go along with the plan but he was not completely convinced that Lukyanov would play ball, as he tended to prevaricate.[5] Hence, two days before the attempted coup, the comrade who was to play the key role in legitimising their unconstitutional act, Yanaev, did not yet know the role he was to play, and had not agreed. Eventually, Yanaev, Pugo and Lukyanov came on board. Presumably, what won them over was being told that the coup was certain to succeed. When Gorbachev phoned Yeltsin on 14 August, he sensed that the Russian President was having doubts about signing the treaty. He was under pressure to impose some more conditions. Gorbachev's instinct told him he should return to Moscow.[6]

On Sunday 18 August Gorbachev made the final amendments to his speech at the signing ceremony, in consultation with Georgy Shakhnazarov, who was at the nearby Yuzhny sanatorium. It was the last telephone call he was to make. All communications went dead at 16.30 hours. Just before 17.00 hours, he was surprised to be told that he had visitors.

He had invited no one, but Baklanov, Shenin, Boldin, General Valentin Varennikov (chief of ground forces) and General Yury Plekhanov (head of the KGB's ninth directorate, responsible for the personal security of the leadership) wanted to see him. They had been allowed into the dacha, which was strictly against orders, because Plekhanov and Boldin were accompanying the group. The head of Gorbachev's own security at Foros, also a KGB officer, was nonplussed. Gorbachev's immediate reaction was to phone Kryuchkov to find out what was going on. The line was dead. All five lines, including the strategic communications line, were out of action. He then told Raisa Maksimovna to expect the worst. They called their daughter, Irina, and their son-in-law Anatoly and told them what had happened. They were to bring the grandchildren in. All this took just over half an hour.

The guests had come up to the second floor, uninvited. They acted as if they were lords of the manor. Baklanov stated that an emergency committee had been set up. 'You must sign the decree on the declaration of a state of emergency.'[7] There were several versions of documents, ready for signature. Baklanov listed the members of the emergency committee, including Lukyanov. He stated that Yeltsin was under arrest and then that he would be arrested on his return from Almaty. Baklanov suggested that if Gorbachev did not want to sign the emergency decree himself, Yanaev could do it for him. After the necessary 'dirty work', Gorbachev could return to Moscow as President. When Gorbachev rejected this course of action, Varennikov enquired: 'Why don't you just resign?'. Mikhail Sergeevich then lost his cool, called them criminals, and swore at them as only a Russian can. He decided against arresting them on the spot as the mastermind was in Moscow.

The conspirators met on Sunday evening. Pavlov and Yanaev had already been hitting the bottle. Kryuchkov reported that Gorbachev had not signed any declaration. He stated that the President could no longer carry out his duties since he was ill. Lukyanov then interjected that, if he were ill, a medical certificate or his own statement was necessary. Kryuchkov's response was to say a medical certificate would be obtained later. Lukyanov then panicked and demanded that his name be removed from the list of conspirators. At 22.15, Shenin, Baklanov, Boldin and Plekhanov arrived.

Varennikov had flown to Kiev to ensure the Ukrainians did not act unwisely. Yanaev was suffering a fit of nerves. He declined to sign the document making him acting President, arguing that Gorbachev should come back to Moscow, recover, and then resume his duties. He did not feel up to the job. Eventually, he did sign, just after 23.00 hours.

Then Yazov, Pugo, Kryuchkov, Pavlov and Baklanov signed order no. 1 of the state committee on the state of emergency, which declared a six-month state of emergency. Aleksandr Bessmertnykh, summoned from a holiday home in Belarus, arrived just after the documents had been signed. He was taken aback when he found his name on the list and struck it off. Kryuchkov mentioned, in passing, that some of the democrats would be locked up and he listed over ten names. Pavlov, in an inebriated voice, advised: 'Arrest a thousand!'. Shortly after midnight, they all went home.[8]

Just before 05.30 hours on 19 August, TASS (the official news agency) announced the state of emergency, that Yanaev was acting President and that the state committee for the state of emergency had taken over. All state bodies were subordinate to it, all political parties and movements were suspended, all strikes and demonstrations banned and the independent media silenced. Two more joined the emergency committee on 19 August: Aleksandr Tizyakov, an enterprise director who had vigorously opposed Gorbachev, and Vasily Starodubtsev, a kolkhoz chairman and president of the USSR Peasant Union, which strongly opposed private agriculture. They gave the impression that industry and agriculture were behind the committee. Vladimir Zhirinovsky immediately enthusiastically endorsed the committee, as did the pro-Moscow Parties in the Baltic republics. Another famous supporter was Marshal Sergei Akhromeev, who rushed back to Moscow from his holiday in the Crimea and offered his services.

Yeltsin was not arrested on his arrival from Almaty, late on 18 August, and repaired to his dacha at Arkhangeskoe, on the outskirts of Moscow. He was simply under the surveillance of the KGB's crack Alpha unit. Yeltsin was woken up by his daughter, Tanya, early on the morning of 19 August. He immediately telephoned republican leaders. Nazarbaev and Kravchuk would not commit themselves without further information. He could not get through to Yanaev or

Gorbachev. Yeltsin summoned Russian government officials to his dacha and they drafted an appeal to the Russian people. Mayor Anatoly Sobchak stayed a while and then left for Leningrad. The Alpha unit merely observed Yeltsin and others leaving for the White House. They made the White House, through the streets of Moscow, past columns of military vehicles and troops, at about 10.00 hours, issued the appeal and began saving Russia, and also Gorbachev. Yeltsin then went down to talk to the Taman division, ordered to take up positions outside the building, and mounted one of their tanks. The resultant photograph became one of the most famous of the decade.

At Foros, a double ring of guards was placed around the dacha.[9] Warships approached the shore where they were detained, stayed a while, and then sailed away. The Gorbachevs managed to tune into the BBC World Service, the Voice of America and Radio Liberty, in Russian, on a Sony transistor. They learnt about Yanaev taking over because of Gorbachev's ill health. Anatoly Chernyaev arrived from Yuzhny sanatorium and was very glum. A nurse told Raisa Maksimovna that Pugo and his wife had been staying at the Yuzhny sanatorium but had left suddenly the day before, 18 August. 'They say that he and his wife had food poisoning.' Suddenly the television began working again. At 17.30 Gorbachev instructed Chernyaev to contact Yanaev and demand again the restoration of communications and an aircraft to fly back to Moscow.

The Gorbachevs were able to watch the emergency committee's news conference. Yanaev, Pugo, Baklanov, Starodubtsev and Tizyakov appeared, but not Kryuchkov and Yazov. They were all nervous, especially Yanaev who kept on drumming his fingers on the table. He insisted that their actions were only temporary. When asked about what specific illness Gorbachev was suffering from, Yanaev could not come up with an answer. A journalist asked if it was clear to them that they had staged a *coup d'état*? Another wondered if they had consulted Chile's General Pinochet. The general impression they radiated was that of frightened rabbits. They did not look like ruthless dictators who would rule with a rod of iron. The general public relaxed, only fearing that by some accident the White House might be stormed, covering the emergency in blood.

The committee received some encouragement from the republics, with Uzbekistan and Belarus supporting them. However, demonstrators, despite the ban, were beginning to assemble outside the White House, and by the evening there were tens of thousands there. Some said afterwards that they felt they had to do something to defend Russia and democracy. Yeltsin had called a general strike but there was little response, until the Kuzbass miners came out. Pavlov ordered Yazov to arrest them. The minister did nothing as he thought the Prime Minister was drunk. Gorbachev managed to make a video for posterity, just in case he did not survive. The recording was in four parts. Each part was packaged separately and hidden in a different part of the house.

On 20 August the Gorbachevs feared that the food coming in from outside could be contaminated. They decided to use only existing food and to boil everything. Kravchuk spoke on Ukrainian television but only appealed for calm and observance of the law and did not mention Gorbachev personally. Nazarbaev stated the actions of the committee were illegal. Someone arrived with news that all of Mikhail Sergeevich's demands would be met. All communications had to go through Plekhanov. The committee was disintegrating. Pavlov had taken to his bed and the bottle and Yanaev was nowhere to be found. Lukyanov reported to the plotters that he had concluded from discussions with Supreme Soviet deputies, the day before, that there was not a two-thirds majority to legitimate the emergency committee. The promised bulletin on Gorbachev's health did not appear. Vadim Bakatain and Evgeny Primakov, members of the Security Council, issued a statement declaring the activities of the committee illegal. Aleksandr Bessmertnykh, another member of the Council, was invited to join them but declined. This led to his being sacked after Gorbachev returned to Moscow.

Rumours spread that there was going to be an attack on the White House on 19 August, but they proved false. Another rumour put the attack the following evening. Civilians adopted the same tactics as those outside the television tower in Vilnius in January: they surrounded it. The military could easily have taken the White House, but only at the cost of a river of blood. Kryuchkov ordered the arrest of Yeltsin and the defenders on 20 August but no commander would obey

him. Even the KGB Alpha unit shied away from the task.
Three young men did die, run over by a tank on a ring road
nearby. On 21 August, at 15.00 hours, Yazov ordered military
units back to their barracks and Kryuchkov phoned Yeltsin
to tell him there would be no assault of the White House.

The Gorbachevs learnt from the BBC that Kryuchkov had
permitted a delegation to fly to Foros to see for themselves
that Gorbachev was gravely ill and incapacitated. They, especially Raisa Maksimovna, feared the worst. At about 17.00
hours, Yazov, Kryuchkov, Baklanov, Ivashko, Lukyanov and
Plekhanov turned up and requested an audience with Mikhail
Sergeevich. 'Let them wait. There will be no negotiations
until communications are fully restored.' They were, at 17.45.
The plotters made repeated attempts to arrange a meeting,
but in vain. Then Yeltsin phoned:

> Mikhail Sergeevich, my dear fellow, are you alive? We have been
> holding firm here for forty eight hours! George and Barbara
> Bush sent their greetings to me, said they had been praying for
> us for the last three days.

Then the Russian delegation arrived, Vice-President Rutskoi,
Prime Minister Silaev, Bakatin, Primakov, and others. The
mood was a mixture of joy and relief.

The members of the emergency committee and their closest aides were arrested. Pavlov and Yanaev did not resist
arrest, they were blind drunk. Pugo was not taken into custody. He and his wife shot themselves on 22 August. Marshal Akhromeev wrote a detailed report on his activities for
Gorbachev, a farewell note to his family, left 50 rubles to
pay his outstanding bill at the staff canteen, and hanged
himself with his belt. An officer was expected to commit
suicide by shooting himself, but he had handed in his service revolver. A tragic end for a very able officer. He once
confided that whereas his head accepted the new military
relationship with the US, his heart refused to change. On
19 August he had acted according to his heart, and it had
cost him his life.

Gorbachev felt most bitter about the betrayal of the Party.
Ivashko, his deputy, could have demanded a meeting with
the boss, together with the Party leadership. Yet he did not
raise his voice. The CC Secretariat ordered local Party bodies

to support the attempted coup. The Communist Party of Ukraine endorsed the activities of the emergency committee. Only Presidents Yeltsin and Akaev, of Kyrgyzstan, had come out unequivocally against the attempted coup from the beginning. The others had preferred to wait and see. Not only republican leaders hesitated.

President Bush, when he met the press on 19 August, was defensive and hinted that he thought that the coup had been successful and that he would have to deal with the emergency committee. This was seized upon by the committee and broadcast over and over again. He declined to telephone Yeltsin. Things were put to right that evening when Bush declared that the attempted coup was illegal and unconstitutional. He then contacted Yeltsin. One of the reasons for the confusion was that the able American ambassador in Moscow, Jack Matlock, was back in America after completing his term of duty.[10] President Mitterrand, unfortunately, was also too quick to adjust to the post-Gorbachev era. On French television, on 19 August, he spoke of the 'new leaders' several times.

. . .

A REVISIONIST VIEW

Amy Knight is the leading revisionist historian who remains unconvinced by the official version of the coup.[11] There are inconsistencies in the testimonies and statements which were made and then retracted. For instance, the time when communications at Foros were cut off was given, by various sources, as 16.00, 16.30, 16.32 and 17.50 hours. However, during Gorbachev's arrest some of his guards phoned home from the administrative building, about 100 metres from Gorbachev's dacha, the special telephones in the President's cars were working and the garage was open. Gorbachev was aware that some guards had phoned their relatives on these phones. If Gorbachev were to be kept isolated, why were Shakhnazarov, his wife and son allowed to join Gorbachev from the Yuzhny sanitorium, about 12 km from the dacha? Gorbachev had 32 guards in the dacha, yet they were kept subdued (they retained their weapons) by only five supporting the plotters.

Knight claims that the KGB never intended to storm the White House. Kryuchkov claimed, in a letter to *Pravda*, that there had never been any threat to the White House and that Yeltsin knew this all the time. The reason for the myth of the threatened attack was to portray Yeltsin as a hero.[12] Yeltsin, in his memoirs, admitted that he had received a phone call from Kryuchkov on 20 August stating that the White House was not under threat, but that he had not trusted him. The commander of the KGB's Alpha unit, which would have carried out the attack, categorically denied having received orders to storm the building. Sergei Stepashin, who sided with Yeltsin, accepted that the KGB had never ordered the arrest of Yeltsin or the storming of the White House. Knight concludes that 'all these discrepancies suggest strongly that Gorbachev was not a captive and might have easily left Foros or at the very least communicated with the outside world'.[13]

However, there is evidence supporting the Gorbachev version. The traumatic shock suffered by Raisa Maksimovna, and her poor health during the subsequent two years, suggests that she was taken completely by surprise. It is highly unlikely that Gorbachev was plotting with the plotters without discussing the matter with her. Had he kept it from her until the attempted coup, he could then have spared her anguish by informing her of it when the plotters arrived.

· · ·

WHY DID THE COUP FAIL?

Paradoxically, Gorbachev's failed perestroika ensured that the plotters failed. The general secretary had so transformed the political culture that it was no longer possible for a hard man like Kryuchkov to wave his rod and expect obedience. Had he eliminated Gorbachev in Foros, he would have failed miserably to refashion the Soviet Union in the pre-1985 image. The economy was in a state of collapse and a new stabilisation programme by Pavlov would have only had cosmetic effect. Little foreign aid would have been forthcoming in such an environment. The republics were claiming control over their assets and would no longer accept dictates from Moscow. Significantly, Gosplan was transformed into a Ministry for Forecasting.

The organisation of the attempted coup was astonishingly inept. This may have had something to do with the Popov leak which forced the conspirators to meet in a narrow conclave. They had to plan the event and then issue orders. The military and KGB turned out to be unreliable. Yeltsin's relentless campaign to promote Russian interests and to stoke the fires of a Russian consciousness had had some effect. Officers and men had to decide where their loyalties lay, with the Soviet Union or Russia. A factor in their decision not to spill blood outside and inside the White House was that, for the first time, they would be involved in shedding Russian blood. Many were willing to shed Georgian, Azerbaijani, Lithuanian and Latvian blood, but not Russian blood. This also implies that had the coup succeeded the instruments of coercion would not have proved reliable forces to reimpose Moscow's will on the Soviet Union.

Perhaps the main reason why the attempt to put the clock back failed was the lack of clear thinking in the junta. They did not possess a single dominant, inspiring idea which could have been used to rally support. The decree put out by them was remarkable for its absence of socialist or communist rhetoric. The main thrust was an appeal to save the country from disaster, larded with promises to improve everyone's lot. Given the disillusionment with Gorbachev's perestroika promises, there was little likelihood that such promises would have enthused anyone. The junta was put together very late in the day. Only when a dithering Yanaev signed up late on 18 August was it certain to go ahead. They had no clear fallback position when Gorbachev refused to cooperate. They lacked the ruthlessness of a Stalin who would, most probably, have liquidated Gorbachev, disguising it as suicide.

The failure to arrest Yeltsin and his associates was a major tactical blunder as it would have decapitated Russian resistance. Kryuchkov had not comprehended the revolution which had occurred in the country. People were no longer afraid of the KGB or the Party or the authorities. He appeared to believe the slanted reports he had been feeding Gorbachev. All that was required to restore authority was a strong hand. He and a cabal of others had been badgering Gorbachev to introduce presidential rule since late 1990. Kryuchkov did not understand that the policies of the past were no longer viable. He epitomised the bankruptcy of the system which had prevailed so long. Gorbachev, inadvertently, had wrecked the country and in so doing made it safe for a different future.

. . .

THE AFTERMATH

The Gorbachevs returned to Moscow at 02.00 hours on 22 August. The strain showed. Mikhail Sergeevich looked drawn and grey. Raisa Maksimovna had to be helped down the steps and appeared to have suffered a slight stroke. It was to take her two years to overcome the effects of the past few days. Their daughter Irina suffered a nervous breakdown.

Symbolically, they were escorted back to Moscow by Vice-President Aleksandr Rutskoi. They had left the Soviet Union but had returned to Russia. No statement was made to the press that night. On 23 August, on his way to the Kremlin, Gorbachev told reporters: 'I have come back from Foros to another country, and I myself am a different man now'.[14] Just how much had changed that he had not comprehended emerged at the subsequent press conference. Invited to comment on the fact that the Party was out of touch with the current mood of the country, Gorbachev put his foot in it. He declared that his most important duty was to rid the Party of its reactionary elements:[15]

> On the basis of this new programme we have put forward, I believe that there is a possibility of uniting all that is progressive, all the best thinking . . . We must therefore do everything to ensure that the party is reformed and becomes the living force of perestroika.[16]

He later made clear that he was a convinced 'adherent of the socialist idea'. These statements caused an intake of breath among the audience. Mikhail Sergeevich had demonstrated that he had not grasped the immense changes the attempted coup had wrought. He was still talking about reforming the Party which had betrayed him! That was the moment when his glittering political career came to an end. It was clear that he had not been very well briefed or that he had not bothered to acquaint himself, in detail, with what had happened.

Instead of thoroughly analysing events, he busied himself with finding replacements for those officials who had blotted their copybook. Perhaps it was the after-effect of the shock he had suffered at Foros. The psychological impact was greater since he had not had the slightest inkling of what was afoot. To find that some of his most trusted subordinates were conspirators was devastating. He addressed the nation on television the same evening and avoided mentioning the Party and socialism. The goals were the same as before: the signing of a Union treaty, a new Union Constitution and then presidential and parliamentary elections. The security forces would have to be looked into. They had proved 'insufficiently reliable'. On 24 August Gorbachev chose Vadim Bakatin to undertake a thorough reorganisation of the KGB. Furious crowds tore down the statute of Dzerzhinsky, the first head of the KGB, outside the Lubyanka, while KGB officers destroyed as much incriminating evidence as they could before Bakatin took over.[17]

On 23 August Yeltsin applied the *coup de grâce* to Gorbachev. At the Russian Supreme Soviet, he placed the minutes of a meeting of Gorbachev's government, on 19 August, before him and insisted that he read them aloud from the rostrum. It was a tale of betrayal. The only minister who was resolutely opposed to the attempted coup was Nikolai Vorontsov, Minister for the Environment, who just happened to be the only member of the cabinet who was not a Party member. Yeltsin signed a decree suspending the activities of the Party and banned *Pravda* and other Party newspapers, sealed the CC Secretariat building (in so doing turfing out unceremoniously the secretaries and officials and not permitting them to take any papers with them), and banned the Russian Party. Gorbachev protested, but in vain. Yeltsin stood above Gorbachev and pointed his finger down at the general secretary. He was now taking calculated revenge for all the insults of the past.

On 25 August Gorbachev resigned as general secretary of the Party and instructed local soviets to take over Party property. Party activity was also to cease in the armed forces, the militia, the KGB and all other state institutions. Ivan Silaev, Russian Prime Minister, chaired a committee, with Grigory Yavlinsky as his deputy, to administer the Soviet economy. Russia was now running the Soviet Union. Gorbachev appointed General Mikhail Moiseev to succeed Yazov but Yeltsin objected. So Marshal Evgeny Shaposhnikov, who had threatened to bomb the Kremlin if the White House were stormed, took over.

. . .

A UNION: TO BE OR NOT TO BE?

Tactically, Yeltsin had the upper hand on Gorbachev. After his return on 22 August, Gorbachev was always chasing events, always reacting to Yeltsin's initiatives. To provide himself with some breathing space, Yeltsin declared that a Union treaty could be signed and implemented. This kept the negotiations going while the Russians worked out where their interests lay. The attempted coup had changed the guidelines for the new Union. The emergency committee had intended to apply martial law to the Baltic republics and scotch all aspirations for independence. Estonia responded on 20 August by declaring independence and Latvia followed suit on 21 August. Previously they had never dared to go as far as Lithuania in declaring independence. Russia immediately recognised Estonian and Latvian independence, having already recognised Lithuanian independence, on 31 July 1991.[18] Gorbachev held back and argued that only the Congress of People's Deputies could take such a step. However, he did decree that all Baltic citizens serving in the Soviet armed forces were to be demobbed and KGB property passed to the respective governments. On 6 September the USSR State Council unanimously recognised the independence of the Baltic republics. *De facto* independence had become *de jure* independence. Foreign countries recognised them with the United States holding back a few days, in deference to Gorbachev. They then entered the United Nations.

The exit of the Baltic republics was accompanied by a rush by other republics to declare their independence. This paralleled the previous race for sovereignty and again the question was raised: what did it mean? By the end of August, Ukraine (subject to a referendum on 1 December, the outcome of which was a foregone conclusion), Belarus, Moldova, Azerbaijan, Kyrgyzstan and Uzbekistan had all declared independence. By the end of September, Georgia, Tajikistan and Armenia had followed suit. Turkmenistan waited until

October, when there was no other option. Hence, the only republics which had not formally declared independence were Russia and Kazakhstan. The latter was in a delicate position as almost half its population were Slav. Independence, except for the Baltic states, was only on paper. They continued to trade and use the ruble and negotiate about a future Union.

The only republic in which power changed hands as a result of the failed coup was Belarus. Nikolai Dementei, the speaker of the Supreme Soviet, prevaricated on 19 and 20 August, and on 21 August, with execrable timing, the Belorusian Party supported the emergency committee. When Gorbachev suspended the activities of the CPSU and ordered an investigation into its activities during the attempted coup, the Belarusian Party leaders became nationalists overnight. They joined their natural opponents, the Popular Front, which had about one-tenth of the seats in parliament, and voted for independence. Dementei was outvoted and replaced by Stanislau Shushkevich as speaker. This made him head of state as Belarus had not adopted a presidential system.

The Congress of People's Deputies convened for the last time on 2 September to assess critically the results of the attempted coup. Deputies accepted the inevitable and voted for the establishment of a Union of Sovereign States. The leaders of the ten republics, who now made up the State Council, recommended this course of action. In so doing, the deputies accepted that they had voted themselves out of existence. The pill was sugared by assuring them that their salaries and privileges would run until 1994, the end of their legislative period. The interim institutions, to serve until the treaty was signed, were the State Council, consisting of the leaders of those republics which wished to sign the treaty, and chaired by Gorbachev; a new Supreme Soviet; and an inter-republican economic committee. An astute decision was that those states which did not wish to sign the Union treaty could belong to the economic committee. This provided a forum for economic cooperation during a time of political divorce.

These institutions were, in reality, stillborn. Gorbachev preferred to consult individually or with advisers and devoted little time to the State Council. He never permitted a successor institution to the Politburo to acquire any influence.

First there was the Security Council, then the Presidential Council, and finally the State Council. The membership of the State Council, on paper, was most promising. Vadim Bakatin, Nikolai Petrakov, Aleksandr Yakovlev, Evgeny Velikhov (the nuclear physicist), Gavriil Popov, Yury Ryzhkov, Anatoly Sobchak (mayor of St Petersburg) and Egor Yakovlev (the editor of *Moskovskie novosti*, who was now to take over Central TV). Eduard Shevardnadze declined to serve.[19]

The Russian elites could not agree on the future of Russia. Yeltsin suffered a mild heart attack in late September, went off to convalesce and did not return until mid-October. There were political and economic conflicts. Yeltsin's team consisted of trusted associates from Sverdlovsk (Ekaterinburg), managers from industry and young democrats. He needed insiders to outmanoeuvre Gorbachev's insiders. The question was whether Russia should be understood as the Russian Federation or as the whole of the Soviet Union, minus the Baltic states. The insiders favoured a loose confederation, dominated by Russia. The democrats, mindful of the fact that the ideological nomenklatura was strong in the other republics, favoured Russia on its own. There was also division over economic direction. Some thought that the big bang could only be successfully implemented in Russia. Attempting to do so in the rest of the former Soviet Union would slow down the whole process and be a drain on resources. Others thought that a single economic space should be retained as the Soviet economy was so intertwined that it would be destructive artificially to split off. The single space would have a single currency, under the control of the Russian Central Bank.

Gaidar favoured the former strategy and Yavlinsky the latter. Ivan Silaev, chair of the inter-republican economic committee, decided to resign as Russian Prime Minister. This revealed him as a supporter of the single economic space group. Presumably, he had perceived that the Gaidar group was going to win and jumped before he was pushed.

Yeltsin took Gaidar's advice and on 28 October presented a radical economic programme to the Russian Congress of People's Deputies. He also requested a year's special powers to introduce a market economy by decree and also appoint provincial governors. Congress granted him his wish. On 4 November the State Council voted to dissolve all Soviet ministries, except defence, foreign affairs, railways, electricity, and nuclear power. On 6 November Yeltsin assumed the position of Russian Prime Minister and appointed Gaidar to head the economic ministries. Now an attempt would be made to introduce monetarism to Russia. Legally, since no Union treaty had been signed, many financial institutions in Russia were still subordinate to Soviet institutions.

Yeltsin rectified this on 15 November when he decreed that Soviet financial institutions on Russian territory pass to Russia. A mistake was made by the Russian government when it did not object to the Russian Central Bank becoming subordinate to parliament. This oversight was to cost Gaidar and Yeltsin dear over the next two years. Yeltsin took his revenge on the CPSU and the Russian Party on 6 November, traditionally the day when a festive speech was delivered, celebrating the October Revolution. He banned both within Russia.[20] The Party had attempted to drum him out of political life in October 1987. Now he drummed the Party out of political life. Revenge was sweet. By late November, all that was left of the Soviet Union was a President and a renamed foreign ministry, the Ministry of External Affairs, armed forces and political police in disarray, and courts and judges which were ignored. They were all desperately trying to find a new paymaster who would pay their wages.

Only in foreign affairs did Gorbachev still have a role to play. Many foreign visitors traipsed through Moscow to make their own soundings about the future of the Union. Given a choice, they would have preferred to deal with Gorbachev rather than Yeltsin. Nostalgia for Gorbachev and the Union were great in certain quarters. But reality was reality and everyone had to be polite to Yeltsin and receive him when he went abroad. Nazarbaev made a successful visit to Great Britain in October 1991. James Baker, in September, saw the two Presidents in Moscow, but also took in Kiev, Almaty and the Baltic states. Gorbachev was most accommodating. Arms supplies to all sides in Afghanistan were ended and the remaining Soviet troops were to be recalled from Cuba. Then Vadim Bakatin provided the US ambassador with a detailed diagram, indicating where KGB listening devices had been planted in the US embassy.[21]

The last great showcase event for Mikhail Sergeevich was the opening of the Madrid conference on the Middle East on 30 October. He co-chaired it with President Bush. The irony was not lost on the participants. A President, representing the strongest power on earth, sat side by side with the President of a country many regarded as non-existent. Before the conference, Gorbachev had had his last summit with 'dear' George Bush. The American President told Mikhail Sergeevich what he wanted to hear. He was backing him and hoped that a Union would emerge. Bush, evidently, was reluctant to take on board that the more important man in Moscow now was Boris Yeltsin. Gorbachev had a warm discussion with the Spanish Prime Minister, Felipe González, his favourite western politician. González could tell Mikhail Sergeevich home truths that no other politician would dare to utter. Gorbachev loved to hear Felipe talking about socialism, even though it was western-style social democracy, as it confirmed his own socialist faith. After the conference, the President's party made for President Mitterrand's rustic retreat near Bayonne. There among the roosters, donkeys and sheep, Mikhail Sergeevich was back home, back to his youth. Mitterrand did his best to make up for his gaffe, on 19 August, when he had spoken about his guest in the past tense.

In mid-November Eduard Shevardnadze was talked into becoming Minister of External Affairs during the death throes of the Soviet Union. Yeltsin had his eyes on the ministry, demanded a savage cut in personnel, and then merged it with the Russian Ministry of Foreign Affairs.

. . .

GORBACHEV, YELTSIN AND THE END OF THE UNION

Yavlinsky drafted outline economic institutions for the inter-republican committee in September. He assumed a single economic space, a single Central Bank, a single currency, open borders, private property, and the Soviet hard currency debt burden was to be shared. By the time the republics had had their say there was practically nothing left. Yavlinsky, in shock, was not sure whether his patient, the Union, was still alive.[22] Nevertheless, a treaty on an economic community of sovereign states was signed on 18 October. All the hard questions had been fudged. All the time,

Gorbachev was discussing an IMF loan to get the Soviet Union out of its self-imposed mess. Yeltsin kept on insisting that he favoured a Union, a confederation. He adopted Gaidar's economic programme on 28 October, without consulting Gorbachev, and it was based on a radically different economic strategy. Did the two go together?

Yeltsin maintained that he had no desire to establish Russian armed forces and even talked about establishing a new Union state. Then he claimed that the new Union did not need a constitution. On 14 November, at the State Council meeting at Novo-Ogarevo, Yeltsin opposed the creation of a unified state, calling the new entity a confederation. Gorbachev and Nazarbaev were appalled: 'If we reject a unified state, we will have something that is indefinite and non-binding, something that serves no useful purpose whatever'.[23] He then came up with the old chestnut of a Union but it was rejected. 'In the end, the decision is yours. I am convinced we must preserve a unified state. If we do not, we'll bring ruin on our country and on the rest of the world', warned Mikhail Sergeevich. Shushkevich observed that a confederation would have unified armed forces. Yeltsin chipped in with transport, the space programme and the environment. Gorbachev would have nothing of it: 'If there are no effective state structures, what good are a President and a parliament? If that's your decision, I'm prepared to go.'[24] Yeltsin rejoined: 'Now you're getting carried away', but Gorbachev countered: 'Nothing of the sort. I'm too exhausted for that.' He got up, a spring in his step, and stated that if they wanted a figurehead or a doormat, he was not their man. He claimed that the country needed a strong leader as a counterweight to decentralisation but that he did not aspire to the position. Then he turned to Yeltsin: 'Boris Nikolaevich, you must realise where they're leading us – the people who suggest that Russia should leave everyone behind in the dust and proceed on its own'. He was referring to Burbulis and others who had argued that a Russian state, heir to the Soviet Union, should be established. Yeltsin did not want confrontation. 'I don't support extremists. Let's spell it out: a confederal state.' Gorbachev could then not resist a dig at Yeltsin, who had given ground. 'I am guided by principles, whereas the first thing you think of is what other people will say.'[25]

They began drafting amendments. The future President would be directly elected by the people; the parliament would be bicameral, with deputies from republics and other territories; and there would be a government and a capital. The office of speaker of parliament was important and a trustworthy man had to be found. Then Gorbachev inserted one of his biblical allusions: 'But even among Jesus's disciples, one traitor turned up'.[26] Since there were only seven around the table, it was assumed there could be no Judas there. On the economic side, Yeltsin mentioned that the Russians had calculated Ukraine's debt to them, at world market prices, to be about US$80 billion. He then decided he could be magnanimous: 'If Ukraine agrees to join the Union, we can forget about this little debt. Otherwise, they can pay up!'[27]

Shushkevich suggested that another meeting be held so that each member of the State Council could approve the final version and defend it in his own parliament. They agreed it should be signed before the end of the year. 'But this time, let's not tell anyone the date', quipped Nazarbaev. Yeltsin told the assembled journalists, 'We have agreed that there will be a Union: a democratic, confederal state'.[28] He then remarked to Gorbachev that he did not always understand him. 'That's all right, as long as you eventually catch on', Gorbachev rejoined. The draft treaty had many defects. It proclaimed that the new Union was a subject in international law, but it also stated that member states were also subjects in international law. Who took precedence when they clashed? There would be unified armed forces and central control of nuclear forces. There would be a President, a Prime Minister, a small government, a Supreme Court, a Court of Arbitration, and a procurator general. There was scope for much conflict. Nevertheless it was quite an achievement by Gorbachev to have got as far as this.

With Yeltsin off on an official visit to Germany, Gorbachev felt that he had to compete for media attention. He headed for Siberia and Kyrgyzstan. It was a sobering experience as Mikhail Sergeevich discovered that he was not addressing the nation, but some locals. Short reports of his tour were carried by the media but everything was low key.

Reality arrived like a cold douche on 25 November, the day for the signing of the draft treaty by the members of the State Council. The television cameras and the journalists

251

were there to record a historic occasion. Yeltsin caused a sensation by declaring that he could not sign the draft treaty in its present form. The Russian Supreme Soviet was not willing to ratify a unified state, or even a confederal state. Defining the Union as a confederation of democratic states might be acceptable.

Gorbachev could hardly believe his ears. He told Yeltsin that he was wiping out all they had agreed together. Shushkevich then came in on Yeltsin's side and suggested postponing the proceedings. The Vice President of Kazakhstan (Nazarbaev was not present) spoke up for Gorbachev. However, President Karimov of Uzbekistan sided with Yeltsin. This revealed that the Russians had been engaged in intensive lobbying to stifle the draft treaty. Gorbachev warned everyone that if a draft treaty were not signed, the consequences could be irreparable.

Shushkevich tried to smooth Mikhail Sergeevich's feathers by saying that it was advisable to postpone the signing for about ten days, without making any major changes to the text. Belarus would then 'sign and ratify the agreement without any problems'.[29] Yeltsin then played what he believed to be his trump card. It would not be wise to sign the agreement without Ukraine being present. 'That might push them into making decisions that would wreck the Union once and for all.' Gorbachev thought differently. It was necessary to demonstrate to the 'separatists' that the Union was going ahead. Then he applied moral pressure:

> I am obliged to note, that the leaders of the republics, at this serious and even dangerous juncture, are engaging in political intrigue and are changing their positions. Under these circumstances, they should have told me frankly that they no longer want a Union. Personally, I think that by acting in such a way as to cause the ruin of the state, you are taking on an extremely heavy burden of responsibility.[30]

They still remained unmoved. So he concluded:

> I feel a profound sadness and disappointment. I don't understand how you can go on. You know that by creating a kind of poorhouse instead of a unified state, you're going to make society suffer tremendously. We're already drowning in shit.

Gorbachev's use of expletives revealed how frustrated and depressed he was. Gorbachev announced a break and when Yeltsin met him again, he announced that he had been sent by the others to kowtow to the Tsar, the great khan. Gorbachev kept his temper and replied: 'Fine, fine, Tsar Boris'.[31] All the members signed a joint communiqué, which turned out to be the death certificate of the Soviet Union.

Had Yeltsin and Shushkevich already decided to do without the Union before the meeting or did they reach that decision during the discussions? Gorbachev and his aides think that the two were playing a foxy game, stringing the negotiations along but ensuring the signing was always pushed into the future. Yeltsin and Shushkevich maintain that Gorbachev's behaviour at the meeting shocked them. They were always seeking a compromise but, especially as far as Ukraine was concerned, Gorbachev would not listen. When Gorbachev called a break and marched out of the room, that was the last straw. They decided to meet in Belarus and invite Kravchuk to join them.[32] At the end of the meeting Gorbachev told the journalists that the republican leaders had taken a step backward. That proved to be an understatement. The State Council never convened again.

It was a foregone conclusion that Ukrainian voters would opt for independence on 1 December. Some 90.3 per cent did so, even ethnic Russian areas revealing a majority in favour. Leonid Kravchuk was elected President with an impressive 61.6 per cent of the votes. Russia immediately recognised Ukrainian independence, thus ending over 300 years of union. No attempt was made to negotiate special conditions for the 11 million ethnic Russians living in the republic. It was a hard decision for Russia as many Russians did and do not regard Ukraine as foreign but as part of the motherland.

Ukraine had been very useful to Yeltsin because he had always been able to point to the republic's reluctance to sign up for the Union as a cover for his own policies. Ukraine could be blamed for destroying the Union, not Russia. On 5 December the Ukrainian Supreme Soviet voted to annul Ukraine's signing of the treaty of 1922 which had created the Soviet Union. On 6 December it resolved not to sign any Union treaty and to set up its own armed forces.

Kravchuk underlined this before he left for Minsk to meet Shushkevich and Yeltsin. Ukraine would not sign a Union treaty which had a central governing body.[33] Gorbachev had always insisted on central institutions at State Council meetings of republican leaders. It was no secret that Yeltsin and Kravchuk were going to Minsk but it was assumed they were going to discuss mainly economic issues, as Russia had announced that it was freeing many retail prices on 16 December (this was eventually postponed until 2 January 1992).

Yeltsin met Gorbachev on 6 December. Later, Gorbachev was told the following story by one of Yeltsin's supporters. After returning from Belarus, Yeltsin called together a group of deputies close to him to ensure that the CIS agreement was ratified. When asked about the legality of the move, Yeltsin broke into a long monologue, the essence of which was that he had duped Gorbachev. He had misled him about the purpose of the Minsk visit. He intended to do the opposite of what he told the Soviet President: 'We had to get Gorbachev out of the way'.[34]

After meeting Yeltsin, the Soviet President offered a confident assessment of the independence vote. It placed Ukraine on a par with other republics. 'I am certain that in Ukraine today people are thinking about the Union, just as people in other corners of our vast country are.'[35] He was clearly unaware of what Kravchuk had said earlier in the day. He was naïve right up to the end.

When Yeltsin and Kravchuk arrived at Minsk airport on 7 December, they were whisked off to Belovezh forest where they met in the seclusion of a hunting lodge. All three leaders later denied that they knew in advance what the outcome of the summit would be.[36] Belarus needed open borders with Ukraine. Russia had been toying with the idea of a commonwealth with Ukraine since late 1990. Yeltsin later stated that he had asked Kravchuk if the draft Union treaty could be amended in such a way as to induce Ukraine to sign. The Ukrainian President had retorted: 'No'. This implied that the commonwealth to be created could not be a state or a subject of international law. It was not to restrict the sovereignty of its members in any way.

A draft was worked out during the night and on the morning of Sunday 8 December the three leaders decided to invite Nazarbaev, who had just arrived in Moscow, to join them. The flight to Brest-Litovsk would only have taken about an hour. He agreed and immediately phoned Gorbachev. He then changed his mind. He later stated that his reason for not going was that he felt he would be presented with a *fait accompli*. He also did not wish to associate himself with what appeared to many to be a conspiracy. In so doing, his sure political touch deserted him. He mistakenly still stuck with Gorbachev. Had he gone to Belovezh forest, he might have been able to insert a few clauses in favour of Kazakhstan. Yeltsin and Shushkevich thought he was coming and had set up a splendid table and invited journalists to observe the signing. They then went off to the airport to receive him.

When he did not turn up they went ahead on their own and signed a joint declaration and the agreement on establishing a Commonwealth of Independent States (CIS). The declaration stated that the agreement was open to all states of the former Soviet Union, if they shared the 'aims and principles' of the agreement.[37] They then suggested Shushkevich, the host, phone Gorbachev with the news. Yeltsin was to phone President Bush. Shushkevich did not immediately phone Gorbachev as, he claimed later, there were no secure phones at the hunting lodge, but wanted to get back to Minsk before he phoned the President.[38] Yeltsin then phoned President Bush and gave him the news.

When Shushkevich did eventually phone Gorbachev, from Minsk, the President's first question was: 'What happens to me?'.[39] Then he exploded. 'You talk to the President of the United States of America and your own President doesn't even know what's going on! That's a disgrace!'[40] He then asked for the receiver to be passed to Yeltsin. 'What you have done behind my back, with the consent of the US President, is a crying shame, a disgrace!'[41]

The Soviet President demanded to be briefed in full and they agreed to meet the following day. The CIS capital was to be Minsk but no institutions were agreed at the founding meeting. The commonwealth was a voluntary association. Any decision reached was not binding on member states, and the CIS could not collect any taxes. However, it was agreed that there would be a joint unified command of nuclear forces and a common security space. Existing boundaries were recognised. The successor states acknowledged their responsibility to be bound by and to implement the international obligations entered into by the Soviet Union. Each state would decide its own responsibilities. They agreed that the Soviet Union would now cease to exist.

Yeltsin met Gorbachev personally on Monday 9 December to go through the agreement. Nazarbaev was also there, to Yeltsin's annoyance. The Russians argued that the agreement was to 'save what could be saved' of the Soviet Union. This did not go down well with the Soviet President and he stated, on television the same evening, that the claim that the Soviet Union was ceasing to exist was wide of the mark. Perhaps the CIS agreement and the draft Union treaty could be debated in the republican parliaments, the Soviet Supreme Soviet, and there could also be a referendum.[42] Nazarbaev still defended the draft Union treaty. The CIS agreement could be discussed along with the treaty. Some of Yeltsin's supporters also opposed the CIS agreement, such as Gavriil Popov, Anatoly Sobchak and Nikolai Travkin. Nevertheless, it was ratified quickly by the respective parliaments.

Deputies from the three states were not to attend the Soviet Supreme Soviet or Congress of People's Deputies. This was the kiss of death, because it deprived these representative institutions of a quorum. Nazarbaev had to accept the inevitable. The Kazakhstan Supreme Soviet declared independence on 16 December so that the republic could negotiate as an equal with the others. On 13 December the Central Asians, in Ashghabat, agreed to seek CIS membership.

On 17 December the Russian Supreme Soviet displaced the Soviet Supreme Soviet in the Kremlin. The following day, the Soviet Supreme Soviet acknowledged that it was dead. On 21 December, in Almaty, eleven states signed the CIS agreement. Only Estonia, Latvia, Lithuania and Georgia declined to attend. However, Georgia later joined. Point five of the agreement stated baldly that the Soviet Union and the institution of the presidency of the Soviet Union no longer existed.

These weeks were deeply frustrating for Gorbachev. He was a bit player, and did not appear on stage for the important events. The republics rushed to claim Soviet assets on their territory and gradually stripped Mikhail Sergeevich bare. He gave vent to his anger and changed his mind about the CIS agreement. The emergency committee's attempted coup in August 1991 was now on a par with Belovezh forest. The only difference was that, whereas the former had failed miserably, the latter had succeeded brilliantly. He had some live ammunition but it never hit the mark. There was the fact that the dissolution of the Soviet Union was never put to a referendum in the three signatory states. The Soviet Congress of People's Deputies should have met to terminate legally the Union. Russia, Ukraine and Belarus had claimed the right to end the Union since they had set it up. This was not quite true, as there had been a fourth signatory, the Transcaucasian Soviet Federated Socialist Republic (Azerbaijan, Armenia and Georgia). They were not invited to attend or comment.

The impression given was that the Slav states wanted to reach an agreement and then present it to others. Since these three republics accounted for over 85 per cent of the Soviet GDP, their dominance was overwhelming. Russia's behaviour was understandable. Logically, it could only implement, what became known later as shock therapy, on its own. The other republics were hostile to the implementation of the big bang. Vice-President Rutskoi was also hostile to the big bang, as were many in the Russian Supreme Soviet. Yeltsin had taken the fateful decision not to draft a new Russian Constitution, and hence a new parliament, after August, concentrating his efforts on demolishing Gorbachev's political base. Had the Union continued into 1992, Gorbachev would have provided a focus for many Russians alienated by shock therapy.

.   .   .

ADIEU

Gorbachev formally resigned on 25 December 1991, addressing the nation and the world on television from his office in the Kremlin. He used the occasion to reiterate his opposition to the decisions taken at Almaty: 'I am convinced that decisions of such importance should have been made by the popular will'.[43] Things had not worked out as planned: 'The old system tumbled down before the new one could begin functioning'. That can serve as his epitaph. He set reforms in motion without understanding where they could lead. Never in his worst nightmare could he have imagined that perestroika would lead to the destruction of the Soviet Union and his own unemployment.

His speech annoyed Yeltsin who was to meet him in the Kremlin to receive the decree transferring control over the armed forces to the Russian President. Instead, Marshal Evgeny Shaposhnikov was given the briefcase containing the nuclear codes, and Gorbachev requested he take it to its new owner. The original agreement had been that Gorbachev would vacate his Kremlin office by 30 December. However, on 27 December he received a phone call from the Kremlin reception room informing him that Yeltsin, Khasbulatov and Burbulis had taken over his office at 08.30 hours and had held a party there, downing a bottle of whisky. Gorbachev was told to vacate the presidential residence and country dacha within three days. The post-Soviet era had already begun. The Soviet Union, in international law, was laid to rest at midnight on 31 December 1991.

It was painful for Gorbachev to leave the Kremlin and power. The manner of his going was 'uncivilised' and the open wound of his relationship with Boris Yeltsin has yet to heal. He set up his own foundation for socio-economic and political studies, the Gorbachev Foundation. This enabled him and his associates, including Chernyaev, Yakovlev and Shakhnazarov, to lead research, publish and hold seminars and conferences on the burning topics of the day. The new Russian President and government were never given the benefit of the doubt.

Gorbachev's popularity remained undiminished in the west and he was a sought-after and welcome guest in many countries. He and Raisa also devoted more time to charitable activities, specialising in child health.

A personal affront was the amnesty, by the Duma, of the plotters of the attempted August 1991 coup. As he points out in his memoirs, by accepting the amnesty the plotters acknowledged, *de facto* and *de jure*, that they had been guilty.[44] Another event which shocked him was the attack on the White House on 4 October 1993. He regarded this as another coup. The only difference between this one and the last was that it succeeded. Yeltsin knew how to conduct a coup, Kryuchkov did not.

A major undertaking after leaving office was to write his memoirs. He needed to give his version of events as other participants were adept at presenting their side of the story. It was team effort with topics being addressed systematically. He dictated the memoirs and this is quite clear from his discursive style. They were published in Russia in 1995 and predictably received a frosty welcome. On the other hand, the German translation sold very well. There was also a Japanese edition. The publication of the English version in October 1996 was a major event. Gorbachev gave several interviews and addressed, along with Raisa, a large meeting in London. He performed with great skill and was a hit with the audience. On television, he demonstrated his quickness of mind, humour and repartee on the Clive Anderson show. He made one profound statement. When asked what event in Russian history he would change, he replied: 'Ensure the continuation of the February 1917 revolution'. This breathtaking choice implied that he was rejecting the revolution of October 1917 and the whole Bolshevik experiment. He was confessing that he had devoted his life to a utopian myth. His performances on the media demonstrated that he could have had a very successful media career, had he so chosen.

In Russia he was less well regarded. Determined to stay afloat politically, he tirelessly gave interviews and wrote articles, bemoaning the state of the country. However, the new communists, the Communist Party of the Russian Federation, would have nothing to do with him. He insisted on contesting the Russian presidential elections in June 1996, but only received less than 1 per cent of the votes in the first round. His political life in Russia had come full circle and he had failed as a democratic politician.

. . .

NOTES

1. This section is partly based on Jack F. Matlock, Jr., *Autopsy on an Empire: The American Ambassador's Account of the Collapse of the Soviet Union* (New York, Random House, 1995), pp. 578–602. Matlock accepts that Gorbachev was not a party to the attempted coup, as many of the conspirators were later to claim in their defence.

2. Mikhail Gorbachev, *Memoirs* (London, Doubleday, 1996), p. 628.

3. Boris Yeltsin, *The Struggle for Russia* (New York, Random House, 1994), p. 39. When Yeltsin suggested that the room might be bugged the others just laughed.
4. Valentin Stepankov and Evgeny Lisov, *Kremlevsky zagovor* (Moscow, Izdatelstvo Ogonek, 1992), p. 84.
5. Ibid., pp. 85–6.
6. Gorbachev, *Memoirs*, p. 629.
7. Ibid., p. 631.
8. Stepankov and Lisov, *Kremlevsky zagovor*, pp. 89–91.
9. Gorbachev, *Memoirs*, pp. 632–40.
10. He had left Moscow on 11 August. He was not consulted by President Bush during the attempted coup.
11. Amy Knight, *Spies Without Cloaks: The KGB's Successors* (Princeton, NJ, Princeton University Press, 1996), pp. 17–28.
12. *Pravda*, 11 July 1992.
13. Knight, *Spies Without Cloaks*, p. 24.
14. Gorbachev, *Memoirs*, p. 642.
15. Only three CC secretaries, Galina Semenova, Andrei Girenko and Egor Stroev, supported Gorbachev. The overwhelming majority of the CC Secretariat and regional Party bodies deserted the general secretary. He found this 'disgraceful'. Gorbachev, *Memoirs*, p. 642.
16. FBIS-SOV-91, 23 August 1991, p. 28.
17. Vadim Bakatin, *Izbavlenie ot KGB* (Moscow, Novosti, 1992), p. 59. Bakatin discovered there were 250,000 KGB officers and employees. Another 240,000 border guards were under KGB control.
18. In July 1990, in Jurmala, Russia agreed to draft treaties with each of the three Baltic republics, recognising their sovereignty. Those with Estonia and Latvia were signed in January 1991, but the treaty with Lithuania was postponed because of the January events and was eventually signed in Moscow on 29 July 1991 and ratified by the Supreme Council of Lithuania on 19 August 1991.
19. Matlock, *Autopsy on an Empire*, p. 614.
20. Gorbachev's suspension of Party activity on 24 August had not been followed by a legal ban. He opposed the banning of the Party but would have been happy to ban Party bodies, ibid., p. 802.
21. Ibid., p. 622. The ex-ambassador maintains that the Americans had already worked out for themselves where the devices were.
22. Ibid., p. 623.
23. Andrei S. Grachev, *Final Days: The Inside Story of the Collapse of the Soviet Union* (Boulder, CO, Westview Press, 1995), p. 107.
24. Ibid., p. 108.

25. Ibid., pp. 108–9.
26. Ibid., p. 110.
27. Ibid., p. 111. Kravchuk was not present. Grachev calls them, ironically, the Magnificent Seven, after the film starring Yul Brynner and Steve McQueen.
28. Ibid., p. 112.
29. Ibid., p. 120.
30. Ibid., p. 122.
31. Ibid., p. 123. The great khan was the ruler of the Mongol Tatars, who dominated Russia from about 1240 to 1480. Tsar Boris was Boris Godunov, who was elected Tsar in 1598, but fell out with the nobility and also failed to alleviate famine and epidemics, 1601–3. A pretender to the throne found support in the south, in 1604, but Boris died in April 1605. The country then degenerated into civil war and suffered foreign intervention, known as the Time of Troubles. These ended with the assumption of power of the Romanov dynasty in 1613. Hence Tsar Boris, in Russian minds, is associated with anarchy and suffering.
32. Matlock, *Autopsy on an Empire*, p. 629.
33. *Izvestiya*, 6 December 1991.
34. Gorbachev, *Memoirs*, p. 658.
35. *Rossiiskaya gazeta*, 7 December 1991.
36. Matlock, *Autopsy on an Empire*, p. 635.
37. *Rossiiskaya gazeta*, 10 December 1991.
38. Matlock, *Autopsy on an Empire*, p. 636.
39. Ibid., p. 636.
40. Grachev, *Final Days*, p. 145.
41. Gorbachev, *Memoirs*, p. 659.
42. *Izvestiya*, 10 December 1991.
43. Gorbachev, *Memoirs*, p. xxvi.
44. Ibid., p. 682.

Chapter 7

CONCLUSION

Reform requires leadership. The more fundamental the reforms, the greater the demands made on leadership. Was Gorbachev a great reformer, was he a great leader? Is it possible to be a great reformer and a failure as a political leader? He certainly was a great reformer, in the sense that the reforms initiated under his leadership transformed the Soviet communist system out of all recognition. Indeed, reform surgery was so radical that the patient, the Union of Soviet Socialist Republics, died under the knife. However, this was not Gorbachev's goal. A man who loved power, the trappings of power and jealously guarded his power would not consciously have undermined it to the extent that he was humbled and unceremoniously stripped of power. He complains, in his memoirs, that he was not even granted an honourable discharge. There was no ceremony marking the demise of the Soviet Union. It just passed away. Russia, its successor state, could not wait to bury the corpse.

Hence, when Gorbachev began his reform journey in March 1985, he believed he was heading for a certain destination. He ended up somewhere totally different. Indeed, his sleek perestroika train crashed into the buffers. There is no question that he was a great reformer. What, however, was he reforming? Reform always involved, first, destruction, and then, construction.

. . .

ASSESSING PERESTROIKA

Perestroika is an elusive concept, deliberately so in Gorbachev's eyes, but it is worth attempting a definition. The concept

262

evolved and eventually meant something radically different over time. This study divides the Gorbachev era into three main periods.

- Perestroika Mark I can be seen as concentrating on economic reform, an important prerequisite to political reform. Mark I was an attempt to reform the economic mechanism (power relationships in the economy) by devolving greater decision-making power to management and labour. Workers were to be drawn into decision making to an extent never before envisaged under a command-administrative system. It was assumed that their interests were the same as those of managers and the Party.

- Mark I believed that contradictory goals could be achieved. Living standards would rise while there would be structural reform, benefiting most of all the machine-building sector. Even though greater investment was required, there would be more funds available for consumption. Two key problems were not addressed: ownership and prices. Instead of growth, there was an economic slowdown. Consumption could not be sacrificed to increase capital investment.

- Mark I was intended to stimulate and motivate the workforce but it produced increasing resentment.

- Mark I's failure led to Mark II. This was founded on the perception that the reason for Mark I's limited impact was the resistance of the upper-level ideological and economic nomenklatura. The solution was to initiate reform from below. Glasnost was to give the people a voice to criticise the conservative leadership. Political reform was seen as the answer to economic stagnation. The Party was taken out of economic management and the pillars of the communist system were undermined. There was no pressure from below for this. It was the conscious decision of the Gorbachev leadership. The soviets were to take over from the Party organisations. The Congress of People's Deputies was the first step in the rebirth of politics in the country. No longer could the Party maintain that there was only one opinion, its opinion. Gorbachev informed communist deputies that the rules of Party discipline no longer applied.

- Mark II was a political revolution which gradually revealed the ills of Soviet society. Democracy began at a time of economic decline.
- Mark II gave way to Mark III during which Gorbachev acted as executive President and attempted to achieve a consensus in society about the future. Desperate efforts were made to find an answer to the economic ills and radical market solutions were discussed. However, the President realised that a market solution was too radical but the damage had been done. The republics understood that a market economy meant that they would acquire control over assets on their territory. This made negotiating a Union treaty all the more difficult.
- Mark III saw the President lurching to the right and adopting some desperate solutions to keep the Union together. In Lithuania, persuasion failed and the President declined to condemn the use of force when it was applied. When the latter was unsuccessful he had no policy options left. Other republics supported Lithuania and this undermined the position of the President. The key player was Russia and it may have been attempting to dismantle the Union, and Gorbachev, from the summer of 1990 onwards. Economic stabilisation, at long last, was attempted in early 1991, but failed. A Union of Sovereign States became a possibility. This galvanised the conservatives to attempt to force Gorbachev to introduce a state of emergency so as to restore conservative order and keep the Union together. The failure of the attempted coup sentenced the Soviet Union to death.

Perestroika went through various phases but was much more politically than economically radical. A composite definition might be:

- Radical reform of the economic and political system. Initially, in the economy, emphasis was placed on reforming the economic mechanism (ownership and prices were expressly excluded). This, in essence, was a search for ways to motivate labour and make management more effective.
- The failure to ameliorate the economy led to discussion of market mechanisms and cooperatives and private trade development. However, the state sector was to remain dominant. Private ownership was eventually permitted

but much too late. Reform of prices was too sensitive to adopt before early 1991, when it was too late.

- Economically, perestroika was an abject failure resulting in economic decline, shortages, large budget deficits and rising inflation.
- Politically, the vision was of a reformed, strengthened Party leading the way forward to economic plenty.
- Democratisation, but not democracy (the right to choose the political system), was an integral part of this transformation. Until 1988, Party officials, accountable to elected bodies, were the beacons of the future, leading, guiding and motivating the population. Their lack of commitment to political reform led to their being marginalised, with soviets replacing them.
- Gradually, democratisation prepared the ground for democracy. The beginnings of parliamentary democracy undermined the leadership's authority and the lack of clear separation of powers, especially between the legislature and the executive, compounded the growing confusion.
- The country gradually became less and less governable as political power at the centre weakened due to the lack of executive institutions to implement the decisions of the leadership.
- Tension built up as economic decline accelerated.
- Perestroika exacerbated ethnic tension and led to calls for independence by some republics. State-inspired bloodletting alienated more and more non-Russians. Eventually the state failed to mediate a transition to a new Union.
- Conservatives viewed perestroika as a failure because it was too radical, and radicals also regarded it as a failure because it was not radical enough.
- Perestroika promoted the plurality of opinions, then socialist pluralism, then political pluralism. It began as within-system reform and ended as extra-systemic reform.
- Initially, it was to improve the existing system, finally it was destructive of that system. In attempting to achieve so many contradictory goals, it satisfied few and alienated many.
- In the eyes of most Soviet citizens, it failed.

Perestroika can be understood as a transitional system, beginning with a functioning communist system but failing to escape successfully from it. It was astonishingly radical in its goals which eventually were akin to establishing a western social democratic order. There was no pressure from below until 1989 to reform, but then the leadership was subjected to increasing pressure from below. The leadership, until 1989, was leading perestroika. During and after 1989, it was propelled forward from below. The lack of consensus among the leadership led to a confrontation which proved fatal. Since perestroika changed its emphasis so often, it put enormous pressure on the leadership and made the management of reform incredibly difficult.

. . .

GORBACHEV AND LEADERSHIP

Before assessing whether the leadership, first and foremost Gorbachev, succeeded or failed, it is necessary to attempt a definition of leadership. Leadership consists of defining the goals to be achieved, after detailed analysis of existing problems. The next stage is to devise a route map to achieve these reforms, based on the strengths and weaknesses of the existing system. Then the leader needs to choose the team which agrees with his objectives and is capable of implementing them.

An important component is risk management. However, risk management is based on individual actors believing that they are, to some extent, free agents. Since one is never certain, one is always ignorant to some degree. Much of the information available is either incorrect or incomplete. When initiating radical changes in society caution is of the utmost importance because one cannot predict the consequences. This is a non-Marxist analysis.

Marxists are determinists and believe they can predict the future. Hence one could predict that the more ideological the Soviet leadership was in 1985, the less likely it was to succeed, given that the human factor (or, put simply, human unpredictability) was a component part. The converse may also be true. Hence Gorbachev, with light ideological baggage, was better placed to initiate reform.

The leadership perceived that the country was falling behind technologically and hence believed that accelerated growth of the machine-building sector would go a long way to solving the problem. The other aspect was the human factor, the motivation of labour. Gorbachev saw no contradiction in attempting simultaneously to accelerate investment in producers' goods and raise living standards. Neither succeeded and a search for a scapegoat was on. The leadership concluded that the fault rested, not with the original concept, but with the upper echelons of the Party and state bureaucracy. They resisted change for their own selfish reasons. The solution was to take the Party out of economic management and replace it with local soviets. Elections to the soviets would demonstrate who had the public's confidence. In this way, officials would become publicly accountable. (Party officials were accountable, not to the public, but to the Party leadership in Moscow.)

The next stage of reform was to establish a Congress of People's Deputies, a people's parliament, which would propel perestroika forward. Glasnost gave the people a voice. It was never doubted that the people were behind perestroika. Until this stage, the leadership was not under pressure from below to reform. The creation of the parliament, responding to the aspirations of its constituents, applied pressure from below. From this point on, the leadership attempted to put a brake on the increasing radicalism of parliament.

Gorbachev then became executive President to provide firm, clear leadership, since he could not exercise it through parliament. Until late 1989, he was the most popular man in the country, then his ratings began to suffer in favour of the most radical parliamentary deputies. From late 1989, he was less radical than the population. He found it increasingly difficult to deal with ethnic and economic problems thrown up by mismanagement of the economy and glasnost.

There was no clear leadership from early 1990 onwards. During 1990 Gorbachev wavered between market and traditional reform, but between October 1990 and April 1991 he sided with the traditionalists, the conservatives. Then he moved back towards market reform and a new confederal Union. During the winter of 1990–1 he was under intense pressure from the conservatives to declare a state of emergency. He survived by giving the impression that he was considering that option.

However, this unfortunately led to the tragedy of Vilnius in January 1991. The lack of firm leadership encouraged the conservatives to believe that they could create a situation which would force him to declare a state of emergency. The same situation prevailed in August 1991, when the traditionalists, led by Kryuchkov, believed that they could force him to resign or take extended leave until they had established 'order' in the country. This misunderstanding was the consequence of weak, indecisive leadership. After he returned from Foros, Gorbachev was a leader chasing shadows. Yeltsin set the agenda and Gorbachev danced to his tune. He failed to achieve any of his goals concerning a Union treaty.

Hence Gorbachev's leadership record is mixed. He began with great self-confidence and received enthusiastic support from the population. The tide began to turn in 1989 and in 1990–1 he lost his self-confidence and consequently was often quite indecisive. One of Ryzhkov's criticisms of his leadership is that he listened to too many opinions before making up his mind. A reason for this could be that he did not know what to do. During the winter of 1990–1 all sides implored him to do *something*.

The fact that he managed to survive despite being pilloried by the conservatives and the radicals testifies to his enormous tactical skill. He outmanoeuvred his critics over time, at least until August 1991. He began as the champion of the Party, seeking to strengthen its role, and ended by destroying it. It is astonishing that it never turned on him. This appears to have been due to his skill at giving the impression he was going to act as the conservatives desired, his warnings that an attempt to remove him which failed would end the political careers of the conspirators, and the extraordinary cult of the leader which prevailed in the Party. At the end of the day, the general secretary could demand and get obedience. This, of course, was only at the centre. The conservatives behaved as they thought fit in their regions. The need to balance so many conflicting forces is an explanation for the weak leadership of 1990–1.

An important component of leadership is clarity of vision, providing a sense of direction. This applied during the initial period of perestroika but faltered in 1989 and was missing in 1990–1. From 1989 onwards, other members of the leadership were often not aware what policy was. This applies, to an even greater extent, to Party officials.

The policies adopted to ameliorate the situation, from 1985 onwards, were defective. Perestroika was built on false foundations. The Soviet Union was in systemic decline when Gorbachev took over but he and other leaders were unaware of this. The reforms adopted accelerated decline. The removal of the Party from economic management had catastrophic consequences. It was the institution which provided the glue which kept the whole system together. No alternative institution was set up to replace it. One of Gorbachev's failures was that whereas he destroyed the old system, he did not put a new one in its place. Under him, the Soviet Union hovered between the old and the new, between the past and the future. A major drawback was Gorbachev's inability to grasp the essence of market economics. As late as the G7 meeting in July 1991, he still thought that the rationalisers and the big bangers could be brought together.

. . .

HOW DID GORBACHEV FORMULATE POLICY?

How does one explain the fact that clarity of vision was often missing? How did Gorbachev formulate policy? When he came into power in March 1985 he had over one hundred situation papers on various aspects of the economy on his desk. He had good advisers but those who stayed with him were all lawyers or politics specialists, such as Shakhnazarov. He never retained economists who favoured moving to the market. He fell out with all the leading mathematical economists. Hence it was very unlikely that he would evolve a coherent economic reform package.

He was much more skilled at tactical, short-term policy than strategic, long-term thinking. He manipulated his opponents brilliantly but then he had to move on to the next contest. He was given to making policy on the hoof. He liked taking a subject and developing it as he went along, often changing direction as he did so. This did not make for coherent leadership or policy-making. He lacked the rigorous intellectual training for such an exercise. The American ambassador calls these verbal *tours d'horizon*, soliloquies. Often off the subject, they became irritating if the interlocutor wished to discuss a specific problem.

There was an authoritarian streak in Gorbachev's make-up and, from 1989, he consulted less and tried to impose his faulty policies. It is striking that the bodies which took over from the Politburo, the Presidential Council, the Security Council and the State Council, besides a secretary, possessed no staffs to implement decisions. It was as if Gorbachev regarded them as necessary nuisances. A workaholic, he consulted with smaller and smaller groups, often only individuals, from 1989.

As a politician, Gorbachev was difficult to get close to. He had no close friends, except Raisa Maksimovna, with whom he discussed everything. Gorbachev had difficulty in assessing the consequences of his actions, perhaps his most serious shortcoming. One can say that he was often the victim of the law of unintended consequences. The information on which he based his judgement, of course, was sifted by his advisers. Since he did not perceive that Boldin and Kryuchkov were misinforming him, this may explain, to some extent, his lack of sound judgement.

Gorbachev, as others since, found Vytautas Landsbergis a difficult interlocutor. A more sympathetic, problem-solving approach was adopted by Kazimiera Prunskiene. Her evaluation of Gorbachev is revealing:

> I would have acknowledged Gorbachev's style of work, his constantly changing efforts to balance political forces in order to control the ever changing situation, as the discrete talent of a creative politician, had I found a positive answer to one decisive question. Was he really planning to reform the communist empire, to free nations and peoples, to build a *Rechtsstaat* [law governed state], and to introduce justice and democracy?[1]

The damning conclusion she arrives at, is that he was not. She understood him as a politician who had liberated forces which he tried to control but could not. The 'political reins slipped from his hands' because he lacked clarity of vision.

Shevardnadze felt betrayed by his leader and bitterly remarked that Gorbachev was a prisoner of his 'own nature, his conceptions, his way of thinking and acting. Sometimes I think a man has no more dangerous an enemy than himself.

270

Before finding friends around you, you must find a friend within yourself.'[2]

Shevardnadze regarded Gorbachev as a poor judge of people and indifferent to his allies. He was bitter at the lack of protection he and others received.

> It remains a mystery to me why he was so passive. He knew that in certain questions I was right, 100 per cent right, but he remained silent. I asked myself: a minister, a close adviser, who thought as he did, and a devoted friend is trampled upon and persecuted – why not defend him? After all, the same thing happened to Yakovlev and to others as well . . . The President should have protected us. Not only us but also our cause.[3]

Foreign policy making was much more successful than domestic policy formation. There was a coherence, a clarity of vision and a dynamism which were lacking in internal policy. This is related to the fact that he adopted western, especially American, criteria, in foreign policy. The espousal of universal human values meant the end of zero game diplomacy, the end of a class approach to policy. He took on board the American view that progress in arms control, then arms reduction, could only take place when the two superpowers shared the same vision for the world. He often rambled when discussing domestic problems but hardly ever in foreign policy.

One notable example was his soliloquy to George Bush, in July 1991, which led the US President to question Mikhail Sergeevich's grasp of reality. He wilted under domestic pressure in 1990–1 but was transformed when he switched to foreign policy. During his 'lurch to the right', from October 1990 to March 1991, he remained radical in foreign policy. Indeed, he can be criticised for devoting too much time to external affairs at a critical juncture.

The outside world took him to its hearts because he wanted the same as it did: peace in our time. He will always be a hero in Germany because he agreed to reunification. He permitted eastern Europe to choose its own path. Looked at differently, he undermined the superpower status of the Soviet Union. He really had no other option since the systemic decline of the Soviet Union was terminal.

. . .

HOW DID GORBACHEV MANAGE HIS TEAM?

No leader can succeed without a team which is in tune with his thinking. Initially, Gorbachev had to duck and weave to strengthen his position. He had to fashion a Politburo which would accept his policy initiatives. Ligachev, Yakovlev, Yeltsin, Ryzhkov and Shevardnadze made a formidable group. By December 1990, all of them had fallen out with him. Gorbachev never permitted his associates complete control of a policy area. Ligachev and Yakovlev were always competing for control of the media, then Yakovlev moved into international affairs, but there he ran into Shevardnadze.

There were instances when Gorbachev gave the impression he did not trust his closest allies. He appeared to be jealous of his primacy. He wanted the limelight for himself. He could not tolerate someone else as an equal. Boldin complains that Gorbachev did not like to delegate, preferring to do things himself. This alienated the apparatus. The radicals suggested that Gorbachev as President and Yeltsin as Vice President would be the dream ticket but it was never a possibility. Gorbachev's relationship with Yeltsin is a study in itself. It is tempting to regard Gorbachev's jealousy of Yeltsin's charismatic populism as the root of the problem.

The comrades he chose as successors to the above were all inferior to them. Over time the quality of top officials declined. Pavlov was a caricature of a Prime Minister. Was he attractive to Gorbachev because he had a poor public image? Bessmertnykh was a professional diplomat and had no authority as a politician. Pugo was a poor substitute for Bakatin. He chose Kryuchkov to succeed Chebrikov and always trusted him. Kryuchkov, as a skilled intelligence man, fed Gorbachev the information he knew the President thrived on. Boldin, his chief of staff, worked against him, as did Oleg Shenin. He never realised their true intentions until the attempted coup. This revealed a lack of shrewdness in judging character. Poor judgement was also revealed in promoting Lukyanov as chair of the Supreme Soviet, the attempt to foist Vlasov on the Russian Supreme Soviet, thereby opening up the way for Yeltsin, the desperate search for an opponent to Polozkov as head of the Russian Party, but all in vain because he had misread Polozkov.

Gorbachev's natural allies were the democrats. Yet, time and again, he perceived them as his opponents, even enemies. He even accepted Kryuchkov's suggestion that they were going to storm the Kremlin in March 1991. Yakovlev did his best to disabuse him of this absurdity but he failed.

Gorbachev was sometimes his own worst enemy. In trying to sack Starkov, the editor of *Argumenty i Fakti*, he turned an ally into an opponent. In doing so, his love affair with the creative intelligentsia came to an end. He was often too self-confident. He waved aside the attempt by Pavlov and other ministers, in June 1991, to usurp some of his power. In July 1991 he laughed at Yeltsin's suggestion that the room might be bugged by the KGB. It almost beggars belief that it never occurred to him that the KGB was bugging him. This from a man who received daily briefings from an organisation, demonstrating it could eavesdrop on anyone. He read the KGB reports carefully and wrote remarks in the margin.

Gorbachev discarded some of his team and they bitterly resented it. One was Nikolai Ryzhkov who was very aggrieved at being dropped in late 1990. Some complained that he was brusque and unappreciative of their efforts on his behalf. He was a good listener, especially where foreign interlocutors were concerned. However, especially in 1990–1, he was inclined to ignore much sound advice.

Can one justify the attempted coup by Kryuchkov, Pavlov, Yazov, Pugo et al.? Gorbachev assumed that since he had appointed them they would be loyal to him. Here he made a crucial mistake. Their loyalty was not to Gorbachev personally but to the Party and the state. When they concluded that he was undermining both they decided to act. Arguably, as their prime loyalty was to the Party and the state, they had to move against the President and the general secretary.

. . .

DOES GORBACHEV BEAR RESPONSIBILITY FOR THE BLOODLETTING?

How culpable was Gorbachev for the bloodletting in Tbilisi, Baku, Vilnius and Riga? The Tbilisi massacre occurred because of a breakdown in the line of command from the centre to the Georgian capital. Had Shevardnadze travelled to Tbilisi, the whole tragedy might have been avoided. There is no reason to doubt his statement that he had been assured by the Georgian Party leader that things were under control. Gorbachev can only be held responsible as the final decision-maker, the buck stopped with him. Hence he only bears indirect responsibility for the massacre.

Baku is much simpler. Gorbachev was involved and sanctioned the use of violence. He was appalled at the extent of the bloodletting. This appears to be due to his false assumption about how easily the separatists could be put down.

Vilnius is the most sensitive and difficult event. He consistently believed that Landsbergis and Sajudis represented only a minority of Lithuanian opinion, when in reality they had majority support. He placed faith in the words of the pro-Moscow Party and ignored the Party led by Brazauskas. The latter, in fact, had some influence, whereas the former had none. He went along with conservative advice that pressure should be applied to Lithuania to force it to retract its drive towards independence. By sending his telegram of 10 January, he deliberately exacerbated the situation. The Lithuanians were told to cease their efforts to restore 'bourgeois order'. They would be responsible for what happened if they did not restore the Soviet constitution, etc. Did he not think through the ultimatum he had delivered to Vilnius? What would happen if the Lithuanians failed to respond positively to his orders?

Little effort was made by Moscow to discover what the response would be before force was used. Kryuchkov had worked out that presidential rule would be imposed, a puppet Prime Minister and government installed and Lithuania brought back into the Soviet fold. Was Gorbachev unaware of this scenario? The Congress of People's Deputies had passed a law in March 1990 which established a constitutional basis for the Soviet President to invoke extraordinary powers. From then onwards, constitutionally, presidential rule was an option. President Bush had warned Gorbachev many times of the consequences of using force in the Baltic republics. Gorbachev did not want bloodletting in Vilnius and was stunned by what had happened. He can be criticised for not thinking through the consequences of his telegram. Surely it made violence more likely? Again, he can be held indirectly responsible for the disaster. Yakovlev and others advised him to fly to Vilnius, meet Landsbergis, lay a wreath in memory of those killed, and condemn the massacre. He declined to do so.

Riga is much more simple. The killings were initiated by an officer acting without direct orders from Moscow. The implication was that the President had lost control of his instruments of coercion in Vilnius and Riga.

. . .

WAS GORBACHEV A GREAT REFORMER, A GREAT LEADER?

Was Gorbachev a great reformer, a great leader? This can be approached from three angles: Gorbachev personally, the Soviet Union, and the west. Is it possible for a political actor to be a great reformer, a great leader, and end up with no country? He reformed the Soviet Union out of existence. From his own point of view, he was a failure because his reforms made him unemployed. This then condemns his leadership.

From the point of view of the country, the view is quite different. He took over a declining power and managed the beginning of the transition to a post-communist society. The Party lost power, the world communist movement was dealt a mortal blow, the Soviet empire disintegrated, the Warsaw Pact disbanded and the power of the centre was broken. Politics was reborn. The Soviet Union passed away and was succeeded by 15 states, without civil war. The tragedy of another Yugoslavia was skilfully avoided. The intelligentsia was liberated and intellectual life revitalised. Democracy could begin to grow alongside private enterprise. The self-imposed exile from the rest of the world ended and Russia and other states could join the world community with shared goals. The above is a huge achievement and Gorbachev will sometime in the future be given some recognition in Russia for his craft. This analysis is based on the assumption that the command-administrative system could not be reformed successfully. The only question in 1985 was: will it be slow or rapid decline? The Party could not be democratised and remain a Marxist-Leninist Party. Inevitably, it would split into left and social democratic wings. The ideological and many of the economic nomenklatura would reject the above analysis. The Gorbachev era for them was a disaster since they lost power. On balance, he was a great reformer but not appreciated as a leader, after 1989.

From the point of view of the west, Gorbachev is a great reformer and a great leader. He had the insight to realise that the system in 1985 was moribund and had to be reformed. He began with economic reform which failed because it ignored the lessons of a market economy. He then engaged in breathtakingly radical political reform which transformed the country. His goal was not to retain or increase his own power, otherwise he would have reverted to a conservative agenda, but he put society and the country first. When he found power slipping away from him, he did not attempt to recapture it by using violence. In foreign policy, he worked wonders and transformed the world. He was voted the man of the year and the man of the decade.

With the wisdom of hindsight, what should he have done to stay in power? Introduce a market economy, permit the Baltic republics to leave the Union and negotiate a federation of sovereign states? The process of demonopolisation, price reform, the introduction of new market-oriented institutions to regulate a burgeoning market should have been initiated by the centre, by Moscow. A common market might have emerged. This would have made reaching political consensus easier as each republic would have grasped that a common economic space was in everyone's interests. Gorbachev never espoused the market economy and was more concerned with political questions at a time of rapid economic decline. Hence giving primacy to economic rather than political reform would, probably, have produced better results. He never saw eye to eye with Ryzhkov and this was a major drawback. It meant that there was no agreed economic reform policy. He was happy with Pavlov because he was a political lightweight. He needed a strong number two, a chief of staff, who agreed with his policy vision and had the administrative skill and clout to implement it. Gorbachev liked the high ground of policy, but he became bored with the nuts and bolts of policy implementation. This was a glaring weakness.

CONCLUSION

. . .

GORBACHEV AND PROSPECT THEORY

A possible explanation for Gorbachev's 'lurch to the right'
between October 1990 and March 1991 comes from prospect
theory.[4] This theory suggests that whereas persons are quite
willing to engage in risk, they are even more driven to avoid
losing. Loss aversion is stronger than risk-taking. Once a
politician has acquired a certain level of political power, he
will be very loath to lose any of it. The loss of a small part
of it may produce irrational reactions and leave lingering
feelings of frustration.

If this is applied to the Soviet Union under Gorbachev,
he was riding high until 1989. As the Congress of People's
Deputies got into its stride, Gorbachev should have welcomed
burgeoning democracy. After all, he was promoting the
human factor, the individual playing a greater role in society.
He was greatly irritated by criticism and mortally offended
when he read that opinion polls revealed the most radical
deputies to be the most popular with the electorate. He had
taken a risk in convening the Congress but the unexpected
side-effect was that he was losing a part of his authority. This
led to the establishment of an executive presidency, another
calculated risk. Again it did not work out as expected. Instead
of welcoming the democrats as allies, he saw them as com-
petitors, even opponents. Any perceived loss of power was
resented.

The move to the market, evidenced by the promotion of
the Shatalin–Yavlinsky 500-day programme, was another calculated risk. Gorbachev initially thought it would strengthen
his position and help him to claw back some of his lost power.
When he discovered that it was the big bang under another
name, he immediately lost interest. The big bang involves the
state playing a non-interventionist role in the economy. It
should restrict itself to providing the framework and permit
economic actors to engage in their preferred activities. He
was in favour of the Ryzhkov–Abalkin version which involved
the state playing a major role in running the economy. This
outcome was predictable, given Gorbachev's premises.

The same applies to his attempts to negotiate a Union
treaty. His main objective was to minimise his power loss, so

277

he attempted to create powerful central institutions which would dominate the new federation. Successive drafts of the treaty whittled away central power, something which Gorbachev was forced to acknowledge by August 1991. His tactics throughout can be classified as loss aversion. He was a negative rather than a positive negotiator. It was a painful exercise for him as it involved the loss of his power. This behaviour applies *a fortiori* to ethnic problems. Separatist aspirations had to be resisted as they were perceived as destructive of the Soviet Union.

Loss aversion can be applied to the Baltic republics where Gorbachev would not accept Yakovlev's suggestion that since they had been brought forcibly into the Union in 1940, they represented a special case. Independence was a feasible option. Yakovlev could suggest this option since he would not suffer any loss of his power, if implemented. On reflection, Gorbachev would have been much better off following this counsel but he could not bring himself to concede voluntarily any of his power.

Prospect theory also suggests that an actor, when taking a decision involving risk, is influenced by the amount of wealth or power he already possesses. A powerful leader is less likely to take a calculated gamble since it might diminish his power. When a leader begins to lose power, he will risk more to recapture his former position. Therefore, a politician who is sinking may become a gambler and put everything at risk. Gorbachev's conservative phase, from October 1990 to March 1991, saw him gamble most. He took immense risks and failed. Afterwards he never recovered the position he had enjoyed in October 1990. Had he espoused a market economy in October 1990, he might still be a President. On the other hand, the Party conservatives and economic nomenklatura might have removed him from office. His policy of loss aversion cost him his political career.

Gorbachev's lasting legacy is that he led his people out of the kingdom of certainty into the kingdom of uncertainty. They thereby ceased to be prisoners of an inevitable future. Uncertainty then made them free. The beginnings of risk management also appeared as citizens perceived, for the first time in Soviet history, that they were, to a certain extent, free agents. How they manage the risks inherent in their everyday existence is their responsibility but Gorbachev gave them something precious, the right to think and manage their lives for themselves.

. . .

AN ALTERNATIVE STRATEGY: DENG'S PERESTROIKA?

The Chinese conversion to capitalism was born out of need. Mao Zedong's flawed legacy threatened social instability. The traditional command economy, inherited from the Soviet Union, was not proving capable of delivering higher living standards for China's growing millions. Zhao Ziyang, the Prime Minister, was able to convince the conservatives in the leadership that experimentation with market-oriented reforms would not undermine the political monopoly of the Communist Party of China.[5] The reforms began in the countryside in the late 1970s and were a great success. There was no overall economic reform strategy. The Chinese leadership was flexible and pragmatic. When it found that a certain policy failed, it drew lessons and moved on to the next reform. Naughton has coined the expression 'growing out of the plan' to characterise the Chinese approach.[6] The plan is retained to resolve immediate economic problems. Administrative coordination accompanies market coordination and hence avoids catastrophic failure. Chinese reforms proceeded by diversifying options. The temptation was resisted to put all their reform eggs in one basket. Economic transition was successfully negotiated through diversification. Chinese economic growth took off and was sustained. The Chinese model works.

Chinese experience demonstrates that a gradual change of the command economy is feasible. The argument that a big bang has to be engineered to move to the market is not valid. In the early stages, from 1978 onwards, the Chinese went down many false alleys in search of viable options. This produced gradual reform which turned out to be successful as it was based on what worked in practice.

A crucial link in the reform process is the relaxation of the state monopoly over industry. Once the monopoly is relaxed, the attractiveness of monopoly profits in that sector brings in new entrants. These new enterprises work according to market prices and gradually force the state sector to realign its prices. They also provide competition and state enterprises must react. A major factor in relaxing the state monopoly over industry was that Beijing had never exercised detailed control over industry. Locally operating industrial activity, independent of the central planners, had always been a reality. The vast size of China was also an important factor.

Thousands of local communities were now empowered to engage in competition with other areas. Cities competed with cities. The state sector was forced again to respond. The entry of new firms grew at a phenomenal rate, even in the absence of well-defined property relations. Since planned economies are always shortage economies, small firms rushed in to fill the gaps and respond to consumer demand. The result was a virtuous circle of development. The Chinese government tried over many years to reform prices but failed. New entrants and competition led to a fundamental realignment of prices during the 1980s. Gradually the state was confronted with a fiscal crisis as the system was not sophisticated enough to collect taxes from all the small private firms. It then began to put pressure on state enterprises to become more profitable.

Economic expansion led to growing demands for political reform and the democracy movement severely embarrassed the Chinese government in 1989. Beijing's response was the massacre of Tiananmen square, and repression elsewhere in China. The conservatives engaged in macroeconomic austerity, recentralisation of public finance, enhanced central planning control and preference for state-run industry. The results were disastrous. Local government vitiated fiscal recentralisation and enterprises suffered under state interference. Real gross national product growth in 1989 fell to 4.3 per cent and to 4 per cent in 1990. This resulted in a consensus among Chinese leaders that a market economy was the only feasible approach to economic growth. The conservative economic policies followed in and after 1989 were shown to be bankrupt. No present or aspiring Chinese leaders could intellectually defend the discredited command model. China then returned to the market. In 1992 growth was up to 12.8 per cent.

The Chinese are pursuing a double-track approach. The plan is retained but gradually the market sector is growing.

The eventual goal is for China to move to a full market economy. A major drawback for China is the continuing failure to address political reform. Taiwan and South Korea reveal that it must come.

What are the lessons of Chinese reform for the Soviet Union? Could Gorbachev have learnt from and followed some of these reforms? The most enthusiastic advocate of Chinese-type reforms was Academician Oleg Bogomolov, director of the Institute of the Economy of the World Socialist System, USSR Academy of Sciences. At the CC conference on economic reform in June 1987, he proposed that economic reform should begin in agriculture, as it had done in China.[7] Gorbachev reacted at the CC plenum in June 1987 by advocating that 800,000 deserted homesteads in the non-black earth zone of Russia should be leased to town dwellers so as to reactivate them.[8] A decree was published but it only provided for 600 square metres of land per farm.[9] This made the whole undertaking economically unviable. Gorbachev had been overruled and it was clear that the leadership did not favour the leasing of land.

Another proponent of China's introduction of the market to the countryside was Aleksandr Yakovlev, but Gorbachev did not listen to him. Bogomolov supported selling shares and bonds to workers, as in China. Workers could buy loss-making enterprises from the state and turn them into cooperatives.[10] The Soviet press printed positive articles on private enterprise in China and some east European countries. The Soviet law on cooperatives bears testimony to careful scrutiny of the experience of China and other socialist states. It would appear that Gorbachev took to heart Chinese agricultural experience and consistently advocated private family farming. He did so at the 27th Party Congress in February 1986, during a speech in August 1987 and at CC conferences on agricultural leasing in May and October 1988.[11] The fact that it never got off the ground points to his failure to convince a conservative leadership. Putting Ligachev in charge of agriculture after the 19th Party Conference was a final admission of defeat. Egor Kuzmich was a passionate believer in socialist agriculture and tirelessly promoted the renaissance of kolkhozes and sovkhozes.

Chinese reform began with agriculture because over 80 per cent of the population lived in the countryside.

Collectivisation had destroyed the entrepreneurial peasant in the Soviet Union and there was a large economic bureaucracy suffocating agriculture. They conspired with the conservatives in the leadership to suffocate private agriculture. Another aspect of Chinese thinking which appealed to the Russians was free economic zones and a lively debate developed about these. Tangible results were minimal, however.

Gorbachev, in his memoirs, considers the Chinese option and predictably rejects it.[12] 'All attempts at any kind of serious economic transformation in our country were stifled and choked by political retrogradism.' For him, political reform had to precede economic reform. Others disagree. Nikolai Ryzhkov, still smarting from his perceived shabby treatment by Gorbachev, finds that perestroika did not originate with Gorbachev but goes back to Andropov:

> I also believe that one can say with considerable certainty that under Andropov's leadership quite different methods of transforming the country economically and socially would have been adopted. Would they have been similar to what is now being done in China? . . . This question can only be answered affirmatively.[13]

Here Ryzhkov is engaging in *ex post facto* rationalisation, or put simply, being wise after the event. In office, he never revealed any predilection for the Chinese road to the market. He clearly does not understand that China was introducing a market economy, not his preferred regulated market.

Laszlo Csaba has compared China and eastern Europe and highlighted the differences and lessons.[14] China enjoys an advantage denied Russia. It can draw on, annually, US$20–25 billion in foreign direct investment (FDI), mainly from overseas Chinese. Thus there is not the hostility to inward investment in China which is so evident among Russians. The FDI is targeted and China benefits from the know-how of the overseas community. The Soviet economy was dominated by the military-industrial complex whereas the military burden in China was light. The Soviet Union had a developed, inefficient, industrial economy, dominated by large enterprises. China was essentially a rural country and hence industrial expansion had to be financed at the local level, mainly from agricultural savings. Agricultural expansion had to come first, in order to generate a surplus. Chinese industrial experimentation was in the coastal free economic zones, well away from the capital, Beijing. These coastal regions responded to global markets and they all had access to the sea. China's equivalent of Gosplan never acquired the control over the economy the Soviet version had. Chinese reform is widening the gulf in incomes and wealth and building up tension between the rural and coastal regions.

Should one agree with Gorbachev that the Chinese model was inappropriate? Was the ideological nomenklatura too powerful to permit successful economic reform without first embarking on political reform? The answer lies in the timing. It was only in 1987 that Gorbachev and the leadership realised there was a crisis. The conclusion they drew was that political reform was necessary to promote economic reform. In 1989 it was quite clear that this analysis was defective. There was an economic crisis. The debate about the new economic model then began. There was the rationalising economic reform model and the big bang approach. Then there was the Chinese model which involved a double-track approach (fixed and market prices with the latter gradually taking over) and a growing out of the plan. The latter would gradually fade away as the market economy took over. The end goal was a full market economy. This was the third way between the rationalisers, whose reforms had always failed in the past, and the big bangers, who wanted to gatecrash the market overnight.

The irony of the situation was that, at the point when the Soviet Union had to decide on the way forward, China was reversing from the market. The conservative backlash of 1989–91 appeared to confirm that there was no third way. Beijing appeared to agree with the rationalisers, that the economy had to be managed from the centre. Hence Gorbachev decided to go with the rationalisers in October 1990 and reject the market path. In 1991 the Chinese returned to the market but it was too late for the Soviet Union. Had China in 1985 reached the stage it had in 1992 or 1995, there would have been a powerful case for the third way, a gradualist approach to economic reform. The argument about what type of market, the regulated market of Ryzhkov–Abalkin or the free market of the big bangers, would have been won by the latter.

Deng Xiaoping rejected political reform as an accompaniment to economic reform. However, relaxation and democratisation built up tensions which exploded in Tiananmen square in June 1989. Repression became the order of the day. Yet it has had little effect on economic policy. The flexible and pragmatic Chinese leadership chose to return to the market while holding the fort against political reform. The latter is bound to come, as the experience of Taiwan and South Korea have demonstrated. Public accountability cannot be evaded for ever.

Gorbachev was unfortunate in that he had to make his decision in 1990. It was predictable that he would agree with the rationalisers. That decision precipitated the collapse of the Soviet Union. The Chinese, third way is viable but this was not clear in 1990. China is the only socialist state to have undertaken economic transformation without precipitating an economic crisis. Is this experience unique to China or can it be copied elsewhere? We shall never know.

. . .

NOTES

1. Kazimiera Prunskiene, *Leben für Litauen* (Berlin, Ullstein, 1992), pp. 191–2.
2. Eduard Shevardnadze, *The Future Belongs to Freedom* (New York, The Free Press, 1991), p. 198.
3. *Literaturnaya gazeta*, no. 4, 22 January 1992.
4. Daniel Kahneman and Amos Tversky, 'Prospect theory: an analysis of decision under risk, *Econometrica*, vol. 47, no. 2, 1979, pp. 263–91; P. L. Bernstein, *Against the Gods: The Remarkable Story of Risk* (New York, Wiley, 1996), pp. 272–5.
5. This section is partly based on the splendid study of Chinese economic reform by Barry Naughton, *Growing Out of the Plan: Chinese Economic Reform 1978–1993* (Cambridge, Cambridge University Press, 1995), see especially pp. 309–26.
6. Ibid., pp. 8–9.
7. *Pravda*, 13 June 1987; Anders Åslund, *Gorbachev's Struggle for Economic Reform: The Soviet Reform Process, 1985–88* (London, Pinter, 1989), p. 100.
8. *Pravda*, 26 June 1987.
9. *Pravda*, 1 August 1987.
10. *Literaturnaya gazeta*, 16 September 1987.
11. Åslund, *Gorbachev's Struggle*, p. 179.

12. Mikhail Gorbachev, *Memoirs* (London, Doubleday, 1996), pp. 494–5.
13. Mikhail Nenashev, *Poslednee Pravitelstvo SSSR* (Moscow, Krom, 1993), pp. 23–4; Vladimir Mau, *The Political History of Economic Reform in Russia, 1985–1994* (London, Centre for Research into Communist Economies, 1996), p. 118.
14. Laszlo Csaba, 'The political economy of the reform strategy: China and eastern Europe compared', *Communist Economies and Economic Transition*, vol. 8, no. 1, 1996, pp. 53–65.

GLOSSARY

ABM Treaty Anti-ballistic missile treaty, signed by the US and the Soviet Union in 1972; part of the Strategic Arms Limitation Treaty (SALT I).

Agitprop Department of Agitation and Propaganda, CC Secretariat. Originally written and oral propaganda, the task of the official was to mobilise the population to achieve the economic goals set by the state by raising Party awareness.

All-Union Ministries could be either All-Union, i.e. responsible for the whole of the country, or republican, responsible for their own republic but subordinate to Moscow. Hence there was a USSR Ministry of Agriculture and 16 republican Ministries of Agriculture.

Alma Ata Meeting See CIS.

Anti-Party Group Those in the Presidium (Politburo) in 1957, almost all representing government ministries, who opposed the transfer of responsibility for the implementation of economic plans from the government to the Party. Khrushchev was almost defeated but after victory he removed all his opponents from the Presidium. The Party dominated economic decision-making until 1988 when Gorbachev, at the 19th Party Conference, removed it from economic management.

Apparatchik Paid Party or state official.

ASSR Autonomous Soviet Socialist Republic. A territory, within a Soviet republic, inhabited by non-Russians, indeed non-Slavs (Russians, Belorussians and Ukrainians) (e.g. Komi ASSR), which had its own government. The Communist Party organisation in an ASSR was equivalent to an obkom. In reality an ASSR was totally subordinate to the capital of the republic in which it was situated. Hence autonomous did not mean independent. Most ASSRs were in the Russian Federation.

August Coup The attempted coup of 19–21 August 1991. An eight-man emergency committee, led by Kryuchkov (KGB), Pugo

(MVD), Lukyanov and Yanaev, declared Gorbachev deposed as Soviet President on 19 August (due to ill health), placed him under arrest at Foros, his dacha in the Crimea, declared a state of emergency and put troops on the streets. They demanded that all administrative organs throughout the country implement their instructions. The timing of the attempted coup was linked to the proposed signing of an agreement to establish a Union of Sovereign States which would have devolved much of the centre's powers to the republics, thus establishing a genuine federal state. The putsch collapsed and reform was given a powerful boost, the Communist Party was fatally weakened and Russia dominated the political scene with an agenda which favoured an independent Russian state.

Belovezh Agreement See Minsk Agreement and the CIS.

Bolsheviks When the Russian Social Democratic Labour Party (RSDRP) split in 1903, those in the majority were known as Bolsheviks. In October 1917 the Bolsheviks or Communist Party took power.

Brezhnev Doctrine The right of the Soviet Union to intervene unilaterally if it deemed socialism to be in danger. It was renounced officially by Gorbachev during a speech in Yugoslavia in March 1988. Spheres of influence were abandoned, officially, in July 1989.

Cadres Personnel. Party cadres were Party officials. Stalin coined the expression 'Cadres decide everything!'.

Candidate Member (a) Before a person could become a full member of the Communist Party he (she) had to serve a probationary period during which he (she) was referred to as a candidate member. (b) Candidate members of the Party Central Committee and Politburo could attend, speak but not vote.

Central Committee Central Committee of the Communist Party; this body acted in the name of the Party Congress when the latter was not in session. It contained all the most important Party officials, governmental ministers, leading army and navy personnel, top ambassadors, academics, etc. It was elected at each Party Congress.

Cheka The All-Russian Extraordinary Commission for Combating Counter Revolution and Sabotage. Founded in 1917, it was the first Bolshevik secret police force whose task was to ensure the Bolsheviks stayed in power. It changed its name several times and under Gorbachev was known as the KGB.

CIS Commonwealth of Independent States. Established on 8 December 1991 by Russia, Ukraine and Belarus in Belovezh Forest, near Brest-Litovsk, Belarus. They reasoned they had the right to dissolve the Soviet Union because they had been the original signatories setting up the USSR in 1922. At a meeting in Almaty, Kazakhstan, on 21 December, other states were admitted: Armenia, Azerbaijan, Kazakhstan, Kyrgyzstan, Moldova, Tajikistan, Turkmenistan and Uzbekistan. Eventually Georgia also joined and this left Estonia, Latvia and Lithuania outside.

Classes   There were two classes in the Soviet Union: the working class and the collective farm peasantry (kolkhozniks), and a stratum, the intelligentsia.

CMEA   See Comecon.

Collectivisation   Common ownership of the land had begun in 1917 but had made little progress by 1929 when peasants (there were about 25 million peasant households) were not given a choice about joining a kolkhoz or collective farm. On land not previously farmed, sovkhozes or state farms were set up. Collectivisation was completed in 1937. The Soviet state never developed socialist agriculture to the point that the demand of the population for food was met.

Comecon   Council for Mutual Economic Assistance. Set up in 1949 by Stalin it came alive after his death to assume the function of a socialist Common Market. It was dissolved in June 1991.

Communist   A member of the Communist Party. By 1990 there were about 25 million members.

Communist Party of Russia, also Communist Party of the Russian Federation   For most of the Soviet period Russia was not permitted to have its own communist party since Lenin believed this would allow Russians to dominate the young Soviet state. There was a Russian Bureau under Khrushchev but it was dissolved in 1965. The RCP was founded in 1990 and elected Ivan Polozkov its first secretary, much to the disappointment of Gorbachev who regarded the Russian party as a bastion of conservatism.

Conference   Differed from a Party Congress in that not all Party organisations were represented (an exception was the 19th Party Conference, 1988). In the early years of the revolution logistics made it difficult to convene a Congress rapidly to deal with urgent business. A conference did not have the right to elect members to the Central Committee and the Politburo.

Congress   Most important meeting of the Party, soviet, trade union or other organisation. At a Congress, which had to meet once during a five-year period, the Communist Party reviewed its record over the period since the previous Congress and laid down goals for the future. A new Central Committee was elected and it, in turn, elected a new Politburo and Secretariat. The last Party Congress, before it was banned by Yeltsin, was the 28th, in July 1990.

Conventional Forces   Non-nuclear forces.

CPSU Communist Party of the Soviet Union. The Party was founded in 1898 as the Russian Social Democratic Labour Party (RSDRP) (until 1917 all social democratic parties were Marxist) but split at its 2nd Congress, in 1903, into Bolshevik (majoritarians) and Menshevik (minoritarians) factions. It assumed the name of Russian Communist Party (Bolsheviks) in 1918, and adopted the name CPSU in 1952.

CPSU Programme The agenda of the Communist Party. The 1961 Party Programme, envisaging the foothills of communism being reached in 1980, was still valid when Gorbachev became general secretary. It was urgently in need of revision but this became a battleground between radicals and conservatives.

CSCE Conference on Security and Cooperation in Europe. The inaugural meeting was in Helsinki on 3 July 1973. The foreign ministers of the 33 European states (Albania was absent), as well as the United States and Canada, participated in the follow-up conferences. The CSCE developed into a forum for east–west debate on political, economic, social, cultural and security issues. On 1 January 1995 it became the Organisation for Security and Cooperation in Europe (OSCE).

Democratic Platform A radical group within the Communist Party whose programme was published in *Pravda* in March 1990, which demanded, among other things, the renunciation of a single state ideology and that the Party should reject communism as its goal. Its leading members were expelled and others resigned and some founded other parties, such as the Republican Party of the Russian Federation.

DemRossiya The Democratic Russia movement came into being in 1990 in order to support democratically minded candidates during the elections to the RSFSR Congress of People's Deputies, especially those associated with Yeltsin. It was an umbrella organisation which contained a wide range of parties and movements of views and failed to develop into a viable political party. One of the issues on which it could not agree in 1991 was whether Russia would be better off if the Soviet Union were destroyed or not. Their views were close to those of the Inter-Regional Group and Memorial. They became the largest opposition group to the communists in 1990, having, before their splits, over 4,000 members. Among leading members were Boris Yeltsin, Yury Afasanev, Anatoly Sobchak, Gavriil Popov, Nikolai Travkin and Sergei Stankevich. Yeltsin's victory in the presidential election of June 1991 owed much to the support of this movement. By 1996 it had shrunk to a small group.

Five Year Plan The first Five Year Plan spanned the period October 1928–December 1932, the second, 1933–7, and so on.

Plans were drafted by Gosplan and had the force of law. Non-fulfilment of the plan was, therefore, a criminal offence.

G7 Group of advanced industrial states, consisting of the United States, Japan, Great Britain, France, Italy, Germany and Canada. The Soviet Union wished to join and transform it into G8. Gorbachev attended the G7 meeting in London during the summer of 1991.

GDR German Democratic Republic. In 1945 the eastern part of Germany was occupied by the Red Army and was called the Soviet Occupied Zone of Germany. In 1949 this territory was re-named the GDR in response to the establishment of the Federal Republic of Germany. It was also known as East Germany and its capital was East Berlin. The ruling communist party was called the Socialist Unity Party of Germany (SED) and there were other parties, such as the Christian Democratic Union of Germany, which were subordinate to the SED. The GDR merged with the Federal Republic in October 1990.

Glasnost A key element of Gorbachev's reforms which involved openness in economic and political decision-making and the open discussion of all questions and freedom of information. This latter aspect led to vigorous debate about the Soviet past, including the crimes of the Stalin era. Glasnost was a key theme at the 19th Party Conference and was confirmed in the conference resolutions.

Gorkom City Party committee, headed by a first secretary.

Gosplan State Planning Committee of the USSR Council of Ministers responsible for drafting economic plans and checking on their implementation. Founded in 1921, it continued to 1991. It produced Five Year Plans, annual plans, quarterly plans, etc. Each Soviet republic had its own Gosplan whose task was to provide inputs for USSR Gosplan in order to draft the next plan and check on plan implementation. After 1985 Gosplan lost influence as the Soviet economy gradually fragmented. In 1990, when Gorbachev replaced the USSR Council of Ministers with a Cabinet of Ministers, Gosplan became the Ministry for Economics and Forecasting.

Ideologists Those Party officials and academics who were concerned with propagating and developing Marxism-Leninism. Every university student was required to pass an examination in Marxism-Leninism before graduating. Gorbachev complained, with justification, that the great majority of these communists merely justified the present and did not attempt to develop creatively the ideology. However, under Brezhnev the concept of developed, mature or ripe socialism was coined and Gorbachev began with developing socialism. The negative western term for these officials is ideologues.

IMF The International Monetary Fund, based in Washington, which is concerned with macroeconomic issues. It was founded in 1945 as a result of the Bretton Woods agreement.

INF Intermediate-range nuclear forces.

INF Agreement Signed on 8 December 1987 by the United States and the Soviet Union to eliminate a whole category of nuclear weapons, land-based nuclear intermediate-range weapons with a range between 500 and 5,500 km.

Inter-Regional Group Deputies in the USSR Congress of People's Deputies and the USSR Supreme Soviet who formed the group in the summer of 1989 and who defended human rights, the introduction of private property, a multi-party system and a democratic rule of law state. Its members included Boris Yeltsin, Andrei Sakharov, Yury Afanasev and Gavriil Popov.

KGB Committee of State Security. Established as the Cheka in 1917 by Lenin to ensure that the Bolsheviks stayed in power; under Stalin its task became to keep him in power. There was a USSR KGB and each Soviet republic had its own KGB, subordinate to the KGB whose headquarters were in the Lubyanka, Moscow. The KGB was responsible for domestic and foreign intelligence. In the military, the GRU was responsible for intelligence gathering but the KGB checked on the political loyalty of the armed forces.

Kolkhoz Literally, collective economy; members farmed the land as a cooperative but, in reality, had little say in what was produced as this was laid down in the annual state plan. Before 1966 there was no guaranteed wage; if the farm made a profit wages were paid, if not, no wages were paid. Most peasants preferred to concentrate on their private plots.

Komsomol Lenin Young Communist League. For those between 14 and 28 years, except for the organisation's leadership. Most young people belonged to it and almost everyone who joined the Communist Party had previously belonged to the Komsomol. There was a USSR Komsomol and one in each Soviet republic. Like the Communist Party its leadership were full-time officials. In the early 1980s the Komsomol had over 40 million members.

Krai Administrative sub-division of a Soviet republic containing within it a territory inhabited by another (non-Slav) nationality, called an autonomous oblast. Can also be translated as territory.

Kraikom Krai Party committee, headed by a first secretary.

Kulak Peasants were divided into poor, middle and rich by Lenin and the Bolsheviks. The poor peasant did not have enough land to live off, the middle peasant did and the rich produced a surplus for the market. In west European terms the kulak would have been a moderately well-off farmer.

Memorial Society Formed to remember the victims of Stalin's oppression. Politically it became active in early 1989 and concentrated on making public the Russian and Soviet past and laying bare the crimes of the Stalin period. It later became part of DemRossiya.

Minsk Agreement This agreement between Russia (Boris Yeltsin), Belarus (Stanislau Shushkevich) and Ukraine (Leonid Kravchuk) was the death blow to the further existence of the Soviet Union under Gorbachev. The agreement states that the Soviet Union as a subject in international law has ceased to exist.

MVD Ministry of Internal Affairs responsible for law and order. There was a USSR MVD and each Soviet republic had its own MVD, subordinate to Moscow.

NATO North Atlantic Treaty Organisation, founded in 1949.

NEP New Economic Policy. Introduced in 1921 by Lenin as a compromise after War Communism (1918–21) had failed and the country was facing economic ruin and the fear that the peasants would not deliver food to the cities. Under NEP the commanding heights of the economy (energy, communications, heavy industry, etc.) stayed in state hands while light industry and agriculture reverted to private ownership. Trade was again legal. There was great interest during the Gorbachev era in NEP and it was seen as an option for the Soviet Union as it had been a mixed market economy under socialism. Stalin's Five Year Plan eliminated the market. In reality NEP was not an option for Gorbachev as Stalin had destroyed private farming and few farm workers in the 1980s wanted to farm on their own. Also during NEP there was a developed system of producers' and consumers' cooperatives, and a vibrant tradition of cottage industries, but all this was destroyed deliberately by Stalin who forced peasants to join collective (kolkhoz) and state (sovkhoz) farms, mainly to ensure that the state could feed workers during the industrialisation drive.

Nomenklatura Nomenclatura or nomenclature: consisted of (a) the list of positions which the Party regarded as important and which required Party assent to be filled; (b) the list of persons capable of filling these positions. There was the Party nomenklatura and the state nomenklatura. Each Party body, from the obkom upwards, had a list of nomenklatura appointments it could fill. The longer a first Party secretary remained in an oblast, for example, the greater the number of posts he could influence. In this way nepotism and corruption crept into the Party apparatus. For example, important Soviet ambassadors – to Washington, Bonn, etc. – were on the nomenklatura list of the Politburo. Nomenklatura officials were full-time.

Novo-Ogarevo Gorbachev's dacha near Moscow at which republican leaders (including Yeltsin) debated the formation of a genuinely federal state to succeed the Soviet Union with President Gorbachev during the spring and summer of 1991. The outcome was the draft Union of Sovereign States. These talks were also referred to as the Nine Plus One, nine republican leaders and Gorbachev. The Baltic republics never participated in these deliberations, having demanded their independence.

Obkom Oblast Party committee, headed by a first secretary.

Oblast Administrative sub-division of a Soviet republic; oblasts were sub-divided into raions, as were cities. Can also be translated as territory, province.

Politburo Political Bureau of the CC. It was the key decision-making body of the Communist Party; set up formally at the 8th Party Congress, in 1919. It was called the Presidium between 1952 and 1966. In 1987 there were 14 full and 6 candidate members, with Russians predominating.

Presidium Inner council or cabinet, hence supreme body. The Politburo of the Communist Party was known as the Presidium, 1952–66. The USSR Supreme Soviet Presidium contained all the worthies in the state and Party. The chairman of the Presidium of the USSR Supreme Soviet was the head of state, hence he was sometimes referred to as President. The term President officially entered the Soviet Constitution in 1989 when Gorbachev was elected Soviet President. The USSR Council of Ministers (Soviet government) also had a Presidium, consisting of key ministers – hence it was similar to a cabinet.

Procurator General The top law official in the Soviet Union, he headed the USSR Procuracy. Each Soviet republic had its own procuracy, as did each raion, oblast and krai.

Raikom Raion Party committee, headed by a first secretary.

Raion Administrative sub-division of an oblast, krai and city. Can be translated as district.

RSDRP The Russian Social Democratic Labour or Workers' Party was founded in Minsk in 1898 but it split in 1903 into Bolsheviks and Mensheviks. It was modelled on the German SPD and until 1917 all social democratic parties were Marxist.

RSFSR Russian Soviet Federated Socialist Republic or the Russian Federation or, simply, Russia. It was the largest of the 15 Soviet republics and its capital was also Moscow.

RSFSR Congress of People's Deputies First convened in March 1990, with Yeltsin as speaker. It was a super-parliament and it elected from among its members a RSFSR Supreme Soviet with a rotating membership which exchanged some members at each new Congress. Russia was the only Soviet republic with a Congress as all the others declined to elect one and proceeded directly to the election of a Supreme Soviet which then enjoyed popular legitimacy. It was dissolved by a presidential decree in September 1991.

SALT Strategic Arms Limitation Talks. Discussions on the limitation of nuclear weapons which got under way in 1969 between the US and the USSR. In 1972 the SALT I treaty was signed and in 1979 the SALT II treaty emerged. Due to the Soviet invasion of Afghanistan the Americans did not ratify SALT II.

Secretariat The administrative centre of the Communist Party. It was set up by the 8th Party Congress, in 1919, and Stalin was elected the first general secretary, but at that time the post was not regarded as conferring much power on the incumbent. Its key officials were called CC secretaries and the leading one general secretary. Between 1953 and 1966 the top man was called the first secretary. The Secretariat had various departments, each headed by an official, and the handful of CC secretaries each supervised a group of departments. After 1957 the Secretariat assumed responsibility for the economy and a CC secretary was senior to a USSR Minister. It was responsible for ensuring that CC decisions were implemented. In 1987 there were 11 secretaries, including Gorbachev. When Gorbachev became general secretary in 1985, Ligachev was elected to chair the secretaries' meetings and he became known unofficially as second secretary.

Soviet a) Council b) citizen of the USSR c) name of the country. Soviets first emerged during the 1905 revolution and then blossomed after the February 1917 revolution. Gorbachev attempted to reinvigorate them in 1988 but by then the Party boss ruled the localities. He hoped they would take over from the Party at local level and implement perestroika but they lacked the skill and personnel to do this.

Soviet–German Non-Aggression Pact or Stalin–Hitler Pact Signed by Molotov and Ribbentrop on 23 August 1939 (Stalin and Hitler never met). It envisaged that the Soviet Union and Germany would not attack one another and that if war did ensue elsewhere both states would remain neutral. The key part of the agreement was the secret protocol which the Soviets denied existed, until the late 1980s. It divided Europe up into zones of influence with the Soviet Union taking eastern Poland, Latvia, Estonia, Finland, Lithuania (as the result of an amendment) and Bessarabia. Germany bagged the rest of Europe.

Soviet Republic There were 15, of which the Russian Federation was the largest and Estonia, Latvia and Lithuania had been the last to join, in 1940. Each republic had its own government, many ministries and its own communist party which was, of course, part of the CPSU. The local communist party had its own Central Committee and a Bureau (playing the same role as the central Politburo) (Ukraine was the exception and had a Politburo). The communist parties split in many republics into pro-nationalist communist parties and pro-Moscow communist parties. This occurred in all three Baltic republics. The pro-nationalist communist parties then supported the bid for independence. Under glasnost, many informal associations (so called because they were not officially registered) sprang up and these included popular fronts, especially in the Baltic republics.

Soyuz Union. People's deputies at all levels were members. Established in December 1990 to defend the integrity of the Soviet Union, it argued that a state of emergency was the only way to restore order and ensure the survival of the Soviet Union. Its leading members were Yury Blokhin, Viktor Alksnis, Evgeny Kogan and Sergei Baburin. Among the membership were representatives of the military-industrial complex, the KGB, the MVD and the Party apparatus. In the USSR Congress of People's Deputies and the USSR Supreme Soviet Soyuz was the largest anti-reform faction but did not command a majority.

Staraya Ploshchad Old Square, the headquarters of the Party CC until August 1991. It is very near Red Square.

START Strategic Arms Reduction Talks. Negotiations on the reduction of strategic weapon systems, between the United States and the Soviet Union, then Russia, which resulted in the START I agreement in 1991 and the START II agreement in 1993.

State Procurements Output bought by the state and laid down by the plan in advance. In industry this applied to most of an enterprise's output but in agriculture it could vary. Kolkhozes and sovkhozes had to meet state procurement plans first before they disposed of any of their produce. Naturally they attempted to keep back as much for themselves as possible, sometimes stating that they did not have enough to meet the plan. The person responsible for ensuring that farms met their state obligations was the first Party secretary.

Strategic Nuclear Weapons Those nuclear weapons which can be fired from one continent to another.

Supreme Soviet Set up by the 1936 Soviet Constitution, the USSR Supreme Soviet was bicameral, consisting of the Soviet of the Union and the Soviet of Nationalities. The number of deputies in the former was based on population, while the number of the latter was fixed; the houses were of equal status and often met in joint session. It was a parliament only in name (until 1989), key decisions being taken by the Communist Party and the government. The chairman of the Presidium of the USSR

Supreme Soviet was Soviet head of state. Each Soviet republic and autonomous republic had its own Supreme Soviet but they were unicameral. Each house had its own commissions and committees were joint bodies. All important state legislation was passed by the USSR Supreme Soviet which normally only met twice a year, for a few days at a time. In 1989 the USSR Congress of People's Deputies elected a USSR Supreme Soviet with a rotating membership, some members being dropped and others elected at each new Congress. The RSFSR Congress of People's Deputies, convened in 1990, also elected an inner RSFSR Supreme Soviet, again with a rotating membership.

Tactical Nuclear Weapons Short- and medium-range nuclear weapons for the theatre of war.

Union of Sovereign States Gorbachev intended it to be the successor state to the USSR but the attempted August coup was timed to prevent its signature. Afterwards it was too late and the dissolution of the USSR and the establishment of the CIS consigned it to the dustbin of history.

USSR Union of Soviet Socialist Republics; also known as the Soviet Union.

USSR Congress of People's Deputies Convened during the early years of the revolution, it was resurrected in March 1989 as the supreme agency of state power. Its 2,250 deputies were elected for five years and there was to be Congress every year. Of the 2,250 deputies, two-thirds were directly elected, and there were to be multi-candidate elections, with open campaigning beforehand. The other 750 deputies were elected indirectly, according to lists proposed by political and social organisations. For instance, the Communist Party received 100 seats. Gorbachev chaired it. It was a super-parliament and from its membership it elected a USSR Supreme Soviet, or standing parliament, with a rotating membership which exchanged some members at the next Congress. According to the amendments of the Soviet Constitution, the Congress could amend the Constitution, if a two-thirds majority approved. The Congress elected Gorbachev President of the Soviet Union. The Congress, on 5 September 1991, voluntarily dissolved itself and conceded power to the RSFSR Congress of People's Deputies but there were deputies who were members of both.

USSR Council of Ministers The Soviet government, headed by a chairman or Prime Minister. The USSR Council of Ministers was dissolved in 1990 and replaced by a Cabinet of Ministers, headed by a Prime Minister.

USSR Council of the President or Presidential Council It was established in March 1990 and functioned until December 1990 with all members being nominated by Gorbachev. It was dominated by the power ministries (Security, Internal Affairs, Defence) but its precise functions were unclear. It was replaced in early 1991 by the newly constituted USSR Security Council which lasted until the attempted coup.

USSR Soviet (Council) of the Federation Established under Gorbachev as a supra-government for the Soviet Union, consisting of the President, Vice-President, and senior representatives from each of the 15 Soviet republics. It ceased to exist in August 1991 and should not be confused with the Council of the Federation, the upper house of the Russian parliament, established in December 1993.

USSR State Council The successor to the USSR Soviet of the Federation but again was only consultative.

USSR Supreme Soviet Founded in 1936, it was the supreme agency of state power in the Soviet Union, according to the Constitution. It was bicameral, consisting of the Soviet of the Union and the Soviet of Nationalities, and in 1985 had 1,500 members. It was elected for four years and had to meet twice a year, amounting to about a week altogether. It elected a Presidium (39 members since 1977) from among its members and the chairman was the head of the Soviet state. Until Podgorny became chairman of the Presidium in 1964, the position had never been politically significant. Brezhnev made himself head of state in May 1977 and Podgorny was sent packing. Andropov and Chernenko also made themselves head of state but Gorbachev, in July 1985, suggested Gromyko for the post and he remained there until 1988 when Gorbachev himself took over. The USSR Supreme Soviet was superseded by the USSR Congress of People's Deputies in March 1989. Confusingly the Congress then proceeded to elect its own USSR Supreme Soviet but the latter was subordinate to the former.

Warsaw Pact Organisation The Pact was founded in 1955 as a response to the Paris Treaties of October 1954 which had admitted the Federal Republic of Germany to NATO. The original members were the Soviet Union, Poland, Czechoslovakia, Hungary, the GDR, Bulgaria, Romania and Albania. Albania left in 1961. The Pact had also a Political Consultative Committee which was attended by foreign ministers. The Pact never permitted the east German Volksarmee to set up its own General Staff, for instance. All advanced military technology was manufactured in the Soviet Union and the Soviet Army was the best equipped. The Pact was dissolved on 1 July 1991.

White House The seat of the Russian parliament in Moscow.

CHRONOLOGY

THE GORBACHEV ERA: IN THE ASCENDANCY, 1985–1989

1985

10 March: Konstantin Chernenko dies.

11 March: Mikhail Gorbachev is elected general secretary of the CC, CPSU.

7 April: Gorbachev halts Soviet missile deployment but insists they will restart in November if NATO does not stop its deployment.

23 April: The April CC plenum accepts Gorbachev's vague reforms. Chebrikov, Ryzhkov and Ligachev become full members of the Politburo, and Minister of Defence Sergei Sokolov becomes a candidate member.

15 May: Gorbachev visits Leningrad and evokes much support for his policies and his frankness.

16 May: Aspects of the anti-alcohol campaign are announced, including reducing production of strong drink and increased penalties for drunken driving.

1 July: CC plenum removes Grigory Romanov from the Politburo, Eduard Shevardnadze is elected a full member of the Politburo and Boris Yeltsin and Lev Zaikov become CC secretaries.

2 July: Andrei Gromyko becomes chair of the Presidium of the USSR Supreme Soviet, head of state, and Shevardnadze succeeds him as foreign minister.

25–27 September: Shevardnadze visits the US to prepare the ground for a Reagan–Gorbachev summit.

2–5 October: Gorbachev visits France, his first official visit to the west as leader. He uses the term 'reasonable sufficiency' for the first time, does not link INF negotiations to anything else and

298

rejects ideology as the basis of foreign policy. He proposes that the superpowers reduce their strategic arsenals by a half.

19–21 November: Summit meeting in Geneva between Mikhail Gorbachev and President Ronald Reagan; they agree to meet in the future.

24 December: Boris Yeltsin replaces Viktor Grishin as first secretary of the Moscow city Party committee.

1986

8 February: In an interview in *L'Humanité*, the French Communist Party newspaper, Gorbachev describes Stalinism as a 'concept thought up by opponents of communism and used on a large scale to smear the Soviet Union and socialism as a whole'.

18 February: A CC plenum discusses the 27th Party Congress and the economic plan for 1990–2000. Viktor Grishin leaves the Politburo and Boris Yeltsin is elected a candidate member.

25 February–6 March: The 27th Party Congress opens with a long keynote speech by Gorbachev in which he advocates the radical reform of the economic mechanism. He refers to the war in Afghanistan as a 'bleeding wound' and the Brezhnev era as 'years of stagnation'. On 6 March Lev Zaikov becomes a full member of the Politburo. Yeltsin addresses the Congress on the sensitive subject of Party privileges.

26 April: An explosion at the Chernobyl nuclear reactor, Ukraine, turns out to be the worst in Soviet history. However, the initial response of the leadership is to play down its extent.

28 July: Gorbachev arrives in Vladivostok to tour the Soviet Far East and states that six regiments will be withdrawn from Afghanistan and that talks have begun with Mongolia on the withdrawal of Soviet troops.

10 October: Gorbachev arrives in Reykjavik for a two-day summit with President Reagan. They agree on most arms reduction issues. They almost agree on substantial cuts in offensive arms and even the elimination of nuclear weapons.

19 October: Five US diplomats are expelled from the Soviet Union in retaliation for the expulsion of Soviet UN officials.

21 October: The US expels 55 Soviet diplomats from the Soviet Embassy in Washington and the Soviet Consulate General in San Francisco and establishes personnel quotas for each.

22 October: The USSR expels five more US diplomats and withdraws Soviet employees from the US Embassy and Consulate General.

6 November: The USSR Ministry of Defence states that the withdrawal of six regiments (about 6,000 men) from Afghanistan has been completed and they will not be replaced.

28 November: The US deploys the new B52 bomber which violates the START II treaty.

1987

28 March–1 April: British Prime Minister Margaret Thatcher visits the Soviet Union and stresses human rights and calls for the withdrawal of Soviet troops from Afghanistan.

28 May: Mathias Rust, a young west German, lands his Cessna light aircraft near Red Square, having penetrated Soviet air defences without being noticed.

30 May: Many top military changes in the light of Rust's achievement. General Dmitry Yazov replaces General Sergei Sokolov as USSR Minister of Defence.

28–30 June: The USSR Supreme Soviet session is devoted mainly to economic reform. Ryzhkov calls the central management of the economy 'obsolete' and advocates radical changes. A law on the state enterprise which affords enterprises autonomy over their budgets is adopted and is to be implemented on 1 January 1988.

24 September: A Politburo resolution permits small shops to be run by individuals and cooperatives, a very radical reform.

12 October: In Leningrad, Gorbachev champions perestroika and glasnost and warns that if the Party leadership does not support reform, the Party could lose its leading role.

21 October: At a CC plenum, Boris Yeltsin breaks a Party taboo that leaders do not criticise one another in public, and blames Gorbachev and Ligachev for the slow pace of reform. Gorbachev reacts very sharply. Yeltsin requests permission to resign as a Politburo member and as first secretary of the Moscow city Party committee. Geidar Aliev is removed from the Politburo.

1 November: Gorbachev's book, *Perestroika and the New Political Thinking*, is published in Moscow. It is translated into many languages and is a huge bestseller.

11 November: Boris Yeltsin is attacked by Gorbachev and others at a meeting of the Moscow Party committee. Lev Zaikov takes over as first secretary. On 18 November Yeltsin is made first deputy chair of the state committee on construction.

5 December: Gorbachev travels to London and meets Margaret Thatcher.

7–10 December: Gorbachev in Washington for meetings with President Ronald Reagan. In Washington he signs the treaty banning intermediate-range nuclear missiles (INF) (8 December). It is his first visit to the United States and becomes a huge personal triumph; Gorbymania has appeared.

1988

1 January: Law on the state enterprise becomes effective and affords factories considerable autonomy (this reform loosens central control of the economy and leads to increasing inflation and shortages).

28 February: Armenians and Jews are attacked in Sumgait, Azerbaijan, and 26 Armenians and six Azeris are killed.

13 March: *Sovetskaya Rossiya* publishes Nina Andreeva's letter attacking perestroika and those critical of Stalin.

14 April: Agreements on the ending of the Afghan war are signed in Geneva. The Soviet Union and the US guarantee the agreements and promise not to interfere in the domestic affairs of Afghanistan and Pakistan.

29 May–2 June: President Reagan visits Moscow to meet Gorbachev for their fourth summit. Reagan also meets dissidents and praises freedom in an address to students at Moscow State University.

June–July: Continuing conflict in Nagorno-Karabakh. On 15 June the Armenian Supreme Soviet votes to incorporate Nagorno-Karabakh but the Azerbaijani Supreme Soviet rejects this on 17 June. On 20 July the USSR Supreme Soviet rules that the Armenian incorporation of Nagorno-Karabakh cannot be accepted.

15 June: The Armenian Supreme Soviet votes to annex Nagorno-Karabakh.

28 June–1 July: The 19th Party Conference opens in Moscow and Gorbachev proposes a presidential system for the country, the removal of the Party from economic management and the convening of a USSR Congress of People's Deputies with contested elections.

25 July: Shevardnadze, addressing a conference in the USSR Ministry of Foreign Affairs, rejects the class struggle as the basis of Soviet foreign policy.

5 August: Egor Ligachev reiterates, during a speech in Gorky (Nizhny Novgorod), that class struggle is the basis of Soviet foreign policy.

12 August: Aleksandr Yakovlev, in a speech in Vilnius, Lithuania, espouses universal human values or the common interests of mankind.

19 August: The draft programme of the Estonian People's Front is published in an Estonian newspaper.

21 September: A state of emergency is declared in parts of Nagorno-Karabakh after disorders.

30 September: At a CC plenum a large number of members retire (having lost their posts which afforded them CC status). Gromyko and Solomentsev retire from the Politburo. Ligachev is placed in charge of a CC commission on agriculture, a clear demotion. Aleksandr Yakovlev takes over the international department in the Party secretariat.

1 October: Gorbachev is elected chair of the Presidium of the USSR Supreme Soviet, head of state, by the USSR Supreme Soviet.

16 November: The Estonian Supreme Soviet declares sovereignty and claims the right to give Estonian legislation precedence over Soviet legislation.

26 November: The USSR Supreme Soviet annuls the Estonian declaration of sovereignty and takes control of state property in the republic.

1 December: The USSR Supreme Soviet passes a new electoral law which provides for contested elections and secret ballots.

7 December: Gorbachev, at the UN, announces that the Soviet Union will reduce its armed forces by 500,000 within two years without requiring reciprocal moves by the US or its allies. He also stresses that the common interests of mankind and freedom of choice are universal human principles. Later he meets Reagan and President-elect Bush on Governors Island. Marshal Sergei Akhromeev resigns as Chief of the General Staff and deputy Minister of Defence. Armenia is hit by a massive earthquake with over 50,000 dead. Gorbachev abandons his planned trip to Cuba and flies home.

1989

12 January: Nagorno-Karabakh comes under direct rule from Moscow by decree of the USSR Supreme Soviet. Arkady Volsky is appointed provisional administrator.

17–19 January: The CSCE Review Conference concludes in Vienna with agreement to begin negotiations on the reduction of conventional forces in Europe (CFE).

18 January: Estonia adopts a new language law which requires non-speakers of Estonian to learn the language within four years. On 26 January Lithuania does the same and on 1 February Latvia follows suit. Other republics adopt the same legislation: Tajikistan on 22 July; Kirgizia (Kyrgyzstan) on 24 August; Moldavia (Moldova) on 28 August; Uzbekistan on 21 October; and Ukraine on 28 October.

15 February: The last Soviet troops leave Afghanistan; the Najibullah regime survives until 1992. (Najibullah is killed by Taleban forces in September 1996.)

26 March: Elections are held to the USSR Congress of People's Deputies. Many Party candidates lose and the pro-independence parties win in the Baltic States. Boris Yeltsin wins in Moscow.

9 April: The Soviet army attacks a peaceful demonstration in Tbilisi, killing 20 and injuring hundreds.

25 April: At a Party plenum, 74 members of the Central Committee resign. Soviet troops begin leaving Hungary.

15–19 May: Gorbachev visits China and announces the normalisation of relations between the two states.

25 May: The USSR Congress of People's Deputies opens in Moscow and is televised live. Gorbachev is elected chairman and on 26 May the members of the USSR Supreme Soviet, the new standing parliament, are elected from among the Congress's members. Yeltsin obtains a seat when Aleksei Kazannik stands down in his favour.

6 July: Gorbachev addresses the Council of Europe in Strasbourg and states that the Soviet Union will not stand in the way of reform in eastern Europe.

10 July: Coal miners in the Kuzbass, Siberia, go on strike, followed later by the Donbass, Ukraine.

29 July: The Inter-Regional Group is formed in the Congress of People's Deputies to promote reform. Among the leaders chosen by these 250-odd deputies are Boris Yeltsin, Gavriil Popov and Andrei Sakharov.

23 August: Over two million participate in a Baltic Way demonstration, forming a human chain across the three republics.

31 August: The Moldavian Supreme Soviet decrees Moldavian (Moldovian or Romanian) as the state language and replaces the Cyrillic alphabet with the Latin.

22–23 September: James Baker, US Secretary of State, and Shevardnadze meet in Jackson Hole, Wyoming. Shevardnadze drops the Soviet demand which links reduction in strategic missiles to limits on the Strategic Defence Initiative (SDI) or Star Wars.

25–26 September: President Bush and Eduard Shevardnadze, at the UN, propose the elimination of chemical weapons.

7 October: Gorbachev, in East Berlin, tells the crowds that 'life punishes those who fall behind' and this further undermines the authority of Erich Honecker, the GDR leader. He is replaced by Egon Krenz on 18 October.

8 October: The Latvian Popular Front adopts independence as its goal.

9 November: The Berlin Wall comes down.

19 November: The Georgian Supreme Soviet declares sovereignty and decides that the Soviet occupation of Georgia in 1921 violated the 1920 treaty between Georgia and Russia.

28 November: The USSR Supreme Soviet ends direct rule over Nagorno-Karabakh despite objections by deputies from Armenia and Nagorno-Karabakh.

1 December: Gorbachev has an audience with Pope John Paul II in the Vatican and states that a law on freedom of conscience will be passed and that the Ukrainian (Greek) Catholic Church will be recognised again.

2–3 December: Gorbachev and Bush meet in Malta and Gorbachev states that force will not be used to ensure that east European communist regimes remain in power. Bush agrees to remove most controls on US–Soviet trade.

12 December: The 2nd session of the USSR Congress of People's Deputies opens and Gorbachev refuses to consider amending or removing article 6 of the USSR Constitution guaranteeing the Party a monopoly of political power.

20 December: The Communist Party of Lithuania declares itself independent of the Communist Party of the Soviet Union.

24 December: The USSR Supreme Soviet declares the secret protocol to the Nazi–Soviet Pact invalid but does not comment on the incorporation of the Baltic States and other territories acquired by the Soviet Union as part of this agreement.

．　．　．

GORBACHEV IN DECLINE, 1990–1991

1990

11–13 January: Gorbachev travels to Lithuania to discuss the republic's desire to break away from the Soviet Union. However Lithuanians demonstrate for independence.

19–20 January: Clashes in Baku between Soviet forces and the local population leave many dead. The Azerbaijani National Front loses power.

February–March: Local elections are held throughout the Soviet Union with pro-independence candidates winning in the Baltic States; in Moscow and Leningrad the official Party candidates are rejected.

5 February: At a CC plenum Gorbachev proposes the Party abandon its leading role (article 6 of the USSR Constitution), accept a multi-party system and adopt 'humane, democratic socialism'. These are accepted on 7 February after a stormy debate.

8 February: James Baker visits Moscow and proposes Two (east and west Germany) Plus Four (the US, USSR, Britain and France) negotiations to discuss German unification.

10 February: Chancellor Kohl, in Moscow, gets an agreement in principle on German reunification.

12 February: The foreign ministers of the Two Plus Four meeting in Ottawa agree to begin discussions on German unification.

6 March: The Congress of People's Deputies amends article 6 of the Soviet Constitution, thus ending the Party's monopoly of power.

11 March: Lithuania declares the restoration of independence and elects Vytautas Landsbergis Supreme Council chairman and President.

14 March: Gorbachev is elected Soviet President by the Congress of People's Deputies.

25 March: The Communist Party of Estonia votes to be independent of the CPSU.

28 March: First free elections in Hungary since 1945.

1 May: The May Day parade in Red Square is disturbed by anti-Gorbachev protesters.

4 May: The Latvian Supreme Soviet endorses independence as a goal.

29 May: Boris Yeltsin is elected chairman (or President) of the Presidium of the RSFSR Supreme Soviet.

30 May–4 June: Gorbachev travels to Washington for his second summit with Bush, then visits Minneapolis-St Paul and San Francisco.

8 June: The Russian Supreme Soviet declares sovereignty and states its laws take precedence over Soviet laws.

19–23 June: The founding Congress of the Russian Communist Party convenes in Moscow.

22 June: Ivan Polozkov, a conservative, is elected leader of the Russian Communist Party.

30 June: Deliveries of oil and natural gas are resumed to Lithuania after the Lithuanian parliament temporarily suspends the implementation of its declaration of independence.

2–13 July: The 28th Party Congress convenes in Moscow. Gorbachev is re-elected general secretary but with a significant number of votes against. The new Politburo contains only Party officials and will have no role in governing the country.

16 July: Ukraine declares sovereignty.

20 July: The 500-day programme of the Russian Republic is published. It envisages moving to a market economy in 500 days.

27 July: Belorussia declares sovereignty.

2 August: Iraq invades Kuwait.

3 August: Baker and Shevardnadze sign a joint statement in Moscow condemning the Iraqi invasion.

22 August: Turkmenistan and Armenia declare sovereignty.

25 August: Tajikistan declares sovereignty. The Abkhaz ASSR in Georgia declares independence from Georgia and requests Union republican status within the RSFSR.

6 September: Leningraders vote to restore the original name of the city, St Petersburg (Sankt Peterburg in Russian).

9 September: Gorbachev and Bush meet for a one-day summit in Helsinki and agree to cooperate to end Iraqi aggression in Kuwait.

12 September: The Two Plus Four treaty is signed in Moscow ending four-power control over Germany.

24 September: The USSR Supreme Soviet grants Gorbachev special powers for 18 months to rule by decree during the transition to a market economy but cannot agree on an economic programme.

3 October: Germany is reunited.

20–21 October: The political movement, Democratic Russia, holds its first congress in Moscow.

25 October: Kazakhstan declares sovereignty.

28 October: The Kirgiz Supreme Soviet elects Askar Akaev President of Kirgizia. Pro-independence parties win parliamentary elections in Georgia. The Rukh congress in Kiev accepts Ukrainian independence as a major goal.

30 October: Kirgizia declares sovereignty.

7 November: Shots are fired at Gorbachev during the Revolution celebrations in Red Square.

17 November: The USSR Supreme Soviet accepts Gorbachev's proposal to set up a new Soviet government, consisting of representatives from all 15 Union republics, to be called the Soviet (Council) of the Federation.

19 November: The treaty on Conventional Forces in Europe (CFE) is signed in Paris.

23 November: The draft treaty of a new union is published, to be called the Union of Sovereign Soviet Republics. Most republican leaders criticise it.

1 December: Vadim Bakatin is removed as USSR Minister of Internal Affairs and replaced by Boris Pugo.

20 December: Eduard Shevardnadze, Minister of Foreign Affairs, resigns and warns of the threat of dictatorship.

25 December: Prime Minister Nikolai Ryzhkov suffers a heart attack.

26 December: Gorbachev chooses Gennady Yanaev as the new Vice-President of the Soviet Union but he is rejected on the first ballot by the Congress and accepted on the second the following day. Gorbachev is also afforded greater powers.

1991

11–13 January: Soviet black berets (OMON forces under the Ministry of the Interior) and the KGB Alpha division fire at the main printing press in Vilnius, Lithuania, and on 13 January attack and take the television station there, killing 13 and one of their own dies also.

14 January: Valentin Pavlov is appointed Prime Minister of the USSR.

15 January: Operation Desert Storm, to remove Iraq from Kuwait, begins in the Persian Gulf.

20 January: Three die in clashes between Soviet forces and Latvian police.

9 February: Over 90 per cent of Lithuanian voters favour independence for Lithuania.

12 February: Valentin Pavlov, Soviet Prime Minister, claims there is a plot to undermine the Soviet economy and withdraws 100 ruble notes from circulation.

24 February: The US-led ground offensive begins against Iraq.

25 February: The Warsaw Pact agrees to annul all military agreements, effective as of 31 March, but to continue voluntary political links.

28 February: All military operations against Iraq are suspended.

1 March: Coal miners strike in the Donbass, Ukraine; strikes then spread to other areas.

3 March: Referendums on independence are held in Estonia and Latvia with 78 per cent voting in favour in Estonia and 74 per cent in favour in Latvia.

14–16 March: Baker visits Moscow for discussions and meets Baltic leaders and other republican heads.

17 March: Referendum on the future of the USSR and (in the RSFSR) on the creation of a presidency and (in Moscow) a directly elected mayor. Large majority in favour of retaining the Union.

31 March: The Warsaw Pact is formally dissolved.

4 April: The RSFSR Supreme Soviet votes to give Yeltsin considerable power. Strikes begin in Minsk.

9 April: Georgia declares independence.

22 April: Prime Minister Pavlov presents an anti-crisis programme to the USSR Supreme Soviet.

23 April: In Novo-Ogarevo, the President's dacha outside Moscow, President Gorbachev and the heads of state of nine republics sign a joint statement on speeding up a new Union agreement (the Nine Plus One agreement).

24 April: The RSFSR Supreme Soviet passes a law providing for the election of a President of Russia.

12 June: Boris Yeltsin is elected President of the RSFSR in Russia's first democratic elections. He receives 57.3 per cent of the vote in a turnout of 74 per cent. Zhirinovsky polls 8 per cent. Gavriil Popov is elected mayor of Moscow with 65.3 per cent of the vote.

17 June: Prime Minister Pavlov requests the USSR Supreme Soviet to grant him special powers (without Gorbachev's approval) and is supported in camera (private meeting) by Marshal Yazov (Minister of Defence), Vladimir Kryuchkov (KGB) and Boris Pugo (Minister of Internal Affairs).

20 June: The US ambassador warns Gorbachev of a conspiracy to remove him.

30 June: The last Soviet soldier leaves Czechoslovakia (they had invaded on 21 August 1968).

4 July: Eduard Shevardnadze resigns from the CPSU to co-found an opposition group.

10 July: Boris Yeltsin is sworn in as President of the RSFSR and receives the blessing of the Russian Orthodox Church.

12 July: The USSR Supreme Soviet approves the Union treaty in principle, but suggests amendments.

17 July: Gorbachev meets G7 leaders in London but receives little support.

30–31 July: President Bush visits Moscow, meets Gorbachev and Nazarbaev, and pays a separate visit to Yeltsin.

1 August: President Bush visits Kiev and meets Leonid Kravchuk.

4 August: Gorbachev leaves for his vacation at Foros, Crimea.

．　．　．

THE DEATH THROES OF THE SOVIET UNION, AUGUST–DECEMBER 1991

17 August: Kryuchkov, Pavlov and Yazov agree with several senior Party officials to demand that Gorbachev hand over power to them temporarily, and if he refuses, to detain him and take control.

18 August: Gorbachev rejects the demands of the delegation sent to persuade him at Foros to agree to the take-over. Shortly before midnight, Vice President Gennady Yanaev agrees to support the take-over and signs a decree assuming the powers of the President.

19 August: The emergency committee announces that it has assumed power and demands that all institutions obey its orders. Gorbachev is declared to be unfit to perform his duties for health reasons. A state of emergency is declared for six months. Yeltsin brands the take-over an illegal *coup d'état* and helps rally resistance at the White House.

20 August: Lack of military and state support gradually becomes clear. Estonia declares independence.

21 August: The attempted coup fails; Gorbachev returns to Moscow. The CPSU finally denounces the attempted coup. Yeltsin is given extra powers by the RSFSR Supreme Soviet and takes control of Soviet armed forces on Russian territory. He orders the CPSU to suspend its activities within the Russian Federation. Latvia declares independence.

24 August: Gorbachev suspends the activities of the CPSU and resigns as general secretary. Ukraine declares independence subject to a referendum on 1 December 1991.

25 August: The Belorussian (Belarusian) Supreme Soviet declares political and economic independence.

27 August: Moldavia (Moldova) declares independence.

30 August: Azerbaijan declares independence.

31 August: Kirgizia (Kyrgyzstan) and Uzbekistan declare independence.

September: The oblast soviet of Nagorno-Karabakh and the oblast soviet of Shaumyan (Armenia) establish the Republic of Nagorno-Karabakh. [The Azerbaijani parliament abolishes self-rule in Nagorno-Karabakh in November 1991. On 6 January 1992 the parliament of the Republic of Nagorno-Karabakh declares independence. In response to this, President Mutalibov of Azerbaijan places Nagorno-Karabakh under his direct control. In March 1993 Nagorno-Karabakh troops attack Azerbaijan; on 30 April 1993 the UN Security Council calls for a ceasefire and the withdrawal of Armenian troops from Azerbaijan; on 29 June the UN Security Council calls for the immediate withdrawal of Nagorno-Karabakh troops from Agdam (Azeri inhabited area of Nagorno-Karabakh); on 12 May 1994 a ceasefire is signed by Armenia, Azerbaijan and Nagorno-Karabakh.]

2–6 September: The 5th extraordinary USSR Congress of People's Deputies calls for a new treaty for a Union of Sovereign States; it issues a declaration on human rights and freedoms; legislation to dissolve the Congress is presented.

6 September: Georgia announces the severing of all ties with the Soviet Union. The USSR State Council formally recognises the independence of Estonia, Latvia and Lithuania and supports their application for membership of the UN and CSCE.

9 September: Tajikistan declares independence.

21 September: Armenia declares independence.

11 October: The USSR State Council decides to dismember the KGB and rename it.

19 October: Treaty on the Economic Community of Sovereign States is signed by President Gorbachev and representatives

of eight republics; Azerbaijan, Georgia, Moldavia (Moldova) and Ukraine decline to sign.

28 October: The Russian Congress of People's Deputies elects Ruslan Khasbulatov its chairman and speaker of the Russian Supreme Soviet. Yeltsin is granted power to implement economic reform by decree for one year.

4 November: Republican leaders meeting in the USSR State Council agree to abolish all USSR ministries except those for defence, foreign affairs, railways, electric power, and nuclear power. Yeltsin informs the meeting that Russia does not intend to set up its own armed forces.

6 November: President Yeltsin bans the activities of the CPSU and the Russian Communist Party on the territory of the Russian Federation. President Yeltsin becomes Russian Prime Minister and appoints Gennady Burbulis, Egor Gaidar and Aleksandr Shokhin as deputy Prime Ministers.

14 November: Yeltsin and other republic leaders in the State Council agree that the USSR successor state shall be a confederation.

15 November: Yeltsin signs ten decrees taking control of almost all financial and economic activity in the Russian Federation.

22 November: The Russian Supreme Soviet takes over the USSR State Bank.

25 November: Yeltsin and Shushkevich (Belarus) decline to initial the treaty on the confederation which had been negotiated.

1 December: In a referendum Ukrainian voters confirm Ukrainian independence.

5 December: The Ukrainian parliament formally revokes the accession of Ukraine to the 1922 treaty establishing the USSR.

8 December: In Belovezh forest, near Minsk, the Presidents and Prime Ministers of Russia, Ukraine and Belarus declare the USSR dissolved and found a Commonwealth of Independent States (CIS). Gorbachev describes the move 'dangerous and illegal'.

10 December: Belarus and Ukraine ratify the CIS agreement.

11 December: The Russian Supreme Soviet ratifies the CIS agreement.

12 December: Central Asian leaders meeting in Ashkhabad (Ashghabat) request membership of the CIS as founding members.

17 December: Yeltsin and Gorbachev agree that by 1 January 1992 the Soviet Union will no longer exist.

21–22 December: Eleven former Soviet republics meet in Almaty and the CIS is extended (Estonia, Latvia, Lithuania and Georgia did not attend).

25 December: USSR President Gorbachev resigns and the Russian flag replaces the Soviet flag over the Kremlin.

31 December: At midnight the Soviet Union ceases to exist in international law.

BIOGRAPHIES

Abalkin, Leonid Ivanovich (born 1930), director of the Institute of National Economy, USSR Academy of Sciences, from 1986, becoming an academician (member of the USSR Academy of Sciences), 1987. Deputy chair of the USSR Council of Ministers, 1989–91; worked with Ryzhkov on economic reform.

Afansev, Viktor Grigorevich (1922–94), journalist; editor-in-chief of *Pravda*, 1976–89; chair of the USSR Union of Journalists, 1976–90. He was removed from *Pravda* for his lack of enthusiasm for perestroika and glasnost.

Afanasev, Yury Nikolaevich (born 1934), rector of Moscow State Archive Institute, 1986; radical communist who lost patience with Gorbachev; co-founder of DemRossiya.

Aganbegyan, Abel Gezevich (born 1932), influential economist during the early period of perestroika but then faded. He was academic secretary, USSR Academy of Sciences, 1987–91, and also rector of the Academy of National Economy.

Akaev, Askar Akaevich (born 1944), nuclear scientist; Vice President, 1987–9, then President of the Kyrgyz Academy of Sciences, 1989–90; President of Kyrgyzstan, from 1991; one of the few leaders to condemn the attempted coup from the outset.

Akhromeev, Marshal Sergei Fedorovich (1923–91), first deputy Chief of the General Staff, 1979–84; Chief of the General Staff of the Soviet Armed Forces and first deputy Minister of Defence, 1984–8; military adviser to Gorbachev, 1989–91; committed suicide.

Aliev, Geidar (Haydar) Ali Rza Ogly (born 1923), first secretary, Communist Party of Azerbaijan, 1969–82; first deputy Chair, USSR Council of Ministers, 1982–7; member of Politburo, 1982–7; too conservative for Gorbachev; President of Azerbaijan from 1993.

Andreeva, Nina Aleksandrovna (born 1938), author of the famous letter in March 1988 savaging perestroika; general secretary of the Communist Party of the USSR Bolsheviks, founded in November 1991 in St Petersburg.

311

Andropov, Yury Vladimirovich (1914–84), chair of the KGB, 1967–82; general secretary of the CPSU, 1982–4; chair of the Presidium of the USSR Supreme Soviet (head of state), 1983–4; member of the Politburo, 1973–84.

Arbatov, Georgy Arkadevich (born 1923), director of the Institute for the USA and Canada, from 1967; member of the USSR Academy of Sciences; adviser to Gorbachev on relations with US.

Bakatin, Vadim Viktorovich (born 1937), first secretary, Kirov Party obkom, 1985–7; first secretary, Kemerovo Party obkom, 1987–8; USSR Minister of Internal Affairs, 1988–90; member of USSR Presidential Council, March 1990; chair of the USSR KGB, 1991; bottom of poll in Russian presidential election, June 1991; chair of the inter-republican Security Service, 1991–2.

Baklanov, Oleg Dmitrievich (born 1932), USSR Minister of General Machine Building, 1983–8; secretary of CC (military-industrial complex, chemical industry), 1988–91; one of the conspirators, August 1991.

Bessmertnykh, Aleksandr Aleksandrovich (born 1933), head of the American department, USSR Ministry of Foreign Affairs, 1983–6; USSR deputy foreign minister, 1986–8; first deputy USSR foreign minister, 1988–90; USSR Minister of Foreign Affairs, 1990–1; dismissed for not siding with Gorbachev in August 1991.

Bogomolov, Oleg Timofeevich (born 1927), director of the Institute of Economics of the World Socialist System, USSR Academy of Sciences, 1969; he stressed the relevance of Chinese economic reforms for the Soviet Union; director of the Institute for International Politics and Economic Research, USSR Academy of Sciences, 1990; member of USSR and then Russian Academy of Sciences.

Boldin, Valery Ivanovich (born 1935), adviser to Gorbachev on agriculture, 1985–7; head of the general department, Party CC, 1987–90; Gorbachev's Chief of Staff, 1990–1; member of the Presidential Council, March 1990; one of the conspirators, August 1991.

Brazauskas, Algirdas Mikolas (born 1932), secretary, CC of Communist Party of Lithuania, 1977–88; first secretary, Communist Party of Lithuania, 1988–90; chair, Lithuanian Supreme Soviet (head of state); chair of the Lithuanian Democratic Labour Party, 1990; President of Lithuania, 1992. He and the majority of Party members broke with Moscow in 1990 and supported the independence of Lithuania.

Brezhnev, Leonid Ilich (1906–82), first secretary, then general secretary of the Communist Party, 1964–84; chair of the Presidium, USSR Supreme Soviet (head of state), 1960–4 and 1977–82; member of Politburo, 1957–82.

312

Bulganin, Nikolai Aleksandrovich (1895–1975), chair of USSR Council of Ministers, 1955–8; chair of council of national economy; supported the anti-Party group, June 1957, and this led to his dismissal as Prime Minister, 1958.

Burokiavicius, Mikolas (born 1927), first secretary, CC of Communist Party of Lithuania, 1990–3.

Chazov, Evgeny Ivanovich (born 1929), personal doctor of general secretaries, 1967–87; leading cardiologist in the Soviet Union; awarded the Nobel Peace Prize, 1985; Minister of Health, 1987–90.

Chebrikov, Viktor Mikhailovich (born 1923), chair of the KGB, 1982–8; secretary, Party CC, 1988–9; member of the Politburo, 1985–9.

Chernenko, Konstantin Ustinovich (1911–85), general secretary of the Party, chair of the Presidium, USSR Supreme Soviet (head of state), 1984–5; member of the Politburo, 1978–85.

Chernomyrdin, Viktor Stepanovich (born 1938), Minister of the Gas Industry, 1985–9; Russian Prime Minister, December 1992.

Chernyaev, Anatoly Sergeevich (born 1921), adviser to Gorbachev on foreign affairs, 1986–91; then moved to Gorbachev Foundation.

Dementei, Nikolai Ivanovich (born 1931), chair, Belarusian Supreme Soviet (head of state), 1989–91; replaced by Stanislav Shushkevich after attempted coup, August 1991.

Deng Xiaoping (1904–97), lost posts during Cultural Revolution (1966–76), rehabilitated, 1973; resigned as deputy Prime Minister, 1980; proponent of market reforms; responsible for Tiananmen square massacre; paramount leader of China.

Dobrynin, Anatoly Fedorovich (born 1919), Soviet ambassador in Washington, 1962–86; secretary, Party CC, 1986–8, and head of the international department; this was a demotion since Shevardnadze wanted to cut his direct links to the foreign ministry; he was invited to retire from the CC in October 1988, completing Shevardnadze's demolition of his career.

Efremov, Leonid Nikolaevich (born 1912), first secretary, Stavropol Party kraikom, 1964–70; first deputy chair, USSR state committee on science and technology, 1970–88.

Falin, Valentin Mikhailovich (born 1926), Soviet ambassador to the Federal Republic of Germany, 1971–8; chair of APN news agency, 1986–8; head of international department, Party CC, 1988–91; one of the country's leading specialists on German affairs.

Fedorchuk, Vitaly Vasilevich (born 1918), chair of the Ukrainian KGB, 1970–82; chair of the USSR KGB, 1982; Minister of Internal Affairs, 1982–6.

Frolov, Ivan Timofeevich (born 1929), editor-in-chief, *Voprosy filosofii*, 1968–77; of *Kommunist*, 1986–7; of *Pravda*, 1989–91; member of Politburo; adviser to Gorbachev.

Gaidár, Egor Timurovich (born 1956), director of the Institute of Economic Policy, USSR Academy of Sciences, 1990–1; member of Shatalin–Yavlinsky group drafting 500-day programme; deputy chair, Russian Council of Ministers, 1991–2; Russian Minister for Economics and Finance, February–April 1992; first deputy Prime Minister, March–June 1992; acting Prime Minister, June–December 1992; director of the Institute of Economic Problems of the Transition Period, December 1992; adviser to Yeltsin.

Gidaspov, Boris Veniaminovich (born 1933), first secretary, Leningrad Party obkom, 1989–90; secretary, Party CC, 1990–1.

Gorbunovs, Anatolis (born 1942), secretary for ideology, CC, Communist Party of Latvia, 1985–8; chair of Latvian Supreme Soviet, 1988–90; chair of Supreme Council of the Republic of Latvia, 1990; President of Latvia after independence, 1991.

Grachev, General Pavel Sergeevich (born 1948), Afghan war hero who sided with Yeltsin during the attempted coup, August 1991; he promised to order the military not to use weapons; then appointed by Gorbachev chair of the Russian committee on defence and security; also made deputy USSR Minister of Defence; Russian Minister of Defence, May 1992–June 1996.

Grishin, Viktor Vasilevich (born 1914), first secretary, Moscow Party gorkom, 1967–85; member of Politburo, 1971–86; popularly known as the Moscow godfather because of corruption.

Gromyko, Andrei Andreevich (1909–89), USSR Minister of Foreign Affairs, 1957–85; chair, Presidium of USSR Supreme Soviet (head of state), 1985–8; member of Politburo, 1973–88.

Honecker, Erich (1912–94), succeeded Walter Ulbricht as first secretary of the SED, the east German Party, 1971; chair of the GDR Council of State (head of state), 1976–89; Gorbachev undermined his position in east Berlin in October 1989; Egon Krenz then took over.

Ivashko, Vladimir Antonovich (1932–94), second secretary, 1988–9, first secretary, Communist Party of Ukraine, 1989–90; chair of Ukrainian Supreme Soviet (head of state), 1990; deputy general secretary, Communist Party of the Soviet Union, 1990–1.

Jaruzelski, Wojciech (born 1923), first secretary, Polish United Workers' [Communist] Party, 1981–9; head of state, 1985–9; President of Poland, 1989–90.

Kádár, János (1912–89), first general secretary, Hungarian Socialist Workers' Party, 1956–88; succeeded by Karoly Grosz.

Karimov, Islam Abduganevich (born 1938), first secretary, Communist Party of Uzbekistan, 1989–91; member of CPSU Politburo, 1990–1; President of Uzbekistan, 1990.

Khasbulatov, Ruslan Imranovich (born 1942), first deputy chair (speaker), Russian Supreme Soviet, 1990–1; speaker, Russian Supreme Soviet, 1991–3.

Khrushchev, Nikita Sergeevich (1894–1971), first secretary, Party CC, 1953–64; chair, USSR Council of Ministers, 1958–64; member of Politburo, 1939–64.

Kirilenko, Andrei Pavlovich (1906–90), secretary, Party CC, 1966–82; member of Politburo, 1962–82.

Kolbin, Gennady Vasilevich (born 1927), first secretary, Communist Party of Kazakhstan, chair of the people's control commission, 1986–9.

Kosygin, Aleksei Nikolaevich (1904–80), chair, USSR Council of Ministers, 1948–52, 1964–80; member of Politburo, 1960–80.

Kravchuk, Leonid Makarovich (born 1934), secretary, second secretary, Communist Party of Ukraine, 1989–90; chair, Ukrainian Supreme Soviet (head of state), 1990–1; President of Ukraine, 1991.

Kryuchkov, Vladimir Aleksandrovich (born 1924), head of foreign intelligence, USSR KGB, 1974–88; chair of KGB, 1988–91; member of Politburo, 1989–90; leader of conspirators, August 1991.

Kulakov, Fedor Davydovich (1918–78), first secretary, Stavropol Party kraikom, 1960–4; secretary (agriculture), Party CC, 1965–78; member of Politburo, 1971–8.

Kunaev, Dinmukhamed Akhmedovich (1912–93), first secretary, Communist Party of Kazakhstan, 1960–2, 1964–86; member of Politburo, 1971–87.

Kuptsov, Valentin Aleksandrovich (born 1937), first secretary, Vologda Party obkom, 1985–90; head of department and secretary, Party CC, 1990–1; first secretary, Russian Party, 1991.

Landsbergis, Vytautas (born 1932), chair, Sajudis, Lithuanian independence movement, 1988–93; chair (speaker), Supreme Council (head of state), 1990–2; Sajudis was defeated in the first democratic elections after independence in September 1992; Algirdas Brazauskas became President in February 1993.

Lenin, Vladimir Ilich (1870–1924), leader of the Bolsheviks, 1917; chair of Sovnarkom (government), 1917–24.

Ligachev, Egor Kuzmich (born 1920), first secretary, Tomsk Party gorkom, 1965–83; secretary (personnel, ideology, agriculture), Party CC, 1983–90; second secretary to Gorbachev, 1985–8; member of Politburo, 1985–90.

Lukyanov, Anatoly Ivanovich (born 1930), head of general department, Party CC, 1985–7; secretary, Party CC, 1987–8; first deputy chair, USSR Supreme Soviet, 1988–90; chair, USSR Supreme Soviet, 1990–1; one of conspirators, August 1991.

Maslyukov, Yury Dmitrievich (born 1937), deputy chair, 1985–8, first deputy chair, USSR Council of Ministers, and chair of Gosplan, 1988–91; member of Politburo, 1989–91.

Medvedev, Vadim Andreevich (born 1929), rector, Party Academy of Social Sciences, 1978–83; head, department of science and education, 1983–6; head, department for liaison with communist and workers' parties of socialist countries, Party CC, 1986–8; secretary, Party CC, 1986–8; member of Politburo, 1988–90; he lost all his positions at 28th Party Congress, July 1990; member of Presidential Council, July 1990; adviser to Gorbachev and moved to Gorbachev Foundation.

Mlynar, Zdenek (1930–97), secretary and member of Presidium, Communist Party of Czechoslovakia, 1968; signed Charter 77; emigrated to Italy, 1977; studied with Gorbachev and kept in touch.

Moiseev, General Mikhail Alekseevich (born 1939), Chief of Staff, Soviet Armed Forces, first deputy USSR Minister of Defence, 1988–91; acting USSR Minister of Defence, August 1991.

Molotov, Vyacheslav Mikhailovich (1890–1986), Soviet Minister of Foreign Affairs, 1939–49, 1953–6; first deputy chair, USSR Council of Ministers, 1953–7; member of Politburo, 1926–57; member of anti-Party group defeated by Khrushchev in June 1957.

Murakhovsky, Vsevolod Serafimovich (born 1926), first secretary, Stavropol Party gorkom, 1970–4; first secretary, Karachai-Cherkess Party obkom, 1975–8; first secretary, Stavropol Party kraikom, 1978–85; first deputy chair, USSR Council of Ministers and USSR State Agro-Industrial Committee (Gosagroprom), 1985–9.

Mutalibov, Ayas Niyazevich (born 1938), chair, Council of Ministers of Azerbaijan, 1989–90; first secretary, Communist Party of Azerbaijan, 1990–1; member of CPSU Politburo, 1990–1; President of Azerbaijan, 1991–2.

Nazarbaev, Nursultan Abishevich (born 1938), chair, Council of Ministers of Kazakhstan, 1984–9; first secretary, Communist Party of Kazakhstan, 1990–1; member of CPSU Politburo, 1990–1; President of Kazakhstan, 1990.

Nenashev, Mikhail Fedorovich (born 1929), editor-in-chief, *Sovetskaya Rossiya*, 1978–86; chair, USSR state committee for publishing and the book trade, 1986–9; chair, USSR state committee for television and radio, 1989–91; USSR Minister for the Press and Information, 1990–1.

Nikonov, Viktor Petrovich (born 1929), Russian Minister of Agriculture, 1983–5; secretary (agriculture), Party CC, 1985–9; member of Politburo, 1987–9.

Nishanov, Rafik Nishanovich (born 1926), chair (head of state), Supreme Soviet of Uzbekistan, 1986–8; first secretary, Communist

Party of Uzbekistan, 1988–9; chair, Soviet of Nationalities, USSR Supreme Soviet, 1989–91.

Niyazov, Saparmurad Ataevich (born 1940), first secretary, Communist Party of Turkmenistan, 1985–91; member of CPSU Politburo, 1990–1; President of Turkmenistan, 1990.

Pankin, Boris Dmitrievich (born 1931), chair, All-Union copyright agency, 1973–82; Soviet ambassador to Sweden, 1982–90; to Czechoslovakia, 1990–1; Soviet foreign minister, 1991; one of few diplomats to side with Gorbachev during attempted coup. It was rumoured that he informed President Vaclav Havel of his opposition to the putsch but that he gave advance notice that, should the coup succeed, he would formally request political asylum in Czechoslovakia.

Pavlov, Valentin Sergeevich (born 1937), chair, USSR state committee on prices, 1986–9; Soviet Minister of Finance, 1989–91; Soviet Prime Minister, 1991; one of the conspirators, August 1991.

Petrakov, Nikolai Yakovlevich (born 1937), deputy director, Central Institute of Mathematical Economics, USSR Academy of Sciences, 1971–90; economic adviser to Gorbachev, 1990–1; director, Institute for Market Problems, USSR Academy of Sciences, 1991.

Plekhanov, Yury Sergeevich (born 1930), KGB head of security for the President and leading officials at the time of the attempted coup.

Podgorny, Nikolai Viktorovich (1903–83), first secretary, Communist Party of Ukraine, 1957–63; chair (head of state), Presidium, USSR Supreme Soviet, 1965–77; member of Politburo, 1960–77.

Polozkov, Ivan Kuzmich (born 1935), first secretary, Krasnodar Party obkom, 1985–90; first secretary, Russian Communist Party, 1990–1; member of Politburo, 1990–1.

Popov, Gavriil Kharitonovich (born 1936), professor of economics, Moscow State University, 1977–88; editor-in-chief, *Voprosy ekonomiki*, 1988–90; mayor of Moscow, 1990–2; leading member of Russian Greek community.

Primakov, Evgeny Maksimovich (born 1929), director (Arabist), Oriental Institute, USSR Academy of Sciences, 1977–85; director, Institute of World Economy and International Relations, 1985–9; chair, Soviet of the Union, USSR Supreme Soviet, 1989–90; director, Russian foreign intelligence service, 1991; personal Gorbachev envoy to Saddam Hussein during the Gulf War; Russian foreign minister, 1996.

Prokofev, Yury Anatolevich (born 1939), first secretary, Moscow Party gorkom, 1989–91; member of Politburo, 1990–1.

Prunskiene, Kazimiera (born 1943), chair, Lithuanian Council of Ministers, 1990–1.

Pugo, Boris Karlovich (1937–91), chair, Latvian KGB, 1980–4; chair, CPSU Central Control Commission, 1990–1; Soviet Minister of

Internal Affairs, 1990–1; one of the conspirators, August 1991; committed suicide.

Rakowski, Mieczyslaw (born 1926), chair, Polish Council of Ministers, 1988–9; first secretary, Polish United Workers' [Communist] Party, 1989–90.

Razumovsky, Georgy Petrovich (born 1936), first secretary, Krasnodar Party kraikom, 1983–5; secretary (personnel), Party CC, 1986–91.

Romanov, Grigory Vasilevich (born 1923), first secretary, Leningrad Party obkom, 1970–83; secretary (defence industry), Party CC, 1983–5; member of Politburo, 1976–85.

Rubiks, Alfreds (born 1935), first secretary, Communist Party of Latvia, 1990–1; member of CPSU Politburo, 1990–1.

Rutskoi, Aleksandr Vladimirovich (born 1947), Vice-President of Russia, 1991–3.

Ryzhkov, Nikolai Ivanovich (born 1929), secretary and head of industry department, Party CC, 1982–5; chair, USSR Council of Ministers, 1985–91; member of Politburo, 1985–90.

Sakharov, Andrei Dmitrievich (1921–89), one of the fathers of the Soviet nuclear bomb; academician; USSR people's deputy, 1989; Nobel Prize, 1975; human rights activist.

Savisaar, Edgar (born 1950), founder and chair, Estonian Popular Front, 1989–90; chair, Estonian Gosplan, 1989–90; Prime Minister, 1990–2.

Semenova, Galina Vladimirovna (born 1937), editor-in-chief, *Krestyanka* [Peasant Woman], 1981–90; secretary, Party CC, 1990–1; member of Politburo, 1990–1.

Shakhnazarov, Georgy Khozroevich (born 1924), aide to Gorbachev, 1988–91; USSR people's deputy, 1989–91; member of Gorbachev Foundation.

Shaposhnikov, Marshal Evgeny Ivanovich (born 1942), Commander-in-Chief, Soviet air force and deputy USSR Minister of Defence, 1990–1; Soviet Minister of Defence, 1991; Commander-in-Chief, strategic first strike forces, 1991–3.

Shatalin, Stanislav Sergeevich (1934–97), academician; drafted, with Yavlinsky and others, the 500-day programme; member of Presidential Council, 1990; resigned from Party after Vilnius killings; supported Yeltsin during Russian presidential campaign, June 1991; joined Democratic Party of Russia, June 1991; co-chair, movement for democratic reforms (international), July 1991.

Shcherbakov, Vladimir Ivanovich (born 1949), member, Soviet commission for perfecting administration, planning and the economic mechanism, 1988; chair, USSR state committee on labour and social questions, 1989–91; deputy, March–May 1991, first deputy Soviet Prime Minister, May–November 1991; Minister of Economics and Forecasting, May–November 1991.

Shcherbitsky, Vladimir Vasilevich (1918–90), chair, Ukrainian Council of Ministers, 1961–3, 1965–72; first secretary, Communist Party of Ukraine, 1972–89; member of CPSU Politburo, 1971–89.

Shenin, Oleg Semenovich (born 1937), first secretary, Krasnoyarsk Party kraikom, 1987–90; secretary (personnel), Party CC, 1990–1; member of Party CC permanent commission on renewal of activities of primary Party organisations, 1990–1; member of Politburo, 1990–1; one of the conspirators, August 1991.

Shevardnadze, Eduard Ambrosievich (born 1928), first secretary, Communist Party of Georgia, 1972–85; Soviet foreign minister, 1985–90; Soviet Minister of External Affairs, 1991; member of Presidential Council, 1990–1; member of Politburo, 1985–90; chair (head of state), State Council of Georgia, March 1992.

Shmelev, Nikolai Petrovich (born 1936), pro-reform economist; head of department, USA and Canada Institute, USSR Academy of Sciences, 1982–92; USSR people's deputy, 1989–91.

Shushkevich, Stanislau Stanislauovich (born 1934), chair (head of state), Belarusian Supreme Soviet, 1991–4.

Silaev, Ivan Stepanovich (born 1930), Soviet Minister of Civil Aviation, 1981–5; deputy chair, USSR Council of Ministers, 1985–90; chair, Russian Council of Ministers, 1990–1.

Sobchak, Anatoly Aleksandrovich (born 1937), USSR people's deputy, 1989–91; mayor of Leningrad-St Petersburg, 1990–6.

Sokolov, Efrem Evseevich (born 1926), first secretary, Communist Party of Belorussia (Belarus), 1987–90.

Solomentsev, Mikhail Sergeevich (born 1913), chair, Russian Council of Ministers, 1971–83; chair, Party Control Commission, 1983–8; member of Politburo, 1983–8.

Songaila, Ringaudas-Bronislavas (born 1929), chair, Council of Ministers of Lithuania, 1981–5; chair (head of state), Supreme Soviet of Lithuania, 1985–7; first secretary, Communist Party of Lithuania, 1987–8; his critics referred to him as the 'shame of the [Lithuanian] nation'.

Stalin, Iosef Vissarionovich (1879–1953), general secretary, CPSU, 1922–34, secretary, 1934–53; chair, USSR Council of Ministers, 1941–53; member of Politburo, 1919–53.

Starodubtsev, Vasily Aleksandrovich (born 1931), chair, All-Russian Kolkhoz Council, 1986–91; USSR Farmers' Union, 1990–1; one of the conspirators, August 1991.

Stroev, Egor Semonovich (born 1937), first secretary, Orlov Party obkom, 1985–9; secretary (agriculture), Party CC, 1990–1; member of Politburo, 1990–1.

Suslov, Mikhail Andreevich (1902–82), secretary (ideology), Party CC, 1947–82; member of Politburo, 1952–3, 1955–82.

Talyzin, Nikolai Vladimirovich (born 1929), deputy chair, USSR Council of Ministers and Soviet representative to Comecon, 1980–5, 1988–9; first deputy chair, USSR Council of Ministers and head of Gosplan, 1985–8.

Tikhonov, Nikolai Aleksandrovich (born 1905), chair, USSR Council of Ministers, 1980–5; member of Politburo, 1979–85.

Travkin, Nikolai Ilich (born 1947), deputy USSR Minister of the Construction Industry, 1988–9; USSR people's deputy, 1989–91; co-founder of the democratic party of Russia, 1990; its chair, 1992–3; Russian people's deputy, 1990–3.

Trotsky, Lev Davidovich (1879–1940), worked closely with Lenin during October Revolution; USSR Commissar for War, 1918–25; lost all posts, 1925; deported to Turkey, later went to Mexico where he was murdered, almost certainly on Stalin's orders.

Ustinov, Marshal Dmitry Fedorovich (1908–84), Soviet Minister of Defence, 1976–84; member of Politburo, 1976–84.

Varennikov, General Valentin Ivanovich (born 1923), Commander in-Chief, Soviet border troops, deputy USSR Minister of Defence, 1989–91; one of the conspirators, August 1991.

Velikhov, Evgeny Pavlovich (born 1935), nuclear scientist; vice-president USSR-Russian Academy of Sciences, and director, Kurchatov Institute of Nuclear Energy, 1988–92; adviser to Gorbachev.

Vezirov, Abdul Rahman (born 1930), first secretary, Communist Party of Azerbaijan, 1988–90.

Vlasov, Aleksandr Vladimirovich (born 1932), first secretary, Rostov Party obkom, 1984–6; USSR Minister of Internal Affairs, 1986–8; chair, Russian Council of Ministers, 1988–90.

Volsky, Arkady Ivanovich (born 1932), adviser to Andropov, Chernenko and Gorbachev, 1983–5; head of department of machine building, Party CC, 1985–8; presidential representative, Nagorno-Karabakh, 1988–90; chair, USSR science and industry union, 1988–90; deputy head, committee for management of Soviet economy, 1991; president, union of Russian industrialists and entrepreneurs, 1992.

Vorontsov, Yuly Mikhailovich (born 1929), Soviet ambassador to France, 1983–6; first deputy, USSR Minister of Foreign Affairs, 1986–90; Soviet permanent representative to UN, 1990–1; Russian ambassador to US, 1994.

Vorotnikov, Vitaly Ivanovich (born 1926), chair, Russian Council of Ministers, 1983–8; chair (head of state), Presidium, Russian Supreme Soviet, 1988–90; member of Politburo, 1983–90.

Yakovlev, Aleksandr Nikolaevich (born 1923), Soviet ambassador to Canada, 1979–83; director, Institute of World Economy and

International Relations, USSR Academy of Sciences, 1983–5; secretary (propaganda, culture, foreign policy), Party CC, 1986–90; member of Politburo, 1987–90; adviser to Gorbachev, 1990–1.

Yakovlev, Egor Vladimirovich (born 1930), editor-in-chief, *Moskovskie novosti* [Moscow News], 1986–91; USSR people's deputy, 1989–91; chair, Soviet-Russian state committee for television and radio (Gosteleradio), 1991–2.

Yanaev, Gennady Ivanovich (born 1937), secretary, 1986–9, deputy chair, 1989–90, chair, All-Union Central Council of Trades Unions, 1989–90; secretary, Party CC, member of Politburo, 1990–1; USSR Vice-President, 1990–1; one of the conspirators, August 1991.

Yavlinsky, Grigory Aleksandrovich (born 1952), pro-reform economist; co-author with Shatalin of the 500-day programme; deputy chair, Russian Council of Ministers, 1990; co-leader of Yabloko party.

Yazov, Marshal Dmitry Timofeevich (born 1923), Commander-in-Chief, Central Asian military district, 1980–4; Far East military district, 1984–6; USSR Minister of Defence, 1987–91; one of the conspirators, August 1991.

Yeltsin, Boris Nikolaevich (born 1931), first secretary, Sverdlovsk Party obkom, 1976–85; head of construction department, Party CC, secretary, Party CC, 1985; first secretary, Moscow Party gorkom, 1985–7; first deputy chair, USSR state committee for construction (Gosstroi), 1987–9; chair (speaker, head of state), Russian Supreme Soviet, 1990; President of Russia, 1991.

Zaikov, Lev Nikolaevich (born 1923), first secretary, Leningrad Party obkom, 1983–5; secretary (military-industrial complex), Party CC, 1985–90; first secretary, Moscow Party gorkom, 1987–9; member of Politburo, 1986–90.

Zaslavskaya, Tatyana Ivanovna (born 1927), sociologist, director, All-Union Centre for Public Opinion Research, 1988–92; USSR people's deputy, 1989–91.

Zhirinovsky, Vladimir Volfovich (born 1946), came second in Russian presidential election, June 1991; leader of Liberal Democratic Party of Russia.

Zyuganov, Gennady Andreevich (born 1944), secretary and member of Politburo, Russian Communist Party, 1990–1; leader of Communist Party of the Russian Federation, 1993.

BIBLIOGRAPHICAL ESSAY

DOMESTIC POLICY

Mikhail Gorbachev, *Perestroika: New Thinking for Our Country and the World* (London, Collins, 1987) was immensely successful; his *Memoirs* (London, Doubleday, 1996) reveal the confusion of the last years of the Soviet Union; A. Brown, *The Gorbachev Factor* (Oxford, Oxford University Press, 1996) is an immensely scholarly case for the defence; in V. Boldin, *Ten Years That Shook the World* (New York, BasicBooks, 1995) Gorbachev's Chief of Staff puts the case for the prosecution but is sometimes inaccurate; Y. Ligachev, *Inside Gorbachev's Kremlin* (Boulder, CO, Westview Press, 1996) is the case for conservative communism; in A. S. Grachev, *Final Days: The Inside Story of the Collapse of the Soviet Union* (Boulder, CO, Westview Press, 1996) Gorbachev's clever press secretary is interesting and revealing; E. Shevardnadze, *The Future Belongs to Freedom* (London, Sinclair-Stevenson, 1991) was written hastily but is of some value; Caroline McGiffert Ekedahl and Melvin A. Goodman, *The Wars of Eduard Shevardnadze* (London, Hurst, 1997) reveals how complex Gorbachev's foreign minister is; R. Gorbachev, *I Hope* (London, HarperCollins, 1991) is interesting; Jack F. Matlock, Jr., *Autopsy on an Empire* (New York, Random House, 1995), by the last US ambassador, is shrewd and very enjoyable; G. Ruge, *Gorbachev* (London, Chatto & Windus, 1991) is well informed; A. Sobchak, *For a New Russia* (London, HarperCollins, 1991) is by one of the stars of the democratic firmament who fell to earth in 1996.

On history R. W. Davies, *Soviet History in the Gorbachev Revolution* (London, Macmillan, 1989) is rewarding; A. Nove, *Glasnost in Action* (Boston, MA, Unwin Hyman, 1989) is excellent; Geoffrey Hosking, *The Awakening of the Soviet Union* (London, Heinemann, 1990) is good on social factors; V. Shlapentokh, *Public and Private Life of the Soviet People: Changing Values in Post-Stalin Russia* (New York, Oxford University Press, 1989) is stimulating.

On the travails of the economy, A. Åslund, *Gorbachev's Struggle for Economic Reform*, 2nd edn (London, Pinter, 1991) is by a leading pro-market western economist and, needless to say, finds Gorbachev sadly wanting; A. Aganbegyan, *The Challenge of Perestroika* (London, Hutchinson, 1988) is by the most influential economist in the early Gorbachev era; D. Filtzer, *Soviet Workers and the Collapse of Perestroika* (Cambridge, Cambridge University Press, 1994) reveals the problems facing Gorbachev; V. Tolz, *The USSR's Emerging Multiparty System* (New York, Praeger, 1991) is good on a complex subject; R. Sakwa, *Gorbachev and His Reforms 1985–1990* (London, Philip Allan, 1990) is a valuable source; S. White, *Gorbachev and After*, 3rd edn (Cambridge, Cambridge University Press, 1992) is comprehensive; J. Miller, *Mikhail Gorbachev and the End of Soviet Power* (London, Macmillan, 1993) is interesting but concentrates on political events; D. Remnick, *Lenin's Tomb: The Last Days of the Soviet Empire* (New York, Random House, 1993) is interesting; T. Zaslavskaya, *The Second Socialist Revolution: An Alternative Strategy* (London, I. B. Tauris, 1990) is revealing about the problems Gorbachev had to face.

On the nationality question see A. J. Motyl, *Sovietology, Rationality, Nationality: Coming to Grips with Nationalism in the USSR* (New York, Columbia University Press, 1990); and his edited collection, *Thinking Theoretically about Soviet Nationalities* (New York, Columbia University Press, 1992); B. Nahaylo and Victor Swoboda, *Soviet Disunion: A History of the Nationalities Problem in the USSR* (London, Hamish Hamilton, 1990); G. Smith, ed., *The Nationalities Question in the Soviet Union* (London, Longman, 1990); G. W. Lapidus and V. Zaslavsky, eds, *From Union to Commonwealth: Nationalism and Separatism in the Soviet Republics* (Cambridge, Cambridge University Press, 1992); G. Suny, *The Revenge of the Past: Nationalism, Revolution and the Collapse of the Soviet Union* (Stanford, CA, Stanford University Press, 1993).

On the rebirth of politics, Michael Urban, *The Rebirth of Politics in Russia* (Cambridge, Cambridge University Press, 1997) is very informative; see also G. Hosking, J. Aves and P. J. S. Duncan, eds, *The Road to Post-Communism: Independent Political Movements in the Soviet Union 1985–1991* (London, Pinter, 1992). On religion the leading study is M. Bourdeaux, *Gorbachev, Glasnost and the Gospel* (London, Hodder & Stoughton, 1990). On crime, A. Vaksberg, *The Soviet Mafia* (London, Weidenfeld and Nicolson, 1991) provides many insights. On Gorbachev's summits with Reagan and Bush, R. L. Garthoff, *The Great Transition: American-Soviet Relations and the End of the Cold War* (Washington, DC, Brookings Institution

Press, 1994) is valuable; C. D. Blacker, *Hostage to Revolution: Gor-bachev and Soviet Security Policy, 1985–1991* (New York, Council on Foreign Relations, 1993) is excellent; M. Beschloss and S. Talbott, *At the Highest Levels: The Inside Story of the End of the Cold War* (London, Little, Brown, 1993) is revealing and valuable; M. MccGwire, *Perestroika and Soviet National Security* (Washington, DC, Brookings Institution Press, 1991) is well informed; C. Andrew and O. Gordievsky, *KGB: The Inside Story of its Foreign Operations from Lenin to Gorbachev* (London, Hodder & Stoughton, 1990) is as good as any spy thriller; M. Galeotti, *The Age of Anxiety: Security and Politics in Soviet and Post-Soviet Russia* (London, Longman, 1993) is a critical review; A. Knight, *Spies Without Cloaks: The KGB's Successors* (Princeton, Princeton University Press, 1996) includes a revisionist account of the attempted coup.

. . .

FOREIGN POLICY

On foreign policy the leader is J. L. Nogee and R. H. Donaldson, *Soviet Foreign Policy since World War II*, 4th edn (New York, Pergamon, 1992); S. Bailer, *The Soviet Paradox: External Expansion, Internal Decline* (London, I. B. Tauris, 1985) is good; James A. Baker III, *The Politics of Diplomacy: Revolution, War, and Peace* (New York, G. P. Putnam's, 1995) is comprehensive; A. Dobrynin, *In Confidence: Moscow's Ambassador to America's Six Cold War Presidents* (New York, Random House, 1995) settles some old scores; G. P. Shultz, *Turmoil and Tragedy: My Years As Secretary of State* (New York, Charles Scribner's, 1993) provides many insights; S. R. Ashton, *The Politics of East–West Relations since 1945* (London, Macmillan 1989) is an excellent survey; any book by J. L. Gaddis is worth reading, especially *Russia, the Soviet Union and the United States*, 2nd edn (New York, McGraw-Hill, 1990) and *The Long Peace: Inquiries into the History of the Cold War* (Oxford, Oxford University Press, 1987); J. W. Young, *Cold War Europe 1945–89: A Political History* (London, Edward Arnold, 1991) is interesting; for a more detailed bibliography see J. W. Young, *The Longman Companion to Cold War and Détente* (London, Longman 1993); Ben Fowkes, *The Rise and Fall of Communism in Eastern Europe*, 2nd edn (London, Macmillan, 1995) is good.

. . .

THE YELTSIN ERA 1992–

On the Yeltsin era see B. Yeltsin, *Against the Grain: An Autobiography* (London, Jonathan Cape, 1990); and his *View from the Kremlin* (London, HarperCollins, 1994); J. Morrison, *Boris Yeltsin* (London,

Penguin, 1991) is good; J. Steele, *Eternal Russia: Yeltsin, Gorbachev and the Mirage of Democracy* (London, Faber & Faber, 1994) is sceptical; A. Saikal and W. Maley, eds, *Russia in Search of its Future* (Cambridge, Cambridge University Press, 1995) is very good; R. Sakwa, *Russian Politics and Society*, 2nd edn (London, Routledge, 1996) is the best textbook; A. Saikal and W. Maley, eds, *Russia in Search of its Future* (Cambridge, Cambridge University Press, 1995) is good; J. Dunlop, *The Rise of Russia and the Fall of the Soviet Empire* (Princeton, NJ, Princeton University Press, 1993) is stimulating; S. White, *After Gorbachev*, 4th edn (Cambridge, Cambridge University Press, 1994) is comprehensive; S. White, A. Pravda and Z. Gitelman, eds, *Developments in Soviet and Post-Soviet Politics* (London, Macmillan, 1994) includes interesting material; T. Remington, ed., *Parliaments in Transition* (Boulder, CO, Westview Press, 1994) has excellent material on Russia.

MAPS

Map 1 Political-administrative map of the USSR until 1991
Source: M. McCauley, *The Soviet Union 1917–1991* (London, Longman, 1993)

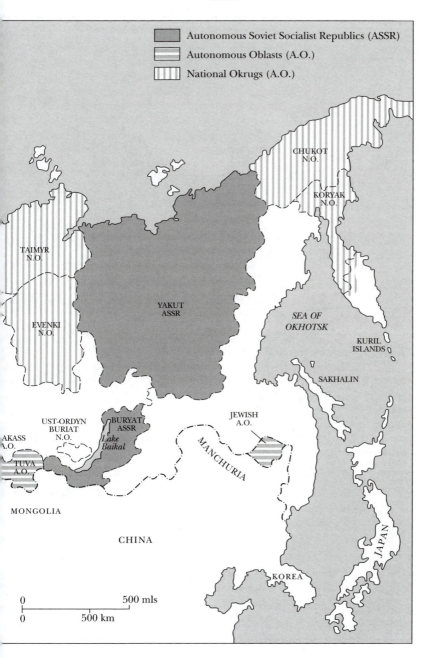

Map 2 The Commonwealth of Independent States
Source: Russia and the Succession States Briefing Service

ARCTIC OCEAN

Chukotsky A.O.

LAPTEV
SEA

Koryak A.O.

Taimyrsky A.O.

Sakha–Yakutia

Kamchatka

Evenki A.O.

SEA OF
OKHOTSK

F E D E R A T I O N

Sakhalin

Ust–Ordynsky Buryat A.O.   Buryatia

kasia

Jewish A.O.

Tuva

Aginsky–Buryat A.O.

SEA OF
JAPAN

0   500 mls

0   500 km

INDEX

Abalkin, L., 110, 182–3, 185, 283, 311
ABM treaty (1972), 140, 286
Achalov, V., 199
Afanasev, V., 94–5, 311
Afanasev, Yu. N., 106, 164, 289, 291, 311
Afghanistan, x, 38, 66, 77, 79, 135, 138, 248, 299–301, 303
Aganbegyan, A. G., 55–6, 70, 119, 185, 311
Agitprop, 286
Agriculture, 23–4, 29–34, 37–9, 67, 125, 282, 288, 291–2, 295, 315–16
  Ipatovsky method, 33–4
Akaev, A., 240, 306, 311
Akhromeev, S., ix, 139–40, 193, 196, 236, 239, 302, 311
Albania, 297
Alksnis, V., 190, 198, 295
Aleksi II, Patriarch, 209, 213
Aliev, G., 42, 300, 311
Alliluyeva, S., 98
Allison, G., 215
Alma Ata (now Almaty), 75, 235–6, 248, 256–7, 288, 310
Andreeva, N., 93–4, 122, 301, 311

Andropov, Yu. V., 11, 14, 35, 37–43, 51, 61, 73, 76, 102, 282, 312
Anti-Alcohol campaign, 60, 62, 114
Anti-Party group, 10, 286
Antonovich, I., 176
Apparatchik, 286
Arbatov, G. A., 71, 96, 312
Argentinia, 137
Arms negotiations, 78–84
Armenia, 116, 119–21, 139, 158–9, 173, 189, 201, 207, 209, 211, 245, 257, 288, 301–2, 306, 309
Ashghabat, 256, 310
Attempted Coup of 18–21 August 1991, 172, 177–8, 233–43, 258, 286–7, 308–9
Austria, 205
Azerbaijan, 42, 116, 119–21, 158–60, 172, 189, 242, 245, 257, 288, 301, 304, 309–11, 316, 320

Baburin, S., 295
Baibakov, N., 39, 134
Bakatin, V., 15, 165, 170, 190, 212, 238–9, 244, 247–8, 272, 306, 312